PONTIFICAL INSTITUTE OF MEDIAEVAL STUDIES

STUDIES AND TEXTS

16

PRINTED BY UNIVERSA — WETTEREN — BELGIUM

STEPHANUS DE LINGUA-TONANTE

STUDIES IN THE SERMONS OF STEPHEN LANGTON

BY

PHYLLIS BARZILLAY ROBERTS

TORONTO

PONTIFICAL INSTITUTE OF MEDIAEVAL STUDIES

1968

For my Parents and Earl

PREFACE

STEPHEN LANGTON, master of theology in the schools at Paris, and archbishop of Canterbury from 1206-28 was a major participant in one of the most formative epochs in English history. His role in the events that led to the drafting of the Great Charter and his efforts to secure the freedom of the English church make him a personage of considerable historical importance whose thought and activities have a special interest. Langton is also known as a notable preacher, whose archiepiscopal sermons were sometimes noticed by English chroniclers. Contemporary manuscripts attest to this reputation. Numerous sermons attributed to Langton bear the rubric: Master Stephen of the Thundering Tongue.

This book has as its purpose the examination of these sermons both as a source of Langton's earlier years in Paris, and as a source in social and intellectual history. Langton's role as an important popular preacher in the evangelical movement in Paris in the last decades of the twelfth century offers additional evidence of the participation of masters in the schools in a program directed toward the education of the laity, reform of the Church, and the reinvigoration of Christian teaching. These interests anticipate those of the mendicant orders who continued the tradition of popular preaching in the high middle ages.

Fundamental to the investigation was the expanded list of manuscripts and *initia* published by Dr. J. B. Schneyer in 1962 which provided the basis for my classification of manuscripts and sermons according to the degree of their reliability, and the preparation of tables of references to all known texts for a future collation of the sermons. I owe a great debt to Dr. Schneyer whose generous assistance has made this work possible. Several parts of this book have their origins in conversations with scholars whose interest and contributions to Langton studies are evident from their published works. Professor C. R. Cheney of Corpus Christi College, Cambridge, pointed out the importance of limiting the study to Langton's Paris period in that this offered a fruitful area for investigation. Miss Beryl Smalley of St. Hilda's College, Oxford, directed me to examining the connections between the sermons and the liturgy, and made available to me the work that she had done on the commentaries of Langton. Dr. R. W. Hunt, Keeper of the Western Manuscripts at the Bodleian Library was most hospitable on my various visits to Oxford, and was most generous in allowing me the use of his work on Alexander Neckham and William de Montibus. I should also like to thank Professor T. J. Brown of King's College, London for his assistance in matters of paleography; and Dr. Nicolai Rubinstein of Westfield College, London who was my tutor at the University of London and whose suggestions were most helpful during the period when most of the research for this book was accomplished. Dr. John Baldwin of Johns Hopkins University has also assisted me on a number of problems connected with Langton's Paris circle. This work was originally accepted by the Department of History, Columbia University, in May 1966, as a dissertation in partial fulfillment of the requirements for the degree of Doctor of Philosophy. Some changes have been made in preparing my dissertation for publication. I am very grateful to Professor J. H. Mundy and Professor N. F. Cantor for their helpful suggestions and criticisms, and to Professor P. O. Kristeller for his valuable advice on difficult textual problems. Any errors or shortcomings in this book are, of course, my own responsibility.

I also acknowledge and thank the keepers of the manuscripts in the following libraries for allowing me to consult manuscripts in their collections and/or assisting me in the obtaining of microfilms or photostats of manuscript materials: The British Museum; Lambeth Palace Library; Lincoln Cathedral Chapter Library; Lincoln Record Office; the Bodleian Library; Cambridge University Library; Peterhouse College Library; St. John's College Library, and Corpus Christi College Library (Cambridge); Bibliothèque Royale (Brussels); Stadsbibliotheek (Brugge); Bibliothèque Nationale, Bibliothèque de l'Arsenal, Bibliothèque Mazarine (Paris); Bibliothèque Municipale (Cambrai); Bibliothèque Municipale (Amiens); Bibliothèque Municipale (Arras); Bibliothèque Municipale (Douai); Bibliothèque Municipale (Troyes); Staatsbibliothek München; Universitätsbibliothek (Leipzig); Universitätsbibliothek (Tübingen). Others were most generous in their responses to my written queries: Archivo de la Corona de Aragon (Barcelona); and the Nationalbibliothek (Vienna). The staff at the Institut de Recherche et d'histoire des Textes (Paris) was most helpful in allowing the use of their catalogue of sermon incipits and access to files of unpublished data. To the librarians of the Institute of Historical Research, London and the Columbia University Library a special word of thanks for their courtesies.

I should also like to express my gratitude to the Fulbright Committee and the American Association of University Women for providing me with the financial assistance to carry out these researches in the European libraries and to purchase large quantities of microfilm and photostat materials.

P. B. R.

Richmond College of the City University of New York
October, 1967

TABLE OF CONTENTS

THE MANUSCRIPTS: SIGLA*

I. *MSS Bearing an Attribution to Langton*

Bg^{1}	Brugge 28
Bg^{3}	—— 278
Bs^{1}	Brussels II. 953
CCC 450	Camb: Corp. Chr. Coll. 450
CCC 459	—— 459
CUL	Camb. Univ. Ee.VI.10
(Le^{1}	Leipzig 364)
Le^{2}	—— 443
LoA	Arundel 292
Lo^{3}	Royal 8.A.x
OM	Magd. 168
Pa^{2}	BN, lat. 3227
Pa^{11}	—— 14859
Pa^{14}	—— 15025
PS	Ste. Gen. 1422
(Ro	Rouen 1468)
Tr^{1}	Troyes 862
Tr^{2}	—— 1100
Tr^{4}	—— 1367

II. *MSS Containing Anonymous Texts*

Am	Amiens, Lesc. 30
Ar	Arras 222
(Bar	Barcelona, Rip. 205)
(Bas	Basel A. IX. 2)
Be	Berlin, lat. fol. 764
Bg^{2}	Brugge 93
Bs^{2}	Brussels II. 957
Bs^{3}	—— II. 962
Ca	Cambrai 588
Do	Douai 495
(Le^{3}	Leipzig 444)
Li	Lincoln 239
Lo^{1}	Royal 3.A.X
Lo^{2}	—— 8.C.VII
Lo^{4}	—— 8.F.IV
Lo^{5}	—— 10.A.VII

* Where a MS citation is enclosed in parentheses, I have relied for a description of its contents on either a communication from the appropriate library authority or a catalogue reference. In most cases, however, I have actually examined the MS and/or a microfilm.

Mu[1]	Munich Clm. 5998
Mu[2]	—— 12660
Ni	Nîmes 42
PA[1]	Arsenal 400
PA[2]	—— 854
Pa[1]	BN, lat. 2915
Pa[3]	—— 3495
Pa[4]	—— 3570
Pa[6]	—— 12420
Pa[7]	—— 14470
Pa[8]	—— 14525
Pa[9]	—— 14593
Pa[10]	—— 14804
Pa[12]	—— 14925
Pa[13]	—— 14957
Pa[15]	—— 15965
Pa[16]	—— 16463
Pa[17]	—— 16502
PM	Mazarine 999
Re	Reims 582
Tr[3]	Troyes 1227
(Va	Vatican, lat. 634)
(Vi	Vienna 1330)

Chapter I

THE LIFE OF STEPHEN LANGTON

IN the Ford lectures delivered at Oxford in 1927, the late Professor Powicke laid the foundations for further inquiry into the career and writings of the archbishop of Canterbury, Stephen Langton, devoting therein considerable attention to the details of Langton's life. These may be briefly summarized here.[1] Stephen, the eldest son of Henry of Langton by Wragby in Lincolnshire,[2] was born *ca.* 1155.[3] The family was probably of Anglo-Danish stock and included besides Stephen two brothers, Simon and Walter.[4] Stephen Langton spent his boyhood years in England, and it was no doubt during this early period that he had some contact with the clergy in the cathedral church at Lincoln.[5]

Ca. 1170, the young Langton went to Paris,[6] where he subsequently spent more than thirty years studying and teaching until he left the schools in 1206. Langton's Paris was not yet the Paris of 1200 when the university

[1] F. M. Powicke, *Stephen Langton: being the Ford Lectures delivered in the University of Oxford ns Hilary Term 1927* (Oxford, 1928); cited hereafter as "Powicke, *SL*." (Particular attention in thii chapter is given to secondary writings published since 1928).

[2] *Ibid.*, 6.

[3] Powicke arrived at this revised date in 1935 in his essay "Stephen Langton," in *The Christian Life in the Middle Ages* (Oxford, 1935), 130-46. In his earlier work, *SL*, *cit. supra*, 8, he had suggested the date *ca.* 1165. Raymonde Foreville, in her article on Langton in *Dictionnaire de spiritualité ascétique et mystique: doctrine et histoire* (4 vols.; Paris, 1937-61), IV, ii, 1495-1502, supports the earlier date, placing it *ca.* 1150-55. On the Langton chronology, see summary in J. F. Veal, *The Sacramental Theology of Stephen Langton and the Influence upon Him of Peter the Chanter* (Rome, 1955), 15-16.

[4] Powicke, *SL*, 6, 8. On Walter, a layman, who died before April 1236, see *ibid.*, 5-8. Simon became archdeacon of Canterbury and acted for Stephen in the negotiations with King John from 1208. He was one of the envoys sent by Stephen to Rome to appeal for the relaxation of the interdict. See letter, Innocent III to Nicholas, papal legate (April-May 1214) in C. R. Cheney and W. H. Semple (edd.), *Selected Letters of Pope Innocent III concerning England, 1198-1216* (Edinburgh, 1953), 188-90.

[5] Powicke, *SL*, 9.

[6] The date, *ca.* 1170, is a revision of the Langton Paris chronology. In 1928, Powicke suggested *ca.* 1180, *ibid.*, 10. In a later article, "Bibliographical Note on Recent Work upon Stephen Langton," *EHR*, XLVIII (1933), 554-57 Powicke summarized the evidence showing that since Langton was master of theology *ca.* 1180, and furthermore, had taught in arts before theology, he must have come to Paris *ca.* 1170.

received its charter, nor was it yet the Paris of Thomas Aquinas. In Langton's day there were only about two hundred students in Paris, and the only schools open to seculars were the cathedral schools in the Island or on the Petit Pont which were subject to the jurisdiction of the chancellor of Notre Dame.[7] Students could pursue a course in the humanities, law, or medicine, but the dominant interest was theology, queen of the sciences. This was, as Powicke has noticed, "a practical, moral theology, closely linked with the careful, but by no means stereotyped, exegesis of the Scriptures."[8]

In the Paris of the closing decades of the twelfth century, Langton undoubtedly had contact with men such as Peter of Poitiers,[9] Alexander Neckham,[10] William of Leicester,[11] Robert de Courçon,[12] Lothar of Segni (later, Innocent III),[13] Peter of Capua,[14] and Prepositinus (Prévostin) of Cremona.[15] Whether Langton was himself a pupil of Peter the Chanter or Peter Comestor has been the subject of considerable scholarly controversy, but recent evidence lends support to the Chanter's role as Langton's teacher.[16]

The Paris period was, furthermore, a fruitful one in Langton's career. To it belong his *Questiones Theologice* (lectures on theological and moral problems); his commentaries on Scriptures; the division of the Bible into its modern chapter arrangement (which is consistently attributed to him); and, indeed, a goodly portion of the sermons that are the subject of this study.[17] Of this Paris period, Powicke wrote:

[7] Powicke, *SL*, 26-27.

[8] Powicke, *Christian life*, etc., 135.

[9] P. Glorieux, *Répertoire des maîtres en théologie de Paris au XIIIe siècle* (2 vols.; Paris, 1933), I, 229-31. See also, P. S. Moore, *The works of Peter of Poitiers* (*Univ. of Notre Dame Medieval Studies*, no. 1, 1935).

[10] J. C. Russell, *Dictionary of writers of thirteenth century England* (*Bull. Inst. Hist. Research, Suppl.* no. 3, London, 1936), 14-17.

[11] *Ibid.*, 196-97.

[12] *Ibid.*, 132-33.

[13] A. Luchaire, *Innocent III* (6 vols.; Paris, 1904-08).

[14] Glorieux, I, 265.

[15] *Ibid.*, 266-68.

[16] Powicke in *SL*, 17, supported Peter the Chanter as Langton's master. Beryl Smalley in *The Study of the Bible in the Middle Ages* (2d ed., rev.; Oxford, 1952), 197, wrote that Langton may have heard Peter Comestor, but not the Chanter. The recent work by Veal, *cit. supra*, summarizes the controversy and returns to Powicke's earlier view. Dr. John Baldwin of Johns Hopkins University is currently investigating the circle of Peter the Chanter, including Langton.

[17] For the most complete lists of Langton's writings and related bibliography, see G. Lacombe, B. Smalley, and A. L. Gregory, "Studies on the commentaries of Stephen Langton," *Arch. d'hist. doct. et litt. du M.A.*, V (1930), 183-212 (cited hereafter as "Lacombe *et al.*"); Glorieux, I, 238-60;

> We get a glimpse of a long life of theological teaching: of a little *scola* with a glossed Bible set on a stand in the middle of the room, of the master's library, containing the chief fathers in full, the works of the Lombard, and some of the writings of his contemporaries, of the master lecturing in course of time on the Scholastic History of the Manducator, the whole of the Bible, and the Lombard on St. Paul, and repeating or extending courses of lectures on theological problems which arose out of this exegesis, and permitted of discussion. By the end of his career as a teacher he was able to re-arrange the books of the Bible and to divide them into new chapters. In addition he was a poet and historian and then, as later, an indefatigable preacher.[18]

This was the Langton whose reputation in biblical scholarship was acclaimed by contemporaries, near-contemporaries, and later bibliographers.[19] This was the Langton named Cardinal-priest of S. Chrysogonus in 1206 [20] by a former Paris schoolmate who had become Pope Inno-

and the most recent F. Stegmüller, *Repertorium biblicum medii aevi* (7 vols.; Madrid, 1950-61), V (1955), 232-302. The *Questiones*, in at least one edition, are assigned to *ca.* 1203-06, although earlier versions can be dated between 1180-85. On the chronology of the various commentaries, see Lacombe *et al.*, 160-66.

18 Powicke, "Bibliographical note, etc.," 557.

19 Note the following as typical of this acclaim: *Annales monastici*, ed. Luard (*Rolls Series*), II, 304: ... in scientia theologica suo tempore nulli secundus. *Caesarius von Heisterbach*, ed. Meister (1901), 10: ... qui nullo theologo huius temporis inferior scientia esse dinoscitur. *Chronica Alberici Monachi Trium Fontium, MGH, SS*, XXIII (Hannover, 1874), 922: ... super omnes sui temporis nominatus theologus. *Roberti Autissiodorensis Chronicon, MGH, SS*, XXVI (Hannover, 1882), 272: .. Virum quidem vita honestum, preclarumque inter Parisienses magistros tam facundia quam scientia scripturarum. *Willelmi Chronica Andrensis, MGH, SS*, XXIV (Hannover, 1879), 737: ...litteris apprime eruditum. Gerald of Wales' dedication to SL of the Itinerary of Archbishop Baldwin through Wales, *Giraldi Cambrensis Itinerarium Kambriae et Descriptio Kambriae*, ed. Dimock (*Rolls Series*), VI, 7: ...tibi, vir inclite, Stephane Cantuariensis archiepiscope, quem religio pariter et literatura commendat. See also the dedication by Peter of Cornwall, prior of Holy Trinity, Aldgate (d. 1221) of his *Liber Disputationum contra Symonem Iudeum* to Langton in R. W. Hunt, *Studies in Medieval History presented to F. M. Powicke* (Oxford, 1948), 153-56. Honorius III, in a letter to Langton (11 July 1226): Cum eminentiam scientiae tibi datae a Domino meditamur... in *Letters of Henry III*, ed. Shirley (*Rolls Series*), I, 547. Gregory IX, confirming the election of Richard of Lincoln, successor to Langton, in 1229: ... bonae memoriae Stephano quondam Cantuariensi archiepiscopo, sanctae Romanae ecclesiae cardinali, viro utique pereminentissime (*sic*) donis scientiae... in *M. Parisiensis Chronica Majora*, ed. Luard (*Rolls Series*), III, 171. Bale in *Hist. litt. de la France*, XVIII (1835), 62: Stephanus Langton... in philosophia aristotelica nulli habebatur secundus. Utramque theologiam, et scholasticam, et interpretativam, ingenio callidus, novo praelegendi genere, per subtilitates docuit; scripturasque sacras multis annis quam superstitiose per allegorisationes et moralisationes exposuit. C. Oudin, *Comment. de script. eccl.* (1722) II, 1695-96: ... ut in celeberrima toto orbe Parisiensi Academia bonis artibus ac studiis vacaret: in quibus adeo brevi excelluit, ut in Philosophia Peripatetica, ac Sacra Theologia nulli suo tempore secundus haberetur, et utramque publice summa cum laude docuerit. J. Brucker, *Hist. crit. phil.* (1766-67) III, 783: ... primo quidem Scholasticae philosophiae et theologiae doctor.

20 As Cardinal-priest, Langton was influential in the Curia, and probably continued his theological teaching at Rome. Powicke, *SL*, 75.

cent III, and this was the Langton who was to become archbishop of Canterbury.

When Hubert Walter, archbishop of Canterbury, died on 13 July 1205, the monks of Christ Church, Canterbury elected Reginald their subprior as his successor.[21] Owing to the irregularity of the election,[22] and subject to royal pressure, the monks subsequently abandoned the first candidate Reginald, and on 11 December 1205 chose instead John de Gray, bishop of Norwich. The pope had then to decide between two archbishops-elect who came to the Curia. Professor C. R. Cheney has called attention to the mystery that still surrounds the events of the disputed election. We do not know, wrote Cheney, precisely how or when Reginald was elected. Nor is it clear what caused the monks to elect John de Gray. There are, moreover, considerable gaps in our knowledge of "the whole truth about Langton's election in the Curia," since, if we accept the previously unknown document as evidence (*cit. infra*), it seems clear that Reginald and his companions were at the Curia before 1 December 1205, and at that time Innocent was "satisfied that Reginald had been chosen by the unanimous will of the convent."[23]

Yet, on or before 21 December 1206, in the presence of Innocent III, Stephen Langton was elected archbishop of Canterbury by a deputation of monks sent from Christ Church, Canterbury to Rome to carry out the archiepiscopal election. Langton was consecrated at Viterbo on 17 June 1207.[24] Several weeks earlier (26 May) Innocent had appealed to John of England to consent to the election, and had outlined to the king Langton's noteworthy qualifications.[25]

Innocent III had good reason to lend support to Langton's candidacy. The two men had been friends in the schools in Paris, and shared an

[21] Stubbs in his introduction to the *Histor. Coll.* of Walter of Coventry (*Rolls Series*) provided the basic account of the events from the disputed Canterbury election of 1205 to the submission of John to the pope. See M. D. Knowles' criticism of the traditional account in "The Canterbury Election of 1205-06," *EHR*, LIII (1938), 211-20.

[22] See C. R. Cheney, "A neglected record of the Canterbury election of 1205-06," *Bull. Inst. Hist. Research*, XXI (1948), 233-38.

[23] *Ibid.*, 233-34.

[24] See letter of 27 August 1207, Innocent III to bishops of London, Ely, and Worcester. Cheney & Semple, 91-95. On the consecration, 93.

[25] *Ibid.*, 86-90. Knowles, in his article on the Canterbury election, *cit. supra*, 220, has shown that Innocent awaited John's approval of the election before proceeding with the consecration. Innocent to John on the character of Langton: ... quod, Parisius diu vacans liberalibus studiis, in tantum profecerit, ut meruerit esse doctor, non solum in liberalibus facultatibus, verum etiam in theologicis disciplinis, ac si per hoc, cum vita concordet doctrinae, dignus est habitus praebendam Parisiensem optinere. M. Paris, *Chron. Maj.*, II, 518.

interest in the reform of the Church. We shall notice Langton's participation in a popular preaching movement that had the support of the papacy. The evidence in his lectures on Scripture and in his theological questions indicates that Langton held generally accepted views about the supremacy of the spiritual power in a Christian society. These were traditional among the high prelates of his day. He would therefore appear most attractive to the pope who sought a candidate who would effectively carry out his program of reform.

Where Langton did take up the question of papal plenitude of power, he does not challenge the doctrine but seems to be more concerned with its use. Obedience to the pope was, in the *Questiones*, couched in very specific terms. In a question, for example, which related to the legitimacy of a particular papal decree on fasting, Langton stated:

> Dicimus quod licitum fuit et acquiescendum summo pontifici quia qui pontifici resistit Dei ordinationi resistit.[26]

Langton's master, Peter the Chanter, had taught in the *Verbum Abbreviatum* that it is a sacrilege to contradict and to censure the works of the lord pope.[27]

At the same time, however, we must notice that there is, in the Chanter's views, a resistance to the increasing number of new laws issued by Rome. When he proclaims the primacy of the gospel and spiritual liberty against the multiplication of precepts,[28] his was the voice of protest against the invasion of local churches by new legislation. It was to the old laws that he looked for inspiration for reform. His pupil Langton spoke of Christ as the head of the Church,[29] and his later career was to bear out his support of reform in the English church.

When Langton was elected archbishop, there does not appear any reason to question his general support of and agreement with overall papal reform policies. Difficulties between the new archbishop and the pope arose, however, over Langton's alleged alignment with the baronial

[26] St. John's Coll., Cambridge MS 57, f. 260ra. See also Powicke, *SL*, 138-39. Notice, however, that in their recent book, *The Governance of Mediaeval England from the Conquest to Magna Carta* (Edinburgh, 1963), 342, H. G. Richardson and G. O. Sayles contend that "Langton was more papalist than the pope."

[27] *Verbum Abbreviatum*, c. 44 (Migne, *PL*, 205, 139): Sacrilegium enim est opera ejus redarguere et vituperare [i.e., domini papae].

[28] *Ibid.*, c. 79 (*PL*, 205, 233-39) cited in M.-D. Chenu, *La théologie au douzième siècle* (Paris, 1957), 264-65.

[29] In the *Questiones*, St. John's Coll., Cambridge MS 57, f. 324rb: de Christo capite, quot modis dicitur caput ecclesie. Also, f. 273ra: De capite ecclesie... et sic filius Dei inquantum homo est est caput ecclesie.

party, and especially over the archbishop's disapproval of the pope's suzerainty over England. These actions brought him into conflict with his Paris friend.[30] There were, in addition, other aggravating factors which related to the freedom of the English church from Rome. The archbishop's attitude toward papal legates was evidenced as early as 1213,[31] and his efforts to bar the presence of a papal legate in England during the reign of Henry III have been hailed by his more enthusiastic admirers as a kind of "nascent Anglicanism."[32]

Opposition to papal legates and criticism of their activities were not unusual in thirteenth-century England. A century earlier, resistance and antagonism to foreign nuncios had led Pope Honorius II, in accordance with a general shift in papal policy, to name the archbishop of Canterbury representative of Rome. This occurred in 1125, when any further attempts at reform of the English church by legatine councils were abandoned.[33] Yet the papal legate sent from Rome was not absent for long. In the disturbances attendant on the reign of Stephen, the pope resumed appointing what legates he pleased, and in 1144, the Cardinal-bishop Imar of Tusculum arrived in England to arbitrate between the disputants to the throne.[34] While such legates often acted in the interests of reform, they were, nonetheless, also viewed by many contemporaries primarily as tax-collectors.[35] Papal taxation was a constant source of irritation and a favorite target for attack — as Matthew Paris attests[36] — as was the

[30] Langton opposed John's submission of the kingdom to the pope and regarded it as something "to be detested throughout the ages." F. M. Powicke, *King Henry III and the Lord Edward* (2 vols.; Oxford, 1947), I, 347. On the submission and the oath of fealty, see *Stubbs' Select Charters*, ed. H. W. C. Davis (9th ed., rev.; Oxford, 1960), 279-81. Also, E. H. Kantorowicz, *The King's Two Bodies* (Princeton, 1957), 349 ff.

[31] In 1213 Langton and his colleagues protested against the papal legate Nicholas who, acting in accord with papal mandate, made appointments to vacant sees disregarding "the wishes of electing bodies or the rights of diocesans." Powicke has suggested that this was probably a reason for Langton's unpopularity with Rome and his temporary suspension in 1215. *Henry III and the Lord Edward*, I, 262. On the papal legates in England from 1207-18, see H. Tillmann, *Die päpstlichen Legaten in England bis zur Beendigung der Legation Gualas* (1218) (Bonn, Diss. 1926), 93-120.

[32] In 1221, Langton succeeded in having Pandulf, papal legate, withdrawn from England. Powicke, *SL*, 146. See also B. Wilkinson, *Const. hist. of Engl.: 1216-1399* (London, 1948), I, 20.

[33] N. F. Cantor, *Church, kingship, and lay investiture in England: 1089-1135* (Princeton, 1958), 312-13.

[34] W. Janssen, *Die päpstlichen Legaten in Frankreich* (*1130-1198*) (Köln, 1961), 39.

[35] C. R. Cheney, "The papal legate and English monasteries in 1206," *EHR*, XLVI (1931), 443. Langton could not have not known that it would remain for a papal legate to carry on the work of reform that he had initiated. This was accomplished by Otto, cardinal deacon of S. Nicola in Carcere who was sent to England by Pope Gregory IX (June 1237-Jan. 1241). Langton died in 1228. Powicke, *Henry III and the Lord Edward*, I, 351-52.

[36] R. Vaughan, *Matthew Paris* (Cambridge, 1958), 140-41 summarizes his views on the papacy.

increasing number of foreigners appointed to canonries and other benefices. Langton took exception to these developments and viewed with particular disfavor Rome's interference with canonical appointments.[37]

This freedom for the English church from Rome, had its counterpart in Langton's independent attitude in his dealings with the Crown. On 21 November 1214, the archbishop received assurances from King John that the canons of a chapter would actually have the right of election.[38] Langton's insistence on free canonical elections ultimately came to be embodied in the first clause of the Great Charter drafted in 1215: *Quod ecclesia Anglicana libera sit...*

Yet, when Innocent had earlier written to John of the new archbishop's qualifications, the king refused to accept Langton as archbishop of Canterbury. His initial response had been to reject anyone who had lived for so long among his enemies. "Anyone who acknowledged Langton as archbishop should be regarded a public enemy," he said.[39] Langton, though born in England, was not very well known in that country, having spent most of his years in the schools at Paris. There have been various interpretations of John's actions. Kate Norgate stressed Langton's later connections with Magna Carta: "It was Stephen Langton who was to give the first impulse to the work which was destined... to make the rule of such a king as John impossible in England forevermore."[40] The late Professor Painter suggested that John insisted on approving the candidate to the archiepiscopal see of Canterbury, it being a political impossibility for the king of England to allow an outside authority to control the election to this important office. John was fearful lest Langton's consecration without the king's consent would set a precedent in other cases.[41]

A more simple and direct explanation relates to John's initial response

[37] Powicke, *SL*, 149-51.

[38] W. S. McKechnie, *Magna Carta* (Glasgow, 1905), 226. See e.g., the Durham election of 1226-28 when Langton insisted on the chapter's freedom of election. Powicke, *Henry III and the Lord Edward*, I, 267-68.

[39] K. Norgate, *John Lackland* (London, 1902), 127. (See W. of Coventry, II, 199; R. Wendover, III, 215-17; Innoc. III, Epp. 1.x. no. 219). Notice that Powicke in his *Loss of Normandy 1189-1204* (2d ed., rev.; Manchester, 1961), 286 has called attention to the idea of treason and alien laws developing in England after the loss of Normandy.

[40] Norgate, 218.

[41] S. Painter, *The reign of King John* (Baltimore, 1949), 169-71, 181. J. E. A. Jolliffe in *Angevin Kingship* (London, 1955), 118 has emphasized the constitutional aspects of the dispute, placing this episode in the larger context of "the internal struggle of the secular state to find its own character... to arrive at a true political monarchy and convert its vassals into subjects." Powicke, *SL*, 78 underlines its ecclesiastical significance, stating that the issue was more than that of freedom of election, but the demand of reformers for canonical and valid elections.

to Langton's appointment, namely the new archbishop's Paris connections. Not too many years before, Normandy was lost to the English monarchy. The Capetian kings were rivals and in fact a worrying threat to John in his troubles with the barons. Langton's long residence in Paris and his associations with a circle of clerics whose pro-Gallic tendencies were pronounced would be adequate reason for John's resistance to the Langton appointment.[42] Peter the Chanter, who was prominent in this circle, had strong pro-Becket sympathies. They were revealed in his praise for Becket's condemnation of simony in the household at Canterbury[43] and in his remarks, reported by Caesar of Heisterbach, that Becket had died the martyr for the liberty of the Church.[44] There was, furthermore, the tradition among certain of these clerics in Paris of the good kings of France and the tyranny of English princes. It was no better articulated than in Gerald of Wales' book on princely instruction.[45] Gerald had been resident in Paris from about 1165-72 and again from 1177-80.[46] His book contains denunciations against Norman and Angevin kings and viciously attacked John himself.[47] (The book did not make an appearance until 1217 after John's death.)[48] This was a climate of opinion which was decidedly hostile to the English monarchy and Langton's associations with it would have been sufficient to arouse John's opposition to the new archbishop.

Assurances by the pope of Langton's loyalty to the king were unavailing.[49] From 1207-13, the pope attempted to negotiate various safe-conducts for Langton[50] (who spent much of this period of exile at the Cister-

[42] Richardson and Sayles in the work, *cit. supra*, view Langton as unsuited to the office of archbishop (363), since he was unfamiliar in the ways of the Curia (353). Granting Langton a measure of "inflexible integrity," they write: "plainly he was not a man of independent thought, but narrow, legalistic, and uncharitable." (338) This, after their statement that Langton's personal qualities were irrelevant to the political struggle under John ! (337)

[43] *Verbum Abbreviatum*, c. 38 (Migne, *PL*, 205, 132): Beatus Thomas Cantuariensis, ut Simoniam a domo sua penitus amoveret, instituens magistrum Arnulphum cancellarium, cum juramento astrinxit, quod nec pac ione, nec sine pactione, usque ad canipulum pro officio cancellariae administrando acciperet. (See also c. 22, col. 81).

[44] Caesarius of Heisterbach, *Dialogus Miraculorum*, viii, 69. (Cited in Powicke, *SL*, 58).

[45] *Giraldi Cambrensis De Principis Instructione Liber*, ed. Warner (*Rolls Series*), VIII. Notice his lavish praises given to Louis VII of France, 132ff; Philip Augustus, 138. Denunciations of Henry II, *passim*; John, 310; William Rufus, 322.

[46] *Ibid.*, xvi.

[47] *Ibid.*, 327: Nullus regum Normannorum... vitam laudabili fine terminavit.

[48] *Ibid.*, xvi.

[49] Letter of 9 May 1208, Innocent III to bishops of London, Ely, and Worcester. Cheney & Semple, 102-03.

[50] In September 1208, John gave Langton a safe-conduct for a visit to England for one week. It was addressed "S. de Langton, Cardinal." Langton refused to come, interpreting it to mean that he was not yet recognized as archbishop. (In Norgate, *John Lackland*, 129, n.6.) In the spring of

cian monastery at Pontigny), and reiterated his request for a guarantee for the archbishop.[51] Efforts by Langton himself to bring an end to his exile were also in vain. In October 1210, the archbishop-elect attempted to reach a personal settlement with the king in an interview with two ecclesiastical envoys sent by John.[52] Two years later, in the winter of 1212, Langton left Paris for Rome with the bishops of Ely and London to register his complaints against the king and to appeal to the pope to bring matters to a conclusion.[53] When he returned to France in January of the following year, Langton turned to Philip Augustus for assistance. Accompanying him was the legate Pandulf who brought a letter from Innocent urging John's expulsion from the throne.[54]

To all of this, John responded with delaying tactics[55] and reasserted his refusal to accept Langton. The interdict in England and Wales (pronounced on Sunday 23 March 1208 and in effect till 2 July 1214)[56] was the papal reply to John's refusal and a move to force royal acceptance of Langton. In two articles published in 1948-49, Professor Cheney underlined the nature of the struggle, in that John's "war" was against the pope and was not directed against the English church or the Christian religion.[57] The interdict was used as a diplomatic weapon,[58] and John's submission

1210, another safe-conduct was sent. This too was irregular in form. When John arrived at Dover on 4 May to meet Langton, the archbishop failed to appear. In his rage, John ordered the woods on all the archiepiscopal manors cut down. See *Annal. Wav.* a. 1211, cited in Norgate, 159.

[51] See letter of 27 Feb. 1213, Innocent to John. Cheney & Semple, 130-36. To the bishops of London, Ely, Hereford, Bath, and Lincoln, *ibid.*, 132-33. See also the letter of 31 Oct. 1213 to archbishop of Dublin *et al.*, *ibid.*, 161-63.

[52] Powicke, *SL*, 78.

[53] Norgate, *John Lackland*, 175.

[54] *Ibid.* (See R. Wendover, III, 241-42; R. Coggeshall, 165). The letter has traditionally been regarded as a papal sentence of deposition, a view upheld by Powicke in *SL*, 78. C. R. Cheney in "The alleged deposition of King John," *Studies presented to Powicke*, *cit. supra*, 100-16 has shown, however, that this was not a formal sentence of deposition, but a threat of such action.

[55] For example, John proposed that instead of his giving Langton the regalia of the see, that these should be placed in the pope's hands. Although the pope was not overly enthusiastic about the suggestion, he, nevertheless, authorized the bishops of London, Ely, and Worcester as his representatives to carry out the scheme. When the bishops tried to seek an interview with John on the proposal, the king put them off. Norgate, *John Lackland*, 129, n. 6.

[56] See letter of April-May 1214, Innocent to papal legate Nicholas, that mentions Langton's envoys sent to Rome to appeal for the relaxing of the interdict. Cheney & Semple, 188-90.

[57] C. R. Cheney, "King John and the Papal Interdict," *Bull. John Ryl. Lib.*, XXXI, no. 2 (1948), 295-317. See also, "King John's reaction to the Interdict on England," *Trans. Roy. Hist. Soc.*, 4th ser., XXXI (1949), 129-50 which deals especially with the problem of John's general seizure of church property in 1208.

[58] Cheney, "King John and the Papal Interdict," 297. Richardson and Sayles, *op.cit.*, 354 call it "a piece of political blackmail."

in 1213 was also a diplomatic move, motivated, no doubt, by his fear of domestic rebellion and foreign invasion.[59]

John's personal excommunication in 1209 was probably a factor as well.[60] He may have feared that the barons might use this as an excuse to withdraw their allegiance and unite against him.[61] There was, furthermore, the threat of deposition. From 1211-13, rumors circulated that John had indeed been deposed.[62] The chroniclers, it appears, transmuted rumor to fact, since, as Professor Cheney has shown, John was not formally deposed but was threatened with deposition should he not submit to the pope by 1 June 1213.[63] That he did. In June or July 1213, Langton landed at Dover with four of his suffragan bishops. They were received at Winchester on 20 July by King John who threw himself at Langton's feet, welcomed him, implored his mercy, swore to uphold the good laws of England, and was thereupon absolved by the archbishop.[64]

By 1213-14, therefore, several of the major issues had been resolved. Stephen claimed his archbishopric. John was absolved of his excommunication. England had become a vassal state of the papacy, and in July 1214 the interdict was relaxed.[65] There remained the grievances of the barons against the king, culminating in the drafting of Magna Carta at Runnymede in June 1215. The history of the Great Charter is well known,[66] but it is relevant to this biographical survey of Stephen Langton that we review his connections with the Charter.

Roger Wendover, the St. Albans chronicler, tells us that on 25 August 1213, Langton informed the barons assembled at St. Paul's in London[67]

[59] Cheney, "King John and the Papal Interdict," 317.

[60] On the excommunicant John and any supporting clergy, see letter of 7 March 1213, Innocent to Langton, and the bishops of London, Ely, and Lincoln. Cheney & Semple, 137, 139-40.

[61] W. L. Warren, *King John* (London, 1961), 174.

[62] Cheney, "The alleged deposition of King John," *op. cit.*, 115.

[63] *Ibid.*, 111.

[64] Norgate, *John Lackland*, 186-87. On John's acceptance of the settlement with the pope, see letter of 6 July 1213, Innocent to Langton and his fellow-bishops. Cheney & Semple, 152-53.

[65] Richardson and Sayles have recently suggested (*op. cit.*, 352-54) that once John and Innocent III had come to terms with respect to the surrender of England to the papacy, that it was Langton who, through his ineptitude and inflexibility, stood in the way of "re-establishing normal relations between the kingdom and the Curia." In short, that Langton, by insisting on full restitution to the Church, bears the responsibility for prolonging the interdict.

[66] For documents relative to Magna Carta, see McKechnie, *op. cit.*, 565-89. See also, Ch. Petit-Dutaillis, "An unknown charter of liberties," in *Studies and notes supplementary to Stubbs' Constitutional History* (2d ed.; Manchester, 1911), 116-26; and J. C. Holt's recently published *Magna Carta* (Cambridge, 1965).

[67] The purpose of the assembly was to give instructions to ecclesiastical dignitaries and the lay magnates "concerning a partial relaxation of the interdict, which he [i.e., Langton] was empowered to grant, pending the arrival of the legate." Norgate, *John Lackland*, 211.

of the laws of Henry I, laying the foundation, therefore, for the reforms embodied in the Articles of the Barons and the Charter itself. Wendover's story has never been conclusively proved, but as Painter noticed it may very well contain an essential truth, in that it was probably Stephen who guided the barons "to seek a general statement of legal principles instead of various benefits for individuals."[68]

Although the barons may have looked to Langton for leadership,[69] it is patent that the archbishop did not, at the same time, abandon the royal cause. Stephen Langton appears as a mediator in the struggle.[70] In August 1213, for example, when Langton tried to intervene between John and the northern barons, he told the king that he should not wage war on his subjects before obtaining a legal judgment against them.[71] John, however, persisted in his plans. With a military expedition imminent, Langton threatened excommunication for every participant except the king.[72] Again in the negotiations of 22 February and 13 April 1215, Langton may be seen working for a peaceful settlement between the disputants.[73] The archbishop's neutrality was further demonstrated when in June-July 1215, the Tower of London was temporarily given in his custody.[74]

Langton's role as mediator in the events of 1213-15 seems clear. Yet the extent to which the archbishop may have been responsible for the actual drafting of the Charter is obscure and subject to controversy.[75] H. G. Richardson, for example, doubts Langton's principal role and questions the veracity of Wendover's story that Langton discovered the Charter of Henry I and handed it over to the barons. The charter, continues this author, was easily accessible in its Latin text and was also available in the vernacular.[76] The argument appears again in the recently published *The*

68 Painter, *Reign of King John*, 276.

69 S. Painter, *William Marshal* (Baltimore, 1933), 177.

70 This was the view reflected in Gervase, II, 109 and Coggeshall, 172. See Warren, *op. cit.*, 232 and Powicke, *SL*, 128.

71 McKechnie, *op. cit.*, 35. The trial was set before the Curia Regis but apparently never took place. (See Coggeshall, 167 and Wendover, II, 83).

72 Norgate, *John Lackland*, 189-90.

73 C. R. Cheney, "The Eve of Magna Carta," *Bull. John Ryl. Lib.*, XXXVIII, no. 2 (1956), 314.

74 McKechnie, 560.

75 On the controversial views, see J. C. Holt, "The barons of the Great Charter," *EHR*, LXX (1955), 1, n. 4. Painter, in 1933 (*William Marshal*, 181), suggested that the Marshal could also have inspired Magna Carta. He came to modify this view in his *Reign of King John*, 303, published in 1949. J. C. Holt, in *The Northerners : a study in the reign of King John* (Oxford, 1961), 111 noticed the moderating influence of both Langton and the Marshal.

76 H. G. Richardson, "The morrow of the Great Charter: addendum," *Bull. John Ryl. Lib.*, XXIX, no. 1 (1945), 189, n. 2; 190.

Governance of Mediaeval England.[77] This emphasis, however, on the technical aspects of the Wendover story seems to miss the essential point. Granted that the charter was available to all and the barons did not require Langton to bring it to their attention, still the problem of baronial leadership remains unresolved by Richardson and Sayles who credit the barons with considerable political consciousness.[78] Thus,

> the barons had been driven to make specific proposals. It needed no *deus ex machina* to formulate them. This was to do no more than the knights and burgesses were to do repeatedly in the Parliaments of Edward III, guided partly by their native wisdom and partly by suggestions from outside.[79]

Although these authors regard the possibility that the Great Charter was the work of Stephen Langton as a "monstrous fable,"[80] they do concede that the inclusion of the clause concerning the freedom of the Church may have been due to his influence, adding, however, that neither the king nor Pandulf, the papal legate, would have objected to its inclusion![81]

This view which ascribes certain portions of the Charter to Langton's influence approaches that of various other authorities. McKechnie had earlier called attention to the inclusion of the chapter on the freedom of the Church, for which, he says, Langton and his friends were largely responsible.[82] Painter emphasized Chapter 39, since Langton held that the "right of a free man to a judgment was the most fundamental of all the baronial demands."[83] Norgate had underlined "the conception of a contract between king and people" and the "carefully chosen phraseology" in the document, crediting these to the archbishop's influence.[84]

Whatever his influence may have been, Langton is named in the Charter. His counsel, along with that of the other prelates, is acknowledged in the preamble:

> ... per consilium venerabilium patrum nostrorum, Stephani Cantuariensis archiepiscopi tocius Anglie primatis et sancte Romane ecclesie cardinalis. ...[85]

Although this may be ascribed to customary usage, the archbishop appears as well as a participant in the machinery of government outlined in Magna

[77] Richardson & Sayles, *op. cit.*, 359.
[78] *Ibid.*, 373.
[79] *Ibid.*, 389.
[80] *Ibid.*, 369.
[81] *Ibid.*, 358.
[82] McKechnie, 50.
[83] Painter, *Reign of King John*, 315.
[84] Norgate, *John Lackland*, 234.
[85] *Stubbs' Select Charters*, *op. cit.*, 292 (Preamble).

Carta. A board of arbitrators including Langton and others, was provided for in Chapter 55 to decide disputes concerning the legality of fines and amercements.[86]

To the pope in Rome, however, the archbishop did not appear to be mediating the dispute between the king and the barons, and his participation in the events surrounding the Charter was cause for criticism and discipline. On 19 March 1215, Innocent wrote to Langton and his suffragans, urging the archbishop to restore agreement between the parties.[87] The pope's tone was sterner in a letter of 7 July wherein he wrote that Langton and some of his fellow-bishops "have afforded him [i.e., John] neither help nor favour against the disturbers of the kingdom which admittedly now belongs, by right of feudal lordship, to the Roman Church: they thus appear as accomplices, if not partners, in a wicked conspiracy."[88] Several weeks earlier (18 June), Langton and his suffragans had been directed to excommunicate the barons unless they came to terms with the king within eight days "post susceptionem litterarum nostrarum."[89] The archbishop refused to act until he had talked with the pope himself. He was subsequently denounced as disobedient and suspended from his office by Pandulf and Peter, bishop of Winchester.[90] In September 1215, an exile once again, a discouraged Langton left for Rome to attend the Fourth Lateran Council.[91]

The deliberations in Rome had a marked effect on the latter part of

[86] *Ibid.*, 300. (c. 55) Omnes fines qui injuste et contra legem terrae facti sunt nobiscum, et omnia amerciamenta facta injuste et contra legem terrae, omnino condonentur, vel fiat inde per judicium viginti quinque baronum de quibus fit mentio inferius in securitate pacis, vel per judicium majoris partis eorumdem, una cum praedicto Stephano Cantuariensi archiepiscopo, si interesse poterit, et aliis quos secum ad hoc vocare voluerit: et si interesse non poterit, nihilominus procedat negotium sine eo, ita quod, si aliquis vel aliqui de praedictis viginti quinque baronibus fuerint in simili querela, amoveantur quantum ad hoc judicium, et alii loco illorum per residuos de eisdem viginti quinque, tantum ad hoc faciendum electi et jurati substituantur.

[87] Cheney & Semple, 196-97.

[88] Addressed to the bishop of Winchester, abbot of Reading and Pandulf, *ibid.*, 207. For the papal bull of 24 August 1215 annulling Magna Carta, see T. Rymer, *Foedera*, I, 203-05.

[89] See G. B. Adams, "Innocent III and the Great Charter," in *Magna Carta Commemoration Essays* (ed. H. E. Malden, London, 1917), 26-45. For text of the letter, 43-45.

[90] See letter of 4 Nov. 1215 wherein Innocent confirmed the sentence of suspension promulgated by Peter, bishop of Winchester, and the legate Pandulf. Cheney & Semple, 220.

[91] Gerald of Wales reported that Langton was so discouraged with the turn of events in England that he had almost decided not only to resign as archbishop but to retire completely from the world in a hermitage or a Carthusian cell. (Gir. Cambr. i, 401. Cited in Norgate, *John Lackland*, 245). For a list of prelates present at the Lateran Council, see A. Luchaire in *Journal des Savants* (Oct. 1905), 557 ff. See M. Gibbs & J. Lang, *Bishops and Reform, 1215-72, with special reference to the Lateran Council of 1215* (Oxford, 1934), 106.

Langton's career, from his return to England in 1218 till his death in 1228. In the ecclesiastical sphere, the first provincial council to legislate in England since the Lateran assembly was held in Oxford in 1222, at which time Langton's canons were read together with those enacted at Rome seven years earlier.[92] Subsequent ecclesiastical councils continued his efforts toward reform of the Church in England and the restoration of order and discipline among the clergy. A provincial council was held at St. Paul's, London on 7 January 1226, and two national councils met later that year on 3 May and 13 October.[93]

Langton devoted himself in this period not only to church reform but also to the administration of his see. In her publication of the *Acta Stephani Langton Cantuariensis Archiepiscopi*,[94] Kathleen Major has considerably increased our knowledge of the diocesan administration at Canterbury and Langton's official activities during his tenure of office. In these documents and elsewhere in the chronicles, we see Langton a busy primate. A few glimpses of the archbishop on several great occasions must suffice. In October 1220, the year of the translation of the relics of Becket, Langton was in Rome and preached a sermon on St. Thomas Becket.[95] In August of the following year, the archbishop welcomed a Dominican mission to England.[96] In 1225, we see Langton at Salisbury where he inaugurated the new choir of the church that had been founded five years earlier.[97]

As primate of England, Langton presided at the coronation of Henry III at Westminster on 17 May 1220 and furthermore had a prominent role as advisor to the young king.[98] It was Stephen who headed the embassy

[92] C. R. Cheney, "Legislation of the English medieval church," *EHR*, L (1935), 208. Individual bishops had, however, reiterated some of the decrees between 1216 and 1222. *Ibid.*, 389. The texts of the Constitutions of Oxford were published in Wilkins' *Concilia* (London, 1737). The need for a new edition has long been recognized and has recently been fulfilled in the publication of F. M. Powicke, C. R. Cheney, edd., *Councils and synods, with other documents relating to the English Church: II, A.D. 1205-1313* (2 vols.; Oxford and New York, 1964), see especially 100-25. See also by Cheney, *English Synodalia of the Thirteenth Century* (Oxford, 1941); *From Becket to Langton: English Church Government 1170-1213* (Manchester, 1956); and "The earliest English Diocesan Statutes," *EHR*, LXXV (1960), 1-29.

[93] Gibbs & Lang, *op. cit.*, 144-45. Powicke & Cheney, *cit. supra*, 155-64.

[94] *Canterbury and York Ser.*, no. 50 (Oxford, 1950). On Langton's diocesan statutes, see Powicke & Cheney, 23-36; 165-67.

[95] Powicke, *SL*, 145. On this and other sermons preached while he was archbishop, see chap. II, *infra*.

[96] *Ibid.*, 153.

[97] C. H. Lawrence, *St. Edmund of Abingdon: a study in hagiography and history* (Oxford, 1960), 123. Edmund was present on that occasion.

[98] The first coronation rite was held at Gloucester, 28 October 1216, while Langton was in Rome. Henry was crowned by Peter des Roches, bishop of Winchester. Powicke, *Henry III and the Lord Edward*, I, 3-4.

to France in 1223, when after the death of Philip Augustus (14 July), an unsuccessful attempt was made to restore Normandy to Henry. Pandulf, who was then in Paris, urged the pope to postpone the coronation of Louis VIII until Normandy was restored to Henry. When Langton arrived, Louis had already been crowned.[99] In the civil war that threatened between the factions who struggled for power during the minority of Henry III (between the supporters of the Justiciar Hubert de Burgh and the opposition led by Fawkes de Breauté), Langton on one occasion wielded the weapon of excommunication against the rebels and was able to maintain the peace by securing strategic castle strongholds for the Crown.[100] The archbishop again made his influence felt in 1225 in the confirmation of the Charter.[101]

His death on 9 July 1228 at Slindon Manor in Sussex[102] brought an end to a life of scholarship and service to the Church of Rome and to his native land. On occasion these allegiances conflicted, but throughout, he was a "devoted lover of Christ," as the Annalist of Waverley recorded in this epitaph:

Presul virtutis Stephanus documenta salutis
Vivens multa dedit, moriens a morte recedit.
Forma gregis, clerique decus, vite speculator
Et speculum, Christique fuit devotus amator.[103]

[99] *Ibid.*, 170. On 28 July 1223, Henry III thus accredited his ambassadors to the archbishop of Reims: ...Mittimus ad vos venerabiles patres dominum Cantuariensem archiepiscopum et Londoniensem et Sarresbiriensem episcopos, rogantes quatinus eos benigne audire et eis credere velitis super hiis que vobis dixerint ex parte nostra, et eadem firma et stabilia indubitanter habere. See Ch. Petit-Dutaillis, *Étude sur la vie et le règne de Louis VIII, 1187-1226* (Paris, 1894), 516.

[100] Powicke, *SL*, 154. See also C. Ellis, *Hubert de Burgh: a study in constancy* (London, 1952), 67, 173.

[101] Powicke, *Henry III and the Lord Edward*, I, 68.

[102] Langton was buried before the altar of the chapel of St. Michael in the Cathedral at Canterbury. The visitor to the Cathedral will notice that a portion of the tomb extends through the east wall and may be seen from outside. Alterations to the chapel in the first half of the fifteenth century made it necessary to replace the coffin under the altar of the chapel, hence thrusting the foot of the tomb through the wall. See C. E. Woodruff and W. Danks, *Memorials of the Cathedral and Priory of Christ in Canterbury* (London, 1912), 201-02. See F. A. Cazel, Jr's recent article, "The last years of Stephen Langton," *EHR*, LXXIX (1964), 673-97, especially on the years, 1227-28. For additions to Langton's itinerary, 697.

[103] *Annal. monas.*, *Wav.*, II, 305. See Powicke, *SL*, 160.

CHAPTER II

LANGTON THE PREACHER AND HIS SERMONS

LANGTON THE PREACHER

THE Annalist of Waverley wrote: "vite speculator et speculum...", one who observes life and is at the same time a mirror, showing people what they are and what they ought to be.[1] This was Langton, the preacher, an aspect of the archbishop's life that has heretofore received scant attention, due no doubt to the mass of sermons in manuscript that have not been systematically explored. Before turning to this sermon material which will be treated in the following chapters, let us examine what evidence we have in the sources of the preacher, Stephen Langton.[2]

In his life of the archbishop, Matthew Paris noted that Langton, in addition to his praiseworthy treatises *On Ecclesiasticus* and *On the Penitence of the Magdalene*, was the author of special theological sermons which he composed in the true manner of a master.[3] A recent study on Matthew Paris has underlined the hagiographical emphasis in this life of Langton. Historical facts were ignored in favor of an emphasis on Langton's piety, his holiness and skill as a preacher and theologian.[4] Langton's biographer regarded him as a saint and represented the archbishop as deploring the submission of England to the pope. Anti-papal sentiments were not uncommon in mid-thirteenth century England, and apparently Matthew Paris found in Langton a spokesman and representative of national feeling against Rome.

Matthew referred to Langton's preaching during the period after the archbishop's visit to Rome in 1215:

[1] Smalley, *Study of the Bible in the Middle Ages*, 245.

[2] Powicke in *SL* (42 ff and Appendix II, 168-76) devoted some attention to Langton the preacher. Miss Smalley, in her *Study of the Bible in the Middle Ages*, 253, noticed Langton's emphasis on the importance of preaching, especially to the laity, as revealed in his Commentaries.

[3] Ad ejus etiam meritum et memoriam spectat immortalem, quod quosdam tractatus laudabiles *Super Ecclesiasticum* et *De Penitentia Magdalene* et alias scripturas cum sermonibus specialibus theologicis magistrales tam magistraliter composuit. ... F. Liebermann, ed., "M. Parisiensis Vita sancti Stephani archiepiscopi Cantuariensis," *Ungedruckte Anglo-Normannische Geschichtsquellen* (Strassburg, 1879), 329. Excerpts of the *Vita* may be found in *MGH, SS*, XXVIII (Hannover, 1888), 441-43.

[4] Vaughan, *op. cit.*, 160-61. See also Russell, *Dictionary of writers*, etc., 83-84.

> How Archbishop Stephen rid Italy and France in great part of usurers, according to master Gervase of Melkeley. ...[5] [He preached], moreover, in northern Italy, in France — especially in Arras and St. Omer — and in parts of Flanders. Aiding him in his attacks and persecutions of usury and usurers was Robert de Courçon, a most learned man and cardinal of the Roman church. Together they rooted out the practice [of usury] and miraculously cleansed the French kingdom of the evil.

The account also mentions that the sermons of Langton, Robert de Courçon, and Jacques de Vitry were to be found in the *Liber Additamentorum* at St. Albans.[6]

Although we may accept Matthew Paris' statements about the preaching of Langton and de Courçon, and the sermons of Jacques de Vitry, the evidence presents certain chronological difficulties, if we are to believe that they were in fact preaching in the same region at the same time. Langton was in northern Italy, France, and Flanders during the years 1216-18. Robert de Courçon, however, who had studied in Paris with Langton and Innocent III, was not. From 1213-15, de Courçon had preached the crusade against the infidels and Albigensians in France and appeared at councils in Paris, Reims, Rouen, Clermont and Bourges as an ardent foe of usurers. In 1215, the cardinal was in Rome, and in 1218, he left for the Crusade, meeting his death on 6 February 1219.[7]

Notice, furthermore, that Matthew mentioned the sermons of Jacques de Vitry, a contemporary of both Langton and de Courçon. In a passage attacking usurers in his *Historia Hierosolymitana*[8] Jacques likened these two preachers to the "stars in the firmament." Jacques himself preached

[5] On Gervase of Melkeley, see Russell, 37-38.

[6] Qualiter archiepiscopus Stephanus mundavit in magna parte ab usuris Ytaliam et Franciam, secundum magistrum Gervasium de Melkeleie... In partibus autem Cisalpinis et in regno Francorum, maxime apud Atrabatum et Sanctum Aodemarum et in partibus Flandrie, iuvante eum... videlicet Roberto de Curcun, viro scientissimo, ecclesie Romane cardinali, adeo usuras eliminando usurarios persequebatur... usum radicitus extirparet et regnum Francorum ab illa eluvie mirabiliter emundaret. Cuius sermones, parabolas et virtutes, quas Dominus pro eodem archiepiscopo et magistro Roberto memorato necnon et magistro Iacobo de Vitriolo, que speciales exigunt tractatus, qui legere desiderat, Librum additamentorum annalium que apud Sanctum Albanum sunt, adeat inspecturus. Liebermann, *Vita*, 327-28. No entries of this kind are extant in the surviving volume of the *Liber Additamentorum* (Cott. MS Nero D.I). Powicke, *SL*, 41, n. 2.

[7] Marcel et Christiane Dickson, "Le cardinal Robert de Courson, sa vie," *Arch. d'hist. doct. et litt. du m.a.*, IX (1934), 61.

[8] Inter quos principales et maiores nominis fuerunt, quasi stelle in firmamento caeli, Venerabilis Pater Magister Stephanus Cantuariensis Archiepiscopus, et Magister Galterus de Londonia et Magister Robertus de Corchon, qui postea factus est Cardinalis. Iacobi de Vitriaco, *Hist. Hieros.* (Duaci, 1597), II, c. 9, 289. Robert de Courçon did not become cardinal till 1212. Dicksons, 61.

against the "Gallicos hereticos," but not at the time Langton was in Flanders or France. In 1216, Jacques de Vitry was preaching in Milan.[9]

The three preachers — Langton, de Courçon, and de Vitry — are mentioned again in Matthew Paris' *Chronica Majora*, where it is suggested that Robert Grosseteste heard them preach against the usurers in France.[10]

Langton and de Courçon, therefore, both preached against usurers sometime during the five year period, 1213-18. It is likely that Matthew Paris, who was writing at a much later date, was in error when he wrote that they preached at the same time in Flanders. That Jacques de Vitry is also mentioned in the same passage is relevant since that preacher had expressed praise for the others. Furthermore, if the sermons of the three preachers were, at one time, to be found in the *Liber Additamentorum*, as Matthew attests, perhaps this led the Chronicler to group them together.

Elsewhere in the chronicles, there are scattered references to Langton's preaching, and in fact to particular sermons which he delivered as archbishop. The Annalist of Waverley, for example, tells us that on 25 August 1213 at St. Paul's (when Langton allegedly informed the barons of the Charter of Henry I), the archbishop "...sermonem fecit ad populum, quo sic incepto, 'In Deo speravit cor meum et adjutus sum, et refloruit caro mea...'"[11] Later that year on 19 November, Langton was at Bury-St-Edmunds and addressed the chapter, saying: "... si separabiles et superabiles, et si inseparabiles insuperabiles usque reperiemini." This sermon, according to the brief account, dealt with the "rector" of a city and its inhabitants.[12]

The funeral of William the Marshal at the Temple in London in May 1219 also afforded the occasion of another of Langton's sermons. The archbishop paid tribute to the Marshal, calling him "the best knight in the world."[13]

9 Jacques de Vitry, born between 1160-70, studied in Paris *ca.* 1187. On his preaching, see P. Funk, *Jakob von Vitry: Leben und Werke* (Leipzig-Berlin, 1909), 176-84.

10 Caursini enim manifesti usurarii, quos sancti patres et doctores nostri, quos vidimus, et audivimus, videlicet magister eximius in Francia praedicator, abbas (Eustace) quoque de Flay Cisterciensis ordinis, magister Jacobus de Viteri, Cantuariensis archiepiscopus Stephanus exulans, magister Robertus de Curcun.... M. Paris, *Chronica Majora*, V, 404.

11 *Annal. monas.*, *Wav.*, II, 277. This sermon has been published by G. Lacombe, "An unpublished document on the Great Interdict," *Catholic Historical Review*, XV (1930), 408-20. See Troyes MS 862, *infra*.

12 Finito tandem sermone super hoc, qualis est rector civitatis, tales et inhabitantes in ea... . *Memorials of St. Edmund's Abbey*, ed. Arnold (*Rolls Series*), II, 39. The recently published Latin-English edition of *The Chronicle of Bury St. Edmund's, 1212-1301*, ed. A. Gransden (Nelson's Medieval Texts 1963) contains no reference to this sermon in the entry of the year 1213 (1-2). A notice of Langton's death appears under the year 1228 (6).

13 There is no mention of a *sermon* as such, nor does the word *preach* appear, but the funeral of so

In the later years of his archiepiscopate, other grand occasions were marked by Langton's preaching. These were usually noticed briefly by some chronicler, or possibly ignored by another. Such was the case when on the occasion of the second coronation of Henry III at Westminster (Pentecost, 17 May 1220), the Annalist of Dunstaple remarked that Stephen, archbishop of Canterbury, celebrated the mass and preached a sermon to the people.[14] One wonders what sort of sermon it was, since the account in Walter of Coventry fails to mention it.[15]

The latter, however, did not forget to mention the sermon that Langton preached on Thomas Becket in October 1220 at Rome.[16] The translation of the saint's relics in July of that year had been noted by Matthew Paris, but there is no mention of a sermon.[17] The dedication of the new Lady Chapel at Salisbury Cathedral on 29 September 1225 was also marked by Langton's preaching to the people.[18]

With the possible exception of the sermon preached at St. Paul's in August 1213 (which has special importance because of its connections with the interdict) none of these other sermons, preached in England, appears to be extant.[19] Langton's preaching at coronations, church dedications, state funerals and other public occasions has importance for the history of eloquence, both ecclesiastic and secular. Although most of these sermons have not been preserved, this is not the case of the great bulk of sermons

prominent a personage could well have occasioned the speech attributed to the archbishop. For the description of the funeral, see *L'histoire de Guillaume le Maréchal*, ed. P. Meyer (3 vols.; Paris, 1891-1901), II, 325-26, ll. 19047-84: Quant li cors dut estre enterrez, / Li archevesques dist: "Veez, / Seignor, comme li secles vet: / Quant chascuns est a sa fin trait, / Ne puet l'en en lui nul sens querre,/ N'est puis fors atretant de terre. / Veez ici a la roonde / Le meillor chevalier del monde... . See also Painter, *William Marshal*, 289.

14 ... et S(tephano) Cantuariensi archiepiscopo missam celebrante, et sermonem ad populum faciente... . *Annal. monas.*, *Dunst.*, III, 57.

15 In illo die igitur sacramentali, scilicet Pentecostes, in praesentia domini Pandulphi legati, Stephanus Cantuariensis archiepiscopus, astantibus ejusdem ecclesiae suffraganeis aliisque ecclesiarum praelatis, cum magnatibus regni plurimis, in ecclesia Sancti Petri Westmonasterii, a rege Henrico sacramentum exegit, scilicet quod ecclesiam Dei tueretur, pacemque tam cleri quam populi et bonas regni leges custodiret illaesas. *Walteri de coventria*, ed. Stubbs (*Rolls Series*), II, 244.

16 *Ibid.*, 246.

17 Eodem tempore, levatum est de lapide marmoreo corpus beati Thomae archiepiscopi et martyris a Stephano Cantuariensi archiepiscopo, praesente rege et omnibus fere episcopis totius regni, cum abbatibus, prioribus, comitibus, baronibus, clero et populo multo, in crastino octavarum Apostolorum Petri et Pauli. *Chronica Majora*, III, 59.

18 Die Sancti Michaelis sequenti, fecit dominus Cantuar. sermonem ad populum, qui quidem multus erat valde... . *Register of St. Osmund*, ed. W. H. R. Jones (*Rolls Series*), II, 39.

19 Another possible exception may be the treatise on the translation of the relics of Becket. It has been suggested that the treatise is an expanded version of the sermon preached on that occasion. *Infra*. I plan to treat Langton's preaching on Becket in a separate study.

attributed to Langton, and which, as we shall subsequently demonstrate, probably belong to his Paris period. Langton came to Paris *ca.* 1170 as a student and remained there studying, teaching, writing, and, we might add, preaching, for over thirty years until his consecration as archbishop of Canterbury in 1207. Stephen, archbishop of Canterbury, was a later title. From 1180, when he became master of theology, he was known as *magister*, as many sermons in French manuscripts (e.g. BN MS, lat. 14859) attest.

We propose to show that most of Langton's extant sermons were composed sometime within the priod *ca.* 1180 and 1207, that they were preached in various churches in Paris — to audiences clerical and popular, and that having already established a reputation as a preacher of note, these sermons came to be repeated elsewhere — singly or with others — under the later title — Stephen, archbishop of Canterbury. That Stephen Langton was an historical personage of some note is clear. An investigation of this unexplored sermon material affords yet another dimension to Langton's scholarship and career. Stephen Langton was not only master of theology at Paris and archbishop of Canterbury. He was also a preacher whose renown was echoed in the contemporary phrase — *Stephanus de Lingua-Tonante*,[20] "Stephen of the thundering tongue !"

The Problem of Sermon Research

The task of investigating this sermon material is not without its difficulties and problems peculiar to the *genre*. The sermons attributed to Langton appear among thousands of medieval Latin sermons extant in the manuscripts of the twelfth through the fourteenth centuries.[21] Most are unpublished, and in their present state in the manuscripts, it is difficult to disentangle a given preacher's sermons from those of other prelates.[22] Sometimes, as Haskins put it, many of these medieval sermons in the "condensed and desiccated form in which most of them have come down to us" do not make very interesting reading.[23]

Sermons are, nonetheless, a largely untapped source in social and intellectual history. The value of sermon research has long been recognized

[20] Ste-Gen. MS 1422, fol. 1.

[21] Ch.-V. Langlois, "L'Éloquence sacrée au moyen âge," *Revue des Deux Mondes*, CXV (1893), 172.

[22] See Powicke, *SL*, 41 particularly on the problem of Langton's sermons. Also, J. B. Schneyer, "Beobachtungen bei der Sammlung von Predigtinitien des 13. Jahrhunderts," *Scholastik*, XXXII (1957), 72-81.

[23] C. H. Haskins, "The University of Paris in the sermons of the XIIIth century," *AHR*, X (1904), 4.

by scholars who have noticed their potentiality as historical sources.[24] Langlois, for example, called the sermon a particularly important source for the history of manners and popular fables.[25] Likening the sermon of the thirteenth century to the popular press, the same author wrote that for a knowledge of the "spiritual state" and the customs of the age, there are no contemporary texts as alive as those sermons addressed to laity and clergy.[26] Owst, author of studies in medieval preaching in England, has also emphasized the important contribution of sermons to our knowledge of social life and thought.[27] Other writers underscore the value of the sermon as a source for the study of medieval Latin[28] and for the history of theological thought.[29]

Given the limitations of the *genre*, the historian can use these sermon texts fruitfully. Their use as sources requires application of standards of historical criticism. We shall, in subsequent chapters, treat the form of the sermon in the light of rhetorical theory; the relation between the spoken and written sermon; and the question of the vernacular and Latin sermon. Consideration of these special problems is necessary to any meaningful study of the sermons. Although Haskins would deny their historical value,[30] the historian who is wary of the special pitfalls of sermon literature — (first, the essential hortatory nature of the sermon that demands the exposure and criticism of the evils of society,[31] and second, that anecdotes, *exempla*, and similitudes are often borrowed and rarely based on personal

[24] For a recent survey of the problem, see J. B. Schneyer, "Die Erforschung der scholastischen Sermones und ihre Bedeutung für die Homiletik," *Scholastik*, XXXIX (1964), 1-26.

[25] Langlois, "L'Éloquence sacrée au m.â.," *op. cit.*, 172.

[26] Ch.-V. Langlois, "Sermons parisiens de la première moitié du XIIIe siècle contenus dans le ms 691 de la Bibliothèque d'Arras," *Journal des Savants* (nouv. sér. 1916), 549.

[27] G. R. Owst, *Preaching in medieval England* (Cambridge, 1926), x. See also his *Literature and pulpit in medieval England* (2d ed. rev.; Oxford, 1961).

[28] Thus, in A. Lecoy de la Marche, *La chaire française au moyen âge, spécialement au XIIIe siècle* (2d ed.; Paris, 1886), 269, who adds, for "modern" French as well. Ch. S. Baldwin, *Medieval rhetoric and poetic* (N.Y., 1928), 250 agrees: "Medieval sermons, for the defects of transmission, offer ample and various demonstration of the force and beauty of medieval Latin."

[29] M. Grabmann, *Die Geschichte der katholischen Theologie seit dem Ausgang der Väterzeit* (Freiburg-in-Br., 1933), 48.

[30] Haskins, *cit. supra*, 3: "By their very nature sermons are not historical but hortatory; their purpose is to edify, not to record; and the preaching of the 13th century, with its elaborate subdivisions, its piling of text upon text, its senses literal and allegorical, tropological and anagogical, would seem peculiarly barren of information upon the life of its age." Haskins does concede that *exempla* and stories selected by preachers do afford some insight into the popular religion and practices of the day.

[31] See, e.g. Lecoy de la Marche, *op. cit.*, 341-76 on the church and the religious world as seen in thirteenth century sermons.

experience)[32] — may still obtain a glimpse of the thought and mores of the society which the preacher mirrors in his sermons. Stephen Langton and his sermons offer such an opportunity.

The Langton Sermons: A Bibliographical Survey

References to the sermons of Stephen Langton in the secondary literature are scattered, and in view of the mass of material involved, very sketchy indeed. The bibliographer Oudin[33] referred to several manuscripts containing Langton sermons:

> Item in Valle Lucensi ejusdem Ordinis [i.e. Cisterciensis], MSS insuper *Sermones Stephani de Linguatona*, pulpito 23. Littera G. quorum multa quoque in Bibliotheca Victorina Parisiensi, quae brevitatis caussa (*sic*) omittimus.[34] Item in Catalogo impresso MSS. Codicum Bibliothecae Lipsiensis fol. 150. n. 36. *Sermones Stephani Cantuariensis Archiepiscopi de tempore et de sanctis. Sermones item ad Sacerdotes* De decem plagis, et alii.[35] Ejusdem *Sermo in Assumptionem Beatae Mariae Virginis*, qui incipit *Vidi, et super firmamentum* etc. MSS in Regia Galliarum Bibliotheca, Cod. MS 4126, pag. seu f. 158.[36] Vide et Catalogum MSS. Codicum Lipsiensis Bibliothecae, pag. 97.[37]

In another eighteenth century collection, Cave[38] repeated the data concerning the MSS noted above, adding however, the following reference to a catalogue of a monastic library in Flanders that was published in 1638:

> Sermones varii habentur MSS. in bibliotheca Dunensi apud Sander. biblioth. Belg. MSS. p. 183.[39]

This apparently refers to Brugge MSS 28 and 93 that originated in the abbey library at Dunes.[40]

[32] Owst, in his *Preaching in medieval England*, 6 noticed the lack of autobiographical details in the medieval sermon. R. W. Hunt in "Alexander Neckham" (unpubl. thesis, Oxford D. Phil. 1936), 97 also commented on the failure of the sermons to tell us much about the life of the author.

[33] Oudin, *Comment. de script. eccl.*, *op. cit.*, II, 1701.

[34] *Cf.* BN MS, lat. 14859 whose provenance was the Abbey of St. Victor in Paris, and Troyes MSS 1100 and 1367, Clairvaux MSS. On these MSS that contain attributions to Langton, see *infra*.

[35] See Io. Feller, *Cat. Cod. MSS Bibl. Paulinae in Acad. Lipsiensi* (Lipsiae, 1686). Now Leipzig MS 443.

[36] *Cat. Cod. MSS Bibl. Reg.* (4 vols.; Paris, 1739-44), III, 389. Now BN MS, lat. 3227.

[37] Feller, *cit. supra*. *Cf.* Leipzig MS 364. See also Th. Tanner, *Bibl. Brit.-Hiber.* (London, 1748), 468.

[38] W. Cave, *Script. eccles. hist. lit.* (2 vols.; Oxford, 1740-43), II, 282.

[39] A. Sanderus, *Bibl. Belg. Manuscripta* (Insulis, 1641), 183. The *Index Librorum MSS Bibl. Monasterii Dunensis. Ord. Cister. in Flandria* is dated 1638. See also Tanner, 468.

[40] On the Brugge MSS 28 and 93, see *infra*.

Feret noticed an additional manuscript — Ste. Geneviève D.I.27 £.[41] Of the more recent scholarship on the Langton sermons, the late Professor Powicke was one of the first to compile a summary list of the known MSS.[42] Georges Lacombe added to the Powicke list in the *Studies on the Commentaries of Stephen Langton* (1930) and underscored the importance of studying the estimated 500 sermons for the light they might shed on Langton's career. He added that he hoped to work on the problem.[43] In his *Répertoire*, Glorieux also listed the then-known MSS, and cited several sermons individually, e.g. *Sermones in Ave Maris Stella.*[44] Those sermons that had been published were noted as well: *Sermo in translatione S. Thomae Cantuar.*[45] and the sermon on the French song, *Bele Aliz matin leva*, which has been attributed to Langton.[46]

This was the bibliographical situation until the most recent work of

[41] P. Feret, *La faculté de théologie de Paris et ses docteurs les plus célèbres: Moyen Age* (4 vols.; Paris, 1894-97), I, 279. On this MS, now Ste-Gen. 1422, *infra.*

[42] Powicke, *SL*, App. II, 168-76.

[43] Lacombe *et al.*, 6-7. Powicke mentioned Lacombe's intention to devote himself to a study of the Langton sermons in the article, "Bibliographical note, etc." *cit. supra*, 556, published in 1933. Apparently Lacombe was unable to fulfill this promise. In the years prior to his death in 1934, Lacombe was engaged in the editing of the catalogue of the Latin Aristotle. Miss Smalley, who collaborated in the *Studies*, informs me that it was quite unlikely that Lacombe had proceeded very far with the sermons. Inquiries at Catholic University of America where Lacombe taught in the early 1930's appear to confirm this. The estimate of 500 sermons also appears in J. H. Baxter *et al.*, *Index of British and Irish Latin Writers* (Paris, 1932), no. 350, 49; in Glorieux, *Rép.*, I, 259; and was repeated by R. Foreville in 1961 in her article, *cit. supra* in *Dict. Spirit.*, col. 1499. See also the comments on the sermons in J. de Ghellinck, *L'essor de la litt. lat. au XII*e *s.* (2 vols.; Paris, 1946), I, 228-29. (References to particular MSS by Powicke, Lacombe, and Glorieux are incorporated in the section on the MSS, to be found in the Appendix. The following authors have also mentioned individual MSS which are also listed, according to each MS: Lecoy de la Marche, *op. cit.*, A. M. Landgraf, *Einführung in die Geschichte der theologischen Literatur der Frühscholastik* [Regensburg, 1948] and B. Hauréau, *Notices et extraits de quelques manuscrits latins de la Bibliothèque Nationale* [6 vols.; Paris, 1890-93], II).

[44] *Rép.*, I, 255. See BM MS, Roy. 8.A.X, f. 36r, *infra.*

[45] Glorieux, *Rép.*, I, 256. See the treatise *Stephani Langton Arch. Cant. Tractatus de translatione Beati Thomae* (Migne, *PL*, 190, 407-24; also published in J. A. Giles, "Vita S.. Thomae," *Patres Ecclesiae Anglicanae* [Oxford, 1845], II, 269-97) which, according to K. Norgate (*DNB*, XI, 568), probably represents an expanded version of the sermon preached on the occasion of the translation. See H. Wharton, *Anglia Sacra* (London, 1691), I, 48; Cave (1743), II, 281; Io. Fabricius, *Bibl. lat. med. et inf. aet.* (6 vols.; Leipzig, 1754), IV, 243; and *Materials for the history of Th. Becket, Archbishop of Canterbury*, ed. Robertson (*Rolls Series*), IV, 426-30. Also, the more recent R. Foreville, *Le Jubilé de Saint Thomas Becket du XIII*e *au XV*e *siècle, 1220-1470: Études et documents* (Paris, 1958), 3-11. For a description of the ceremonies, see Woodruff & Danks, *op. cit.*, 75-77.

[46] Glorieux, *Rép.*, I, 259 listed this sermon with spurious writings. See BM Arundel MS 292, f. 38r, *infra.* Ed. M. de la Rue, *Archeologia*, XIII (1800), 231. See also Norgate, *DNB*, XI, 568 on this sermon.

Dr. J. B. Schneyer of the University of Freiburg, whose interest in medieval Latin preaching is demonstrated in the compilation and publication of the valuable lists of *initia* and MSS, without which further sermon research would be well-nigh impossible.[47] Fortunately for Langton scholars, Dr. Schneyer has provided the necessary groundwork for further study of the sermons of Stephen Langton. His article, published in 1962, "Eine Sermonesliste des Kardinals Stephan Langton Erzbischofs von Canterbury,"[48] was a pioneering study which included an expanded and corrected list of MSS (as against the lists of Powicke, Lacombe, and Glorieux, *cit. supra*) and an alphabetical list of the sermons — arranged according to theme, incipit, and explicit. Dr. Schneyer also included rubrics (where available) noting the occasion of the sermon and a MS reference for each text. These researches have an incontestable value for any further investigation of the Langton sermons, and we are indeed grateful to him.

Dr. Schneyer has, furthermore, assisted us by pointing out the kinds of problems that need researching and the importance of continued study of the Langton sermons. We must, for example, in order to arrive at some notion of the number of sermons involved, distinguish between *different versions* of the same sermon on a given theme and *different sermons* on the same theme. Only a close look at the texts themselves can offer a solution to this question. An additional problem of anonymous texts besets the sermon investigator. Only a comparison with authenticated texts can suggest possible attributions.

Dr. Schneyer has thus taken us one step further on the way to unravelling the obscurities of the Langton sermons, by making numerous additions and corrections to earlier researches. These *Studies in the Sermons of Stephen Langton* aim to proceed with the investigation and to use Dr. Schneyer's published findings as the key to solving some of the problems delineated earlier. To this end, we shall in the succeeding pages of this chapter describe the following:

1) *Classification of manuscripts:* Dr. Schneyer has listed MSS which bear

[47] See bibliography.

[48] *Recherches de théologie ancienne et médiévale*, XXIX (1962), 159-205. (I am indebted to Dr Schneyer for his generosity in sending me this article in typescript a year before its publication. His continued interest in these researches has earned this writer's heartfelt gratitude). Dr. Schneyer's *Wegweiser zu lateinischen Predigtreihen des Mittelalters, Bayerische Akademie der Wissenschaften* (München, 1965) contains an alphabetical listing of themes and incipits of many preachers of the high and late middle ages, including Stephen Langton. Numerous references to Langton's sermons appear in the *Wegweiser*, but the earlier study (1962) is more complete. Where Schneyer has repeated the sermon and MS reference, I have indicated this in the lists in the Appendices, as *Weg.*, and page number.

an attribution to Langton and which are anonymous. A description of the criteria I have used to classify these MSS follows in this chapter, and is intended as an introductory explanation of the more complete catalogue of MSS that appears in the Appendix. Such a catalogue, with appropriate bibliography, has not, to my knowledge, appeared previously in the literature on the Langton sermons. For each MS listed, there is also given a tabulation of the sermon texts in that MS to show where copies and/or variants appear elsewhere. This is an effort to provide a more complete picture of each MS involved, whereas Dr. Schneyer's list was, of necessity, restricted to giving a single textual reference (or, at the most two references). We cannot underestimate the value of each of these entries in the Schneyer List. It was possible with this information to go to the MS reference, to read the text and compare it with texts found in the other MSS cited. We were in effect using two important instruments, i.e. the list of MSS where Langton sermons were to be found, e.g.

Paris, Nat. lat. 2915, f. 53^{v}, 60^{v}; 3227; 3495, f. 176ss.; 3570, f. 185; 3995, f. 196; 12420; 14470; 14525, f. 240; 14593; 14804, f. 164; 14859; 14925; 14957, f. 69; 15965, f. 12ra; 16463, f. 26ra-96ra - ?; 16502, f. 104ra; 16875.

Land the alphabetical list of themes and incipits where at least one copy of each text could be located, e.g.

Attendite vobis, etc. - Terret me latebras... Paris. Nat. lat. 16463, f. 142rb.

The result was the preparation of a detailed classification of the sermons themselves.

2) *Classification of the sermons*: In these pages is to be found a description of the process whereby I have classified the individual sermons according to the criteria based on the attribution or anonymity of the MSS. I have also given examples in this section of the use of *different versions* of the same sermon on a given theme, and *different sermons* on the same theme. The lists of the sermons appear in the Appendix and include the various MS references where copies and/or variants of a given text may be found. This is a refinement and expansion of the published list by Dr. Schneyer and is essential first, to sorting out what can, at this stage of research, be reliably assigned to Langton for the purposes of this study; and second, to locating all known texts to facilitate the collating and editing of the sermons.

3) *A brief description of sermons erroneously attributed to Langton*, as indicated by Dr. Schneyer in his article.

4) *A compilation of references to sermons apparently no longer extant*, but indicative of the extent to which Langton's sermons were known.

Classification of the Manuscripts

A first task, therefore, is to examine the known MSS.[49] These have been divided into two major groups:

I. MSS containing an attribution to Langton;
II. MSS containing anonymous texts.

Tables describing each of these MSS are to be found in the Appendix. Under each MS heading and description are collated bibliography and other details relevant to the MS and the sermons therein, e.g. catalogue reference, authors who have mentioned the sermons in the MS, and most important (for Group I), evidence of attribution in the MS. In those cases where a microfilm and/or file of unpublished data are available at the *Institut de recherche et d'histoire des textes* in Paris, this is noted by the abbreviation, *IRHT.*

Each table includes a tabulation of the data drawn from the classification of the sermons (also to be found in the Appendix). It is necessary to account for each sermon in the series attributed to Langton. A number of the sermons in the attributed series do not appear in the Schneyer List. If they have been otherwise identified, or if the author remains unknown, this information is indicated in sub-section (1).

In sub-section (2) there follows a numerical analysis of the remaining sermons ascribed to Langton in the MS series, according to the following criteria: those sermons where copies and variants appear in other named MSS; those sermons having copies (only) in other named MSS; and those sermons having variants (only) in other named MSS.

The following example will illustrate this procedure: A sermon on the theme *Aqua frigida bonus nuntius* (*Prov.* 25.25) — *Isaias de filio Dei incarnando prophetans primo de beate virginis nomine designans...* appears in Troyes MS 1100 (f. 260vb), a MS which has an attribution to Langton. Copies of this sermon may be found in Arsenal MS 400 (f. 76rb) and Mazarine MS 999 (f. 135va), but these are anonymous. If we want to use this sermon for further study as a *Langton sermon*, it should be substantiated by a copy in another named MS. And we find it in Ste-Gen. MS 1422 (f. 53^{v}).

That is not to say that there is no possibility for error in using this method. It is, however, far more likely that a sermon is Langton's if it

[49] Schneyer, "Sermonesliste, etc.," 161. These MSS are known from the printed catalogues or from the literature on the subject. I have, in addition, checked the following catalogues: A. M. Bandinius, *Catalogus codicum latinorum Bibliothecae Mediceae Laurentianae*, (5 vols., Florence, 1774-78). G. Mazzatinti *et al.*, *Inventari dei Manoscritti delle Biblioteche d'Italia* (82 vols., 1887-1957). J. Valentinelli, *Bibliotheca Manuscripta ad S. Marci Venetiarum*, (6 vols., in 2, Venice, 1868-73).

has an attribution than if it does not, and the chances of a correct attribution are increased by the presence of the same copy or a variant in another named MS.[50]

Returning to our example of *Aqua frigida bonus nuntius*, the likelihood of its being Langton's is further enhanced by the presence of the same sermon in other versions in other named MSS. Thus, Brussels MS II. 953 (f. 116vb) and Leipzig MS 443 (f. 148vb). With two copies and two variants in named MSS, this sermon can be used with more assurance than one which falls into the next category, i.e. a sermon appearing in only one named copy and in anonymous copies.

A sermon drawn from BN MS, lat. 14859 will serve as an example. The MS contains sermons whose authors are individually cited. Langton is mentioned as author of the sermon on the theme *Solve iubente Domino terrarum Petre cathenas — Gloria mea semper innovabitur...* (f. 282rb). An anonymous copy of the sermon has been found in Reims MS 582 (f. 54^{v}); and an anonymous variant of the sermon in BN MS, lat. 12420 (f. 101ra). The summary table for the MS, BN lat. 14859 indicates that of the thirty-five sermons having Langton attributions, twenty-three of these have been verified by copies and/or variants elsewhere. Although it is likely that the remaining few are authentic as well, it is necessary to notice that these have not satisfied the above-described criteria, and we should require additional internal evidence before accepting their authenticity.

A similar doubt attaches to sermons that appear in the Schneyer List but are found only in single copies in the named MSS. These too might be Langton's since they appear in series that contain a majority of verified texts. Notice, for example, the case of a sermon in the same BN MS, lat. 14859 that we have cited earlier. The text on f. 216vb on the theme *Ecce Dominus vocat nos ad fletum* (*Is.* 22:12) bears an attribution to Langton, but so far as I have been able to determine, is not to be found in any of the other named MSS or indeed in any of the more numerous MSS containing anonymous texts.

In still other cases, sermons appearing in the Schneyer List have, through these subsequent investigations, been found to have been erroneously attributed to Langton. This is also indicated (where applicable) in the MS summaries.

These analyses provide, therefore, some guide to the reliability of the named MSS. Where an overwhelming majority of the texts have clear

[50] Langlois commented on the problem, stating that the only possibility for identifying anonymous sermon texts, is where there are a number of copies and some have attributions. *Journal des Savants*, *op. cit.* (1916), 548, n. 2. On anonymous sermons, see Lecoy de la Marche, 180-201.

support in other attributed MSS, we can then proceed with greater assurance that we are dealing, in fact, with a Langton sermon.

The sermons of Stephen Langton are not, however, limited to the named MSS but are to be found in the far more numerous MSS containing anonymous sermons. The procedures described above pertaining to the summaries of MSS in the first group of attributed MSS, also apply to the summaries of the MSS containing anonymous texts, with the exception that only those sermons that *appear* to be Langton's (based on a comparison with the Schneyer List) were examined; namely those on themes generally associated with Langton's preaching. These were then tested by the established criteria.

The importance of this additional body of material should not be ignored. Dr. Schneyer called attention, for example, to the previously unknown Arras MS 222 that contains a book of anonymous sermons. There are 106 sermons extant in the MS. All but five have been listed by Dr. Schneyer who has assigned the remaining 101 sermons to Langton. Further investigations of these 101 sermons indicates that 66 sermons in the MS appear in copies and/or variants in named MSS; 26 sermons appear only in Arras MS 222; 5 have other anonymous copies; and 4 have been otherwise attributed.

A careful survey of anonymous texts has an additional value. Noting the various anonymous texts and comparing them with named texts not only helps to establish their reliability but also provides the basis for a future collation and edition of the Langton sermons.

Classification of the Sermons

Having examined the manuscripts in the two major categories — those that have some attribution to Langton and thosel that are anonymous — our next task is to have a closer look at each of these sermon texts to notice: (1) in which group of MSS does the sermon belong; (2) in what group of MSS are copies and/or variants to be found; and (3) whether theme and different *incipit* classify the text as a variant of another sermon with the same theme, or a different sermon entirely.[51] In order to establish the identity between two works, we have collated incipits, explicits, and some other passage.[52]

The basis for this division is Dr. Schneyer's alphabetical list of the ser-

[51] The importance of knowing both theme and incipit cannot be overemphasized. A themei n itself is an insufficient mark of identification in the view of Schneyer, "Beobachtungen, etc." *cit. supra*, 74.

[52] A procedure recommended in Lacombe *et al.*, 167, n. 3.

mon themes and incipits. We have, however, divided this list in the following categories in order to have a clearer idea of the kinds of sermons involved, and in order to arrive at a body of material which will serve the purposes of this study.

Class I — Sermons appearing in more than one named copy. — Sermons that appear in more than one named copy and/or variant are the most numerous. To this category we assign one hundred and twenty-two sermons. (Notice in the appropriate list in the Appendix that a distinction has been made between *different versions* of the same sermon on a given theme, and *different sermons* on the same theme).

Class II — Sermons appearing in only one named copy. — Eighty-two sermons are assigned to Class II. These include twenty that are *individually* cited as Langton's, e.g. BN MS, lat. 14859. The others appear in series that bear a general attribution to Langton, but as in the case of Troyes MS 1367 may include sermons of other masters of Paris.

Class III — Addenda: sermons appearing in only one named copy. — To Class III, we assign twenty-five sermons. (In four cases Langton is specifically cited as author). In this category are listed those sermons that have *themes* that appear elsewhere in named copies but are *different sermons* that have neither copies nor variants in *other named MSS.* Notice, by way of illustration, the sermon on the theme *Accingere cilicio.* The text beginning *Dilectissimi, indignus ego scientia,* etc. is to be found in the named MS Leipzig 443 but differs from the sermon on the same theme, with different incipit — *Ad predicationis officium me,* etc. — which appears in two named copies, Ste-Gen. MS 1422 and Troyes MS 1100.

Class IV — Sermons appearing only in anonymous copies. — There are fifty-one sermons that fall in Class IV. For the most part, these appear in single copies, but where other copies or variants have been found, these too are anonymous. Notice this example that will illustrate our procedure: The sermon on the theme *Obtulerunt Magi Domino — Dicit Eccli: Splendidum in panibus,* etc. may be found in the anonymous MSS, Arras 222 and Amiens, Fonds Lesc. 30. A variant, with the incipit, *Si quis (gravatus) egritudine,* etc. appears in two other anonymous MSS, BN, lat. 3495 and lat. 14925.

Class V — Addenda: sermons appearing only in anonymous copies. — To Class V may be assigned seventeen sermons. In this category we list sermons whose *themes* appear elsewhere in named copies but whose *incipits* differ and furthermore introduce entirely *different sermons,* having neither copies nor variants in named MSS. For example: The theme, *Ecce rex venit, occurramus Salvatori nostro* appears several times. The text whose incipit is *Nota sex homini necessaria esse,* etc. is to be found in four anonymous copies

(MSS Arras 222, BN, lat. 12420, lat. 14470, and lat. 14593). A second, but different sermon, on the same theme has the incipit, *Pater omnipotens*, etc. and appears in the anonymous MS, Arsenal 400. There is still another sermon on the same theme that begins, *Fratres karissimi, anime peccatrici*, etc. This sermon differs from the two cited above and appears in three named copies, MSS Leipzig 443, Troyes 1100, and Troyes 1367. (See Class I, above).

Class VI — Sermons that have been otherwise attributed. — A remaining twenty sermons that Dr. Schneyer listed have, in these subsequent investigations, been tentatively assigned to other preachers.

Classification of the Sermons: Summary

Class	I	122
	II	82
	III	25
	IV	51
	V	17
	VI	20
		317

The previous estimate of Langton's sermons numbering about five hundred has clearly been exaggerated. Dr. Schneyer called attention to this,[53] but left the problem open for further investigation, since it was necessary to ascertain whether the repetition of a theme meant a different sermon or another version of the same sermon. This has been a major consideration in arranging the classifications described here, and in drawing up the lists of the sermons that appear in the Appendix.

If we put aside the sixty-eight sermons that remain in the anonymous categories and those twenty that have been otherwise attributed, two hundred and twenty-nine sermons remain in named copies (Classes I, II, and III). It has, as we have seen, been necessary to distinguish between those extant in one named copy only (107 in Classes II and III), and those sermons appearing in several named copies and/or variants (122 in Class I). In the former case, all but twenty-four that are individually cited as Langton's appear in series which are generally assigned to this author; but these series, as shown elsewhere in this study, also contain texts that remain anonymous and/or sermons of other preachers. A sermon, therefore, that appears in only one of these named copies must then

[53] Schneyer, "Eine Sermonesliste, etc.," 164.

be subjected to further analysis to prove through internal evidence that it can be regarded as a Langton sermon. Comparisons of style, the use of *exempla* and *similitudines*, and similarities in content and sources will undoubtedly shed further light on the correct assignment of these texts to Langton. The same procedures may usefully be applied to those sermons that remain anonymous. Such a study, however, is beyond the scope of these present investigations. The author shall concentrate, therefore, in these *Studies in the Sermons of Stephen Langton* primarily on those sermons, one hundred twenty-two in number, that appear in several named copies and/or variants and may be regarded as Langton sermons and a reliable source for his thought.

Sermons Erroneously Attributed to Langton

Not so reliable are two manuscripts which contain sermons that have traditionally, but as Dr. Schneyer has proved, erroneously been attributed to Langton.

BM Royal 2.D. XXXVII. — Bale, in his list of Langton's works, cited a text beginning: "Sacerdotes nescientes Dominum neque officium suum...,"[54] first of a series of fifteen sermons appearing in MS Roy., 2.D. XXXVII, ff. 142rb-55. The manuscript which is described as a thirteenth century, vellum copy contains Langton's *Commentary on the Minor Prophets*,[55] (f. 28). The presence of Langton's *Commentary* in the MS perhaps led Bale to attribute the subsequent text to Langton. The description in the *Catalogue of Royal MSS* contains the attribution, and in fact, suggests that the whole collection of the sermons can be assigned to Langton.[56]

Powicke included the MS reference in his list,[57] and Lacombe repeated

[54] J. Bale, *Index Brit. Script.*, ed. R. L. Poole with M. Bateson (Oxford, 1902), 418. Noted also among Langton's writings by C. de Visch, *Bibl. Script. Sac. Ord. Cist.* (Duaci, 1649), 243 and Io. Pits, *De illust. Angl. Script.* (Paris, 1619), 304.

[55] G. F. Warner & J. P. Gilson, edd., *Catalogue of western manuscripts in the Old Royal & King's Collections* (2 vols.; London, 1921), I, 61.

[56] *Ibid.* None of the following incipits appears in the Schneyer List of Langton sermons: (142rb) Sacerdotes nescientes Dominum neque officium suum; (143va) Discipuli cum Domino appropinquantes; (144rb) Magnum quidem et difficile est; (144vb) Heri, fratres karissimi, de bono conscientie vobiscum; (145ra) O homo, hominis attende dignitatem; (145va) Quatuor reges adversus quinque; (146rb) Salomon fecit sibi tronum ex ebore; (147vb) Dominus eduxit filios Israel de Egipto; (148rb) Intravit Iesus in quoddam castellum; Mundus, fratres karissimi, leges sibi a Deo positas; (149rb) Aiel de Bethel edificavit Iericho; (149vb) Ait Dominus, ecce ego demetam posteriora Basaci; (151ra) En lectulum Salomonis abiciunt sexaginta fortes; (151va) Hodie, dilectissimi, si vocem eius auditis; (152ra) In die illa sibilabit Dominus musce que est in extremo fluvii Egipti; (152vb) Sanctorum vita, fratres, ceteris est norma vivendi.

[57] Powicke, *SL*, 170.

it in *Studies on the Commentaries*.[58] Notice, however, that Lacombe did question the authenticity of the attribution, and suggested Robert Pullus as author.[59]

That this series of sermons has been erroneously attributed to Langton was made clear by Dr. Schneyer, who in the compilation of the list of Langton sermon themes, demonstrated that none of the fifteen themes in the Royal MS appears elsewhere in the Langton sermons. He has called attention to the similarity of the sermons in this series to those in BN MS lat. 18096, ff. 48-74.[60]

Lambeth MS 71. — Dr. Schneyer's researches also revised the traditional attribution of the series of sermons in Lambeth MS 71 to Langton.[61] *A Catalogue of the Archiepiscopal MSS in the Library at Lambeth Palace*, published in 1812, listed the contents of the MS:

1) Petri Cantoris... Commentarius in Psaltorium...
2) Stephani Langton Cant. Archiepiscopi Commentarius in Isaiam...
3) Ejusdem Sermones de Tempore.[62]

The inscription on the flyleaf of the MS, written in a later hand, may well have been the source for the catalogue attribution. Thus Lacombe listed Lambeth MS 71 in the *Studies on the Commentaries*,[63] and the reference was repeated as recently as 1961 by the author of the article in the *Dictionnaire de Spiritualité*, who referred to this "systematic collection" of *Sermones dominicales* as Langton's.[64]

It should be noticed, however, that the description of the manuscript in the revised catalogue of medieval MSS at Lambeth Palace (published in 1932), omits Langton's name in connection with the series of 114 sermons in the MS.[65] It was Dr. Schneyer who discovered a similar series of sermons in the Hatton MS 37, which contained the following attribution in a contemporary hand (f. 267rb): "Sermones magistri Rogeri de Salesburia de dominicis diebus."[66]

[58] Lacombe *et al.*, 6.

[59] *Ibid.*, 7. Schneyer ("Eine Sermonesliste, etc." 162, n. 16) identified three preachers with the series: (144vb) Robert Pullus; (145va) Petrus Manducator; (147vb) Hildebert de Lavardin (?).

[60] Schneyer, *loc. cit.*

[61] Schneyer, 162; n. 15.

[62] P. 8.

[63] Lacombe *et al.*, 6.

[64] Foreville, *cit. supra*, col. 1499.

[65] M. R. James, *A descriptive catalogue of the MSS in the library of Lambeth Palace: the medieval MSS* (Cambridge, 1932), 115-16. The MS, described as on vellum, contains two volumes in twelfth and thirteenth century hands.

[66] My thanks to Dr. Schneyer who called my attention to the Hatton MS. See F. Madan *et al.*, *A summary catalogue of western manuscripts in the Bodleian Library at Oxford* (Oxford, 1937), II, ii, 837.

Miscellaneous corrections. — The BN MS lat. 16875,[67] appears in the Schneyer List[68] of MSS possibly containing Langton sermons. This thirteenth century MS containing various sermons and homilies (following the *Liber Pastoralis* of Gregory the Great and the *De Miseria Hominis* of Innocent III)[69] had been previously cited by Lecoy de la Marche,[70] Lacombe in *Studies on the Commentaries*,[71] and Glorieux in his *Répertoire*.[72] I have examined ff. 180-226 which contain these sermons. None of these can apparently be identified as a Langton sermon.[73]

A further error of attribution appears in the case of BN MS lat. 3995, f. 196 which first appeared in Hauréau, *Notices et extraits*.[74] The reference was repeated in the Schneyer List,[75] but must be corrected to BN MS lat. 3495, f. 196^{v}, *Noli timere, filia Sion - Fratres, si coram nobis positus*, etc.

Sermons Apparently No Longer Extant

The late Mgr. Lacombe listed in the *Studies on the Commentaries* several lost works of Stephen Langton and called attention to the frequent mention of sermon collections which had disappeared.[76] These present investigations into the sermons of Stephen Langton have yielded several references to sermons apparently no longer extant, which are of interest as an indication of the diffusion of the archbishop's sermons.

Bale referred to *Sermones lx*, probably a series of sixty sermons contained

My own reading of some forty of the sermons in the Lambeth series indicates that these sermons are more complex in structure than those of Langton. The attribution to Roger of Salisbury, a preacher who flourished in Paris in the second decade of the thirteenth century, appears very likely. On Roger, see Russell, *Dictionary of writers*, etc., 146-47.

67 L. Delisle, *Inventaire des mss latins de Notre-Dame... nos. 16719-18613* (Paris, 1871), 13.

68 Schneyer, 161.

69 *Liber regulae pastoralis* (Migne, *PL*, 77, 13-128); *De contemptu mundi sive De miseria conditionis humanae* (Migne, *PL*, 217, 701-46).

70 Lecoy de la Marche, 539.

71 Lacombe *et al.*, 6.

72 Glorieux, I, 255.

73 The following are the incipits of the sermons in this MS: (180) Vie Syon lugent — Qui tangit vos; (183) Refulsit sol in clipeos — Dominus appellatur pastor; (187) Ascendam in palmam — Dicitur quod pauper; (192) Iob procul adoratur bellum — Cum demones vident; (196) Surge aquilo — Consuetudo est hominis; (202) Non est hic aliud nisi domus Dei — Tria sunt; (208) Valde ammirandum est... Castrum fuit mundus iste; (216) Feriam vobiscum — Cum aliqui populi; (221) Misericordia et veritas obviaverunt sibi — Quidam paterfamilias; (223bis) Peccata mea Domine sicut sagitte — Hodie plorat mater ecclesia.

74 II (1891), 110.

75 Schneyer, 161. BN MS lat. 3995 contains *Hostiensis in decretales.*

76 Lacombe *et al.*, 10-12. He indicated that this would "... be reserved for an article on the sermons," which apparently was never written.

in one book in the Cambridge University Library. He cited the opening word, *Filia*, but failed to shed further light on this collection.[77] The reference appeared again in Tanner as, *Filia Sion, ecce rex tuus.*[78] The Catalogue of Boston of Bury had referred to a "book of sixty sermons" whose *explicit* was given as "... studeamus."[79] We learn, in addition, that manuscript copies had, in the fifteenth century, been in the monastic libraries at Bury (Burgh) and Cogeshale (*sic*).[80]

We are, therefore, led to seek a manuscript book that had originated in the libraries at Bury or Coggeshall and had at one time been noticed by Bale in the Cambridge University Library. In Ker's *Medieval Libraries of Great Britain*,[81] an entry for the Cistercian abbey of Coggeshall indicates two Langton MSS, now in the collection of Corpus Christi College, Cambridge — namely, MSS 31 and 89.[82] Neither of these is the MS we seek, and furthermore, we have been led by Bale to the Cambridge University Library.

Ker's reference to Bury-St-Edmunds apparently takes us closer to our source. There we notice that MS Ii.vi.5, now in the Cambridge University Library, has a pressmark "S" (i.e. *Sermones* ?), and that the present manuscript book was formerly bound with a book of sermons, no longer extant.[83] In the description of the MS in the *Catalogue of the MSS... in the library of the University of Cambridge*, there is mention of a table of contents on the fly-leaf of the MS that indicates that the volume formerly belonged to the monastery at Bury-St-Edmunds and that the MS had once contained several theological works (sermons ?), no longer extant.[84]

[77] Bale, *Index*, 417. *Cf.* De Visch, *op. cit.*, 243: "Sermonum sexaginta, lib. 1. Filia Sion, ecce Rex tuus."

[78] Tanner, 468 ; also in Pits, 304.

[79] *Catalogus scriptorum* (1410) *ecclesiae a Johanne Bostono Buriensi monacho conscriptus* (ed. Tanner, *Bibl. Brit. Hibern.* London, 1748), xxxix.

[80] *Ibid.*, xxiv-xxv.

[81] N. R. Ker, *Medieval libraries of Great Britain: a list of surviving books* (2nd ed., London, 1964).

[82] *Ibid.*, 53.

[83] *Ibid.*, 17.

[84] *A catalogue of the MSS preserved in the library of the University of Cambridge* (6 vols.; Cambridge, 1856-67), III, 500-01. The MS in its present form consists of 125 leaves, written in a thirteenth century hand; and begins with the *Liber Constantini Monachi Cassinensis qui dicitur Viaticum...*, followed by miscellaneous scientific treatises. On Constantinus Africanus (1098), see historical and literary notes in Migne, *PL*, 150, 1559-66. In a recent article, R. H. Rouse has identified the author of the *Catalogus Scriptorum Ecclesiae* as the fourteenth century monk of Bury-St-Edmunds, Henry of Kirkestede, who apparently was responsible for introducing such innovations as the class-mark and the contents listed on the flyleaf of the MS to this monastic library. "Bostonus Buriensis and the Author of the *Catalogus Scriptorum Ecclesiae*," *Speculum*, XLI (1966), 488, 490.

Similarly, in the library of Christ Church, Canterbury, there is evidence of numerous sermon collections that have since disappeared. M. R. James, in *The Ancient Libraries of Canterbury and Dover*,[85] has published the titles of books in the library of Christ Church during the period when Henry of Eastry was Prior (1284-1331).[86] The following titles have relevance to these studies on the sermons of Stephen Langton:

No. 940 Interpretaciones hebraicorum nominum... In hoc vol. cont: Sermo Stephani Archiepiscopi Cantuar...[87]
1177 Sermo S(tephani) Archiepiscopi, *Viderunt*[88]
1178 Item sermo eiusdem, *Vidi super*... Vel de mortalitate rerum qui dicitur *angelus.*[89]
1229 Concordantie veteris et novi Testamenti. In hoc vol. cont... Item Sermones S(teph). Archiepiscopi.[90]
1253 Sermo S(teph). Archiepiscopi. *Fornacem.*[91]
1262 Sermo S(teph). Archiepiscopi. *Vidi.*[92]
1295 Sermo S(teph). Archiepiscopi. *Aperite.*[93]
1296 Sermo eiusdem. *Stelle dederunt.*[94]
1345 Item sermones et themata S. Archiepiscopi.[95]
1604 Sermo S(teph). Archiepiscopi.[96]
1736 (Libri Roberti Poucin) Sermo S(teph). Archiepiscopi.[97]

From the Catalogue of the Library of St. Augustine's Abbey, Canterbury,[98] we notice:

No. 490 Tractatus Stephani Cantuar. Archiepiscopi super ympnum *aue maris stella.*[99]
760 ... Tract. Steph. Cant. Arch. super ymnum (*sic*) Ave maris stella.[100]

[85] M. R. James, *The ancient libraries of Canterbury and Dover* (Cambridge, 1903).

[86] See the catalogue of the library of Christ Church, Canterbury in Cotton MS, Galba E.IV, ff. 128-47 (14th cent.).

[87] James, *cit. supra*, 91. A book called *Interpretationes nominum Hebraicorum*, variously attributed to Remi of Auxerre and Stephen Langton appears in F. M. Powicke, *The medieval books of Merton College* (Oxford, 1931), 131, No. 347.

[88] James, 105. *Cf.* (?) Viderunt eam hostes... (*infra*, Sermon No. 118).

[89] James, 105. *Cf.* BN MS, lat. 3227, f. 158r (*infra*).

[90] James, 108.

[91] *Ibid.*, 109.

[92] *Ibid.*, 110. *Cf.* (?) no. 1178, n. 89 *supra.*

[93] James, 112. *Cf.* (?) Aperite portas nobis... (*infra*, Sermon No. 5).

[94] James, 112.

[95] *Ibid.*, 115.

[96] *Ibid.*, 132.

[97] *Ibid.*, 139. None of these preceding items has been identified by James in App. C, 505-11.

[98] In MS Trinity Coll., Dublin 360 (Bernard 285), 15th cent.

[99] James, 252. *Cf.* Tanner, 468: In ave maris stella. Salutationem angelicam. Olim in bibl. monast. S. Aug. Cant. See, BM, Roy. MS 8.A.X, f. 36r (*infra*).

[100] James, 275.

805 ... Steph. Cant. super ymnum aue maris stella.[101]
810 ... Tract. Steph. Cant. arch. sup. ymn. a.m.s.[102]

In addition to these notices in the catalogues, there are in two of the named manuscripts (Oxford, Magdalen MS 168 and Troyes MS 1367) that contain series of identified Langton sermons, indications that the MSS at one time contained sermons that are no longer extant. The MSS have tables of contents that list themes and/or rubrics. In Magdalen MS 168, for example, such a table is to be found on ff. 50ᵛ-51ᵛ. There are listed *seven* themes of sermons, attributed to Langton. *Five* of these appear in other named MSS (*infra*).

...xli M. Stephani Cantur' in unius confessoris - Iustus cor suum tradidit ad.
xliii ——. Estote imitatores mei sicut...
lviii M. Stephani in die Penth.' Veni sancte Spiritus reple tuorum.
lix Eiusdem [M. Stephani] in festo apostolorum Petri et Pauli. Bonum certamen certavi cursum.
lx Lectio M. Stephani Cantuar' in exodo: Legimus filios Israel profectos de Eg (ipto).

One appears only in this MS:

liii M. Stephani in nativitate Domini. Vidi angelum fortem descen(dentem).

One appears to be repeated only in an anonymous copy:

lxiii M. Stephani in sollempnitate apostolorum Petri et Pauli — In ingressu oraculi.

In the second of these MSS, Troyes 1367, *four* sermons that are no longer extant are indicated by theme and rubric in the table on f. 2ʳ and correspond to Langton sermons appearing in other named MSS (*infra*):

... lxxxi	Noli timere filia.	In ram. palm.
lxxxii	Viri Galilei quid.	In ascensione Domini
lxxxiii	Que est ista.	In assumpt. beate Marie
lxxxiiii	Beati pauperes	Omnium sanctorum

To conclude these notes on sermons that are apparently no longer extant, we should also mention Vitry-le-François MS 75 which appears in the lists by Lacombe,[103] Glorieux, [104] and most recently, Schneyer.[105]

[101] *Ibid.*, 281.

[102] *Ibid.*, 282. None of these preceding items has been identified by James in App. C., 515-22. *Cf.* C. E. Woodruff, *A catalogue of the manuscript books in the library of Christ Church, Canterbury* (Canterbury, 1911). James wrote that of the 108 volumes described in the catalogue, only about 20 can be identified with certainty as having once formed part of the important library of the ancient priory of Christ Church, Canterbury. (James, 3-4).

[103] Lacombe *et al.*, 6.

[104] *Rép.*, I, 255.

[105] Schneyer, 161.

The MS was described as being a thirteenth century parchment copy, comprising 391 folia,[106] and containing *Biblia sacra*.[107] According to information obtained at the *Institut de recherche et d'histoire des textes*, MSS 19-175 in the Vitry-le-François collection were destroyed during World War II. Included in this group we might add Vitry-le-François MS 73, described as being a thirteenth century parchment copy of 201 folia.[108] On f. 122, according to the catalogue description, the sermon: Magister Stephanus de Langetone. Estote imittatores mei... (*sic*).[109]

CONCLUSION

We have, in this examination of "Langton the Preacher and his Sermons," an added dimension of the life and career of Stephen Langton. Known to his contemporaries as *Stephen of the Thundering Tongue*, Langton was, as master of theology and archbishop of Canterbury, a preacher of note. His sermons — extant and those long since disappeared — attest to the extent and fame of his preaching.

The Langton sermon tradition is a long, though frequently confusing one, since his sermons often came to be collected with others, or, as we have also seen, the sermons of others came to be assigned to him. Our attempt to sort out these sermons according to MSS, the availability of copies and variants, and the location of the texts is aimed at establishing a body of material which can be used as a reasonably reliable source for Langton's thought.

It has been necessary, until this point, to concern ourselves with the Langton sermon as an isolated phenomenon. This aspect of our study was essential to disentangling Langton's preaching from that of his contemporaries. We must now address ourselves to the Langton sermon as part of the medieval preaching tradition.

106 *Cat. gén. des mss des bibl. publ. de France: Dép. XIII: Vitry-le-Fran., etc.* (Paris, 1891), 38.

107 There is no mention of sermons in the catalogue description.

108 The MS has not, to my knowledge, been heretofore cited as having contained a Langton sermon. For a description of the MS, see *Cat... Vitry-le-Fran.*, 37.

109 See *infra* under this theme.

CHAPTER III

LANGTON AND HIS SERMONS IN THE MEDIEVAL PREACHING TRADITION

THE DEVELOPMENT OF MEDIEVAL PREACHING

LANGTON'S career as a preacher coincided with the revival of popular preaching in western Europe. Once the veritable monopoly of the cloister and the schools, preaching by the end of the twelfth and the beginning of the thirteenth century entered an era when masters and doctors of theology, regulars and seculars alike, became increasingly aware of the importance of popular audiences. Their sermons became all the more significant, therefore, as instruments of persuasion and education of medieval folk. These sermons in the numerous contemporary manuscripts attest to the remarkable development of the art of preaching in the high middle ages.

The growth of the art over the earlier medieval centuries had been a gradual one. Although the tradition of preaching was as old as Christianity and its Judaic roots, the early middle ages contributed relatively few preachers.[1] The Fathers recognized the importance of preaching. They had before them Jesus and Paul as models, and numerous parables and *exempla* drawn from Scripture. St. Augustine wrote one of the early guides to preaching in Book IV of his *De doctrina Christiana*,[2] and Gregory the Great's emphasis on the close relationship of exegesis, teaching, and preaching[3] may well have foreshadowed the twelfth century formula of Peter the Chanter who defined the threefold function of the master of theology: *legere*, *disputare*, *praedicare*.[4] Gregory's books of moralities and homilies[5] were, furthermore, a rich source of *exempla* and anecdotes for the medieval preacher.

[1] L. Bourgain, *La chaire française au XII*e *siècle d'après les manuscrits* (Paris, 1879), 370. For a general survey of the preaching of the high middle ages (1095-1361), see E. C. Dargan, *A history of preaching* (2 vols.; New York, 1905), I, 174-288.

[2] Smalley, *Study of the Bible in the Middle Ages*, 27. See *De Doctrina Christiana, Corpus Christianorum, ser. lat.*, 32, lib. IV, 116-67.

[3] Smalley, 35. See e.g. Gregory's *Liber regulae pastoralis* in Migne, *PL*, 77, 13-128.

[4] *Verbum Abbreviatum*, c. 1 (Migne, *PL*, 205, 25).

[5] *Moralium libri sive expositio in librum B. Iob* (Migne, *PL*, 75, 509-1162 and continued in 76, 9-782); *Homiliae in Ezechielem prophetam* (*PL*, 76, 785-1072); *XL Homiliae in Evangelia* (*ibid.*, 1075-1312).

These patristic homilies[6] were the raw material of the monastic sermon that dominated the preaching of the tenth and eleventh centuries. The scarcity of early medieval sermons — that has attracted the attention of scholars — probably means that it was common to recite or adapt patristic homilies which often appear in early medieval manuscripts. Delivered twice daily by either abbot or ordinary monk, these early sermons were simple in style and content.[7] This earlier simplicity of style that was so characteristic of the sermons of the cloister also distinguished the sermons of the first half of the twelfth century. A theme drawn from Scripture, generally based on the daily liturgy, was the point of departure. (The theme was not, however, followed by the protheme which was a creation of the thirteenth century.[8])

These twelfth-century sermons were distinctive in yet another aspect, namely the predominance of theological themes, e.g., grace, the sacraments, and redemption.[9] Observations on society were traditional. Beryl Smalley summed it up in her recent study of fourteenth-century sermons: "Society still appears as a hierarchy. The preacher continues to prescribe the duties and denounce the sins of men on each rung of the ladder, with special reference to the duties and sins of prelates. It is all the old stuff again, little changed since the twelfth century."[10] *Plus ça change, plus c'est la même chose!*

The preachers of the period included regular and secular clergy. Bernard of Clairvaux, whose sermons attest an orator of spontaneity and originality, was one of the best of the twelfth-century sermon makers.[11]

[6] Changes in terminology reflect the development of the sermon. *Homilia* in its early meaning applied to a commentary on the evangel of the mass. Homily then became the generic term pertaining generally to utterances of a religious character. It was, however, to be replaced by the term *sermo* which was almost solely used in the thirteenth century. By this period, differences between homily and sermon lay in their length and methodical form. Lecoy de la Marche, 271.

[7] See J. Leclercq, "Recherches sur d'anciens sermons monastiques," *Revue Mabillon*, XXXVI (1946), 2-3, 7-8, 13. Sermons preached in the morning (*Sermones in mane*) must be distinguished from those preached in the evening (*Sermones post prandium* or *Collationes*). The latter terms owed their origin to the questions and responses raised after the evening meal. A sermon might also be separated into two parts: *in mane* and *in collatione*. This distinction particularly applied to sermons preached in Benedictine houses. Lecoy de la Marche, 220-26.

[8] Notice, e.g., Alexander Neckham's use of an introduction following the scriptural text, usually from the day's epistle or gospel reading. The introduction was unlike the protheme. Hunt, *A. Neckham*, 93. (On sermon construction, see Chap. IV, *infra*).

[9] M.-M. Lebreton, "Recherches sur les principaux thèmes théologiques traités dans les sermons du XIIe siècle," *Recherches de théol. anc. et méd.*, XXIII (1956), 6, 8.

[10] B. Smalley, *English friars and antiquity in the early fourteenth century* (Oxford, 1960), 39.

[11] Bourgain (*op. cit.*, ix) has noticed, however, that outside the monasteries of his Order, Bernard had little influence on preaching. For the sermons of Bernard, see H. M. Rochais, *et al.*,

Other regulars whose preaching was noteworthy and whose extant sermons reflect the life of the cloister included the Benedictines Guibert de Nogent[12] (d. 1124) and Peter de Celle[13] (d. 1183); the Cluniacs Peter Abelard[14] (d. 1142) and Peter the Venerable[15] (d. 1156); the Cistercians Alain de Lille[16] (d. 1202) and Adam de Perseigne[17] (d. 1204); and from the Abbey of St. Victor, Hugh[18] (d. 1141), Richard[19] (d. 1173), and Peter Comestor[20] (d. 1179).

Clerical audiences also dominated the preaching of the secular clergy who include in their ranks some of the most distinguished names in twelfth-century intellectual history: Anselm, archbishop of Canterbury[21] (d. 1109); Yves of Chartres[22] (d. 1116); Hildebert, bishop of Mans and archbishop of Tours[23] (d. 1134); Peter Lombard[24] (d. 1160); Stephen of Tournai[25] (d. 1203); Geoffrey Babion[26] (d. 1112); and Peter of Blois[27] (d. 1198). Not to be ignored is Alexander Neckham (d. 1217) whose presence in Paris in either 1175-82 or 1185-92[28] makes him a contemporary of Langton. Neckham preached at Oxford, but his sermons are, nonetheless, a part of the late twelfth-century tradition of sermon-making and were addressed, in the main, to "scolares" or "scolares et laici."[29]

The distinguishing mark of this preaching was that it was essentially preaching by clerics for audiences of clerics. This is not to say that popular

S. Bernardi Opera, I: Sermones super Cantica Canticorum 1-35 (Rome, 1957), and various sermons in Migne, *PL*, 184, *passim.*

[12] *PL*, 156, *passim.*

[13] *PL*, 202, 637-926.

[14] *PL*, 178, 379-610. See D. Van den Eynde, "Le recueil des sermons de Pierre Abélard," *Antonianum*, XXXVII (1962), 17-54.

[15] *PL*, 189, 954-1006.

[16] See his *Summa de arte praedicatoria* (*PL*, 210, 109-98) and his *Sermones, ibid.*, 197-228.

[17] *PL*, 211, 579 ff.

[18] *PL*, 175, 113-256. See J. Châtillon, "Sermons et prédicateurs victorins de la seconde moitié du XIIe siècle," *Archives d'histoire doctrinale et littéraire du moyen âge*, XXXII (1965), 7-60.

[19] *PL*, 196, *passim.*

[20] *PL*, 198, 1721-1844.

[21] *PL*, 158, 585 ff.

[22] *PL*, 162, 505-610.

[23] *PL*, 171, 339-964.

[24] *PL*, 191-92, *passim.*

[25] *PL*, 211, 567-76.

[26] See, e.g., BM MS Roy. 8.A.XI, f. 64ff; and W. Lampen, "De sermonibus Gaufredi Babionis scholastici Andegavensis," *Antonianum*, XIX (1944), 145-68.

[27] *Sermones de tempore*, *PL*, 207, 559-776. On these various preachers of the regular and secular clergy, see Bourgain, *passim.*

[28] Hunt, *A. Neckham*, 6. On the sermons, see 171-80.

[29] *Ibid.*, 13-14.

audiences were ignored in the early middle ages. There was, in fact, legislation in the Capitularies of Charlemagne urging preaching to the people in the language they would understand.[30] The real impetus to popular preaching, however, coincided with the offensive taken by the Church against its enemies, be they Saracens or heretics. Those preachers of the first half of the twelfth century who declared for God's justice and invoked the faithful to join the Crusade included hermits who lived in the forests that then covered France. Bernard de Tiron (d. 1117) was one of these. He left the Île de Chausey to preach in the provinces of Normandy.[31]

This revival of popular preaching in the twelfth century was rapidly extended in the first decades of the thirteenth.[32] The prelates assembled at Rome for the Lateran Council in 1215 (including Langton as well) underscored the importance of the office of preaching and, in the tenth canon adopted by the Council, emphasized the responsibility of the bishop to name men suited to fulfill the important task of edifying the flock by word and example.[33] Langton's Paris friend, Innocent III, himself a renowned preacher, exemplifies an age when the sermon was coming into its own as an effective instrument not only against the enemies of the Church, but also in winning popular support for his plans of reform.[34]

The men whose responsibility it was to take up the task were like Langton, doctors and masters. Langton was part of that circle in Paris which included Maurice de Sully, Peter the Chanter, and Robert de Courçon whose interests were directed toward the reinvigoration of Christian teaching. The importance attached to popular preaching, already evident in Langton's Paris, anticipates the formation of the mendicant orders whose rapid diffusion in the cities of western Europe in the first decades of the thirteenth

[30] De officio praedicationis, ut iuxta quod bene vulgaris populus intelligere possit, assidue fiat. *MGH, Legum*, I (Hannover, 1835), c. 14, 190.

[31] Bourgain, 140, 144. See Migne, *PL*, 172, 1363-1446 for the *Vita S. Bernardi de Tironio.*

[32] The revival of popular preaching in the twelfth century was particularly emphasized by B. Smalley in her *Study of the Bible in the Middle Ages* (244), and appears to be a revision of Lecoy de la Marche's (11) view that popular preaching, with some exceptions, was rather neglected at the end of the twelfth century, in favor of sermons addressed primarily to clerics and monks.

[33] Inter caetera quae ad salutem spectant populi Christiani, pabulum verbi Dei permaxime sibi noscitur esse necessarium... . Unde cum saepe contingat, quod episcopi propter occupationes multiplices... per se ipsos non sufficiunt ministrare populo verbum Dei, maxime per amplas dioeceses et diffusas, generali constitutione sancimus, ut episcopi viros idoneos ad sanctae praedicationis officium salubriter exequendum assumant, potentes in opere et sermone, qui plebes sibi commissas... eas verbo aedificent et exemplo. *Conciliorum Oecumenicorum Decreta* (Freiburg-Rome-Vienna, 1962), 215.

[34] F. Hurter, *Geschichte Papst Innocenz III* (4 vols.; Hamburg, 1834-42), IV, 506. For the sermons of Innocent III, see Migne, *PL*, 217, 313-688.

century must be seen as a continuation and extension of the effort to educate and persuade the laity.[35]

Popular preaching may be regarded as only one aspect of the preaching office. Of equal importance was its teaching function, since in the language of the thirteenth century church, preacher and doctor were synonomous.[36] Masters who were preachers had not only to deal with the instruction of the Christian community; they also were responsible for the education of clerics, which had reached a critical stage by this period. The increasing concentration of scholars in major centers such as Paris deprived the general ranks of the clergy of adequate leadership and instruction. The ecumenical councils of 1179 and 1215 aimed to correct this situation by providing for masters who would give free instruction to clerics and poor scholars. Initially directed at cathedral churches, the ruling was extended in 1215 to other churches.[37] Attempts to upgrade the level of clerical instruction may also be seen in the increasing importance attached to preaching handbooks and models of sermons which could be consulted by parish clergy.

The literature of the *artes praedicandi* (which we shall discuss below) reflects that aspect of preaching that was susceptible to rules and formal instruction. The fundamental character of medieval preaching, the teaching of moral theology is, however, admirably illustrated in the *quodlibet* literature,[38] where the intimate connections between preaching and theology are most evident. Preaching was essentially a religious function, engaging the whole person and life of the preacher. The preaching office was pastoral (a *cura animarum*), consisting of instructing one's flock in the elementary truths of Christianity and exhorting them to the good. Masters who were also preachers were thus pastors of souls. They were by their own learning and virtue eminently qualified to preach. Masters were, furthermore, also suited to teach. The medieval conception of the preaching office meant that masters in turn prepared clerics to preach. Scripture and theology provided the inspiration and subject matter. Masters them-

35 On Dominican and Franciscan preachers, see Lecoy de la Marche, 110-51. On preachers of other orders, e.g., Cistercians, etc., 152-80.

36 On the preaching office and the role of masters in preaching, see P. Mandonnet, *Saint Dominique* (2 vols.; Paris, 1938), II, 83-100 and J. Leclercq, "Le Magistère du Prédicateur au XIIIe siècle," *Archives d'histoire doctrinale et littéraire du moyen âge*, XXI (1946), 105-47.

37 ... per unamquamque ecclesiam cathedralem magistro, qui clericos eiusdem ecclesiae et scholares pauperes gratis doceat, competens aliquod beneficium assignetur, quo docentis necessitas sublevetur et discentibus via pateat ad doctrinam. *Lat. III*, c. 18, *Conciliorum, etc.*, 196. *Lat. IV*, c. 11, *Ibid.*, 216: Verum quoniam in multis ecclesiis id minime observatur, nos praedictum roborantes statutum, adicimus ut non solum in qualibet cathedrali ecclesia sed etiam in aliis... .

38 Leclercq, *cit. supra*, 136 ff.

selves gave an example of piety and learning to their students. Their handbooks and manuals formulated the rules of preaching and often furnished models of sermons. The preacher-doctor of the high middle ages gave instruction on two levels — as pastor to his flock, and as master to clerics who would preach to the people.

The changes in the orientation of medieval preaching required new techniques in the formulation of the sermon. To the masters of the high middle ages, the art of preaching was modern and therefore required up-to-date techniques. No longer could sermon-making be left to divine inspiration alone or to the kind of patristic homilies that had characterized the preaching of the earlier era. The new masters needed a *forma praedicandi*, which outlined the choice of theme and various subdivisions of the sermon according to certain conventional rules.[39] Their needs were met by the development of the preaching manual, whose numbers steadily increased in the course of the thirteenth and fourteenth centuries, and which became indispensable guides to the complexity of the contemporary sermon.[40]

The first examples of such manuals appeared in the twelfth century and were compiled by Guibert de Nogent, the *Liber quo ordine sermo fieri debeat*, and Alain de Lille, *Summa de arte praedicatoria*.[41] The Universal Doctor's *Summa* also contained homiletic models for preachers. As master of theology at Paris and later at Montpellier, Alain de Lille addressed his sermons to monks, scholars, and *ad populum*.[42] Some of his sermons are to be found scattered among those of Langton in named manuscripts.[43] Another of

[39] Th. M. Charland, *Artes praedicandi* (Paris-Ottawa, 1936), 9. Robert Holcot (d. 1349) was one such English preacher whose *Moralitates* contain *exempla* for use by other preachers. See B. Smalley, "Robert Holcot O.P.," *Archivum fratrum praedicatorum*, XXVI (1956), 6, 8. On later masters of preaching, see Smalley, *English friars...*: Thomas Waleys, 75-108; John Ridevall, 109-32; and Robert Holcot, 133-202. See also H. Caplan, *Medieval artes praedicandi: a handlist, Cornell Studies in Classical Philology*, nos. 24-25 (Ithaca, 1934-36).

[40] Smalley, *Study of the Bible in the Middle Ages*, 244. See, e.g., Jacques de Vitry (d. 1240) who gives advice to orators in the prologue to his *Sermones de tempore*, in BN MS, nouv. acq. lat. 1537, f. 1, cited in M. M. Davy, *Les sermons universitaires parisiens de 1230-31* (Paris, 1931), 29. See also the treatises listed by Lecoy de la Marche, 288: Etienne de Bourbon, Humbert de Romans, Hugh de Saint-Cher, Pierre de Tarentaise, and Humbert de Prully.

[41] Guibert de Nogent (Migne, *PL*, 156, 21-32); Alain de Lille (*PL*, 210, 109-98). See also the treatise attributed to William of Auvergne (bishop of Paris, 1228-49), published by A. de Poorter, "Un manuel de prédication médiévale, le ms 97 de Bruges," *Revue néo-scolastique de philosophie*, XXV (1923), 192-209.

[42] Lecoy de la Marche, 152-55 and 496 on the MSS.

[43] See BN MS, lat. 14859, ff. 233ra-240rb. On this MS, see M.-T. d'Alverny, *Alain de Lille: Textes inédits, Études de Philosophie Médiévale*, LII (Paris, 1965), 14, 121ff. On the *Summa de arte praedicatoria*, *ibid.*, 109-19.

Langton's Paris contemporaries who compiled a manual for preaching was Maurice de Sully (d. 1196). Named bishop of Paris 12 October 1160 and himself an illustrious preacher, Maurice's sermons were arranged in the order of the ecclesiastical year, on saints' and special feastdays, in the manner of a handbook for priests in the diocese. At the beginning of the collection of model sermons, the prelate counselled his clergy concerning their instruction to the laity.[44]

The *Artes Praedicandi* that grew out of these earlier efforts to provide some guide for the medieval preacher, illustrate the important influence of dialectical studies on medieval thought, and more specifically, on a particular literary *genre*.[45] Their general form was dictated by relatively circumscribed rules of composition, but the treatises themselves varied in scope and content. Some had as their object to discuss the moral conduct of the preacher. Others were collections of materials — handbooks of themes, distinctions, authorities, concordances, and examples — that undoubtedly formed a useful reference library for the preacher.[46] Most of the treatises considered the technique and composition of the sermon;[47] some also gave attention to matters of voice, gesture, and delivery.[48]

The development of this *ars praedicatoria* and the diffusion of these *artes praedicandi* obviated the necessity for separate instruction in the art of preaching. Although the master did not devote much time in his lectures to *instruction* on preaching (this apparently was the function of the preaching handbook),[49] the close connections between preaching, sermon-making, and the study of Scripture in the schools (and later in the university) is evident.[50] Many of the outstanding French preachers of the thirteenth century had some connections with the university.[51] Prepositinus or Pré-

[44] Lecoy de la Marche, 42-50, and 520-23 on the MSS. See also C. A. Robson, *Maurice of Sully and the medieval vernacular homily* (Oxford, 1952). (I am grateful to Dr. J. Baldwin for calling my attention to this reference).

[45] Charland, 9.

[46] See, e.g., the collections of themes for sermons by Nicolas de Gorran, O.P. (d. 1295); Gui d'Evreux, O.P. (d. *ca.* 1300); and Humbert de Romans, O.P. (d. 1277), Lecoy de la Marche, 331. Also, H. G. Pfander, "The medieval friars and some alphabetical reference books for sermons," *Medium Aevum,* III (1934), 19-29.

[47] Charland, *op. cit.*, gives special attention to the composition of the sermon.

[48] Notice Thomas Waleys' treatise, discussed by Charland, 219-23.

[49] Charland (110) has noticed that the diffusion of preaching handbooks corresponds to the intensity of university life. They appear most profusely in France in the thirteenth century, in England in the fourteenth, and in Germany in the fifteenth. Caplan, *cit. supra,* has also listed numerous *artes praedicandi* of Italian origin.

[50] Smalley, *Study of the Bible in the Middle Ages,* 368.

[51] Haskins, *op. cit.*, 5.

vostin of Cremona, for example, was chancellor of Notre Dame and at the same time (1206) chancellor of the University of Paris. He too was a contemporary of Langton, and his sermons also appear mingled with those of the later archbishop of Canterbury[52]. Prévostin was preaching in 1193, when he was *magister* (as the MSS indicate).[53]

Masters in the Faculty of Theology were in fact directed to preach on certain days and in specified places in the capital.[54] Stephen Langton as master of theology also preached. He commented on the Bible and his lectures are full of the scriptural quotations, the allegories and moralities that were shared by twelfth-century sermons.[55] His sermons, however, were not the simple kind of homiletic exposition that had been characteristic of preaching in the earlier part of the century. Langton's sermons, like those of many of his famous contemporaries in Paris, are more complex and well on the way to obtaining the fixed form of later medieval sermons. Preaching was no longer the monopoly of the cloister. Popular preaching, as we have seen, had come into its own, and the kind of audience addressed helped to determine the general schema of the sermon. Various indications point to Langton as a popular preacher. An examination of Langton's audiences will, therefore, be useful to establish whether this was in fact the case.

Audiences

Sermons have, from the earliest times, been informed by their divine and human characteristics. Although their essential purpose is the instruction of the faithful in matters of religion, their form and manner reflect, nevertheless, the tastes and needs of their listeners according to the circumstances and requirements of the moment.[56] These listeners in Langton's day included clerical and lay assemblies which in turn affected not only the matter of the language of preaching (*infra*) but also the selection of material and method of presentation. While a more elevated and "polished" style was generally reserved for the clergy, familiar and practical explanations characterized those sermons addressed to predominantly lay audiences. Since the preaching of this period was pri-

[52] See BN MS, lat. 14859, ff. 212ra-215vb; 251vb; 274ra; 287rb.

[53] Lecoy de la Marche, 75-110 and 526 on the MSS; and G. Lacombe, *Prepositini Cancellarii Parisiensis* (*1206-10*) *Opera Omnia, I: La vie et les œuvres de Prévostin* (*Revue des sciences philos. et théolog.*, 1927).

[54] Échard I, 97 (*ex libro rectoris universitatis*), cited by Lecoy de la Marche, 25, n. 1.

[55] Lacombe, *et al.*, 182.

[56] Bourgain, 197.

marily instructive, sermons were highly colored by the inclusion of allegory, satire, elegy and rhymes.[57] These were teaching devices found to be effective for audiences lay and clerical.

Langton had earlier remarked on the two types of preaching in his *Commentaries*:

> This makes clear that a preacher should not always use polished, subtle preaching, like Aod's sword, but sometimes a ploughshare, that is, rude, rustic exhortation. Very often a popular story (*exemplum vulgare*) is more effective than a polished subtle phrase. Aod killed one man only with a two-edged sword, Samagar six hundred with a ploughshare; so, whereas the laity are easily converted by rude, unpolished preaching, a sermon to clerks will draw scarcely one of them from his error.[58]

The distinction between audiences of clerics and laity was carried over into Langton's sermons as well. Sermons to laymen, gathered in either parish church or cathedral, are sometimes identifiable in the manuscripts by the rubric, *ad populum*, attached, for example, to the famous sermon preached at St. Paul's in August 1213, which contains the following counsel: "Because you are layfolk, it is your business to believe that your prelates are men who do all things discreetly and with counsel."[59]

The rubric *ad populum* is, however, relatively rare in the class of sermons appearing in more than one named copy (Class I). Although it appears in the general title of the series of sermons in Troyes MS 1367 (i.e., *Incipiunt sermones... ad populum*), this all-inclusive rubric is useful only as partial evidence that the sermons had popular audiences. Other indications must be noted: e.g., the frequency of popular commonplaces and proverbs, modes of address (*infra*). The rubric, in itself, is clearly not altogether reliable, since at least two sermons in the series were addressed to clerical audiences.[60]

Elsewhere, in individual sermons, a rubricator noted *ad populum*, in at least one version of the sermon on the theme, *Sint lumbi vestri* (*Luc.* 12.35); another copy has been identified as a sermon on confessors.[61] Three other

[57] *Ibid.*, 231; Lecoy de la Marche, 206-07.

[58] Quoted in Smalley, *Study of the Bible in the Middle Ages*, 253-54. These sermons were also compared to two kinds of grain — wheat (sermons to clerks), the more precious; and barley (popular sermons), the more fertile and useful.

[59] Quoted in Cheney, *From Becket to Langton*, 155. Although Powicke (*SL*, 42) noted that this sermon is a Latin translation of one originally preached in the vernacular, the text offers no conclusive evidence for this judgment. The problem of the language of the sermons is treated *infra*.

[60] Sermons incorrectly assigned are nos. 9 (addressed to priests or prelates in synod) and 99 (also to a clerical assembly).

[61] (Sermon references shall appear as follows: the number of the sermon in Class I, the appropriate MS sigla, and the fol. no.). Thus, 100^{a}, Pa^{11}, 267ra and 100^{bc}.

sermons which bear the descriptive rubric, *Sermo communis*, may also be taken to have been addressed to largely lay audiences.[62]

These contemporary assemblies were generally numerous. Lecoy de la Marche has described the enthusiasm of the faithful in the thirteenth century as they surrounded their preachers.[63] Grouped separately, men on one side, and women on the other (as dictated by traditional pratice), lay audiences of the period usually sat during the preaching of the sermon — the majority on benches, but noble ladies on folding chairs, or on cushions carried by their servants.[64] In special circumstances when an especially large crowd was in attendance, the sermon might deliberately be removed from the confines of the church and preached in a public place.[65]

Clerical audiences, on the other hand, were less numerous and were generally seated in the choir of the church or on the stone benches that ran the length of the walls along the sides of the chapel.[66]

Clerical audiences, such as these, heard sermons preached in Latin. These are the sermons, *ad clericos*, as the manuscripts denote. They were secular clergy assembled in synods, councils, or in the schools; and regular clergy, addressed in the cloister or monastic chapel.[67] Langton's sermons also follow this pattern. In the sermon, for example, on the theme *Attendite vobis et universo gregi* (*Act.* 20:28), prelates meeting in synod were Langton's audience: "You, who are entrusted with the dispensation of the ineffable sacrament of the body and blood of our Lord... ought to be the chosen race, the royal priesthood. ... Attend to your flock by example; to yourselves by living well and to your flock by teaching well... my lords and fathers."[68] Langton went on to comment briefly on the Greek word

[62] See nos. 50[a], 83[a], 91.

[63] Lecoy de la Marche, 206.

[64] *Ibid.*, 209. In the age of Augustine, not only was the bishop seated when he addressed the people, but they were as well. (See Augustine's *De catechizandis rudibus*, c. XIII: Usus audiendi verbum Dei sedendo, in quibusdam Ecclesiis receptus. Migne, *PL*, 40, 309-48). Nobles had their own chapels, but ecclesiastical authorities exhorted the nobility to attend parish churches. Lecoy de la Marche, 227. There appear to have been variations of custom in regard to posture. References in sermons indicate that in some cases people were standing; while in others, they sat. See Dargan, *op. cit.*, I, 193.

[65] Preaching outside the church was later proscribed in France, well before the beginning of the Reformation. The council of Angers in 1448 condemned it. Lecoy de la Marche, 228-29.

[66] *Ibid.*, 210.

[67] Baldwin, *op. cit.*, 232.

[68] 9, Pa[16], 143[ra]-144[vb]: Vos estis quibus dispensatio ineffabilis sacramenti corporis et sanguinis Domini commissa... sed vos qui debetis esse genus electum, regale sacerdotium (*I Petr.* 2:9)... Attendite... gregi per exemplum. Attendite vobis bene vivendo. Attendite gregi bene docendo... igitur patres mei et domini...

episcopus, observing that *speculator* is its Latin equivalent. By this did the preacher Stephen underline the supervisory function of the office of his listeners.[69]

In yet another sermon addressed to priests in synod — this on the theme *Sumite de optimis terre frugibus* (*Gen.* 43:11) — Langton compared his audience spiritually to the brothers of Joseph who brought the youngest son Benjamin down to Egypt:

> Your youngest brother are the layfolk — simple and untutored — who have been entrusted to you by your father ... If, therefore, the laity are good, and if simple clerks are better, it is consistent that priests be best... and furthermore, that prelates of churches be most courageous in the fulfillment of their office, and most skilled in spiritual combat... .[70]

A rubricator has enabled us to identify still another audience of seculars, this more closely associated with the schools. The sermon beginning *Legimus filios Israel profectos de Egypto* (variously called an *Epistola* or *Lectio mag. Steph. de X plagis*), is, in at least one manuscript cited as Stephen's inaugural lecture as master of theology.[71]

Nor were regular clergy absent from Langton's audiences. Rubrics such as *Sermo... ad monachos*[72] and *In ascensione Domini claustralibus et scolaribus*[73] point up instantly the audiences addressed by Langton in these sermons.

These rubrics indicating secondary categories within the general divisions (*ad clericos* and *ad populum*) classify audiences according to the particular listeners and circumstances of the sermon. Specified categories were especially common in the sermons of Alain de Lille, Jacques de Vitry, Humbert de Romans, and Guibert de Tournai, whose sermons *ad status* were addressed, *inter alia*, to princes, nobles, bourgeoisie, students, workers, merchants, peasants, sailors, regular and secular clergy, women and children.[74] The one hundred and eight classifications that have been

69 *Ibid.*, 144vb: Episcopus grece latine speculator, et ut alludat vocabulo, dicitur quasi superintendens... . (Notice the variations in the rubric of this sermon: *In synodo; Ad sacerdotes; Ad episcopos et pastores; In synodo ad prelatos;* and *Sermo quomodo prelatus se habeat et de non appetenda prelatione*).

70 102, Pa^{16}, 81vb-82ra: Fratres inde Ioseph: vos estis spiritualiter... frater vester minimus populus est laicorum simplex et indoctus, qui vobis est a patre commissus... Si enim boni sunt laici, si simplices clerici meliores, congruit ut sacerdotes sint optimi... congruit enim ut ecclesiarum prelati sint in operatione fortissimi, et in spirituali pugna doctissimi. (Variants of this rubric: *Sermo in sinodo ad omnes et maxime ad presbyteros; In sinodo ad sacerdotes*).

71 48, Pa^{14}, 222vb (Contemp. hand, XIII): Lectio M. Stephani de Long. quam fecit in sua inceptione... (See the text of this sermon in the Appendix).

72 77^{b}, CUL, 108^{r}.

73 121, Pa^{8}, 233^{v}.

74 Lecoy de la Marche, 207-09. Sermons addressed especially to penitents were also common.

assigned to the last three of these preachers are a rather fine elaboration of status, not to be found in such precision in the extant Langton sermons. Diversification according to persons and circumstances was to some extent apparent in Langton's preaching as well, not however, uniformly or exactly identified always by rubric. The few examples of *specific rubrics*, cited above, indicate that for some judgment relating to the audiences of the bulk of Langton's sermons, we must turn to internal evidence.

His sermons to the clergy included seculars, prelates, and priests, as we have already seen. In two sermons referred to earlier, the occasions were special synods. Other sermons were addressed to seculars in more ordinary circumstances. Notice for example in a sermon for Pentecost, the address: "Domini et patres reverendi. ..." "You are the royal priesthood, the chosen race, and holy people," continues Langton.[75] To an audience of clerks during Lent, he admonished: "There are certain simple folk who would willingly hear how they ought to love God and to follow Him, but they are without instruction in doctrine. You, [however], who so often hear the teachings of theologians cannot allege this excuse. You are not lacking in education. ..."[76] Sometimes a phrase such as *ad vos clericos*[77] appears in the text itself, and like a rubric, is a valuable aid in identifying the audience.

Regular clergy, as we noticed earlier, were also among Langton's audiences. They might be so indicated by rubric, but for the most part, we must search the texts. In a sermon preached on Assumption Sunday, Langton addressed an assembly of monks: "You, therefore, my brothers and lords... are the most beloved disciples of Jesus Christ... . Humble yourselves, dearest ones, to your prelates..."[78]

Modes of address frequently offer a key to the kind of audience and may indicate the status of the listener. *Bona gens*, in a sermon for Ascension Sunday,[79] or *bone gentes* in a text for Easter,[80] suggest popular audiences.[81] The most customary forms of address in contemporary sermons were

[75] 2, Bs[1], 149[va]: Domini et patres reverendi... Vos etenim estis regale sacerdotium, genus electum, gens sancta... .

[76] 38[b], PA[1], 109[va-vb]: Quidam enim simplices libenter audirent qualiter Deum diligere deberent et eum sequi, sed doctrina carent. Vos non potestis pretendere hanc excusationem qui tociens theologorum instructiones auditis. Non deest vobis instructio... .

[77] 98[b], Ar, 19[rb].

[78] 77[b], Pa[16], 145[vb]-146[va]: Vos igitur fratres mei et domini... Karissimi discipuli estis Ihesu Christi... Humiliamini etiam karissimi prelatis vestris... (*Cf.* CUL, 108[r], *Ad monachos*).

[79] 17[a], Pa[11], 259[vb].

[80] 56, Bs[1], 133[va].

[81] I would base this judgment on the evidence of the vernacular sermons of the period, which as Lecoy de la Marche has shown (211), used the following forms of address for popular audiences: *bele gens; bele segnors; bele douce gent; segnors et dames.*

fratres or *fratres karissimi.*[82] There are several variations, e.g., *karissimi;*[83] *fratres mei;*[84] *dilectissimi;*[85] *fratres dilectissimi;*[86] and *viri fratres.*[87] These forms of address cannot, however, in themselves be taken to indicate one type of audience over the other. Examples of their use in sermons clerical and lay are not unusual. *Karissimi,* said Langton, to priests gathered in synod;[88] and *fratres karissimi,* to monks and scholars.[89] Yet in a sermon preached before Ascension Day, Langton called his listeners, *fratres,* adding later, "Vos laici dicitis quod omne bonum de terra [est]..."[90]

Lay audiences of the faithful might indeed speak up, for it was not unusual for a preacher to be interrupted by questions or objections from his audience. The practice was a reminder of the primitive homilies and conversations during which the bishop interrogated the people and responded to their questions. The sermon was not only a theological exercise to mark an occasion in the ecclesiastical year, but was also a significant teaching device. It was not unheard of in the thirteenth century to hear a voice raised in the midst of the sermon asking for clarification or contesting an assertion made by the preacher.[91]

So far as I have been able to judge, Langton's sermons do not yield any information about such interruptions. There is, however, testimony in a contemporary chronicle of one such incident. In the case of the sermon addressed *ad populum* at St. Paul's in August 1213, the Annalist of Waverley has preserved the account of a listener who challenged the relevance and accuracy of Langton's theme: *In Deo speravit cor meum, et adjutus sum, et refloruit caro mea*; calling out in a loud voice that the archbishop was a liar — in response to which the prelate was silent for a moment and then, without further delay, the troublemaker was ousted from the cathedral.[92]

[82] *Ibid.* See, in Langton's sermons, e.g., 6[b], Bs[1], 117[ra] and 6[c], Le[2], 148[vb].

[83] 1[b], Pa[7], 248[rb].

[84] 3, Tr[2], 262[vb].

[85] 36[c], Ar, 133[vb].

[86] 62, Tr[2], 239[vb].

[87] 115[a], Ar, 8[ra].

[88] 102, Pa[16], 82[va].

[89] 121, Tr[2], 271[rb].

[90] 64[a], Bs[1], 144[vb].

[91] Lecoy de la Marche, 216.

[92] *Annal. monast.*, *Wav.*, II, 277: ... sed in primis apud Sanctum Paulum sermonem fecit ad populum; quo sic incepto, 'In Deo speravit cor meum, et adjutus sum, et refloruit caro mea,' etc., surgens quidam verbis hujuscemodi alta voce respondit, 'Per mortem Dei,' inquit, 'mentiris, nunquam cor tuum speravit in Deo, nec refloruit caro tua.' Hoc audito tacuit archipraesul, obstupescentibus omnibus; nec mora, irruente in eum populo, flagellatus est, custodiaeque traditus; ut ni die sequenti, qua temeritate hujuscemodi proferret sermonem, innotesceret.

Nor were audiences of the clergy silent. In assemblies of monks, for example, protestations and contradictions to the words of the preacher were not unusual.[93] In the twelfth century, moreover, monks actually participated in the presentation of a sermon by asking the abbot for clarification of certain passages of Scripture.[94]

To sum up. Various items of evidence must be assessed before determining the audiences that Langton addressed. Where there is a clear statement in a rubric and/or an otherwise identifying title of address in the text itself, this is evidently the most dependable form of identification. In other instances (notably the majority of cases), we must weigh the use of ambiguous modes of address (e.g., *karissimi*, *fratres mei*, etc.) against other evidence (e.g., the general rubric in Troyes MS 1367,[95] the predominance of commonplace examples that characterize sermons to primarily lay audiences; the use of phrases such as *vulgariter dicitur* or *vulgo dici solet quod*), to venture some estimate as to Langton's listeners on a given occasion.

The number of examples can be multiplied, but the evidence appears overwhelming that by far the majority of the sermons examined in this category (i.e., appearing in more than one named copy) were addressed to predominantly lay audiences. Fewer were delivered to clerical assemblies, and some of these on occasions of ecclesiastical councils. Our extant Langton sermons seem to indicate that Stephen Langton, master of theology and later archbishop of Canterbury, for the most part preached to the people in less unusual circumstances, on the Sundays and festivals of the liturgical year.[96] These sermons are written in Latin in the manuscripts. Were they also spoken in Latin?

The Language of the Sermons

The kind of audience addressed determined the language of preaching. Although it is generally agreed that sermons preached to monks and seculars were delivered in Latin,[97] whether this was also necessarily true of sermons addressed to popular or mixed audiences has been a subject of

[93] Lecoy de la Marche, 217.

[94] Bourgain, 23-24.

[95] See Appendix A: Sermons classified by audience.

[96] *Cf.* Powicke, *SL*, 42.

[97] Bourgain (186) listed the following as audiences for Latin sermons: *ad clericos, ad sacerdotes, in synodo, ad monachos, ad moniales, ad sanctimoniales, ad monachas, ad scholares.* Eileen Power shows evidence to the contrary, regarding female religious. In her *Medieval English Nunneries: c. 1275 to 1535* (Cambr. Univ. Pr., 1922, repr. 1964), 246, 249 she concludes that the majority of nuns during the period studied, knew no Latin. She refers to visitation sermons of the first half of the fifteenth century, preached in the vulgar tongue in various nunneries.

debate, first raised in 1873 by the French scholar Hauréau. Noting that most of the sermons in the manuscript collections were *written* in Latin, Hauréau questioned whether they were not also *spoken* in Latin. His thesis, in effect, held that popular audiences were able to comprehend Latin and that it was unreasonable to suppose that, after preaching in the vernacular, a preacher would then translate the sermon into Latin, rendering it less intelligible to the average priest.[98]

Hauréau, however, appears to have been the lone dissenter against popular preaching in the vernacular. Most scholars believe that the evidence supports the view that medieval preaching had a dual character determined by the clerical or lay composition of the audience.[99] Manuscript evidence also supports this duality of language. Translations by the compilers of the sermons for the manuscripts substantiate the claim.[100] Latin, the language of the manuscripts, had a "universality of appeal" in all Christendom.[101] The practice of publishing in Latin sermons composed and preached in the vulgar tongue had always been in the tradition of the Church.[102] Moreover, the vernaculars, in this period, could scarcely compete with Latin which afforded a uniformity in the written texts which the diversity of dialects, barely literate in character, could not begin to approach.

A tradition of vernacular preaching in the middle ages also argues against the Hauréau thesis. It had long been established that Bernard of Clairvaux addressed his monks in Latin and the people in the vernacular.[103] Nor were sermons in the vernacular unusual before the twelfth and thirteenth centuries. We have earlier referred to the Capitulary of Charlemagne (published in 813) which advised that popular preaching

98 B. Hauréau, "Sermonnaires," *Hist. litt.*, XXVI (Paris, 1873), 388-89.

99 Representative of the consensus are Bourgain, 196; Lecoy de la Marche, 235, and L. Stinglhamber, "Prédicateurs au moyen âge," *Nouv. rev. théol.*, LXIX (1947), 651-52.

100 Both Bourgain (192, n. 1) and Lecoy de la Marche (239-41) cite the manual of sermons by Maurice de Sully. The sermons had been preached in French, but the Latin texts were prepared by Maurice himself for the use of the clergy in his diocese. Contemporary French texts that are also extant were later adaptations of the manual by preachers in different provinces. See Robson's recent study on Maurice de Sully, *cit. supra.*

101 See Owst, *Preaching in medieval England*, *op. cit.*, 223-24. H. G. Pfander in *The popular sermon of the medieval friar in England* (New York, 1937), 7 noticed that sermons given in English were written down in Latin.

102 Langlois, "L'Éloquence sacrée au m.â.," *op. cit.*, 173: "L'usage de publier en latin des sermons composés et récités en langue laïque a toujours été de tradition dans l'Église."

103 This had been established by Mabillon. Studies of the sermons of St. Bernard, extant in Latin and French texts, indicate that Latin was the original and French, a translation. Bourgain, 170, 188.

be done in the language understood by the people.[104] It seems obvious then that preachers spoke to their congregations in the language they best understood. In an age when the formal study of Latin was restricted to monastic or cathedral schools, the general population in a preacher's audience could only be expected to understand preaching in the vulgar tongue.[105]

If we apply this question of language to the Langton sermons, it is of interest to notice what evidence is available in the texts that would support the generally accepted view that these sermons, overwhelmingly popular in their audience, were originally preached in the vernacular.[106]

While the condition of the sermon texts renders the problem all the more complex, there are nevertheless, some helpful clues. It has been suggested that many extant texts may, in the case of vernacular sermons, represent a report by a cleric who has reproduced the text in Latin. Or, a preacher might himself have redacted his sermons in Latin, possibly to satisfy the desire of his admirers, to offer model sermons to his colleagues, or confer on his works a possible fame that the use of the vernacular would not permit.[107]

In any case, it was not unusual to clarify certain Latin words or expressions by giving the vernacular counterpart, possibly to facilitate the use of the text by another preacher. Contemporary manuscripts show frequent usage of common expressions, e.g., *scilicet vulgare dicitur*, or, *quod dicitur* (followed by the French expression), or *gallice*.[108] Langton's sermons have similar examples. Thus in a text for Advent:

> Item domus Domini *gallice* dicitur *hospitale*... .[109] (Emphasis mine).

This phraseology is more apparent in Langton's rendering of popular proverbs into Latin. In a sermon for the Sunday after Epiphany:

> Item vulgari proverbio dicitur: Bonus est denarius qui cum lucro revertitur... .[110]

104 See section on audiences, *supra*.

105 Bourgain, 176-77. By the time of the high middle ages, monastic schools concentrated mainly on the training of their novices and cathedral schools — that accepted all those who had received or intended to receive even minor orders — provided instruction in Latin not only for those who entered the priesthood, but also for those who needed Latin for law, medicine, or administration. See R. R. Bolgar, *The Classical Heritage and its Beneficiaries* (Harper Torchbook, 1964), 194-95.

106 There seems to be no doubt that Latin was the language of Langton's sermons to the clergy. (On the correspondence between the written record and that which was allegedly spoken, see the section below on transmission of the sermons).

107 Stinglhamber, 651.

108 Lecoy de la Marche, 253-56.

109 33[a], Ar, 77rb. Godefroy, *Dict. de l'anc. langue française*, IV, 500 gives *hospitale* as an alternative to the other French forms *hospital, hospitalerie.*

110 19[c], Le[2], 41va.

Elsewhere in the same text: *Vulgariter dicitur. Male consilium accipit qui non credit.*[111] And in a sermon on the Vigil of St. John: *Vulgare dicit proverbium quod amor qui cito adquiritur cito amittitur...* .[112] In another instance, a proverb appears in French in one copy of the text, and in Latin, in another:

> Debet igitur quilibet solus sedere et beneficia Dei lugens numerare timoremque iudicii ad memoriam revocare. Ita sancti lugent sed mali gaudent in presenti. Hic est cantus. *Melius est unum in presenti habes, quam tria que expectas.*[113] (Emphasis mine).

Compare this with the following rendering:

> ... proponitur cuilibet homini utrum velit in presenti ridere et in eternum lugere vel econverso. Multi sunt qui ridere eligunt et per consequens in eternum lugebunt. Sicut gallice dicitur vel vulgariter. *Miels vaut uns tien que deus tu l'auras.*[114] (Emphasis mine).

Whatever the phrase: *vulgariter dicitur,*[115] *vulgo dicitur,*[116] or *usu vulgari*[117]— the evidence suggests that like other contemporary sermons preached *ad populum,* Langton's sermons were probably also preached in the vernacular and written in Latin in the manuscripts. This evidence is not in itself conclusive. The fact that some vernacular phrases appear in the text of a Latin sermon does not *prove* conclusively that the entire sermon was originally delivered in the vernacular. It might even be argued that Langton could have used a Latin script for a vernacular delivery. One might maintain, moreover, that phrases such as we have cited might be appropriate to audiences of clerks as well. We submit, however, that the presence of similar expressions in contemporary sermons demonstrated to have been delivered in the vernacular to the people, and the remarkable absence of Latinity among the populace at large, lead us to conclude that Langton was a popular preacher who addressed his audiences in the vulgar tongue. The late Professor Powicke who knew only a small portion of the now known sermons of Stephen Langton, thought otherwise: "Those sermons of Langton which do remain in manuscript are for the most part addresses originally given in Latin to audiences which could

111 *Ibid.*, 42rb.

112 72^{a}, Tr^{2}, 277vb. For examples of popular proverbs given in Latin, see Lecoy de la Marche, 251, n. 2.

113 13^{a}, Le^{2}, 44^{ra-b}.

114 13^{a}, Ar, 151va. *Cf.* 13^{a}, Lo^{1}, 100vb: ...sicut gallice dicitur. Meuz ualt unten ke deus tu l'aueras.

115 19^{c}, Le^{2}, 42rb.

116 65^{a}, Tr^{2}, 254rb.

117 54^{b}, Ar, 58vb.

follow them in that language."[118] Whether the sermon was preached in Latin to clerics, or in the vernacular to the people and then written in Latin in the manuscripts, raises questions relating to the trustworthiness of the translations and problems of reporting, to which we must now turn.[119]

Transmission of the Sermons

The problem of the transmission of the sermons is closely related to that of language, for in the course of the final rendering of the sermon into Latin — whether by a cleric or by the author himself — the text might, in its final appearance, be the whole of the sermon or a digest.[120] Even if the spoken sermon were in the vernacular, this does not mean that the written Latin sermon was always a direct later translation. The intervention of a time interval and/or reporter must be taken into account.[121]

We have earlier referred to the suggestion that the sermons extant in the manuscripts may represent a *reportatio* by a cleric, who has reproduced in Latin the sermon given in the vernacular; or, that the author himself may have brought together a collection of his sermons, translating them into Latin, possibly to serve as a kind of manual for other preachers. The book of sermons that comes down to us under the name of Maurice de Sully, bishop of Paris, exemplifies this practice. Other preachers who collected their sermons in similar fashion, introduced by a preface addressed to

[118] Powicke, *SL*, 42. While Powicke acknowledged that popular sermons would be delivered in the vernacular and that *several* of these survive in Latin translation, this appears to be true of *most* of the Langton sermons.

[119] Bourgain (193) has called attention to one further influence of the vernacular in these sermons, namely in vocabulary. Medieval Latin, as a living language, was susceptible to change. In order for the Church to express its theology and liturgy, it was often necessary to create new words and extend its vocabulary. The vernaculars assisted in this as well as in matters of construction and the all too frequent neglect of syntax. Examples such as the following (though certainly not limited to sermons) point to the infiltration of the language by words of patristic and medieval derivation: de *feudo* beate virginis... (58[a], Ar, 83[va]); ... quomodo in facie primo Maxentio *ydolatre* restitit (46[b], Le[2], 188[rb]).

[120] Baldwin, *op. cit.*, 233.

[121] Lecoy de la Marche (320-21) has distinguished between those sermons published by speech, and those published by the written word. Although the second ordinarily followed the first, the two forms of publication were not necessarily joined. Spoken sermons of the thirteenth century generally followed any of four different procedures, i.e., improvised sermons, prepared sermons, sermons recited from memory, and sermons that were read. Improvised sermons, though rendered quite frequently, were not often preserved or reproduced. A listener, or sometimes the orator himself might record such sermons. The prepared sermon, on the other hand, is much more frequent in the MSS. Method and general appearance, citations of texts and commentaries, indicate great pains taken in their preparation.

colleagues, include Jacques de Vitry, Jean d'Abbeville, and Guibert de Tournai.[122]

Most frequently, however, the sermon was written down by a listener, either at the time of hearing or afterwards. Certain priests carried notebooks or tablets with them when they listened to the preaching of their colleagues, taking notes, either for their own use, or for the benefit of others. These copies by second hand are often the only ones we have.[123]

The writing down of the sermon by *reportatio* had close connections with the teaching of the schools. As Lecoy de la Marche observed:

> It is, in effect, from the instruction of the schools that this practice [i.e., *reportatio*] was extended to the teaching of the pulpit. The University had scribes specially charged with noting down the sermons of its members: hence it is according to their notes that so many of the collections of diverse provenance and nature were formed — these set forth with no order or solely according to the ecclesiastical year.[124]

The author went on to mention some examples of these "collections of diverse provenance and nature." These include manuscripts from the Sorbonne and the Abbey of St. Victor,[125] sources which coincide with the history of many of the Paris manuscripts which we have examined for Langton sermons. Notice, for example, the following manuscripts whose provenance was the Sorbonne, but are now among the Latin manuscripts of the Bibliothèque nationale: 15965, 16463, and 16502. The canons of St. Victor also have left collections of the same *genre*. Manuscripts bearing the St. Victor *ex-libris* and containing Langton sermons include the following: BN MSS, lat. 14859, 15025, 14470, 14525, 14593, 14804, 14925, and 14957.[126]

122 Lecoy de la Marche, 325. On Jacques de Vitry, see *supra*, p. 19, n. 9; on Maurice de Sully, *supra*, p. 45, n. 44. Jean Halgrin d'Abbeville (d. 1237) was a younger contemporary of Langton who rose in the ranks of the church hierarchy from deacon in the church at Amiens to become cardinal-bishop of Sabine. His sermons, collected in the *Summa sermonum de tempore et sanctis*, enjoyed great vogue, despite their alleged mediocrity. See Lecoy de la Marche, 60-64 and 516 for MSS. Also, Glorieux, *Rép.*, I, 272-73.

123 Lecoy de la Marche, 325. Jacques de Vitry tells of the masters and scholars of Paris writing down the words of Foulques de Neuilly, in order to repeat them in their turn. (*Hist.*, II, vii, cited in *ibid.*, 325, n. 3).

124 *Ibid.*, 326. Lecoy de la Marche adds (328) that series of sermons such as these were transcribed, based on notes, or simply by memory. Similarly, in sermons of the Dominican Jordan of Saxony, the texts are probably compilations from notes taken by a reporter. See A. G. Little & D. Douie, "Three sermons of Friar Jordan of Saxony," *EHR*, LIV (1939), 3.

125 Lecoy de la Marche, 326.

126 We should also mention BN MS, lat. 12420 which was previously in the library of St. Germain-des-Prés; and Ste. Gen. MS 1422, still in that collection. For the details of the contents of these MSS, and relevant bibliography, see the section on the Classification of the MSS, *infra*.

Many of the collections of sermons contained in these manuscripts appear to be the result of the practice described above, i.e., the work of a copyist who has transmitted a number of texts second-hand. In some, the common denominator appears to have been the association of the authors of the texts as masters in Paris. Certainly the group of named sermons in BN MS, lat. 14859[127] meets this description, as do those sermons in Ste-Gen. MS 1422. In the former, individual sermons bear the names of their authors; in the latter, Langton's name is prominent in the general rubric: *Incipiunt sermones mag. Steph. de Linguatonante.*[128] An attribution to one author can also be misleading. In BN MS, lat. 16463, the name of Maurice de Sully appears to be associated with the *ninety sermons* in the series. *Thirty-eight* of these are clearly Langton's.[129]

The most characteristic feature of the collections that have been cited above is the assembling of a group of sermon texts of diverse authorship, and notably personalities associated with Paris and its schools. This intermingling of texts, so often rendered homogeneous by an unknown reporter-copyist, and alas, anonymous by later copyists, has created untold difficulties to one who would seek to use sermon literature as historical evidence. Given a sermon by Stephen Langton or one by Alain de Lille or a third, by Jean d'Abbeville, one is impressed by the external features of homogeneity engraved on the text by the transmitter. These sermons look very much alike in the manuscripts, beginning with a theme drawn from Scripture, perhaps identified by an appropriate rubric, and often drawing on a common stock of examples and similitudes. These preachers were after all of the same school and tradition in sermon-making.

If, however, we pass beyond the externals of the sermon texts and begin to identify them by author (this facilitated by some of the named collections), these texts assume an individuality and a corresponding significance as historical sources. We have noticed, for example, in manuscripts where large numbers of Langton sermons have been found (these notably in libraries outside Paris), that the manuscripts contain copies of texts ori-

[127] Sermons in BN MS, lat. 14859 include those attributed to Prévostin (ff. 212ra-215vb; 251vb; 274ra; 287rb); Peter the Chanter (205ra-209va); Hugh of St. Victor, Maurice de Sully, etc. (188^{v}-195^{v}); Peter, Chancellor of Chartres (230ra; 242vb; 243va; 284ra; 285vb); Alain de Lille (233ra-240rb); Joh. d'Abeville (*sic*) (244ra; 245va; 247ra; 250va; 254rb; 262va; 263vb; 264vb; 273ra).

[128] Notice, however, that some eighteen sermons cannot be conclusively identified as Langton's. See Ste. Gen. MS 1422.

[129] Other sermons in BN MS, lat. 16463 that can be identified include: Stephen of Tournai (2ra-10vb; 96ra-98rb; 98rb-129rb; 131vb-133vb); Geoffroy of Troyes (12rb-14ra); Peter Comestor (16rb-24vb); Guerric, abbé d'Igny (154^{r}-163^{v}); Maurice de Sully (167ra-196vb). See Hauréau, *Notices et extraits*, V, 136-37.

ginally in Paris manuscripts. That furthermore, whereas in the Paris manuscripts, Langton's sermons were frequently mingled with those of other masters, in these other cases, the sermons of Stephen Langton appear to have been deliberately brought together, under his name, and indeed with his title *archbishop*, and arranged according to the ecclesiastical calendar, much in the manner of the sermon manuals mentioned above. Whether Langton himself brought these texts together, or whether the collections are the work of a copyist, we do not know. In the named collection in BN MS, lat. 14859, Langton was called *magister*; in the Leipzig MS 443, he is Stephen, archbishop of Canterbury:

> Steph. Cant. arch. sive Steph. Langthon sive de Linguatona, Sermones de tempore et de sanctis.[130]

This Leipzig manuscript has been found to contain eighty-four sermons identified as Langton's. The rubrics of these sermons, in the order in which they appear in the manuscript, correspond to the church calendar of holidays and saints' days[131] and demonstrate further the process of the transmission of the Langton sermons.

The sermons in Brugge MS 28, where twenty-four texts are Langton's, is another example. The manuscript has this contemporary inscription:

> Sermones magistri Stephani Cantuariensis archiepiscopi... .

The order in which the sermons appear corresponds to the ecclesiastical calendar.[132]

Given these various stages in the transmission of the sermon text: (1) delivery of the sermon; (2) recording of the text (and its translation, where necessary) by author or clerk; (3) collections of texts of various masters (sometimes but not always) arranged according to the liturgical calendar; and (4) gathering together a group of sermons of a prominent preacher — perhaps one such as Stephen Langton, who had become archbishop of Canterbury — we cannot underestimate the problems raised by the transmission of sermons by *reportatio*. We have found, for example, no manuscript containing only sermons by Langton with a preface by him. One must be aware that a sermon transmitted by *reportatio* may contain something of the reporter as well, not to mention later copyists! Glorieux stressed the extent to which we are at the mercy of the copyist in his description of Paris University sermons of 1267-68,[133] but his remarks are

130 Leipzig MS 443, f. 1.

131 See Appendix B: Arrangement of sermons in Le^2.

132 *Ibid.*: Sermons in Bg^1.

133 P. Glorieux, "Sermons universitaires parisiens de 1267-68," *Recherches de théol. anc. et méd.*, XVI (1949), 40.

equally true of the large numbers of anonymous sermons scattered in the manuscripts.

Before criticizing the preacher Langton's style, we must, therefore, judge whether his works have in fact been transmitted by *reportatio*. The final word must await the collation and editing of each sermon text. For our present purposes, we have selected various passages for comparative investigation in the light of several means of identification of the *reportatio* method, e.g. the brevity of developing ideas, the absence of protheme, and of initial and final formulae which were almost always omitted by reporters.[134] Notice, for example, that the account of the slaying of Holofernes by Judith is given at length in one version of a sermon on the theme *Aperite portas nobis* (*Iud.* 13:13); but remarkably abbreviated in another.[135]

In most cases in Langton's sermons, *Pater Noster* (followed by a restatement of the theme) is prominent in the introductory part of the sermon (*cf.* protheme). Thus, *Pater Noster. Est puer unus hic...* .[136] Or, *Pater Noster. Exemplum dedi vobis...* .[137] Sometimes, however, the characteristic *Pater Noster* has been omitted by a copyist: thus, *Orate... Omnis vallis implebitur...*[138] or, *Oremus ergo ut iste cor nostrum et vestra tangat corda...* .[139]

In the matter of closing formulae, the situation varies. Considerably abbreviated as *Quod ipse prestare dignetur, amen,*[140] the formula appears in full as *dignetur qui vivit et regit, per omnia secula seculorum, amen.*[141] In two versions of a given text, the closing formula was lacking in the first, but abbreviated to *Quod nobis prestare* in the second.[142] In another sermon on the theme *Plurima turba straverunt vestimenta sua* (*Matt.* 21:8), in three versions of the text, there were discrepancies in the closing: ... *ad quam perducat salvator noster Jesus, amen*; *Quod ipse, etc.*; and no formula in the third.[143]

Brevity as an outcome of *reportatio* may be puzzling in the attempt to arrive at what the preacher most likely said and hence in understanding his intent. But it is an aid in explaining the variants of the sermons that have survived in several copies.[144] This, coupled with the habit of eco-

[134] Lecoy de la Marche, 330-31.

[135] The lengthier account appears in 5^{b}, Le^{2}, 23va-24va; abbreviated in 5^{a}, Bs^{1}, 136vb.

[136] 38^{b}, Pa^{16}, 109ra.

[137] 40^{b}, Be, 37ra.

[138] 66^{b}, Bs^{1}, 79ra.

[139] 101^{b}, Bs^{1}, 82va.

[140] 38^{c}, Le^{2}, 69rb.

[141] 44^{b}, Le^{2}, 14vb.

[142] *54*^{a}, Pa^{11}, 224ra and *54*^{b}, Ar, 60va.

[143] *70*^{a}, Pa^{11}, 232vb; *70*^{b}, PA^{1}, 61rb; *70*^{c}, Le^{2}, 75vb. There are other examples of the absence of closing formulae in Le^{2}: 88, 109rb; 103^{c}, 140vb; and 105^{a}, 131ra.

[144] Lecoy de la Marche, 331.

nomizing parchment by reporting simple analyses of sermons may also help to account for the texts we have today.[145] Notice, for example, these variations in a sermon for Epiphany, on the theme *Transeamus usque Bethlehem* (*Luc.* 2:15), which indicate a change not only of the words of the passage, but also a notable shift of emphasis from a statement of straight political theory to one on self-government or ethics:

> Rex est quicumque fidelis corpus suum bene regens. Regnum eius est corpus, populus huius regni sunt desideria carnis que militant adversus animam...[146]
>
> Regnum ergo hoc est corpus vel caro. Rex homo, populus huius regni desideria carnis... .[147]
>
> Similiter quilibet homo est rex longinque regionis i.e. carnis, que nos elongat a Deo. Hanc carnem debet anima regere. Populi huius regni sunt illicita desideria.[148]
>
> Nullus poterit venire ad Dominum nisi sit rex. Quomodo autem quis rex sit, Beda ostendit dicens. Reges magni sunt qui se ipsos regunt, et malis temptationum motibus non subcumbunt. Populus talium regum sunt desideria...[149]
>
> Rex ergo potest esse quilibet christianus, licet pauperrimus qui regnum suum i.e. corpus suum sapienter et discrete gubernat. Regni autem huius plebs extrema est motus, carnalia desideria que semper adversus spiritum sunt repugnancia et ideo vix subicienda vel domanda... .[150]

In conclusion, we should emphasize that the means by which the Langton sermons have been transmitted appears to have been by *reportatio.* Supporting evidence is supplied by the brevity of various passages and significant differences in the renderings of standard formulae. This was generally true of contemporary twelfth and thirteenth century sermons, and Langton's preaching does not appear to be exceptional in this respect. The extent to which alterations are an outcome of reporter or copyist or several *reportationes* must remain tentative, pending a complete analysis of every sermon text in all its manuscript copies. Our samples indicate a wide variation in phraseology which suggests that there was a *reportatio* which came to be modified further in the history of the transmission of the text. As our texts came to be recorded and transmitted, they were first included in collections ascribed to various masters in Paris (including our *Magister Stephanus*); and were later gathered under the full title, Stephen Langton, archbishop of Canterbury, in the manner of a sermon manual.

145 *Ibid.*, 336.

146 *109*[a], Tr[2], 299[vb].

147 *109*[b], Pa[7], 230[va].

148 *109*[c], Le[2], 38[va].

149 *109*[d], Le[2], 36[va].

150 *109*[e], OM, 55[v].

This appears to be a departure from the usual practice where the collection of pieces by the same author generally precedes the miscellaneous collection of several authors. We submit further that the remarkable absence of contemporary references in Langton's sermons may be explained by the nature of the sermon manual. A preacher, consulting such a handbook of sermons, might use the sermon as a model and embellish the theme with oral and topical comments that would not necessarily be found in a collection of sermons arranged according to the ecclesiastical calendar.

Kinds and Occasions of the Sermons

The ecclesiastical year formed a continuous drama during which the faithful were instructed in the tenets of religion. Langton preached on the Sundays and feastdays of the church calendar, but his sermons were not limited to these occasions. Like other prelates, Langton preached to the clergy in synod.[151] Pastoral visits also might call for a sermon. Langton's preaching to the chapter at Bury-St-Edmunds in November 1213 may well have been such an occasion.[152] Grosseteste, for example, regularly preached during his visitations in 1238 to monasteries, archdeaconries and deaneries.[153] Extant visitation sermons of the thirteenth century (and indeed sermons urging visitations by prelates as part of their offices) underline the importance attached to the preaching-teaching function of the good pastor.[154]

Special sacred ceremonies likewise afforded opportunities for the pastor to address audiences of the faithful. Ordinations, consecrations, elections, coronations and pilgrimages were frequently highlighted by the preaching of a sermon.[155] Dedications gave preachers an opportunity to initiate the faithful to liturgical practice by explaining the rites of the consecration of a church.[156] Two sermons, *In dedicatione*, may well have been preached by Langton at special ceremonies dedicating a new church.[157] For other

151 See section on audiences, *supra*. On the growth of the Latin synodal sermon in the preaching of Maurice de Sully, see Robson, *op. cit.*, 52-58.

152 The sermon does not appear to be extant, but is referred to in the *Memorials of St. Edmund's Abbey*, *cit. supra*, chap. II.

153 C. R. Cheney, *Episcopal visitation of monasteries in the thirteenth century* (Manchester, 1931), 59.

154 *Ibid.*, 15, 62. Archbishop Pecham who called preaching the principal duty of a bishop preached at state ceremonies and on visitations. D. Douie, "Archbishop Pecham's Sermons," *Studies presented to Powicke*, *op. cit.*, 269 ff.

155 Lecoy de la Marche, 221.

156 *Ibid.*, 372.

157 93[b], Le[2], 128[vb] and 105[a], Le[2], 129[vb]. See also the reference to Langton's preaching at the dedication of the new Lady Chapel at Salisbury Cathedral in September 1225 in the *Register of St. Osmund*, *cit. supra*, chap. II. The sermon apparently is not extant.

grand occasions, we are dependent on the records of chroniclers who marked the presence of Langton and the preaching of a sermon. Notice, for example, Langton's preaching at the second coronation of Henry III at Westminster in May 1220, or on the occasion of the translation of the relics of Becket, two months later at Canterbury.[158]

For the most part, however, Langton's sermons are in accord with the most frequently noticed classification of sermons in the manuscripts, i.e., the division of sermons according to the ecclesiastical year (*Sermones de tempore, de dominicis, dominicales*); and sermons for saints' days (*Sermones de sanctis, de festis, festivales*).[159] A glance at the rubrics of the Langton texts is sufficient to indicate that the sermon for Advent, or Lent, or Easter; All Saints Day, or St. Stephen's Day is his most typical occasion and kind of sermon.[160]

The Sermon and the Liturgy

Preaching to the laity on Sundays and feastdays, or on extraordinary occasions, was an important function of the prelate. Instruction of the people in the principles of the faith had been set forth in the canons of one of the early church councils.[161] Langton himself often commented on the importance of preaching and the essentials of the preacher: "Every preacher ought to have three things; he ought to think in advance about what he should say, he ought to pray to God that what he says is useful for himself

158 See chap. II.

159 *Sermones de sanctis* may also include sermons for special groups, e.g., martyrs, confessors, virgins. Lecoy de la Marche, 274-75. Notice the collection of *Sermones de tempore* in St. John's Coll., Cambridge MS C 12, f. 24 *inc*: Dicite filie Syon, etc. A reference on f. 105[rb] indicates that the speaker was archbishop of Canterbury. (I have checked these sermons against the Langton list and find no evidence to assign them to Langton. I am grateful to Dr. C. H. Lawrence of Bedford Coll., London for calling my attention to the collection). On the MS, see M. R. James, *A descriptive catalogue of the MSS in the library of St. John's Coll. Cambridge* (1913), 82-6. The sermons of Jacob of Lausanne also appear in these divisions, *Sermones de tempore et de sanctis*. See J. B. Schneyer, "Eine Sermonesliste des Jacobus von Lausanne," *Recherches de théol. anc. et méd.*, XXVII (1960), 67-132.

160 We have earlier noticed examples of the *Sermo communis* (called an "exhortation banale et vague" by Lecoy de la Marche, 276) in Langton's preaching. Other miscellaneous types of sermons include the funeral prayer which had been well developed in the twelfth century, and the special form of preaching in rhymed sermons. (*Ibid.*, 277, 279) See comments on Langton at the funeral of William Marshal, *supra*, chap. II. For an example of the rhymed sermon, see BM, Arundel MS 292, Bele Aliz, f. 38[r]. The authenticity of the attribution to Langton has been challenged. (See references in chap. II). See Appendix E for kinds and occasions of the Langton sermons.

161 *Concil. Trullan.* can. 19. (Constantinople 692). See Lecoy de la Marche, 220; Hefele & Leclercq, III, 566.

and his listeners; he ought also to live a good life, so that what he says by word, is fulfilled by the example of good deeds."[162] Drawing frequently and vividly on scriptural similes, Langton likened the preacher to a creditor,[163] a messenger,[164] a legate,[165] a soldier,[166] or to the champion of the Lord.[167]

Scripture was, after all, the basis of preaching and was not limited to providing simile and metaphor. The sermon was in fact an exposition on Scripture, and specifically on the gospel reading of the day. The preaching of the sermon, or instruction of the faithful, took place in the course of the mass, following the reading of the gospel. These were "sacred sermons," and generally contained some reference or exposition of the particular gospel.[168] Fundamental to the sermon, therefore, was a text from Scripture, and most particularly from the reading of the evangel.

This close association between the reading of the gospel and the sermon preached on that occasion raises the question of the liturgy followed in the churches in which Langton preached. Do the themes of his sermons reflect a traditional use in the readings of Scripture? Biblical texts, it has been noticed,[169] did not usually vary. Yet their application for a certain day or for a particular purpose does.[170] Although a degree of uniformity was dictated by the use or rite practiced in the church, a particular preacher such as Langton might imprint his words with distinctive originality. Lecoy de la Marche singled out Hélinand and Langton in this comment

162 109[c], Ar, 135va: Omnis predicator debet habere tria. Debet precogitare quid dicat; debe orare Deum ut illud quod dicit prosit sibi et auditoribus; debet etiam esse bone vite, ut quod predicat ore, impleat bone operationis exemplo.

163 74[a], Tr[2], 246rb: Nomine creditoris predicator intelligitur. Credit enim censum verbi divini auditoribus...

164 72[a], Tr[2], 277[vb]: Omnis predicator nuncius est domini eius mandata nuntians populo. 82[a], Le[2], 52[vb]: Ille qui verbum predicationis aliis elucidat est quasi nuncius missus ad predam tollendam de manibus inimici.

165 87[b], Pa[6], 46[ra]: Ecce ego quasi legatus, licet indignus vobis omnibus. Lac predicationis i.e. verbum salutis ex parte eius propinare paratus sum.

166 82[b], Pa[16], 92[vb]: Qui dicit verbum Domini est quasi miles Domini... sed miles Domini est predicans verbum eius... .

167 38[a], Pa[16], 66[rb]: Predicator pugil Domini est... .

168 Lecoy de la Marche, 223-24, n. 1: Post evangelii lectionem homilia seu exhortatorius sermo ad populum haberi solebat... . A separate category of preaching should be noticed, i.e., those sermons having nothing to do with the gospel or the feast day, or sermons motivated by extraordinary circumstances. These were relegated to the end of the mass and were called "extraordinary sermons." *Ibid.*, 224.

169 *Ibid.*, 271.

170 Notice, e.g., the use of the theme *Viderunt eam hostes* (*Tren.* 1: 7), sermon no. 118 [a-b]. Different versions of the same theme were preached on Christmas and Easter.

> Les Élinand, les Étienne de Langton et beaucoup de leurs collègues savent donner à leur parole un cachet d'originalité... .[171]

Given a degree of originality, Langton, nevertheless, had to operate within some liturgical use. The history of the liturgy has been treated in some detail by Jungmann, who has described the pre-Christian origins of the delivery of the sermon, preached in the vernacular after the reading of the gospel. It had been the custom in the ancient synagogue to follow the Sabbath Bible reading with some clarifying explanation. Early medieval sermons reflected this homiletic character, and the subsequent history of the medieval sermon is, in effect, a history of its increasing independence from the mass. By the high middle ages, the sermon had not only come into its own as an independent *genre*, but it had come more and more to leave the confines of the mass. (This is most evident in the preaching of the mendicant orders.)[172]

The preaching of the last part of the twelfth and the early years of the thirteenth centuries was, as we have seen, a preaching in transition. This was also true of the relationship between the sermon and the liturgy. Sermons of this age were part of the service, prescribed for in the service books of the church. Rules determining the conduct of the service, appropriate gospel readings (from which a preacher might select his sermon theme) were a part of the *Ordines Romani* (from the sixth to the fifteenth century) which described the Roman ceremonial rite or liturgy that was basic to most of the rites followed in the individual churches of the West. The process by which a uniform liturgy was finally accepted in the western Church was a gradual one and was not completed until the promulgation of the papal bull *Quo primum tempore* by Pius V in 1570. Until that time, various provinces and dioceses had individual variations of the Roman rite.[173]

The use in a given church might draw on other elements, the Roman being only one. By the Merovingian era, two liturgies coexisted in the West. The Roman rite prevailed in Rome itself and southern Italy; and the Gallican use was followed in France, Spain, Britain, Ireland, and northern Italy. By the beginning of the seventh century, the Gallican liturgy, like the church of which it was a part, was already in noticeable decline, and the Roman liturgy making considerable inroads. This process was most apparent by the beginning of the eighth century when the Roman

[171] Lecoy de la Marche, 270-71. For the sermons of Hélinand, see Migne, *PL*, 212, 481-720.

[172] J. A. Jungmann, *The mass of the Roman rite* (2 vols.; New York, 1951-55), I, 456 ff.

[173] A. A. King, *Liturgy of the Roman Church* (London, 1957), see Part I, Historical Summary, 3-45, 442.

sacramentary was brought into France, modified and subsequently adopted as the Gelasian sacramentary. A next step in the incorporation of Romanic elements was the remarkable influence exerted by the Gregorian sacramentary, sent by Pope Adrian to Charlemagne sometime between 784 and 791. The changes in the rite in France over the centuries of the early middle ages are reflected in the manuscripts themselves and most evident in the history of the missal.[174]

It was not until the beginning of the eleventh century that we encounter missals, properly speaking. The origins of the missal are to be found in the earlier sacramentary books containing prayers and sacerdotal formulae reserved for the bishop or a priest who was qualified to administer the sacraments. *Sacramenta facere* sums up the function of these early service books. The term *missalis liber* as applied to these sacramentaries first appears in the Carolingian age. Sacramentary and missal continued to coexist well into the eleventh and twelfth centuries. By the thirteenth century, however, the missal had evolved in its fullest sense as a composite, not only of sacramentaries, but also of books of readings from the gospel, directions for chants and responses, and descriptions of the ceremonies.[175]

This rather long digression was necessary to furnish the background for our attempt to get as close to Langton's own experience as possible. To do so, we are led to investigate the kind of rite contained in the missal books of that era, that is to say, the end of the twelfth and the early years of the thirteenth centuries in Paris. Preaching after the gospel reading was already an established part of the Roman rite by the middle of the twelfth century. The first of the Roman *Ordines* noted the reading of the evangel, but made no mention of preaching. The first specific reference to preaching appears in the *Ordo Romanus XI, ca.* 1143:

> Descendentes portant Evangelia obviam pontifici; et pontifex osculatur ea, ascendit in pulpitum, et praedicat Evangelium.[176]

We have already noticed that the Roman rite in its entirety was not uniformly accepted in the West until the sixteenth century. In the high middle ages, there were local variations, but by and large, the basis was the Roman rite, with several relatively unimportant variations in the prayers and deviations in ceremonial.

[174] V. Leroquais, *Les sacramentaires et les missels manuscrits des bibliothèques publiques de France* (4 vols.; Paris, 1924), I, Intro. xiiiff.

[175] See M. Michaud, *Les livres liturgiques: des Sacramentaires au Missel* (*L'église dans sa liturgie et ses rites*, Xme partie; Paris, 1961), *passim.*

[176] Migne, *PL,* 78, 1033.

We are justified, therefore, in examining the Roman rite effective in this period for themes or scriptural texts traditionally associated with the ecclesiastical calendar. *Ordo Romanus XI* suggests several themes that appear among Langton's sermons. *Ostende nobis, Domine, misericordiam tuam* (*Ps.* 84: 8), for example, appears to have been a recommended theme for Advent.[177] Notice its use by Langton in a sermon for Advent, extant in four versions.[178] Another theme in the Roman *Ordo* traditionally associated with Advent (and also used by Langton) was *Aspiciens a longe ecce video potentiam Dei.*[179] *Circumdederunt me gemitus mortis* (*Ps.* 17:5) had customary connections with Septuagesima and thus appears in Langton's preaching on this occasion.[180]

The Roman rite furnished the basis for the local rite. The missal books in use in Paris during this period have been described by the French scholar V. Leroquais.[181] One of these, a missal in use in Paris in the first half of the thirteenth century (now BN MS, lat. 1112), contains a calendar which lists the various Sundays and feastdays peculiar to the capital. Particular saints associated with Paris are mentioned, e.g., Genovefa and Germanus, who are especially prominent in several Langton sermons and offer an excellent example of the connections between Langton's preaching and the kind of missal then in use. Notice, for example, in the missal: *De sancto Germano Parisiensi Episcopo et Confessore*, the passage, *Ecce sacerdos magnus*, which appears as a theme in Langton's sermon on St. Germanus.[182] Was Paris then the locale of most of these Langton sermons?

The Locale of the Sermons

We have heretofore addressed ourselves to the development of medieval preaching, with particular attention to Stephen Langton — the audiences he addressed, the language of his preaching, and how these sermons came to be transmitted in the form in which we find them. We have noticed, in

177 *Ibid.*, col. 1026.

178 Sermon no. 68[a-d].

179 *PL*, 78, 1026. See the Langton sermon no. 7[a-b].

180 *PL*, 78, 1037, and Langton sermon no. 13[a-c].

181 Leroquais, *cit. supra.*

182 BN MS, lat. 1112, f. 171[r] and sermon no. 30[a-c]. Leroquais also described a missal in use at the end of the twelfth century (now Ste. Gen. MS 93) which contains a calendar (that customarily appeared at the beginning of the book), and litanies for saints. A missal of the first half of the thirteenth century (now BN MS, lat. 862) is described as *Missale Parisiense ad usum magnae confratriae in ecclesia parochiali sanctae Magdalenae* and also contains a calendar of Paris. For descriptions of Ste. Gen. MS 93, see Leroquais, I, 344-45; BN MS, lat. 1112, *ibid.*, II, 47-51; BN MS, lat. 862, 68-69.

addition, the kinds and occasions of these sermons, and the degree to which Langton's use of themes was traditional, in accord with the practice of the Roman rite which, with slight variations, was basic to the missal in use in Paris in this period.

Our sources tell us of Langton's Paris and French connections. What evidence do the sermons themselves offer to support the hypothesis that the bulk of these texts were composed, if not in fact, preached in Paris ? Langton's Gloss on the *Historia Scholastica* (1193), for example, contains frequent references to a milieu which he knew intimately — the liturgy of Notre Dame, the architecture of Parisian houses, and reminiscences about Maurice de Sully, bishop of Paris. When the Latin word failed him, he often glossed in French.[183] Our sermons, we submit, offer comparable evidence.

If we turn to our chronology for a moment, we recall that Langton spent over thirty years of his life in Paris as student in arts and theology, and as master of theology. This continuity of experience afforded him time and opportunity to comment extensively on the Bible and to prepare an early draft of his theological questions. The sermons, steeped as they are in the knowledge of Scripture and awareness of human nature, fill out the picture of Langton's Paris period. Furthermore, similarities between Langton's sermons and other contemporary "French" preaching — in matters of audiences, transmission, language, etc. — strengthen the argument that most of the sermons we are here considering were part of his French experience. The presence of these sermons in collections with other masters of Paris in manuscripts of French provenance can lead us to no other conclusion.

The arguments based on external evidence can be supplemented by the importance attached to preaching in the schools and University of Paris, with which Langton was intimately associated. Although Paris did not receive formal recognition as a university until 1200, we may assume that many of the practices embodied in later statutes antedate formal recognition and reflected customary usage in the cathedral schools out of which the university developed. Bulaeus, in his history of the university, mentions the custom of preaching in the schools of Paris in the twelfth century:

> Sermones in scholis Parisiensibus... intelligimus morem iam tum fuisse illis temporibus habere sermones in scholis ad Magistros et Scholares... .[184]

Evidence adduced from Bernard, Peter of Blois, and Alain de Lille substantiates this observation. Bulaeus continues: "These sermons were

[183] Lacombe *et al.*, 21 and nn. 1-4.

[184] Bulaeus, *Historia universitatis Parisiensis* (6 vols.; Paris, 1665-73), II, 374.

held in the schools on all major feast days, in Advent, and on the day of the Nativity of our Lord, in Lent, also on feast days of the Patrons or Saints, chosen as protectors by the Nations, as though [they were] patrons and leaders of their studies, namely the divine Virgin, St. Nicolas, and St. Catherine."[185] Alain de Lille in those days preached two sermons, one on Easter to the masters and clerks of theology, and the other on St. Nicolas day. Nicolas was patron of the lower or beginning scholastics; Catherine, the patron of philosophers and orators.[186]

Bulaeus does not, however, comment on Langton's preaching. He is first mentioned in the history after his election as archbishop:

> ...elegerunt M. Stephanum de Langetona Cardinalem, quo non erat maior in Curia, imo nec ei par in moribus et scientia.[187]

The extent of Langton's learning won praise elsewhere: "He was learned and erudite in Sacred Scripture, and in Aristotelian philosophy, second to none... . As teacher of theology for many years, he was steeped in biblical studies... ."[188]

Turning from this history of the university to the cartulary of the University of Paris, we find that Langton's name appears as the distinguished alumnus called upon by Pope Honorius III on 2 April 1221 to come to Paris to participate in an inquiry into the controversy between the bishop of Paris and the masters and scholars of the university; and furthermore, to make recommendations concerning curriculum.[189]

Denifle-Chatelain have also printed one of the earliest extant calendars

[185] *Ibid.* Habebantur autem illi sermones in scholis, omnibus diebus maioribus, in Aduentu et Natiuitate Domini. In Quadragesima. Diebus quoque festis Patronorum seu Sanctorum, quos pro Patronis delegerant Nationes, quasi studiorum suorum auspices et duces; nempe D. Virginis, S. Nicolai, et S. Catharinae.

[186] *Ibid.* Leguntur inter opera M. Alani de Insulis, qui hisce temporibus Lutetiae magna nominis fama docebat, sermones duo, quorum unus est in die paschae ad Magistros Clericorum Theologiae: alter in die S. Nicolai... nam minorum seu incipientium Scholasticorum Nicolaus semper Patronus habitus est, ut Catharina Philosophorum et Rhetorum.

[187] Bulaeus, III, 37.

[188] *Ibid.*, 710: Stephanus Langton vel de Langetona Anglus... in Divinis scripturis studiosus et eruditus, atque in Philosophia Aristotelica nulli suo tempore secundus. ... Theologiam multis annis gloriose docuit, et primus Scripturam sacram medullitus... .

[189] H. Denifle & A. Chatelain, *Chartularium universitatis Parisiensis* (4 vols.; Paris, 1889-97), I, no. 41: 2 Aprilis 1221 Laterani (Reg. Vat. Honorii III an. 5, ep. 505, fol. 101[b]): Honorius III Stephano archiepiscopo Cantuariensi et Hervaeo Trecensi ac Guillelmo Lexoviensi episcopis mandat ut Parisios accedant et inquirant super querelis episcopi Parisiensis, quas ad apostolicam sedem contra magistros et scholares Parisienses detulit, statuantque quod statui studii et utilitati studentium viderint expedire. *Cf.* no. 45; see also nos. 48, 54 for additional correspondence between Langton and Honorius and Gregory IX.

used at the University of Paris. It is a fourteenth-century document of the Picard nation, but it may be taken to reflect practices in effect throughout the university. Arranged by months, the calendar lists the various feast-days and contains a memorandum whether classes would meet on that day, and in what faculty. For example, on 1 January, *Circumcisio Domini, non legitur in aliqua facultate.* On the 3 January, however, feast day of St. Genovefa: *non legitur in theologia, nec in decretis: tamen legitur in aliis.* Arts students apparently had to go to classes !

The calendar, albeit later than our period, has an interest and importance in showing the dates and feastdays traditionally marked in Paris. We have noticed this already in our remarks on the Paris missal. Here, too, are the saints' days that are noticeable in the Langton sermons:

28 May Germani episcopi et confessoris Parisiensis
4 July Translacio sancti Martini episcopi et confessoris
31 July Germani episcopi Altissiodorensis et confessoris gloriosi
11 Nov. Martini episcopi et confessoris
25 Nov. Katherine virginis et martiris.[190]

If we turn to examine the Langton sermons, many of these saints appear and re-appear. Notice Langton's sermon on the feastday of St. Catherine, who had particular associations with the schools of Paris:

> De sancta Katherina... ut instructissima in omni arte gentilium philosophorum, precipue vero Sacre Scripture litteris informata...[191]

Other Langton sermons were specifically dedicated to saints with distinctive French connections. On St. Genovefa, for example, there is a sermon on the theme *Consideravit agrum* (*Prov.* 31:16);[192] on St. Germanus Altisiodorensis, this comment:

> Sacerdotis magni appellatione significatur episcopus egregius. De isto scil. beato Germano Altisiodorensi cuius festum hodie representat ecclesia... .[193]

The sermon, *In natali S. Martini*, on the theme *Thesaurus desiderabilis et oleum* (*Prov.* 21:20) refers to St. Martin's special treasure:

[190] *Ibid.*, II, no. 1192. *Cf.* no. 1188: Statuta pro omnibus facultatibus (a. 1335): ... (1) Et primo notandum, quod in quinque festis Virginis Marie, duodecim apostolorum, quatuor evangelistarum, et quatuor doctorum, non legitur in aliqua facultate, et *semper debet fieri sermo.* (Emphasis mine). Both Charland and Haskins (*cit. supra*) emphasize that sermons addressed officially and regularly to university students are an invaluable source on the University of Paris and its life.

[191] 46[a], Ar, 62[rb].

[192] 14, Pa[16], 141[rb].

[193] 30[a], Tr[2], 272[rb]. See also 80[a], Ar, 60[va].

> Beatus Martinus... fuit pauper et modicus spiritu i.e. voluntate... . Habuit igitur beatus Martinus thesaurum bone voluntatis; habuit et thesaurum sancte locutionis... .[194]

Notice this reference to St. Germanus in a sermon on the feast day of St. Genovefa:

> Cum beatus Germanus in Britanniam proficiscens... veniret fere universus populus ei obviam occurit.[195]

In his examples dealing with the duties and responsibilities of an earthly king (*rex terrenus*), Langton frequently refers to the French king. (The phrases *rex Francie* and *rex Francorum* are used interchangeably).

> Quid faceremus ut rex Francie fateretur nos esse de cognatione sua ? Audi verbum Dei et eris cognatus summi Dei.[196]

When a king is moved to anger and subsequently conciliated by his mother, Langton makes him a French king:

> Si rex Francie in iram moveretur erga aliquem procerum suorum et mater regis ostenderet qualiter regi conciliari posset, ille libenter consilio utili acquiesceret... .[197]

It is the French king as well who entrusts his treasury for safekeeping;[198] and the French king who indicates the seriousness of a crime by calling together all his subjects to condemn the offenders.[199] In an example pointing up the great love of the Celestial King who sent forth His son to free the human race for whom He shed His blood, Langton's earthly king is the *rex Francie* whose great love for an imprisoned soldier would be demonstrated by sending his son to die in place of the prisoner.[200] A similar example appears in yet another sermon, where the king is called *rex Francorum*.[201]

The King of France is coupled with a remark about the citizens of

[194] 106^{b}, Bs^{1}, 76va. See also 31^{a-b}.

[195] 14, Pa^{16}, 141rb.

[196] 13^{b}, Be, 18ra.

[197] 19^{a}, Tr^{2}, 255rb.

[198] 23^{b}, Pa^{11}, 276rb: Si rex Francie thesaurum alicui commisisset custodiendum... .

[199] 33^{b}, Bs^{1}, 115rb: Nonne scelus magnum esse putaretur, si rex Francie omnes illos qui sub potestate sua constituti sunt in unum congregaret, ut maxime duo genera hominum coram eis condempnaret ?

[200] 68^{a}, PA^{1}, 49ra: Si rex Francie militem incarceratum videret... ut maiorem dilectionem illi ostenderet si permitteret filium suum pro milite sanguinem fundere... Incomparabiliter maior ostenditur misericordia patris qui filium suum misit ut liberaret genus humanum quo sanguinem suum fudit.

[201] 118^{b}, Bs^{1}, 109va: Si ex precepto regis Francorum in carcere, etc... .

Paris in the sermon on the theme *Hec est voluntas Dei* (*I Thess.* 4:3).[202] Other references to Paris are to be found in statements such as these:

> Vinum territorii et Parisiensis insipidum est... .[203]

or,

> Si rex in Monte Martyrum mille marcas proponi faceret in premium currentibus... .[204]

In only one instance, so far as I have noticed, has a reference included a name. The young lord Louis and Paris are so coupled in the following example:

> Si quis cum domino Lodovico in puerilitate esset, et florem pulchrum ostenderet, si flos Lodovico placeret, Parisius pro flore promitteret, vel aliquam rem magnam... .[205]

A final word on the most frequented sanctuaries during this period in Paris. Lecoy de la Marche, in his study of thirteenth-century French preaching, has indicated the abundance of manuscript evidence for the district or parish church or conventual where sermons were preached.[206] The following were selected for their connections with Langton's sermons: (See the lists of sermons in the Appendix).

Saint Germain-l'Auxerrois
Saint Martin-des-Champs
Sainte Geneviève
Sainte Catherine de la Coutoure
Saint Germain-des-Prés.

Conclusion

It becomes increasingly clear as we discuss problems of liturgy, the ecclesiastical calendar, and references to Paris that we must attempt to assign an approximate date to these texts. Let it be said at the outset, that the manuscripts do not themselves give us this information. They are, for the most part, thirteenth-century manuscripts and often contain,

202 42, PA^{1}, 74va: Si rex Francie... aures civium Parisiensium demulceret... .

203 53, Tr^{2}, 241rb.

204 100^{c}, Pa^{6}, 109va. *Cf.* Hauréau, *Notices et extraits*, II, 116 who also cites this passage which suggests that the sermon was pronounced in a church in Paris.

205 23^{b}, Pa^{11}, 276va. The identity of this Louis is unknown. It might be Louis VIII (son of Philip Augustus) who ruled France from 1223-26, but who would be referred to as "the young lord Louis" during his father's reign (1180-1223), during which time these sermons were written.

206 Lecoy de la Marche, 227, n. 1. See also A. Friedmann, *Paris, ses rues, ses paroisses du moyen âge à la révolution: Origine et évolution des circonscriptions paroissiales* (Paris, 1959).

as we have noticed elsewhere, sermons of other preachers, earlier and later than Langton. The bulk of Langton's sermons appear to fall within his Paris period, a conclusion that we can review briefly:

1) preponderance of French manuscripts;
2) appearance of Langton sermons with texts of other French preachers;
3) allusions to the king of France and Paris;
4) frequency of saints having distinctive Paris connections;
5) the importance assigned to preaching in the schools and the later University of Paris.

Langton came to Paris *ca.* 1170 as student and remained there studying teaching, writing, and also preaching, for over thirty years until his conse cration as archbishop of Canterbury in 1207. He was master of theology in 1180. The sermons in BN MS, lat. 14859, for example, call him *magister.* We suggest, therefore, that the majority of these sermons were composed sometime within the period *ca.* 1180-1207, that they were preached in various churches in Paris, to audiences clerical and lay, and that having already established a reputation as a preacher of note, these sermons came to be repeated elsewhere, singly or with others, under the later title, Stephen, archbishop of Canterbury.

This history of most of the Langton sermons composed prior to 1207 indicates the extent to which Langton was part of the medieval preaching tradition. The developments in medieval preaching toward an emphasis on the popular audience and the needs of the laity have an excellent spokesman in Stephen Langton. His role as a popular preacher was enhanced even more by the tools he used in the construction of his sermons and in the store of commonplaces and similitudes that formed its parts. Master Stephen as sermon maker warrants our attention.

CHAPTER IV

LANGTON THE SERMON MAKER

CONSTRUCTION OF THE SERMON

THE preacher took his place on the pulpit, and following the custom that originated in the primitive church, made the sign of the Cross. Before addressing the faithful in their own tongue, he pronounced several words in Latin, i.e. the theme, or the text to be explicated.[1] Sometimes composed of a single phrase, or even less, the theme was treated as an authority. Its origins lay in the patristic homilies in which the preacher commented on successive passages of the gospel reading for the day, interpreting these in their spiritual and moral senses.[2] As the sermon developed in the course of the middle ages, this kind of explication of the gospel gave way to the initial theme, i.e. a text selected from the evangel or elsewhere in Scripture. It was this type that flourished when Master Stephen was preaching. The Langton themes drew widely from the books of the Old and New Testament.[3] The conditions for their selection may well have been these criteria set forth in one of the later treatises on medieval preaching: "It [i.e. the theme] should suit the material about which the preacher

[1] Lecoy de la Marche, 289-90. In university sermons, a theme might be taken up in a subsequent sermon or in the *collation*. The Faculty of Theology required preachers of the university to take up in the evening the theme developed in the morning. Échard I, 97 (*ex libro rectoris univ.*), cited in *ibid.*, 291, n. 1. See Denifle-Chatelain, *Chart.* II, No. 1188 (a. 1335): Item, nota, quod quando unus prelatus vel unus magister in theologia facit sermonem de mane in Universitate in aliquo festo in aliqua domo mendicantium vel alibi: debet accipere illud thema in collatione, quod assumptum fuit per prelatum vel per magistrum, qui fecit sermonem eadem die. Notice, e.g. in the collections of Old English homilies, ed. R. Morris (see bibliography), the statement of the theme in Latin followed by the vernacular text. These sermons belong to the twelfth and thirteenth centuries. Similarly, in the collection ed. by A. O. Belfour, *Twelfth-century homilies in MS Bodley 343* (*Early English Text Soc.* orig. ser. 137, London, 1909) are Latin themes followed by the sermon in the vernacular.

[2] Charland, 112.

[3] Lecoy de la Marche (275) has emphasized the popularity of the Psalms as providing inspiration, especially for the preachers Jean d'Abbeville and Stephen Langton. For the sources of the Langton themes, arranged according to the Vulgate, see Appendix C.

principally wishes to speak... it should be taken from Scripture... it should be to the point... [and] it should be accurately quoted."[4]

Having announced his theme, the preacher invited his listeners to pray with him. The section that followed (sometimes called *protheme*, or more accurately *exordium*),[5] served as an introduction to this prayer, and frequently contained some excuse relating to the preacher's unworthiness. Notice, by way of example, this *exordium* in Langton's sermon for Advent on the theme *Preparare in occursum Dei tui* (*Amos* 4:12):

> Fratres mei, priusquam hoc vobis aperiamus verbum memoriale proponere vobis dignum duxi. Dicit enim Salomon: Pauper et creditor obviaverunt sibi, (*Prov.* 29:13) et Deus illuminator est utriusque. Qui verbum Domini aliis dicit quasi pecuniam non suam, sed Domini, aliis credit... sed quia dictum est vulgariter quod bonum est a divite pecuniam accipere, et non a pauperi, cum pauper sim, sicut et vos et gratia Dei egens, verba mea tanquam minutias Domini de mensa cadentes... suscipite...[6]

Most distinctive of the *exordium* is its conclusion, which consists of an invocation to prayer, repeated simultaneously by the preacher and the audience of the faithful. In the manuscripts, the prayer is indicated by its opening words, i.e. *Pater Noster*, or *Ave Maria.*[7]

By way of illustration, let us have a look at the Langton sermon on the theme *Dominus prope est* (*Phil.* 4:5), followed by this *exordium* and invocation to prayer:

> Sermo Domini clipeus ignitus est sperantibus in se. Viri fratres, iugis et continua pugna est inter hominem et diabolum. Sed memor sit homo verbi Dei ut et audiat et custodiat illud et quasi scuto contra inimicum se muniat. Ante congressum pugilium orant, oculos et manus levant, et sic scutum sumunt et se invicem impetunt. Cotidie Christiani contra diabolum pugnant. Magne

[4] From Thomas Waleys' treatise *De modo componendi sermones* (14th c.) in Charland, 328-403. See esp. c. 2: *De themate assumendo et auctoritatibus allegandis:* ... ut materiae congruat de qua praedicator principaliter loqui intendit... ut thema accipiatur ex Sacra Scriptura... ut... thema non sit multum prolixum... ut... sententia Scripturae non mutetur omnino in sententiam aliam.

[5] This *protheme* or *exordium* is the brief passage that intervenes between the initial statement of the theme and the *Pater Noster*. It is, however, unlike the more complex protheme that developed in thirteenth century preaching. Although Lecoy de la Marche uses both terms, *protheme* and *exordium*, with reference to Langton (291), we should better restrict ourselves to calling this an *exordium*, which more accurately describes the section as an introduction. A glance at the fully developed protheme indicates that it was, in effect, a kind of pre-sermon, with its own introduction relating to the scriptural text; reference to the good preacher; and its own division of the parts of the theme and subsequent confirmation by various authorities. See, e.g. the specimen of the University of Paris sermon on the theme *Justus de angustia liberatus est* in Charland, 181-87.

[6] 74[b], Pa[11], 209[va]. The passage was also cited by Lecoy de la Marche, 293, n. 4.

[7] *Ibid.*, 291, 293-94. Sometimes if the protheme is lacking, this may be ascribed to the reporter or copyist who generally transcribed only the essential parts of the discourse.

> ergo sic gentes oculos et manus in celum levent et verbo Dei quasi clipeo ignito diaboli conatus eludant. Oremus ergo ut ipse qui dignatus est nobis per uterum virginalem appropinquare, sit nobis scutum et munimentum contra insultus inimici. *Pater noster.*[8] (Emphasis mine.)

Once the initial prayer had been pronounced, the preacher restated the theme, a repetition possibly motivated by the arrival of latecomers.[9] Continuing therefore, in the example cited above, Langton reiterated his theme:

> ...Pater Noster. Pauli apostoli verba sunt, *Dominus prope est...*[10]

The typical dominical sermon had, in addition to theme and *exordium*, (with concluding invocation) several other distinctive features, namely, the development of the theme by use of examples and similitudes, a conclusion, and final formulae.[11] The simplicity of this organization is all the more striking if one compares these sermons of Langton to the fully developed sermon construction of the first half of the fourteenth century. Not only had the protheme become virtually a sermon within the sermon that followed, but the intricacies of the development of the theme itself illustrate the extent to which the sermon had become a subject of complex rules of composition which continued to be useful in the preaching of the early modern era.[12]

A. Statement of the theme
B. Protheme
 (1) Introduction;
 (2) Statement on the good preacher;
 (3) Division of the theme; confirmation by authorities.
C. Reintroduction and development of the theme
 (1) Introduction[13] by scriptural or patristic authority, profane author,

[8] 23ᵇ, CCC 459, 148ᵛᵃ.

[9] Charland, 136.

[10] 23ᵇ (*cit. supra*).

[11] On method and style of sermons, see Lecoy de la Marche, Part II, Ch. IV, 289-319. In this opening section of this chapter, I emphasize the matter of the construction of the sermon, particularly to underline its simplicity, in contrast with the later medieval sermon. The nature of the structure, i.e. examples, similitudes, sources and authorities will be considered in greater detail below.

[12] For the following outline, see Charland, 137-217. See also the article by E. Gilson, "Michel Ménot et la technique du sermon médiéval," *Revue d'histoire franciscaine*, II (1925), 301-60. Division of sermons into sub-sections was not limited to medieval preaching, but may also be found in printed English sermons of the seventeenth century. Baldwin, 249.

[13] The introduction followed either the narrative or argumentative mode; the latter differing from the former in its utilization of an argument from which one inferred a conclusion which was other than the theme itself. Charland, 141-42.

popular proverb, or the words of the preacher himself;

(2) Restatement of the theme at the end of the introduction comes not as a conclusion but as a confirmation, thus: *Ideo dicunt verba thematis...* .

(3) Division of the theme into parts facilitated the preacher's organization and presentation of the sermon and enabled his listeners to follow the content and procedure of the speaker with greater ease. It was also possible to subdivide these divisions.

In the medieval university sermon, the division of the theme was accompanied by a declaration and confirmation of its parts. This was done to justify the division made by the preacher and to show that it was well-grounded according to reason and Scripture. Declaration furnished a rational justification; confirmation, a scriptural justification to the division.[14] Similar procedures were followed by medieval theologians in their exegesis and commentary on Scripture. The intimate association between biblical studies and sermon making was personified in the master of theology who commented on the Bible, preached to his students, and like Langton, also preached to the people.[15]

The means by which sermons could be developed were rather elaborate by the late middle ages. Thomas Waleys, a Dominican master at Oxford who opposed John XXII on the matter of the Beatific Vision, indicated three: citation of authorities, arguments, and examples. Robert de Basevorn added *digressio*, i.e. the marginal development of the principal subject, and *correspondentia*, the comparison of various parts.[16] A late medieval tractate on preaching[17] lists these nine methods of expanding a sermon:

1) through concordance of authorities,
2) through discussion of words,
3) through explanation of the properties of things,
4) through a multiplication of senses,
5) through analogies and natural truths,

[14] Notice the following example of theme division and declaration and confirmation in the university sermon, *cit. supra*. *Theme* for sermon for Feast of the Apostle S. John: *Justus de angustia liberatus est* (*Prov.* 11:8): *Division*: In hiis verbis tria tanguntur: in Joanne sanctitas custodita: *justus*, in suo adversario malignitas infrunita: *de angustia*, in Deo propitio bonitas infinita: *liberatus est*. *Declaration of parts*: In *primo*, scilicet in sanctitate, lucet ejus conversatio exemplaris. *Confirmation of this first part by scriptural authority*: Unde bene cum sibi aequalibus describitur *Prov.* 4º: *Justorum semita quasi lux splendens procedit.* Charland, 174-75.

[15] On the connections between Langton's biblical studies and the sermons, see Chapter V.

[16] Charland, 195, 213-14.

[17] Quoted in H. Caplan, "The four senses of scriptural interpretation and the medieval theory of preaching," *Speculum*, IV (1929), 282.

6) through marking of an opposite,
7) through comparisons,
8) through interpretation of a name,
9) through multiplication of synonyms.

The emphasis we have given here to the complexity of subsequent sermon development is not without purpose. For if we return to our earlier period and the Langton sermon, we must be all the more impressed by these relatively unencumbered texts of the late twelfth and early thirteenth century. They are, in fact, the sermon in transition — no longer the simple patristic homily or monastic sermon of the early middle ages, they have taken on the characteristics of the epoch: the symbolical interpretations of proper names and numbers, the use of learned citations, and a predilection for allegory; but this has not been subjected to the intricate rules of composition which informed the late medieval sermon. The practical attitude that medievals had toward their preaching, aiming at instruction rather than emotional arousement, is apparent throughout. Having instructed his flock, the preacher closed with a new prayer, indicated in the manuscripts by the word *Rogabimus* or by the patristic formula (most typical in the Langton sermons): *Quod nobis prestare dignetur qui vivit et regnat Deus per omnia secula seculorum*,[18] which invoked divine blessing for all that had been described in the sermon.

Having examined the edifice of the sermon and the increasingly complex structure it acquired in the high and late middle ages, we must turn now to consider the nature of the structure, that is to say, the various devices the preacher Langton drew on to develop his themes. To this end, we shall treat first of the use of *exempla* and similitudes. The remaining chapters will deal with the kinds of sources indicated by the sermons (with special emphasis on the relationship between scriptural studies and preaching), and the prominent themes treated by Langton in his preaching.

The Exemplum

The study of the *exemplum* has attracted the attention of many scholars since the middle of the nineteenth century.[19] The classic study of the *exemplum* by Thomas Welter traces the origin and development of the

18 This traditional closing from the Fathers was always given in Latin. Sometimes a prayer might be included for the king, bishops, or the sick. These have special interest for allusions to contemporary persons or events. Lecoy de la Marche, 305. (I have not noticed any such additional closing in the Langton sermons).

19 For bibliography, see J. Th. Welter, *L'Exemplum dans la littérature religieuse et didactique du moyen âge* (Paris, 1927), 3.

genre through the high middle ages to its decline in the fifteenth century. The history of the *exemplum*, one might say, parallels the history of the medieval sermon; or, more accurately, is an intimate part of that history, since the *exemplum* furnished the preacher with a plentiful raw material for his text.

The term itself was adopted by theologians from classical works on rhetoric. Quintilian wrote a full chapter on *exempla*.[20] The classical world had in turn inherited the *genre* from ancient oriental peoples whose parables, tales, legends, and fables were the stuff of which *exempla* were made. The continuity of the tradition was strengthened all the more in the Christian world by Jesus' preaching and use of examples and parables.[21]

The word *exemplum* has a variety of application. In its specialized meaning, it may refer to a particular type of anecdote; or, it may also have general reference to any kind of brief narrative used by preachers to illustrate or confirm the teaching of their sermons[22]. Welter has elaborated on the essential elements of the *exemplum* by indicating that it must be narrative or descriptive; it must give moral or religious instruction; and that this must apply to man.[23] Essentially, however, the *exemplum* was a part of the teaching function of the sermon, rendering it all the more effective by including those concrete illustrations by which moral and theological truths were conveyed to the faithful.

The importance of the *exemplum* in its various forms was evident to the Church fathers. Ambrose (d. 397) was the first in the western Church to recommend the use of the *exemplum* in preaching, and, in fact, to make use of it himself.[24] "*Exempla*," he wrote in his comment on *I Corinthians*, "are more persuasive than words alone."[25] Augustine (d. 413) also drew on

[20] See M. D. Howie, *Studies in the use of exempla* (London, 1923), 5.

[21] Welter, 10. J. A. Mosher in *The exemplum in the early religious and didactic literature of England* (N.Y., 1911), 9 has emphasized the importance of these eastern origins. Oriental collections of apologues began to come into Europe from the beginning of the twelfth century. The earliest known western collection of oriental apologues was the *Disciplina clericalis* by Petrus Alphonsus. See the recent *Studies in Biblical and Jewish Folklore* (edd. R. Patai *et al.*, Indiana Univ. Pr., 1960), 29 ff. on some selected *exempla* from Jewish sources.

[22] *Cf.* Welter, 1. Howie, 5. Some authors would apply *similitudo* to the general type of example, and reserve *exemplum* for the illustrative story. See F. C. Tubach, "Exempla in the decline," *Traditio*, XVIII (1962), 408.

[23] Welter, 3. For the various definitions of *exempla* in the literature, see the bibliographical note 1, pp. 1-2.

[24] Welter, 12-13. Howie (6) would accord this honor to Gregory the Great. (For the following references on the history of the *exemplum*, see Welter 13-14).

[25] Migne, *PL*, 17; 236, 254 (*Com. in epist. ad Cor. I*): Exempla subjicit, ut facilius suadeat, quia cui verba satis non faciunt, solent exempla suadere... quoniam exempla facilius suadent quam verba, exemplis commendat per quae facilius assequantur.

exempla in his sermons. His sources included the historical books of the Bible, the lives and miracles of martyrs, the secular literature of classical antiquity, and his own personal experience.[26] Hagiographic *exempla* drawn from the *Acta Martyrum* were especially recommended by Pope Leo the Great (d. 462).[27] The lives and deeds of martyrs were not only in themselves examples of good works, but also were examples to others to do good works. It was, however, in the writings of Gregory the Great that the *exemplum* received its greatest impetus in the early middle ages. Called "Father of the Exemplum in Europe,"[28] Gregory's homilies and dialogues furnished ample opportunity for the use of *exempla* of all kinds, especially those of a pious and hagiographic nature and those based on personal experience. Gregory's *Dialogues* had still another function. They constituted one of the early *exempla* collections for use by other preachers.[29]

The history of the *exemplum*, like that of the sermon, in the era of the barbarian invasions reflects a decline in the intellectual life of the clergy. Eighth century homilaries were little more than simplified imitations of patristic homilies and contained collections of pious instructions for the faithful. For the most part, extracts from the Bible, the *Acta Sanctorum*, and sometimes *exempla* drawn from ecclesiastical history or even the personal experiences of the preacher predominated.[30] New sources, however, were incorporated in the preaching of the tenth and eleventh centuries. Odo of Cluny (d. 942), for example, drew on contemporary events; while Rather of Verona (d. 974) added to the biblical *exemplum*, the fable and parable.[31] *Exempla* were especially well suited to eleventh century polemicists, e.g. Wulfstan, archbishop of York (1002-23), Odilon of Cluny (d. 1049), and Peter Damien (d. 1072), whose emphases on biblical, historical, and hagiographical *exempla* respectively, show a continuity with the earlier patristic tradition.[32]

Until the twelfth century, as we have seen, the sermon had a very simple structure. The preacher developed his subject, drawing on biblical texts, patristic citations, comparisons and descriptions without any precise observance of rules governing good composition. The effort to give the sermon some organic form belongs to the high middle ages and possibly

[26] See the sermons in *PL*, 39, 1568-81, Nos. CCCLV & CCCVI, *De vita et moribus clericorum.*

[27] See *PL*, 54, 435: *In natali s. Laurentii martyris*: ...validiora tamen sunt exempla quam verba; et plus est opere docere quam voce.

[28] Howie, 6.

[29] Welter, 14-16.

[30] *Ibid.*, 16-19.

[31] *Ibid.*, 20.

[32] *Ibid.*, 21-22.

reflects the influence of teaching methods in the theological schools.[33] The sermon had long since outgrown the early medieval *homilia*, and had come to be governed by rules of composition that foreshadowed the later *artes praedicandi*. The *exemplum*, as a story not only from life but also from history, was especially recommended in the sermon handbooks as an effective preaching and teaching device. Alain de Lille, in his *Summa* on the art of preaching, specifically advocated the use of *exempla*[34] as did Honorius of Autun, whose *Speculum Ecclesiae*[35] (containing models of sermons for Sundays and feast days) underlined the importance of the *exemplum* for particular audiences.[36]

The way was prepared for the great blossoming of *exempla* in the thirteenth century, when the *genre* became more important than ever in the contemporary sermon. By the beginning of the century, masters of theology urged the use of *exempla* on their student clerks.[37] The participation of Paris masters in the revival of popular preaching (which we have seen exemplified by Langton and his contemporaries), was instrumental in the extended use of the *exempla*.[38] And once taken out of the schools, the *exemplum* was brought into even wider use by the mendicants who completely revolutionized the art of preaching and who were themselves the main compilers of *exempla* handbooks from the second half of the century on.[39] The spread of popular preaching meant that sermons had to appeal

[33] *Ibid.*, 34.

[34] *PL*, 210, 114: In fine vero, debet uti exemplis, ad probandum quod intendit, quia familiaris est doctrina exemplaris (verbi gratia leguntur exempla virorum forcium ut ad imitacionem provocentur animi infirmorum). (Quoted in Welter, 66-67). Guibert de Nogent, also the author of a sermon handbook, *cit. supra*, had this comment on the *exemplum*: Placere etiam nonnullis comperimus simplices historias, et veterum gesta sermoni inducere, et his omnibus quasi ex diversis picturam coloribus adornare. *PL*, 156, 25. (Quoted *ibid.*, 35).

[35] *PL*, 172, 813-1104. (Cited in Howie, 6).

[36] Howie (9) has called attention to Honorius' use of the *exemplum* for audiences of merchants or husbandmen. Welter (41) singled out this preacher and his use of different types of *exempla* as a precursor of the great popular preachers of the thirteenth century.

[37] Mosher, 15. Miss Smalley has suggested (*Study of the Bible in the Middle Ages*, 256) that Peter the Chanter was the first master to introduce *exempla* systematically into his lectures on Scripture. The *exemplum*, in this period, came to include new sources (e.g. Peter Comestor's *Historia Scholastica*, *PL*, 198, 1054-1722). Its use extended beyond the sermon to treatises of instruction and chronicles, where *exempla* from a variety of sources appear: e.g. the *Speculum historiale* of Vincent of Beauvais; the *Chronica majora* and *Historia Anglorum* by Matthew Paris; the *Policraticus* by John of Salisbury. (For other examples and references, see Welter, 151-53, 189).

[38] Smalley, *Study of the Bible in the Middle Ages*, 256-57.

[39] See Mosher, 84; Welter, 69, 211. See, e.g. Etienne de Bourbon (d. 1260) *Tractatus de diversis materiis praedicabilibus* (in *Anecdotes historiques*, ed. Lecoy de la Marche, *Soc. de l'hist. de France*, Paris, 1877); the *Liber de Abundantia exemplorum* of Humbert de Romans (for MSS, see Welter, 222 ff). For other late 13th and 14th century collections, *ibid.*, 228 ff.

to the masses of the people. The *exemplum* in all its varieties was ideally suited to the popular audiences of the high middle ages. Hence the widespread use of *exempla* and *exempla* collections which, like the *artes praedicandi*, multiplied in the course of the thirteenth century and reached their greatest diffusion in the fourteenth.[40]

The period from *ca.* 1190 to 1225 has been called the golden age of the *exemplum* in western Europe. Among its prominent exponents was Odo of Cheriton (1160-1247), an Englishman who studied in the theological schools of Paris and who drew on the Latin classics and patristic writings for *exempla* in his sermons, *de tempore et de sanctis*.[41] The preacher Jacques de Vitry (d. 1240) added to the types of *exempla* heretofore cited, those based on personal experiences which in turn were models for other preachers.[42] To the earlier sources, Caesar of Heisterbach added his *Dialogus Miraculorum*.[43] To Odo of Cheriton, Jacques de Vitry, and Caesar of Heisterbach as practitioners of the art of the *exemplum* we should add Master Stephen Langton:

> [They were]... all products of the same schools of Paris, [and] may serve as representatives of the new techniques. The popularity of *exempla* at this period is but one sign of the great wave of quickening which marks the opening years of the 13th century as a climacteric period of human progress. In preaching, as in painting and poetry, architecture and legislation, these years are filled with a striving to break through the horizontals of tradition, the Cathedral of Chartres being as powerful a protest against feudalism as the contemporaneus Magna Charta.[44]

Stephen Langton drew, for his biblical commentaries, on *exempla* that appear frequently in thirteenth century collections.[45] The special quality of sharpness and humor which Miss Smalley has emphasized in her

[40] Mosher, 13. Later example books were usually either collections containing unclassified *exempla*, or those arranged under alphabetical topics. On these, see Mosher, 7; Welter, 228 ff. On the example books in use in England in the late thirteenth century, see Mosher, 75 ff. Not everyone was so enthusiastic about *exempla*. Dante in *Paradiso* (Canto XXIX, ll. 99ff) expresses resentment at the excessive use of tales and fables in the sermons of his day. Both Wycliff and Erasmus opposed story-telling in the pulpit. (Cited in Mosher, 16-17).

[41] See Welter, 124-25; Mosher, 68. Odo studied in Paris 1214-21, but might possibly have been at Paris earlier and have known Langton. B. Smalley, "Exempla in the commentaries of Stephen Langton," *Bull. John Ryl. Lib.*, XVII (1933), 122, n. 2. See also Russell, *Dictionary of writers*, etc., 92-94 and A. M. Friend, "Master Odo of Cheriton," *Speculum*, XXIII (1948), 641-58.

[42] Welter, 118, 122-23. Jacques de Vitry studied in Paris, *ca.* 1187. On his preaching, see Funk, *op. cit.*, 176-84, and on his *exempla*, G. Frenken, *Die Exempla des Jacob von Vitry* (Munich, 1914).

[43] Ed. J. Strange (2 vols.; Cologne, 1851).

[44] Howie, 10.

[45] Smalley, "Exempla in the commentaries of SL," *op. cit.*, 122-23.

description of the *exempla* in the commentaries applies, as well, to the *exempla* in the sermons.

For the purposes of this study, we shall take the *exemplum* in its widest sense as any kind of brief narrative used to illustrate or confirm the preacher's message. No attempt has been made to prepare an exhaustive list of Langton's *exempla* in the sermons, nor to limit them to a particular type. Our aim here is to explore the various devices used by Langton the sermon maker, and to offer by way of illustration certain selected examples and their sources. Welter's outline of *exempla* sources is especially useful:

Class I: Literary sources:
- A. *Sacred* — Bible, apocrypha, patristic writings, ecclesiastical writers, hagiography, devotional tracts.
- B. *Profane* — literary, historical, poetic and philosophic works of classical antiquity and the middle ages; chronicles, legends, fables, animal tales, geographical treatises, treatises on natural history, fabliaux.

Class II: Contemporary events of the author; personal memories; contemporary customs and traditions.[46]

Using this outline as a guide, we shall find that Langton's *exempla* in the sermons generally follow these traditional classifications. If we begin with the second category, i.e. those *exempla* that relate to customary practices familiar to the preacher's audience, we notice that this type of *exemplum* is frequently indicated in the manuscripts, either in the text itself or by a gloss. In this passage, Langton used the term in context:

> Cum dominus pius et misericors sit, quomodo vult nos laborare? *Respondeo per exemplum* [emphasis mine]. Cum miles probatus militem novum habet filium, ut eius strenuitatem probet, in locum pugne eum inducit, et ibi ad tempus relinquit, lassatum vero educit et refrigerari permittit, postea si bene pugnat, de illius probitate gaudet et iactat.[47]

This kind of *exemplum* illustrates the use of the device in its most familiar form, that is to say, that the preacher, in his effort to hammer home a particular theological or moral message, offers as an example a concrete situation, in this case, drawn from military practice. A test of strength and endurance was understandable to the preacher's listeners. Notice, however, that this kind of *exemplum* lacks specific and identifying details. Neither the knight nor his son was identified or located in time or place.

A similar ambiguity attaches to this example:

> Sed nos magis ac magis debemus clamare sicut cecus, et sicut potestis videre *per hoc exemplum* [emphasis mine]. Si quis vellet aliquod ferculum facere regi, horam captaret quando rex pauca fercula haberet.[48]

[46] Welter, 83-84. For a list of the sources of *exempla* (patristic and ecclesiastical writings, 85-88; profane literary sources, 95-98).

[47] 38^{c}, Le^{2}, 68rb.

[48] 82^{a}, Le^{2}, 53va.

Exempla in the sermons sometimes bear the tag, "vulgar" or "common," and may very likely reflect contemporary custom and tradition:

> Karissimi non sunt contempnendi pauperes. Ut *vulgari exemplo* [emphasis mine] redditur manifestum. Cum imperator aliquis multos habens milites eos vestibus ornat preciosis, se ipsum autem viliori panno induit, et vestis sue conformitatem alicui suorum impertitur, ille domino suo creditur esse familiarior. Karissimi, pauperes induit dominus sacco sue paupertatis, unde scire possumus quod eos amat quos sibi veste conformat.[49]

The *exemplum* was customarily introduced by any of the following words: *sic*, *igitur*, *ita*; or the preacher might use the general formula: *fertur* or *legitur*. If he has himself witnessed the deeds he is reporting, he may prefix his account by: *sicut ego vidi; ut ego vidi; credo me audivisse;* or *credo me vidisse*.[50] Jacques de Vitry, a notable thirteenth century preacher, introduced his *exempla* by the general formulae: *legimus*, *dicitur*, *unde*, *ut*, or (as we have noticed also in the case of Langton) by the word *exemplum*. Direct information was indicated by: *novi*, *audivi*, *vidi*, or *memini*[51]. Ordinary expressions used by Odo of Cheriton, another of Langton's contemporaries, included: *comparacio*, *similiter*, *hujusmodi*, *ita*, *unde*, and *sic*.[52]

Langton also introduced his *exempla* by many of these customary formulae. We have cited passages above wherein the word *exemplum* was used. Elsewhere, his examples are introduced in an apparently standard fashion, e.g. *Ut ait Origines*[53] or, *Unde Beda*[54] in *exempla* drawn from patristic and ecclesiastical sources. In apparent references to Aristotle: *Unde dicit philosophus gentilis*[55] and, ... *sicut dicit philosophus*[56] are to be found a few *exempla* drawn from profane literary sources.

Notice the expression, *sicut... ut audivi*, used to introduce this story about the oppressive William Rufus:

> Sicut quondam ut audivi pro certo dici de quodam rege Anglie Rufo pauperum et ecclesie oppressore manifeste ostendit. Somniavit enim quadam nocte ille rex, quod esset in ecclesia coram ymagine beate virginis tenentis intra brachia filium suum, et videbatur illi regi quod ipse usque ad scapulam sinistram comedisset filium virginis, et quod ille parvulus scil. virginis filius altera manu percuteret regem in maxilla, ita graviter ut eum cadere faceret ad

49 10, PA[1], 69[ra].
50 Welter, 80-81.
51 *Ibid.*, 121.
52 *Ibid.*, 126.
53 9, Pa[16], 143[ra].
54 40[b], Be, 37[vb].
55 2, Bs[1], 150[rb].
56 30[a], Tr[2], 273[ra].

terram. Quod et fecit, quia crastina die ignominiose ac turpiter mortuus est rex ille.[57]

Sacred literary sources predominate among Langton's *exempla* in the sermons. The most prominent among ecclesiastical writers was Gregory the Great:

> Unde beatus Gregorius de quodam divite Romano loquitur qui vagus per insulam transiit et invenit sanctum hermitam, qui diviti interroganti an sciret rumorem aliquem de Roma, ait quod viderat adductum Romanum tyrannum ad flammigerum os inferni, submersum ibi a Petro apostolo et quodam alio sancto qui in carcere tyranni eius fame perierat.[58]

Exempla drawn from Scripture are most frequent:

> Patet per exemplum memoriale quod in Sacra Scriptura reperitur. Mulier enim quedam oppressa ere alieno ad prophetam accessit, lacrimabiliter conquesta est quod creditor duos eius filios in servitutem redigere voluit, quia ipsa non habebat unde solveret quod mutuo sumpserat. Cui propheta inquit: Habes in domo tua aliquid, et illa: Habeo parum olei. Cui propheta: Vade et accipe vasa vacua mutuo a vicinis tuis, non pauca, et recludas te in domo tua et mitte in quolibet vase partem olei. Quod cum ipsa fecisset excrevit oleum et usque ad marginem vasa replevit. Quo vendito se illius precio a creditorum improba exactione liberavit et de residuo tam sibi quam filiis necessaria procuravit.[59]

Whatever its source, the aim of the *exemplum* was to offer in a palatable and understandable form dogmatic and moral teachings; to stimulate the zeal and piety of the faithful; and to captivate the attention of listeners until the end of the sermon.[60] The *exemplum* often appeared, therefore, near the close of the sermon,[61] intended perhaps to stimulate an audience weary of the lengthy harangue that preceded it. Langton sometimes indicated his intention to end the sermon:

> Fratres karissimi, quod posuit Dominus in ore meo vulgari claudatur exemplo...[62]

or,

> Verbum meum volo exemplo vulgari claudere, propter simpliciores. Cum mercator aliquis emit rem aliquam precio aliquo, nonne carior est ei res precio, alioquin non daret precium pro re.[63]

57 36^{b}, Bs^{1}, 144^{rb-va}.

58 73, Pa^{16}, 84vb. For other *exempla* from Gregory the Great, see 17^{a}, Pa^{11}, 261ra: Item narrat Gregorius, etc. and 43, Le^{2}, 103ra: Gregorius in eadem omelia, etc.

59 *Cf. IV Reg.* 4: 1-7. 42, PA^{1}, 75rb.

60 Welter, 82.

61 Howie, 14.

62 121, Tr^{2}, 272ra.

In other instances, the intention to conclude may not be expressed, but an *exemplum* was especially well suited to the preacher's closing remarks. Notice these in a Langton sermon on the Sunday before Pentecost:

> Item unum exemplum dico vobis. Si alicui datum esset castrum ad custodiendum, et in eo essent familie que proderent castrum, et dominus castri in recessu suo dixisset quod mitteret succursum cito, et hostis fortis sederet ante castrum, certe custos castri esset in timore et multum respiceret versus illam partem unde expectaret succursum. Quilibet nostrum habet castrum custodiendum scil. seipsum, ubi sunt due familie, quarum alia vult prodere castrum, nolit altera scil. familia anime et familia carnis. Familia anime sunt bone cogitationes, familia carnis sunt prava desideria que militant adversus animam. Hostis qui insidiatur huic castro est diabolus. Dominus huius castri est Deus, qui licet recesserit ab hoc castro corporaliter, tamen diligit hoc castrum et mittet ei succursum desursum in die Pentecostes.[64]

The *exemplum* was a totality in itself and varied in length according to the importance of the subject. Sometimes it might be sketched in three or four lines, the details of its development being left to the initiative of the preacher.[65] Generally speaking, however, the normal *exemplum* varied between eight to nine lines, or extended as long as forty lines, where the author assumed the role of a storyteller and aimed more to interest his audience rather than to instruct and moralize.[66] Langton liked to tell the story of the martyrdom of St. Catherine who was buried on Mt. Sinai where the law was given. In one version of the sermon on the theme *Infirma mundi elegit Deus* (*I Cor.* 1:27), the account is given in ten lines; in a second version, the *exemplum* appears in fifty-seven lines.[67]

Manuscript evidence is helpful, therefore, in indicating the extent to which an *exemplum* was known. It might be reproduced in the manuscripts by a few words, or simply indicated by the title, the details being left to the resourcefulness of the narrator.[68] Not only might the length of a given

[63] 9, Pa[16], 145[ra].

[64] 64[a], Bs[1], 145[rb].

[65] Howie (15) has pointed out that "... the brevity of an exemplum may be taken as a mark of its antiquity."

[66] Welter, 80. In Jacques de Vitry's sermons the length of the *exemplum* apparently depended on the importance attached to the subject. Extracts from written sources were usually abridged. The number of *exempla* in his sermons varied from one to four per sermon. *Ibid.*, 121.

[67] *Cf.* this outline of Catherine's confrontation with the idolatrous Emperor Maxentius in 46[b], Le[2], 188[rb]: (... qualis fuit beata Katherina, que ut pateat legendam eius percurre... quomodo in facie primo Maxentio ydolatre restitit ...) to the fuller detail afforded in 46[c], Pa[9], 46[va]-47[ra]: (... accidit ut imperator vir nefandissimus persequitor Christianorum subditos suos omnes Alexandriam sub minatione mortis convocaret ad sacrificandum ydolis, quod audiens beata virgo utpote instructissima in omni arte gentilium philosophorum, precipue vero sacre scripture litteris informata, aggressa est tirannum sevissimum cum aliis sacrificia ydolis celebrantem... .)

[68] Lecoy de la Marche, 299.

exemplum vary in the manuscript copies; so too could details be altered, by omission or addition. There is, for example, in the *Dialogues* of Gregory the Great the well-known story about the priest Constantius, nephew of the bishop Boniface. According to Gregory's account, the nephew had sold his horse and deposited twelve gold *solidi* in a money chest for safe keeping. On one occasion while the nephew was away on business, several poor people came to the house begging for alms. The uncle Boniface, who apparently had not the heart to turn anyone away empty-handed, remembered the coins in the box and accordingly broke open the chest and gave away the money. Nephew Constantius was furiously angry and raised a commotion that brought the entire household to the scene. All attempts by Boniface to calm him were in vain, and the nephew demanded the return of the money. Whereupon, the uncle Boniface took refuge in the Church of the Blessed Virgin Mary, and with arms extended, entreated her to give him the wherewithal to appease his nephew's anger. The folds of his garment were stretched out over his extended arms, and when he looked down at them, he saw, to his astonishment, twelve gold *solidi*. Boniface left the church, went to his nephew, and threw the gold pieces into the lap of the infuriated priest. "Here," he said, "you have the money you demand. But mark my word. Because of your avarice you shall not succeed me as bishop of this church." The prophecy apparently was correct. The priest had, undoubtedly, been putting aside money to obtain the episcopal see. But the words of the God-fearing Boniface prevailed. Constantius never became bishop, but ended his life as a priest.[69]

This *exemplum* was admirably suited to Langton's lesson on the importance of alms-giving. Yet it is told at varying lengths and with some variation in detail, in separate versions of the same sermon. The briefest account, five lines, goes like this:

> Ut refert Gregorius, quod sanctus quidam erat ita largus, Bonifacius nomine, quod omnia que habebat pauperibus erogabat, et cum non haberet quod amplius daret, accepit xii aureos et dedit nepoti suo et dixit: Per avariciam tuam episcopatum istum quem habiturus esses post me amisisti.[70]

The story is here highly abbreviated. To one who was not familiar with the original *exemplum*, the reference would have been almost incomprehensible. Comparisons with other variants show how this deterioration of the story occurs.

[69] *Saint Gregory the Great: Dialogues* (tr. O. J. Zimmerman; NY.: Fathers of the Church, 1959), 38-39.

[70] 83^{a}, Pa^{11}, 280vb.

A somewhat longer version of the *exemplum*, this in twelve lines, appears in another manuscript copy, and begins:

> Legitur enim de quodam qui effuderat omnia que habere poterat in pauperes et erat in domo cuiusdam nepotis sui....[71]

We do not know the source of the *exemplum* (i.e. Gregory) nor is Boniface identified by name or by his office. The money (this version continues) was finally returned to the nephew by his uncle, but there is no mention of the failure of the nephew to become bishop.

In yet a third variation of the same story, in twenty-nine lines, most of the original details appear, save the source and the name of the bishop Boniface:

> Legitur de quodam episcopo qui dederat egenis....[72]

In his use of *exempla* and their sources, Langton was traditional. The manuscript copies of his sermons reflect practices to be found in the sermon texts of other contemporary preachers. Langton's *exempla* were drawn from sources sacred and profane,[73] from Scripture and the writings of the Fathers, from hagiography and classical antiquity, and from the store of medieval legends and tales. Langton drew his inspiration from an ancient *exempla* tradition that reached its greatest flowering in the high middle ages. His examples of a more general nature, reflecting contemporary customs and practices, are also typical of this kind of medieval preaching, whose principal aim was didactic. These *exempla*, whatever their origins, had a particular function: to illustrate and to concretize the more subtle and sophisticated dogmatic and theological teachings the preacher wanted to emphasize. These *exempla* and their use (abbreviated or given in full) are the most telling evidence that this was, in fact, popular preaching.

Similitudes

The *exemplum* was not alone among the devices at the disposal of the medieval preacher. The *similitudo* was another tool, not unlike some of the more general *exempla* noted earlier. Defined as a likening or comparison, a parable or allegory, the similitude had much in common with those *exempla* which lacked specific or historical detail. (Recall the *exemplum* about the knight and his son, without identification as to time and place.

[71] 83^{a}, Pa^{16}, 71vb.

[72] 83^{b}, Pa^{6}, 62va.

[73] For a discussion of Langton's sources, see Ch. V, *infra*.

This kind of generalization was common to some *exempla* and most similitudes).

This is not to say that similitudes did not become standardized and afterwards assembled into useful handbooks. One such collection, the *Similitudes* of Anselm, was assembled by his biographer Eadmer.[74] The following rubrics may give some idea of the nature of these similitudes: *Similitudo inter propriam voluntatem et fontem... . De similitudine inter Deum et quemlibet regem suos judicantem... . Similitudo inter Deum et ignem.... Similitudo inter monachum et potionem, et abbatem et medicum... . Similitudo inter monachum et arborem... . De similitudine cerae... . Similitudo militis* (*miles temporalis et miles spiritualis*).

Such a book of similitudes has, in fact, been attributed to Langton by Pits[7] and De Visch.[76] The reference appeared in the catalogue of Boston of Bury[77] and was repeated among the works attributed to Langton in Glorieux' *Répertoire*.[78] It was described as a book *De similitudinibus*, the incipit being: *Nec miles in bello, nec sacerdos.* Only Glorieux gave a manuscript reference: *Grimesthorpe, Bibl. earl of Ancaster.*

Lacombe and his co-authors of the *Studies on the Commentaries of Stephen Langton*[79] repeated the attribution of a *Similitudinarium* to Langton and called attention to the following item in the *Report of the Historical Manuscripts Commission*: MSS of the Earl of Ancaster:[80]

> Similitudines mag. W. Lincolniensis ecclesie cancellarii in sermonibus edite (46 1/4 pp.)
>
> Similitudinarium mag. Stephani Cantuariensis archiepiscopi (33 1/2 pp.)

The importance of this possible connection between Stephen Langton and William, chancellor of Lincoln, otherwise known as William de Montibus, has special relevance and significance to these studies in Langton's sermons, beyond the similitudes themselves. Some facts relating to the chronology of the two men suggest the possibility that they may have known each other in Paris. William came from Lincoln (Langton's neighborhood); and was in Paris *ca.* 1170-80 (when Langton was a student in the

[74] *Eadmeri Monachi Liber De Sancti Anselmi Similitudinibus* (Migne, *PL*, 159, 605-708). See also, R. W. Southern, ed., *Eadmeri monachi Cantuariensis Vita Sancti Anselmi archiepiscopi Cantuariensis* (*The Life of St. Anselm, Archbishop of Canterbury by Eadmer*, Nelson's Texts, 1963). On the *De Similitudinibus* and its sources, see Prof. Southern's *Saint Anselm and his biographer* (Cambridge, 1963), 221-26.

[75] Pits, *op. cit.*, 304.

[76] De Visch, *op. cit.*, 243.

[77] (Ed. Tanner), xxxviii.

[78] I, 255.

[79] Lacombe *et al.*, 9.

[80] (Dublin, 1907), 482.

schools). He later taught at Lincoln from 1188 until his death in 1213 (when Langton finally returned to England). The nickname, *de Monte*, or *de Montibus*, derives, so Gerald of Wales reports,[81] from William's teaching days on the Mont-Ste-Geneviève. There is no conclusive proof that the two men knew each other, but it does seem likely that the young Stephen Langton, coming from the neighborhood of Lincoln to Paris to study theology, would seek out the master William, whose origins and interests were the same.[82]

The two also shared an interest in preaching. William's influence on the *ars praedicandi* is evident in the kinds of handbooks he prepared.[83] His *Similitudinarius*, extant in a number of manuscripts, may be described as such a sermon book, an aid to preachers. This purpose was made clear in the preface:

> Ad declarandum in sermone quocumque propositum similitudines undecumque Deo donante collegimus, scientes quod propositiones in medium prolatas probant seu dilucidant auctoritates et rationes, exempla et similitudines. Ut autem facilius et citius aliquod simile spectans ad propositum reperire valeamus, tractatum presentem de similitudinibus secundum ordinem alphabeti disponere curavimus et huic operi similitudinarium nomen imponimus.[84]

The arrangement of the similitudes according to the order of the alphabet is not, however, consistent in the various manuscript copies. In the Ancaster manuscript[85] (our principal concern here, owing to the Langton attribution on f. 76 b), the arrangement is similar to that in Peterhouse MS 255[86] where the first group of similitudes (f. 84r-99v) is arranged alphabetically; but the second group (f. 100r-127r) is not. It has been suggested that such a general arrangement in the various manuscripts probably reflects the growth of the work, that is to say, that the

81 *Opera*, i, 93 (cited in Powicke, *SL*, 9).

82 On William de Montibus, see Powicke, *SL*, 9 and Lecoy de la Marche, 512. Powicke has indicated the extent to which the theological school at Lincoln became famous under this chancellor, William of Leicester, who first definitely appeared in the post, *ca.* 1191-92. William de Montibus has been the subject of an unpublished D. Phil. thesis at Oxford (1959): H. MacKinnon, S. J., "The life and works of William de Montibus." (My thanks to Dr. J. Baldwin of Johns Hopkins for originally calling my attention to this essay, and to Mr. Tom Waldman who examined the manuscript for me and reported of its contents). See also R. W. Hunt, "English learning in the late twelfth century," *Trans. Roy. Hist. Soc.*, 4th s., XIX (1936), 21-22 and G. Lacombe in *New Scholasticism*, V (1931), 141, 148-50.

83 See Appendix D for a note on William de Montibus and his writings.

84 Anc. MS, 53ra and in Peterhouse MS 255, 84r.

85 Lincoln Record Office: Ancaster MS 16/1, ff. 53r-92v.

86 Peterhouse, Cambridge MS 255. See description of the MS in M. R. James, *A descriptive catalogue of the manuscripts in the library of Peterhouse* (Cambridge, 1899), 314-21.

second grouping of similitude material represented additions that had not yet been incorporated in the alphabetical list.[87]

Where does Stephen Langton fit into this picture? The detail with which we have surveyed this William de Montibus-Langton association is not without purpose. We suggest, on the basis of the chronology sketched earlier, that the two knew each other in Paris in the closing years of the twelfth century. We are further faced with the fact that William de Montibus was the author of a *Similitudinarius*, extant in a number of manuscripts, including the *Ancaster MS*, where there is in addition, the attribution to Langton. Yet the same texts appear elsewhere *without this attribution to Langton*, as e.g. in Peterhouse MS 255. If we add to these observations the fact that William de Montibus drew freely on the works of others without any indication of authorship,[88] we come closer to understanding how Langton's name came to be associated with William de Montibus' book. Dr. Hunt has shown that extracts from Alexander Neckham's sermons were incorporated in the *Similitudinarius*, without indication of source.[89] We propose to demonstrate that William de Montibus also drew on quotations from Langton's sermons as freely; that these appeared in the Ancaster MS under Langton's name, but elsewhere, as in Peterhouse MS 255, they take on the anonymity of other similitudes. Apparently, however, the extracts from Langton's sermons were familiar as *Langton material* to some copyist. William de Montibus died in 1213, the year of Langton's return to England to take up the duties of his archbishopric. Although the inscription in the Ancaster MS calls Stephen, archbishop of Canterbury, the fact that the book itself was compiled anterior to 1213 lends additional support to our thesis that the sermons from which these similitudes were drawn belong to Langton's Paris period.[90] Comparisons between quotations in this similitude collection and sermons in the French manuscripts, where Langton is called *magister*, lead us to no other conclusion.

Notice, for example, the following extract that appears in the Ancaster

[87] I am indebted to Dr. R. W. Hunt, Keeper of the Western Manuscripts at the Bodleian, for permitting me the use of his notes on William de Montibus. Dr. Hunt has called attention, for example, to the arrangement in New Coll. MS 98, where part of the non-ABC material has been incorporated in the main ABC series.

[88] Gerald of Wales in fact accused him of plagiarism. In a dedicatory letter to the Exposition on the Gospels, William shows that he was conscious of the charge, but that it did not greatly disturb him. His critics, he said, should reflect that it is better to be strong with the strength of others, than to fail as a result of one's own weakness. See Bodl. MS S.C. 2089, f. 1^r. Si autem mei amici adhuc subsannaverint et dixerint me manum ad aliorum laborem misisse... sciant et illi multo melius esse quemlibet ex aliena virtute proficere quam ex propria imbecillitate deficere.

[89] E.g. in Oxford MS, New Coll. 98, ff. 129rb-130va are taken from sermons that appear in Bodl. MS Wood 13, f. 64^v, 120^r, 121^r. (My thanks to Dr. Hunt for these references).

[90] *Supra*, Chapter III.

MS (f. 81rb) and in Peterhouse MS 255 (f. 113r) under the rubric: *Christus puer*:

> Si quis cum Lodowico in puerilitate esset, et florem pulchrum illi ostenderet, si flos Lodowico placeret, Parisius pro flore promitteret, vel aliquam rem magnam. Ita puer natus est nobis scil. Christus magna promittit pro obolo qui datur sacerdoti in oblatione vel pauperi Christi cum bona intentione; pro tali parva re patriam celestem vobis promittit. Posset aliquis dicere. Ita Lodowicus in puerilitate pro parva re magna promittit, si venerit ad adultam etatem rem iterum auferet. Non ita est de domino. Dominus enim rem semel collatam numquam aufert ubi per ipsum steterit cui contulit, peccata enim semel dimissa numquam improperat ubi per illum steterit, testante beato Iacobo, qui dicit omnibus affluenter et non improperat. (*Iac.* 1:5).

The text is quoted, nearly *verbatim*, from the Langton sermon for Advent that appears in BN MS, lat. 14859[91] where the author has been identified as Master Stephen Langton.

The following is another illustration of a similitude, apparently drawn from Troyes MS 1100 (f. 276rb), and appearing under the rubric: *Prelatus ecclesie* in the *Similitudinarius*:

> Rex secularis fidelitatem militum et dilectionis constanciam comperiri machinatur, priusquam eis curam committat castrorum, ut probata fide possit sine dispendio custodiam munitionum eis committere. Ita dominus Petri stabilitatem probare curavit trina questione, de modo diligendi domini proposita, voluit enim ut dilectionem Dei quam habebat in corde confiteretur et ore, quo probato et veritate per responsum notificata, ait Salvator: Pasce oves meas. Sicque animas quasi castra custodiendas egregio militi tradidit.[92]

Similitudes were therefore freely exchanged and borrowed by various preachers. A book such as that assembled by William de Montibus was a handy reference, and his incorporation of similitudes from Langton's sermons attests further to the fame of the master's preaching. The usefulness of the *Similitudinarius* was enhanced by its alphabetical arrangement (e.g. *Amor*, *adventus Christi*, *apis*, *angelus*, etc.)[93] or, if one sought far enough in the unalphabetized section, one might find this simile:

> *De cera*: Cera munda est, liquescit ad ignem, lumen prestat. Sicut cera munda est, ita mundiciam carnis homo amplectatur sicut liquescit igni admota, ita cor hominis emolliri debet ad ignem verbi divini... .[94]

Notice Langton's use of similar material in his sermon on the theme *Sint lumbi vestri* (*Luc.* 12:35):

[91] F. 276va. For other MS references, see sermon no. 23, on the theme *Dominus prope est* (*Phil.* 4:5).

[92] Anc. MS, f. 81va-b and in Peterhouse MS 255, f. 113v. (See sermon no. 8, for other MS references).

[93] Peterhouse MS 255, f. 84r.

[94] *Ibid.*, f. 127r; Anc. MS, f. 78rb.

> Cera est cor hominis... . Cera pura est tractabilis et cum calescit ad ignem. liquescit...[95]

Not all of the similitudes in Langton's sermons can be traced to such accessible collections as we have noted. Yet there are certain distinguishing characteristics of the *genre* that enable us to identify them. The expression, *sicut... ita* (as in *Sicut cera est... ita cor hominis*) appears most frequently:

> *Sicut* mater infantem parvulum cum primo gressibus suis incipit inniti et linguam solvere in humane vocis susurrum, aspicit attente et gressu suo invitat eum ad ambulandum, et [voce sua] ad loquendum. *Ita* Dominus penitentem oculo pietatis intuetur quasi ambulare incipientem et loqui.[96] [Emphasis mine.]

Elsewhere, a similitude may be indicated in the manuscript by the gloss: *simile.* Thus,

> Sicut enim expugnatores castri alicuius ferventibus aquis exscaturizantur sic diabolus lacrima penitentis conficitur.[97]

The appearance of the word *quasi* also indicates a similitude (e.g. Vita viri iusti bonis insignata operibus est *quasi* navis honerata rosis...),[98] as does the expression, *sic... similiter* (... *sic* munita civitas fossis, muris, turribus... . *Similiter* nostra civitas in XL^{a} (i.e. Quadragesima) est premunita fossis, muris....).[99]

Similitudes and *exempla* were the tools, therefore, by which Langton the sermon maker fashioned the edifice of his preaching. In his *exempla*, he appears as a follower of tradition; in the similitudes, the presence of portions of his sermons in the handbook of William de Montibus shows him to be a maker of tradition. The content of these similitudes and *exempla* is not very exciting in itself. Somehow Gregory's credulousness and comparisons of wax to the human heart fail to move us. It is, however, this very simplistic quality of the preaching that affords an insight into the popular mentality of the age and the function of the preacher as teacher of his flock. The sculptures of the medieval cathedral may have been the picture book for congregations that were largely illiterate. *Exempla* and similitudes, for all their naïveté and simplicity, supplemented the teaching of Scripture to the people. Master Stephen's stories and examples were usually drawn from biblical sources. The sermon was, in effect, a commentary and exposition of Scripture. This intimate association between Langton's sermons and Scripture requires further exploration.

95 100^{c}, Pa^{6}, 109vb.

96 1^{a}, Tr^{2}, 262va.

97 *Ibid.*, 262vb.

98 30^{a}, Tr^{2}, 272rb.

99 50^{c}, Pa^{16}, 36va.

CHAPTER V

LANGTON'S SERMONS AND SCRIPTURE

LANGTON AS MASTER OF THEOLOGY

THE predominance of Scripture in sermon making requires some further comment on Langton as master of theology. His contributions to the history of biblical commentary and exegesis have special relevance to these studies in the sermons because of the close associations between the study of the Bible and preaching. The medieval sermon, as we have seen, drew its fundamental inspiration from Scripture. It has been called a theological commentary of an inspired theme.[1] Sermons drew widely on biblical texts which had particular relevance to the teaching of both clergy and layfolk. Like the commentaries, they were transmitted by *reportatio*. Techniques common to instruction in Scripture were carried over into the master's preaching.[2] A master of theology had, furthermore, to prove his capacity as a preacher before becoming a bachelor and receiving the license.[3] He had, as Peter the Chanter put it, a threefold task: reading, disputation, and preaching:

> The practice of Bible study consists in three things: reading (*lectione*), disputation, preaching.... Reading is, at it were, the foundation and basement for what follows, for through it the rest is achieved. Disputation is the wall in the building of study, for nothing is fully understood or faithfully preached, if it is not first chewed by the tooth of disputation. Preaching, which is supported by the former, is the roof, sheltering the faithful from the heat and wind of temptation. We should preach after, not before, the reading of Holy Scripture and the investigation of doubtful matters by disputation.[4]

[1] P. C. Spicq, *Esquisse d'une histoire de l'exégèse latine au moyen âge* (*Bibliothèque Thomiste* XXVI, 1944), 363.

[2] *Ibid.*, 349.

[3] See Denifle-Chatelain, *Chart.* II, no. 1188 (a. 1335): Statuta... de Ordine Legendi... Facultas theologiae... Item, nota, quod bachalarii qui legerunt Sententias, debent postea prosequi facta facultatis per quatuor annos antequam licentientur, *scilicet predicando*, argumentando, respondendo... no. 1189 (a. 1366): Statuta Facultatis Theologiae... Pro baccalariis Sententiarum et biblicis ordinariis. Statuimus quod nullus admittatur ad lecturam Biblie ordinarie aut etiam Sententiarum, nec ad juramenta, nisi prius fecerit in Universitate duas collationes, vel sermonem cum collatione juxta arbitrium illorum qui habebunt de sermonibus ordinare, et in propria persona, *ut in eloquentia et arte predicandi comprobetur*. (Emphases mine).

[4] *Verb. Abbrev.*, c. 1 (Migne, *PL*, 205, 25). Translated in Smalley, *Study of the Bible in the Middle Ages*, 208.

The tools of the exegete were *lectio* and *disputatio*, the latter probably taking place at the end of the *lectio* and dealing with problems that had arisen earlier. Ultimately, however, the two came to be separated entirely. By the middle of the thirteenth century in Paris, the demarcation between *disputatio* and *lectio* was a fact.[5] This separation between *disputatio* and *lectio* occurred in all fields of learning by the thirteenth century. In the history of biblical studies, as Miss Smalley has indicated, "this dwindling of *lectio* has its positive side," in that the literal meaning of the text took supremacy over the old allegories and moralities of the twelfth century.[6] By the thirteenth century, scriptural exegesis came to consist more and more of "the scientific study" of those authors who had commented on the text.[7]

In the preceding century, however, exegesis had not yet reached this "scientific" complexity, and consisted either of commenting on, or glossing the text consecutively, *or* expounding selected passages (instead of the whole of the text). William of Conches had distinguished between the commentator who expounds the sense of the passage, and the glossator who expounds both words and sense. Commentary as a "product of the cloister or the study" joined the gloss, product of the classroom, to furnish the basis of biblical exegesis in the twelfth century.[8] Instrumental in the formulation of this union were the Victorines, who as both *claustrales* and *scholares*, facilitated the transmission of the monastic *lectio divina* into the "academic lecture course."[9]

Two distinct theological tendencies are apparent among twelfth-century exegetes (many of whom we have noticed earlier as prominent preachers). The more theoretical stream was represented by Prévostin and Peter of Poitiers; the more practical, by Peter Comestor, Peter the Chanter, William de Montibus, Robert de Courçon, and Stephen Langton.[10]

[5] *Ibid.*, 210-11. The separation was apparent at Oxford in the second half of the thirteenth century.

[6] *Ibid.*, 284.

[7] *Ibid.*, 293.

[8] *Ibid.*, 120. While gloss was frequently synonymous with commentary in the twelfth century, the following terminology indicates a more specialized development of meaning: a *postilla* (which probably originated from the phrase, *Post illa verba*) was a comment written out as a continuous gloss and set between the various portions of the text; the *glosa* came to refer to marginal and interlinear glosses. *Ibid.*, 270.

[9] *Ibid.*, 196-99. Miss Smalley has emphasized the role of Langton in the continuity of the Victorine tradition, in that the three — Peter Comestor, Peter the Chanter, and Langton — drew their inspiration from St. Victor and have a special interest in the study of the Bible and moral questions of a practical nature. They, in their turn, made individual contributions to biblical studies. Langton glossed the biblical books in the order recommended by Hugh of St. Victor in the *Didascalicon*.

[10] Veal, *op. cit.*, 12.

Master Stephen, the greatest biblical scholar of the later twelfth century,[11] commented on the whole of the Bible. Biblical glosses were read as lectures in the Paris schools and then circulated. Langton's might be described as "medieval best sellers."[12] The method by which these glosses were transmitted was by *reportatio*. Sometimes a work may survive in several *reportationes*. This, however, was unusual, for generally there was an official *reportatio* which the master had corrected and approved. Langton's glosses, for example, seem to be exceptional in that they survived in two or three versions.[13]

Of all the Langton writings, these commentaries afford the closest connections with the sermons. We have already noted how the *exempla* suited commentaries and sermon alike. These brief narratives were useful in formal biblical exposition which was the commentary; and the more "informal" kind of teaching which was the sermon. Yet another aspect of these commentaries, or more exactly the manuscripts in which they are found, deserves our attention. Langton's commentaries contain a great amount of homiletic material which is singled out in many instances in the manuscripts by glosses, either in the margin or in the text itself, which suggest that a given passage of the commentary is suited to a specific sermon occasion. Even if we take into account Miss Smalley's warning that these glosses may have been added by a later copyist, and that these notes were not necessarily in the original *reportationes* of Langton's lectures,[14] the great amount of sermon material furnished by the commentaries is, nonetheless, significant. Is it stretching credibility too far to suggest that the young clerks who listened to Master Stephen's lectures on the Bible, and who would themselves be preaching to audiences, clerical and lay,

[11] Smalley, *Study of the Bible in the Middle Ages*, 181. In addition to his commentaries on Scripture, Langton is credited with the division of the Bible into its present chapter arrangement and order. Trevet and Knighton, later chroniclers, were responsible for this attribution. Accordingly, all the historical books were placed at the beginning, except *Maccabees* which has an intermediary place between the Old and New Testament. The doctrinal books, e.g., *Job* and *Ecclesiasticus* follow; then the prophets. Twelfth-century Bibles lacked standard chapter divisions, and the citation of Scripture by chapter was largely a thirteenth-century innovation. If the tradition ascribing the modern chapter division of the Bible to Langton is true, then it most probably belonged to the end of his teaching career in Paris and was an outcome of his experience in the schools. We know, for example, that the new division was known and used in France in copying one of his glosses (on the Minor Prophets in Troyes MS 1046) in 1203. The division was not, however, used in his lectures. *Ibid.*, 221-24.

[12] *Ibid.*, 182.

[13] *Ibid.*, 200-206.

[14] *Ibid.*, 254, n. 4. (I am most grateful to Miss Smalley for allowing me the use of her thesis on the Commentaries of Stephen Langton, written at Manchester in 1929).

would not draw freely on the master's suggestions of appropriate themes and passages for sermons. Recall how often a college teacher may, in the course of his lecture, point out the need and appropriateness of a given subject for further research and investigation. The student may note such a comment in his lecture notes. Perhaps such a student did likewise in his own notes of Langton's lectures, or in a report corrected and authorized by the master.

Whatever the source for these numerous marginal notes, it is not at all unlikely that the lecture-commentary itself became a source book for sermon making. The commentary itself was clearly too bulky for the purpose. Various methods of annotation, therefore, appear in the manuscripts:

1) Marginal notes or headings which indicate the suitability of certain passages as themes for particular sermons. This might suggest that the lecturer himself may have mentioned the particular occasion ;
2) Indexes by subject sometimes appear in the manuscripts to aid the preacher;
3) The most drastic method was to break up the commentary and then retranscribe it as subject matter for sermons arranged according to the liturgical year.[15]

The first of these methods appears most frequently in the manuscripts of Langton's commentaries. In Corpus Christi Coll., Cambridge MS 55, which contains Langton "super Vetus Testamentum,"[16] we noticed the following marginalia:

In the book of *Genesis*, chapter xlix (f. 31rb): *potest hic elici thema de passione... thema de resurrectione... thema de nativitate.* For *Exodus*, ix (f. 36rb): *Sermo de passione domini*; and chapter xviii, (f. 41va): *Thema de die in ramis palmarum.* The book of *Isaiah* appears to have had special relevance to clerical sermons. Thus, these headings: xxxii (f. 262rb): *sermo ad claustrales*; lx (f. 280ra): *Sermo in sinodo*; (f. 280va): *Thema ad episcopos*; lxii (f. 281va): *Sermo ad prelatos.*

In Brugge MS 28[17] are notes of Langton on the four books of Kings (ff. 35ra-95ra). These too contain glosses indicating themes for sermons, e.g., *I Reg.*, xx (f. 49ra): *Thema ad claustrales*; or in *II Reg.*, v (f. 57rb), where the rubric, *Thema ad prelatos* calls attention to Langton's comment in the text on the important requisites for a prelate: "... vitam, scienciam, et doctri-

[15] Smalley, *English friars*, etc., *op. cit.*, 34-36.

[16] See M. R. James, *A descriptive catalogue of the MSS in the library of Corpus Christi Coll. Cambridge* (2 vols.; Cambridge, 1912), I, 112.

[17] See A. de Poorter, *Catalogue des mss de la bibliothèque publique de la ville de Bruges* (Gembloux-Paris, 1934), 45-47.

nam." Sometimes a passage might be suited to more than one occasion for a sermon. Thus in *III Reg.*, xix (f. 80ra): *Thema de ascensione Domini vel de assumptione beate virginis.*

The commentaries in Peterhouse MS 112[18] are also full of glosses, suggesting the relevance of certain passages to sermons. The book of *Genesis*, chapters 6-9, giving the account of the Flood offers these examples: (f. 10rb) *Sermo in sinodo*, where the ark is compared to the Church:

> ...quia sicut archa tundebatur fluctibus maris et non submergebatur, ita ecclesia tunditur undique persecutione malorum nec submergitur.

The *archa* suggested the Church; the *archus* (rainbow) that appeared after the waters receded designated Sacred Scripture, a text suitable for the Feast of St. Martin: (f. 11rb)

> Ita ad hoc quod bene mittat verba Dei in corda audientium, oportet quod precepta moralia habeat in operis executione... per archum etiam intelligitur predicatio... per archum designatur sacra scriptura, iste archus positus est in nubibus celi, i.e. in doctrina apostolorum et prophetarum... .

In most cases in the manuscripts I have examined, these glosses appear to be attached to a passage from Scripture which is commented on in the text. These are not necessarily themes of sermons. Yet they can be. Notice this passage in *III Reg.*, viii (Peterhouse MS 112, f. 142rb):

> Si quis cognoverit plagam cordis sui. Sermo in dedicatione ecclesie... .

Langton himself preached on this theme. The occasion was the dedication of a church. The sermons are to be found in Troyes MS 1100 (f. 259ra) and Leipzig MS 443 (f. 128vb).[19]

Master Langton in his preaching once compared the preacher to a messenger who announces the mandates of the Lord to the people.[20] He drew for his sources for themes, examples, and similitudes from the fountain of Scripture. The sermons, furthermore, draw abundantly on biblical texts by way of direct quotation (within the texts themselves but not necessarily in the form of *exemplum* or *similitudo*). Here too Langton has drawn widely on the books of the Old and New Testament.[21] Most prominent are the prophetic books, major and minor. Ezekiel, Jeremiah, and Isaiah appear to be special favorites. Among the minor prophets, Joel, Osee, Zacharias, and Malachias are especially noteworthy.

Of all the books of Scripture, preachers most frequently paraphrased the

18 See James, *Cat. of Peterhouse MSS*, *op. cit.*, 129-30.

19 See sermon no. 93a-b.

20 72a, Tr2, 277vb: Omnis predicator nuncius est domini eius mandata nuntians populo... .

21 See Appendix F for the biblical sources of the Langton sermons.

Cantica Canticorum, which was interpreted by medievals to represent the mystical marriage of Christ with the Church.[22] Langton was also not unusual in this respect. His citations from *Canticles* are frequent, as are his references to other didactic books in the Old Testament, notably *Job*, *Psalms*, *Proverbs*, and *Ecclesiasticus*. The phrases *sicut ait Salomon*, or, *de hoc ait Salomon*, or, *Salomon dicit* recur so often, that they have been singled out as typical of Langton.[23]

Fewer, however, are textual references to books of the New Testament which, as we noted earlier, furnished many of the themes of the sermons. All the evangels are represented in the context of the sermons, and there are many references to the epistles of St. Paul, indicated generally by *Paulus dicit*... .[24] References to the *Gloss*[25] are even scarcer in number. We noted only a few examples.[26]

The writings of the Fathers, often themselves commentators on Scripture, furnished another important source for the preacher Langton. The Latin Fathers most frequently cited in twelfth-century sermons were Augustine, Benedict, the Venerable Bede, and Gregory.[27] Gregory[28] and Augustine[29] have special prominence in the Langton sermons. There are several references to Bede[30] and one, so far as I have noticed, to Origen.[31] In his Gloss on the Minor Prophets, Langton had drawn extensively on Jerome's commentary.[32] His quotations from this author in the sermons are frequent.[33]

[22] Bourgain, 239-40.

[23] Schneyer, "Eine Sermonesliste, etc.," *op. cit.*, 162. (See Appendix F for these citations). See also *Wegweiser*, *op. cit.*, 573.

[24] Also in Appendix F.

[25] References to the *Gloss* in Langton's commentaries are to the Ordinary or Marginal Gloss, sometimes the Interlinear. The Antwerp edition (1634) contains both. See B. Smalley, "Stephen Langton and the four senses of scripture," *Speculum*, VI (1931), 66, n. 2.

[26] Sermons No. 1, 50, 79, 118 in Class I.

[27] On the knowledge of the Greek Fathers in the West in this period, see A. Siegmund, *Die Überlieferung der griechischen christlichen Literatur in der lateinischen Kirche bis zum zwölften Jahrhundert* (München, 1949).

[28] *Greg.* Sermons no. 2, 3, 8, 9, 10, 14, 16, 17, 20, 26, 33, 34, 40, 43, 50, 51, 54, 56, 57, 58, 60, 61, 68, 72, 73, 75, 80, 82, 83, 87, 89, 91, 98, 100, 101, 109, 116, 117, 118, 120.

[29] *Aug.* Sermons no. 2, 10, 11, 16, 19, 30, 36, 40, 43, 54, 69, 74, 81, 82, 83, 91, 95, 96, 98, 101, 103, 108, 110, 111, 115, 118, 120, 122.

[30] *Bede* Sermons no. 40, 65, 93, 97, 103, 109, 119.

[31] *Origen* Sermon no. 9.

[32] Smalley, *Study of the Bible in the Middle Ages*, 227.

[33] *Jerome* Sermons no. 2, 9, 10, 14, 26, 59, 62, 70, 77, 98, 102, 109, 115, 120. Veal (*op. cit.*, 13) has noticed these authorities used by Langton in his writings in sacramental theology: Augustine, Ambrose, Gregory, Bede, Rabanus Maurus, Boethius, Aristotle's *Old Logic*.

Medieval commentators cited by Langton are scarcer. We noted a reference to the *Histories*,[34] i.e., the *Historia Scholastica* of Peter Comestor, the great summary of biblical history which formed the subject of lecture courses in the schools. Called by twelfth-century masters, the *Histories* (and its author, *Master of the Histories*), Peter Comestor's work became a classic for cleric and layman alike.[35] A single noted reference to Bernard[36] underscores the paucity of contemporary or near-contemporary sources in these sermons.

Theology, in medieval parlance, was queen of the sciences. Its handmaid, however, was philosophy which culminated the course in liberal arts that preceded the study of Scripture. Students at Paris, like Langton, first studied in the Arts faculty before proceeding to the more arduous course in theology. The study of philosophy was seen as preparation for the student to understand Sacred Scripture and to refute its objectors.[37] Clement and Origen had earlier stressed the value of profane learning for the study of the Bible.

In the matter of classical sources for our sermons, it was not generally customary in the preaching of this period to mix sacred and profane references.[38] The medieval sermon, in this respect, differed from the scriptural commentaries. Sermons contained fewer citations from profane authors and many more *exempla* and *moralitates*.[39] Some preachers, however, were exceptional in their use of classical sources. Peter Comestor, for example, cited many classical authors: e.g., Ovid, Horace, Vergil, Terence, Varro, Plato, Aristotle, Pliny the Elder, Lucan, Cicero, Statius, and Seneca[40] — the poets more frequently than prose writers.[41]

[34] In Sermon no. 66.

[35] *Hist. schol.* (Migne, *PL*, 198, 1054-1722). The book was translated into the vernacular and also rendered into verse. The nickname *Comestor* referred to one who had eaten and digested the Scriptures. See Smalley, *Study of the Bible in the Middle Ages*, 178-79.

[36] In Sermon no. 2. We might note, by way of comparison, numerous citations by Langton of Hugh of St. Victor and Andrew of St. Victor in his commentaries. *Ibid.*, 99, 112. The question of the extent of Peter the Chanter's influences on Langton has been raised elsewhere (see chap. I). Comparisons between the Chanter's *Verbum Abbreviatum* and Langton's *Questiones* suggest a similar sacramental theology and the possibility that Langton may well have been a disciple of the Chanter. Veal, 53-54.

[37] Smalley, *Study of the Bible in the Middle Ages*, 12.

[38] H. Caplan, "Classical rhetoric and medieval theory of preaching," *Classical Philology*, XXVIII (1933), 95; it was not until the Renaissance that preachers drew more extensively on classical authors. On the acquaintance of some fourteenth-century friars with the classics, see Smalley, *English friars*, etc., 45-65.

[39] Spicq, 363.

[40] Seneca was occasionally cited in twelfth-century biblical commentaries, but was quoted more frequently in the thirteenth century. Smalley, *Study of the Bible in the Middle Ages*, 325.

[41] Bourgain, 250-51. See also Lecoy de la Marche, 472-73.

Classical references in these Langton sermons are few indeed. We noticed two to Aristotle (i.e., *philosophus*);[42] one to Josephus;[43] one to Horace;[44] and one to Boethius[45] (whom some would call first of the scholastics !). A more significant classical influence on preaching lay in the form and development of medieval rhetoric which inherited from the classical tradition "the inventional use of the *topos* or commonplace, the artistic finding of the right argument communicable to the right audience in the right circumstances." While medievals were to develop their own scheme of sermon construction, the edifice showed the pervasive influence of principles of Aristotelian logic.[46] The study of Aristotle in the twelfth century was largly limited to his logical writings. Since the study of Arts traditionally preceded Theology, these masters of theology who were also preachers had studied something of Aristotle.

They might also have known some Hebrew since, by the turn of the thirteenth century, Hebrew studies were more common in the Latin West. It is not at all certain that Langton himself knew Hebrew,[47] and it seems more likely that his familiarity with Jewish sources can be traced to Andrew of St. Victor, whose direct acquaintance with the contemporary French rabbinic tradition sets him apart as an important commentator on Scripture.[48]

The few etymologies of Hebrew words that appear in the sermons would not necessarily call for a knowledge of the language. Langton refers to a *Liber de Hebraicis Nominibus*[49] which was probably the source for his explanation of Hebrew words:

> ... et ut legitur in Libro de Hebraicis Nominibus, cebolet interpretatur palee spica... .[50]

42 Sermons no. 2, 30.

43 No. 2.

44 No. 48. (See Appendix G).

45 No. 2.

46 Caplan, "Classical rhetoric, etc.," *cit. supra*, 86, 88. See also J. J. Murphy, "The Medieval Arts of Discourse: an introductory bibliography," *Speech Monographs*, XXIX (1962), 71-78.

47 Smalley, *Study of the Bible in the Middle Ages*, 235. Dr. Hunt mentions in his study on Alexander Neckham, *op. cit.*, that Neckham probably knew Hebrew (119-21).

48 That his consultations were oral is indicated in the texts (*dicunt, tradunt, asserit*). Andrew was also interested in modern Jewish practices which he compared with those in the Old Testament. Smalley, *Study of the Bible in the Middle Ages*, 149, 154.

49 Sermon no. 30. Etymologies of Latin, Greek, and Hebrew words were characteristic of scriptural commentaries and the medieval sermon. Spicq, 363. *S. Hieronymi Presbyteri Liber Interpretationis Hebraicorum Nominum*, ed. P. de Lagarde (*Corpus Christianorum, Ser. Lat.* LXXII, 1959), 59-161. (On the attribution of a similar book to Langton, see chap. II, *supra*, on sermons no longer extant).

50 30[a], Tr[2], 273[ra] (ear of corn = שבלת).

Jerusalem was, etymologically, "vision of peace":

> ...anima fidelis Ierusalem est, scil. visio pacis iuxta nominis interpretationem, quia veram pacem bene considerat et inquirit... .[51]

In this example, Peter's denial of Jesus to the kinsman of Malchus (both Malchus and the kinsman were servants of the High Priest), reminds Langton that the derivation of the Hebrew word *malchus* relates to kings who are kinsmen of pride:

> ...negat Petrus ad vocem cognati Malchi... Unde recte dicitur cognatus Malchi ad cuius vocem negat. [*Cf. Ioh.* 18: 10, 26] Malchus interpretatur rex, regibus autem et potentibus seculi nimis est cognatum et familiare vitium elationis... .[52]

Scriptural sources, therefore, were supreme in Langton's sermons. This emphasis and reliance on biblical authority was an outcome of Langton's experience as student and then master of theology in the schools at Paris. As a master, Stephen Langton emphasized the importance of preaching to his students, and was himself an example of the effective preacher. As a commentator on the Bible, Langton drew on and added to the edifice of biblical commentary and exegesis. The three aspects of the scholar Langton — commentator, teacher, and preacher — were interwoven, one sustaining and furnishing the material and inspiration for the others. In his role as biblical scholar and especially as preacher, Langton also made frequent use of the multiple senses of Scripture, a tradition that deserves special attention in these studies of the sermons.

Senses of Scripture and the Distinctio

Medieval preachers drew on a long tradition of expounding Scripture according to its multiple senses. The Church had inherited the idea of the various senses of Scripture from *haggadic*, Stoic, and Philonic ways of interpretation.[53] Allegory in early patristic writers, as before in Philo, derived from the allegorical interpretation of Greek classical poetry and mythology (e.g. Homer and Hesiod) as practised by Greek philosophers, especially the Stoics and later the Neoplatonists. The first Christian theologians used allegory to bring about a reconciliation of Christianity with the pagan philosophical tradition.[54] To the simple, or literal sense of the word (also called the historical) of Cassian, for example, were added three spiritual

[51] 44^{a}, Tr^{2}, 247va (to see = לראות; peace = שלום).

[52] 9, Pa^{16}, 144ra (king = מלך; royalty, reign or kingdom = מלכות).

[53] H. Hailperin, *Rashi and the Christian Scholars* (Univ. of Pittsburgh Pr., 1963), 255. See also H. De Lubac, *Exégèse médiévale. Les quatre sens de l'Écriture* (4 vols. Paris, 1959-64).

[54] Caplan, "The four senses of scriptural interpretation," *op. cit.*, 284-85.

senses. This fourfold exposition became the standard form in the medieval period.[55] Explanation of Scripture according to its moral, historical, or spiritual significance was a prominent feature in the sermons of Augustine, Jerome, and Gregory the Great.[56] The senses came to be defined as follows:

1) *sensus historicus* or *literalis*, i.e., the simple literal explanation of the words;
2) *sensus tropologicus*, intended for the instruction or correction of morals;
3) *sensus allegoricus*, i.e., exposition by a sense other than the literal, using exemplification by simile;
4) *sensus anagogicus*, used mystically or openly to raise the minds of listeners to the contemplation of heavenly things.[57]

Jewish tradition with its long history of allegorical interpretation in *haggadic* exegesis also enriched the medieval convention of the multiple senses of Scripture. Exegesis in Jewish schools followed two main lines of development before Rashi's time (1040-1105). These were the *halachic*, i.e., the exposition of the Old Testament to deduce a rule of law, or *Halacha*; and the *haggadic*, the midrashic or homiletic method which consisted of the exposition of moral doctrines. To these, Rashi added the literal or rational method, giving special attention to grammar and syntax.[58] The prominence given by Rashi to the literal meaning is reflected in the talmudic dictum which informed his exegesis: "A biblical passage can never [in the final analysis] lose its peshat meaning..."[59]

By the later middle ages, Jews had formulated a fourfold way of interpretation which "was undoubtedly an adoption of the fourfold scheme of the Christians."[60] These senses came to be defined in the *Zohar*, canon of Jewish cabala.[61]

peshat	פשט	(i.e., the simple or literal sense)
derash	דרש	(i.e., tropological or explanatory sense)
remez	רמז	(lit., *hint*, i.e., allegorical sense)
sod	סוד	(lit., *secret*, i.e., mystical sense; *cf.* anagogical sense)

Medieval treatises on preaching came to include comments on the im-

[55] Smalley, *Study of the Bible in the Middle Ages*, 28.

[56] Mosher, *op. cit.*, 10.

[57] Caplan, *cit. supra*, 283.

[58] Smalley, *Study of the Bible in the Middle Ages*, 150-51.

[59] Hailperin, *op. cit.*, 36-37. This author has called attention to the connections between the Victorines and the biblical commentaries of Rashi. *Ibid.*, 105-06, 111, 129. The influence on Langton of the Victorine tradition has already been noted.

[60] *Ibid.*, 258.

[61] Caplan, 285, 289.

portance of the use of the senses of Scripture.[62] Guibert de Nogent, for example, in his handbook on sermon making, urged preachers to use any or all of the four senses of scriptural interpretation.[63] Notice his interpretation of *Jerusalem*, in its multiple senses:

literal — the city of that name;
allegorical — represents Holy Church;
tropological — signifies the faithful soul of one who aspires to the vision of eternal peace;
anagogical — refers to the life of the dwellers in Heaven who see God revealed in Zion.[64]

Hugh of St. Cher, in the first part of the thirteenth century, summed up the manifold senses of Scripture in the following statement:

> ... historia docet quid factum, tropologia quid faciendum, allegoria quid intellegendum, anagoge quid appetendum.[65]

These first two senses are echoed in this comment by Langton in one of his sermons:

> Evangelium duo facit. Facta Christi recitat, et docet quid nobis sit faciendum.[66]

Langton generally followed the threefold division attributed to Hugh of St. Victor, i.e., the literal, allegorical, and moral senses (merging the anagogical sense with the latter two). His use of the terms: *allegorice*, *moraliter*, or *mystice* for either of these is characteristic.[67] The significance of Jesus' hands, perforated on the Cross, is given in the mystical sense in this sermon for Passion Sunday:

> Solet dici quod manus habet perforatas qui omnia dat et pauca retinet. Hoc modo Dominus manus *mistice* perforatas habuit, quia se ipsum pro nobis obtulit, qui uno verbo liberare potuit... .[68] (Emphasis mine.)

Elsewhere in a sermon for the Feast of Mary Magdalene, Sacred Scripture spiritually has the taste of honey:

> ... sapor eius ita *spiritualiter* exprimitur.[69]

[62] See especially in the preaching tracts cited by Caplan in his article, "Classical rhetoric' etc.," *op. cit.*

[63] *Liber quo ordine sermo fieri debeat* (Migne, *PL*, 156, 25-26). Cited by Caplan in "The four senses of scriptural interpretation," 282.

[64] *Ibid.*, 283.

[65] *Ibid.*, 287.

[66] 19^{b}, Bs^{1}, 142va.

[67] Smalley, "Stephen Langton and the four senses of scripture," *op. cit.*, 64.

[68] 81^{c}, Le^{2}, 70va.

[69] 57^{a}, Pa^{16}, 42va.

In his espousal of the spiritual sense,[70] Langton apparently departed from the emphasis on the historical or literal sense by Andrew of St. Victor.[71] Notice this distinction between the historical (or literal) sense and mystical (or spiritual) understanding in Langton's sermon on the theme *Deficiente vino ait mater Jesu* (*Ioh.* 2:3):

> In serie huius evangelii ostenditur manifesta dulcedo benignissime virginis et matris domini... . Evangelium istud egregia gesta salvatoris *historice* narrat, et iuxta dulcem historiam nobis *misticum* intellectum insinuat.[72]

Tropology, or the moral sense, largely affected practical conduct and politics; whereas allegory bore mainly on theological questions.[73] A study of Langton's tropology, therefore, would be useful to understanding his view of society and the world; while his allegory would illustrate and confirm established theological truths.[74] Langton combined these senses — moral and spiritual — in this passage on the colors of the rainbow:

> ... sed ex repercussione solis a nube aquosa provenit yris et notandum quia in arcu duo sunt colores, igneus et aquosus... . Aliter et *moraliter* color igneus significat dilectionem Dei, color aquaticus proximi compassionem. Si ergo predicto modo aliquis fuerit nubes aquosa, ex repercussione radii solis, i.e. ex illustratione gratie spiritus scil. efficietur arcus celi, i.e. movebitur compassione erga proximum et ferventem habebit dilectionem erga Deum. Item notandum quod in tempore pluvioso apparet yris sic et arcus iste apparet *spiritualis* in tempore doctrine...[75]

Senses of Scripture were tabulated and formulated in the *distinctio*, a scheme or table of meanings for each word, according to three or four senses (each meaning frequently illustrated by a text). Biblical scholars probably borrowed the device from canon lawyers and theologians. Richard de Mores of Lincoln, for example, who was in Paris in the 1180's as a student and lecturer in canon law wrote *Distinctiones* (1196-98) which contain references to individual canons in Gratian or to decretals.[76] The use of the *distinctio* in the theological writings of Thomas Aquinas is well known.[77] The earliest examples of these biblical distinctions appear to

[70] Also, Peter Comestor and Peter the Chanter. Smalley, *Study of the Bible in the Middle Ages*, 243.

[71] *Ibid.*, 120.

[72] 19[a], Tr[2], 254[vb].

[73] Smalley, "Stephen Langton and the four senses of scripture," 76.

[74] Smalley, *Study of the Bible in the Middle Ages*, 253. Note that Langton did not usually use allegorical arguments in the *Questiones*, which do discuss theological truths. *Ibid.*, 261.

[75] 79, Pa[16], 87ra.

[76] S. Kuttner and E. Rathbone, "Anglo-Norman Canonists of the Twelfth Century: An Introductory Study," *Traditio*, VII (1949-51), 279-358. On Richard de Mores, see 329-39.

[77] See the discussion in M.-D. Chenu, *Introduction à l'Étude de Saint Thomas d'Aquin*, *Publications de l'Institut d'Études Médiévales*, XI (Montreal, 1950), 146-50.

have been the work of Paris masters and belong to the last quarter of the twelfth century. These distinctions, or symbolical significations, became increasingly frequent in sermons to clergy and people throughout the middle ages.[78]

The *distinctio* form was well suited to Langton's temperament and preaching skill. His observations of all manner of objects and natural phenomena, and his ability to relate these to a particular didactic purpose found ample expression in the *distinctio.* Symbolism was not yet tyrannical, as it was to become in the later middle ages. For Langton, preaching in the late twelfth century, "the thought is still mistress of the language; symbolism is her tool which she chooses and sharpens."[79] This distinction on four characteristics of a cloud was admirably suited to Langton's lesson on mundane vanity:

> Per nebulam vanitatem intellige mundanam, quod per iiii^or [vias] circa nebulam possumus colligere. *Primum.* In nebula dum aliquid conspicitur maius quam sit videtur, sic dum pauperes et in diviciis tenues divites mundane vanitatis gloria circumscriptos intuentur, eos magnos estimant, quia non ad eos sed ad ipsorum divicias oculos inclinant, qui si in die vera viderentur nullius meriti haberentur. *Secundum* est circa nebulam considerare quod eius ingruente caligine viator timet iter ignotum... . Omnes autem viatores sumus, et volentes vel inviti ad mortem currimus. Viam autem nostram fumus mundane vanitatis involvit. *Tercium* in nebula quod dum cadit serenitatis future sit prenuncia, si vero ascenderit, vel turbinem prenunciat tempestatis vel pluviam premonstrat. Quid aliud est alicui nebulam descendere, quam fluxu et instabilitate diviciarum vel honorum que prius affluxerant destitui ? Hec destitutio future et perpetue serenitatis est indicativa. Per pluviam vero lacrima satisfaciens, et per tempestatem futuri comminatio intendatur iudicii... . *Quartum* in nebula est, quod licet multum occupasse videatur, tamen cum cecidit nullum sui

[78] Smalley, *Study of the Bible in the Middle Ages*, 247-48.

[79] *Ibid.*, 260. Among the list of writings no longer extant, but attributed to Langton, are two books which might suggest that Langton may have compiled handbooks for preachers, similar to those of William de Montibus. Among the books of the library of Christ Church, Canterbury, James lists no. 1221: *Distinctiones Stephani Archiepiscopi.* (*Ancient libraries of Canterbury and Dover, op. cit.*, 107). *Cf.* Lacombe *et al.* (10-11), who suggest that this may have been either a commentary on the Psalms or a dictionary on the fourfold sense of words. *Cf.* Glorieux, *Rép.*, I, 255. Another book, no. 1229 in James, 108, is anonymous: *Concordantie veteris et novi Testamenti*, but is grouped with the *Interpretationes Ebraicorum nominum* and *Sermones Steph. Archiepiscopi.* (See chap. II, *supra*). *Cf.* Lacombe *et al.*, 11, and Stegmüller, *Repertorium*, V, 232 on fragments by one Stephanus Anglicus: Allegoriae simul et tropologiae in locos utriusque testamenti selectiores et in ordinem digestae e monumentis unius et triginta auctorum. Since there were no real biblical concordances during this period, the problem of supporting every statement by authority was solved by giving students a table of references. Langton developed a system of making a list of texts which were suggested by the passage he was expounding, or which supported his interpretation of the original text. Such lists were sometimes titled *Concordantia.* Smalley, *Study of the Bible in the Middle Ages*, 241.

> vestigium reperitur. Quid expressius quam mundi huius magnates exprimit, qui dum honoribus gloriantur omnia inferiora occupant, omnium oculos et aures in se convertunt, et ecce cum mors eos discussit, periit memoria eorum cum sonitu, sed dominus in eternum permanet.[80]

In all these aspects — by *distinctio* and by senses of Scripture; by theme and by direct quotation; by similitude and by example — Langton's preaching, like medieval preaching in general, was essentially biblical. "C'est un mode d'exposition scripturaire," wrote Spicq.[81] The Bible was, after all, the main textbook of the middle ages not only for lettered clerks and theologians, but also for those who were unlettered and untaught who could learn its lessons from their preachers. The same masters who taught in the schools preached to the people. These preachers were, furthermore, observers of the society and life about them and mirrored these in their sermons. Their frame of reference was biblical, but the milieu that was reflected was undoubtedly medieval. Although the view might be distorted, or idealized, it is, nonetheless, a precious glimpse into the popular mentality, the *Volksgeist*, of an age. Langton's sermons afford us such an opportunity.

[80] 80^{b}, Le^{2}, 180^{rb-va}. *Cf.* the *distinctio* on the word *nebula* in a thirteenth-century sermon by John de la Rochelle on St. Anthony of Padua. See K. F. Lynch, "Three sermons on the Doctor Evangelicus by John de la Rochelle," *Franciscan Studies*, XXIII (1963), 219.

[81] Spicq, 351.

Chapter VI

LANGTON... VITE SPECULATOR ET SPECULUM

Introduction

VARIOUS aspects of Langton's sermons indicate that this was popular preaching. That the master's audiences were largely popular in their composition has been demonstrated by internal evidence in the sermons and by the kinds of *exempla* that reflected ordinary and familiar activities. A sermon could be most effective if the anecdotes, the moral illustrations, the concrete examples — in short, the conceptual language, mirrored the kind of life experience common to Langton's listeners. The stories told by a preacher might not be original. They were, in fact, rarely so. But they had to be understood, and their importance lies in their selection by a preacher for an audience that would find them meaningful and significant.

There is ample illustration of the way in which Langton's *exempla* were designed to meet the needs of popular audiences. By cloaking lofty moral teachings in the more mundane garb of the earthly *exemplum*, Langton's message could be all the more compelling. Just as there are several ways for an enemy king to besiege a castle, so does the devil lay siege to the soul of man.[1] God's love and solicitude for man and the interest in his welfare were rendered all the more understandable to the preacher's listeners, by comparing these to the mother who watches the first steps of her child;[2] or to the wife who weeps for her absent husband.[3]

Langton drew on other familiar images to teach his lessons: the one who sees good in carnal pleasure is like the child who sees his shadow, and thinking that it is solid tries to touch it. If he does, he finds himself holding

[1] 17[c], Bs[1], 113[ra]: Rex iste tribus modis impugnat castella, que adhuc invenit resistentia. Primo fossoribus pedem muri effodientibus... . Secundo modo impugnat bellico instrumento... et vi brachiorum impellitur ad murum. Tercio modo impugnat petreia, que cum valido ictu magnos et ponderosos emittit lapides.

[2] 1[a], Tr[2], 262[va]: Sicut mater infantem parvulum cum primo gressibus suis incipit inniti... aspicit attente et gressu suo invitat eum ad ambulandum... . Ita Dominus penitentem oculo pietatis intuetur... .

[3] 115[a], Pa[16], 136[vb]: Vir absens si per nuntium audierit de uxore quod contristetur de absentia viri, et quod defleat eum absentem, multum placet ei, quia hoc est certum argumentum magne et firme dilectionis, quam illa habet erga maritum suum.

mud and not his shadow ![4] How warmly we are received by the Divine Host is the teaching of the story of the pilgrim whose reception by an earthly host is dependent upon his condition: if he is rich, the host is most cooperative and is all graciousness; if he is poor, the host leaves him to fend for himself. We are like this poor man, since we possess very little.[5] Our need for visitation by the Holy Spirit is underscored by the comparison with the doctor who tends the sick who cannot himself come for aid.[6] The direction given by the Virgin through the storms and sea of this world is given emphasis by the example of the sailor who makes his way across uncharted waters by fixing his course and direction by the *stella maris*, the star of the sea.[7]

The use of commonplace examples to audiences of layfolk is indicative of still another aspect of Langton's preaching. This relates to his role among that circle of reformers in Paris whose participation in a growing movement to restore Christian teaching lends additional significance to the content of these sermons. During the second half of the twelfth century, several masters in Paris were active in a movement of evangelical preaching and teaching to the people. Robert de Courçon, Peter Comestor, Peter the Chanter, and Stephen Langton were among this group. The idea of the movement was the *vita apostolica*[8] which drew for its inspiration on the ideals of the remote Christian past and the ideology of more recent efforts to reform the Church and society. The apostolic life had, from the age of primitive Christianity, remained an ideal in the Church. Eleventh century Gregorian and monastic reformers gave it further impulse.[9] The *vita apostolica* became a rallying cry to those who would restore the Church and its clergy to an earlier purity.

It had its impact too on the society at large, in the effort to check the

[4] 115[b], Le[2], 89[rb]: Puer umbram suam videns, et solidum aliquid esse putans, attempnat illum tangere, sed non nisi lutum apprehendit. Sic puer est et fatuus, qui in voluptate carnis aliquid boni esse putat... .

[5] 107[a], Tr[2], 286[ra]: Cum quis peregrinus hospitatus est in aliqua villa, si dives est vultum bonum offert ei hospes suus... . Si vero pauper sit is qui hospitatus est, hospes ei nihil extra querit, sed ipsum omnia necessaria sibi querere oportet. 107[b], Pa[9], 79[vb]: Tales pauperes sumus quia pauca bona habemus... .

[6] 116[c], Pa[6], 98[rb]: Ut medicus ad infirmum veniat, cum accedere non possit infirmus ad medicum, visitatione [i.e. Sancti Spiritus] indigent pauperes, infirmi, captivi, vincti, incarcerati... .

[7] 110[b], Le[2], 170[vb]: ... et sciendum quod sicut navigantibus per mare necessarius est certe stelle cursus, ut per eum maris pericula possint evitari. Sic navigantibus in hoc mundo necessarius est certe stelle cursus, et que est ista stella ? Virgo sancta Maria. Nam idem sonat hoc nomen Maria quod maris stella.

[8] Chenu, *La théologie au douzième siècle*, *op. cit.*, 233, 260.

[9] See H. Grundmann, *Religiöse Bewegungen im Mittelalter*, *Historische Studien*, Hft. 267 (Lübeck, 1965), 13-69.

spread of heresy and to intensify the spiritual life of Christians. St. Bernard's role in the second quarter of the twelfth century in furnishing an inspiration and model of the spiritual life was decisive.[10] In many of his sermons (that were also translated into the vernacular), St. Bernard drew on episodes from the life of Christ. In an age when heresy was a danger and reform a necessity for the Church, the constant meditation on the mysteries in the life and death of Christ had a profound influence on the development of Christian life and the spread of medieval piety. One of the most touching manifestations of this phenomenon was the pilgrimage which appeared to be on the increase from the middle of the century. To the holy places in Rome and Italy, to Jerusalem in the Holy Land, and to the shrine of St. James of Compostella in Spain, pilgrims moved in ever growing numbers. In this intensification of Christian piety, popular preaching played a not inconsiderable part. Attacks on the vices and wealth of the clergy were themes in the sermons of Peter Waldo and Arnald of Brescia. The great popular preaching movements that were sweeping France and Italy in the latter half of the twelfth century also had their echoes in the schools. Masters who were preachers responded to the reproaches addressed to the clergy and answered the call for the reinvigoration of Christian teaching and lay piety. The *vita apostolica* movement included among its followers Jacques de Vitry who made its first acquaintance while he was a student in Paris. There he became familiar with the preacher Bishop Maurice de Sully, and came under the influence of the popular preacher Foulques de Neuilly (d. 1202), who had himself been a pupil of the Chanter. The vernacular sermon came to be recognized as an effective weapon fighting against the enemies of the Church, and winning friends and support for its policies. Popular preaching was, furthermore, a part of the effort to improve the religious life of the laity and to effect the spread of lay piety.[11] Given Langton's participation in this movement (which is clearly indicated by the evidence in his sermons), we must notice further how the content of these sermons shows him to have been a reformer of the laity. That is to say, that if we examine the prominent themes treated in these sermons, they indicate a desire to bring about a right order in the individual and in society.

The range of subjects treated in these sermons[12] lends support to this picture of Langton, popular preacher of reform. In his denunciations of

[10] A. Fliche & V. Martin, *Histoire de l'Église depuis les origines jusqu'à nos jours*, IX (Paris, 1944), Pt. I, ch. 6, 150ff, and Pt. II, ch. 4, 353ff which treat various aspects of Christian life in the period 1123-1198. See also in volume X (Paris, 1950), Bk. II, ch. 5 on the Christian life, (1198-1274).

[11] See the chapter, "The education of Jacques de Vitry in Belgium," in E. W. McDonnell, *The Beguines and Beghards in medieval Culture* (Rutgers Un. Pr., 1954), 20-39.

[12] See Appendix H: Index of prominent themes in the Langton sermons.

temporal wealth and avarice, he held up before his listeners the ideal Christian life which meant the renunciation of the things of this world. To the layfolk who heard his sermons, Langton taught the importance of alms-giving and of good works in the fierce and continuous struggle of all men against the devil. He impressed upon his audiences the perils of the sinful life and urged confession, prayer and penitence. The transitory nature of mundane glory and the pitfalls of this world, he compared with the eternal and beneficent qualities of the Holy Spirit and the beatitudes of the future life. The example of the just man who combats the evils of avarice, pride and lust is a frequent theme echoed in these sermons. Langton's preaching emphasized the role of the saints as intercessors with God the King, and continually repeated the lesson of the efficacy of the word of God, reaffirming the special responsibilities of the clergy in the instruction of layfolk. In all these themes, Langton appears as the reformer of the individual Christian, attempting by concrete illustration and example to point the way to a right order in Christian life.

This popular and reform quality in Langton's sermons is a notable characteristic which has not been sufficiently appreciated. As popular preaching, these sermons have a special importance as sources in social history, supplementing the scarce contemporary materials in this field. A preacher such as Langton was an observer of life and his milieu. He offers us in his sermons something of the spirit of medieval society. For all that preaching was full of exaggeration and hyperbole (as indeed it had to be, to point up the evils in man's life and the need to correct them), it represents the real state of spirit and manners.[13] Master Stephen held a mirror up to society and the various social classes that would be found in a medieval audience were reflected in that mirror. The kings and princes, serfs and burghers, clergy and layfolk who fill these sermon texts also filled the medieval world. Their vices might be condemned, but their virtues were also exalted as examples of the right order in society itself. We have selected Langton's observations on medieval social classes for special discussion. These are significant for two reasons: as a source of information about the contemporary social milieu, and as the *exempla* and moral teachings of the reformer preacher.

Vox Populi

Langton's message of reform and the restoration of Christian teaching to the laity applied to the traditional estates in medieval society, all of whom are mirrored in these sermons: nobles and princes, equally at home

[13] Bourgain, 271.

at court or on the battlefield; the clergy in the schools or in the cloister; and the large mass of people, the great "catch-all" that included burghers and serfs alike, in town or countryside. The theme of the right order in society runs throughout these observations on social groups and applies as well to the relationships between man and his neighbor, in business transactions, or in the manorial world of serfs and lords.

We have a glimpse into the rural world of the middle ages, where the major occupation was agriculture that would understandably be adversely affected in time of war and stress. A desire for peace is obvious: "Happy are the farmers in time of peace, when they can best till the soil and gather in the fruits they wish for."[14] This was the world of the serf, his lord, and perhaps a steward acting in the lord's behalf, or as Langton here suggests, his own: "The evil steward does not remember the kindness of his master. He is proud because he oppresses the poor. He despises the command of his master because he knows that he is absent and is a traitor because he makes himself rich from the money usurped from his lord."[15]

Not all were as evil as the *malus villicus* described above. Better examples for his listeners to emulate were the serfs of a lord who kept a careful reckoning and rendered an account of those things entrusted to them.[16] The *bonus servus* could be seen acting in other capacities to show his worth. The good serf gladly received his lord's friends so that he might be the more acceptable to his lord.[17] To such rustics, lords sometimes entrusted the rearing of their sons.[18]

Langton's teaching also touched on filial relationships and sometimes raised questions of property and inheritance. Master Stephen reminded his audience that a son owes his father love, fear and obedience.[19] A father, in his turn, loves his son, but must discipline him, feed him, and leave him an inheritance.[20] Notice how the problem of a lost inheritance figures in this illustration:

[14] 44[a], Tr[2], 247[vb]: Agricole magna leticia reficiuntur, cum proclamatur pacis edictum, quia tempore pacis terram bene possunt colere, et fructus optatos percipere.

[15] 25[b], Ar, 177[ra]: Malus villicus non recognoscit beneficium domini sui. Superbus est quia deprimit pauperes. Contempnit iussum domini sui cum non videt eum presentem. Proditor est quia facit se divitem de usurpata pecunia domini sui... .

[16] 98[d], Bs[1], 75[va]: Omnes autem reddituri sunt rationem de sibi commissis. Unde sicut servus domini terreni diligenter custodit scedulam sue computationis faciende, ita et servus Domini doctrinam sue computationis debet diligenter audire et sollicite custodire... .

[17] 25[b], Ar, 177[va]: Item bonus servus libenter recipit eos, quos scit esse amicos domini sui ut magis sit acceptus domino suo.

[18] 58[b], Le[2], 172[va]: Nobiles enim cum nascitur eis filius, tradunt eum alendam alicui de ruralibus suis... .

[19] 39[a], Tr[2], 267[vb]: Filius autem tria debet patri, amorem, timorem, et obsequium... .

[20] 119, Tr[2], 288[va]: Pater filium suum diligit, castigat, nutrit, hereditatem confert... .

> If someone lost his inheritance and did not dare to fight to recover it, nor had the money to hire a champion, and if someone offered to fight without reward, was victorious and wounded in the struggle, and was then taken into the hospitality of him in whose behalf he had fought, it would be base if he were thrown out of the house before his wounds were healed.[21]

A better example of the faithful friend could be found in one who lent his assistance in any affair to his partner who required it. False is he who fails in the case of need.[22]

There are four kinds of men, observed Langton. Some have wealth and love it; some have it and do not love it; some neither have it nor love it: these are happier than the others. Those who do not have wealth but love it are the unhappiest of the lot.[23] Langton may well have been referring here to the prosperous burghers of the fast growing towns of his day. The bourgeois of Paris in the thirteenth century, for example, already had something of the desire for profit. While he preserved the faith of his fathers, he nevertheless had a certain disdain for sermons and preachers. This attitude was born of his confidence in the advantages given him by wealth and privilege.[24]

Langton, like other of his contemporaries, criticized bourgeois merchant and worker alike. Workers were frequently condemned for fraudulence in the products of their industry.[25] Insofar as the burgher was concerned, the prime interest of the preacher lay in the denunciation of shady business practices and usury. These were moral teachings that especially applied to Langton's town audiences. Usury was likened to theft, and its practitioners to the creations of the devil.[26] All things acquired unjustly by robbery or by usury, or by some other illicit means, are evidence in judgment against the usurer.[27] Elsewhere Langton identified usury with

[21] 17[a], Pa[11], 260[va]: Si aliquis amitteret hereditatem suam nec auderet pugnare pro ea recuperanda nec haberet pecuniam qua conduceret pugilem, si aliquis pugil diceret ei pro te pugnabo sine precio, et pugnaret et obtineret victoriam et vulneraretur in prelio et susciperetur in hospicio illius pro quo pugnaret, turpe esset ei si eiceret eum a domo scil. antequam curarentur vulnera eius.

[22] 114[a], Tr[2], 249[ra]: Fidelis amicus est qui in omni negotio subsidium suum impendit amico postulanti. Fictus qui in necessitate deficit.

[23] 85, Le[2], 91[ra]: Sunt autem quatuor genera hominum. Quidam divicias habent et amant, quidam habent et non amant, quidam nec habent nec amant — isti ceteris sunt securiores. Alii non habent et amant et isti sunt omnibus miseriores.

[24] Lecoy de la Marche, 403.

[25] *Ibid.*, 420.

[26] *Ibid.*, 407, 416.

[27] 54[b], Ar, 59[vb]-60[ra]: Omnia iniuste adquisita per rapinam vel usuram vel alio modo illicito, contra eum [i.e. usurarium] loquuntur testimonium in iudicio.

mortal sin;[28] in still another sermon he called it "dung and filth."[29] Usurers, he said, are condemned to eternal damnation, for the usurer will see cash but he will not see God.[30] The moneylender, like a wolf, devours the poor of Christ.[31]

The reformer must expose and denounce. So did Langton when he condemns the crafty and deceitful business men who do not want to unfold their bolts of cloth, but sell them folded and thus deceive their customers.[32] Not all merchants, however, are bad. Some ply their trade with skill, as we notice in Langton's remark on supply and demand in the market place: "If a merchant brought to the market something that was in great supply, he would be unwise to sell it. Good merchants, therefore, are those who bring those items to market that are not so plentiful, and sell them well because of their scarcity."[33]

Business partnerships do not escape Langton's criticism, in this passage that decries the double standard among Christians:

> It is well known that everyone wants to live with Him, but that there are few indeed who wish to suffer and die with Him. This is not a correct partnership, for even as among merchants, it is not right if one always wishes to participate in the profit and never in a loss or misfortune — if perchance it should occur — so it is not a true partnership if we wish to live with Christ and refuse to die with Him or for Him. But just as in a proper business association merchants share equally in the losses or profits of one of their fellows, so with us a true association (fellowship) with Christ means that as we are ready to live with Christ so also should we be willing to suffer and die with Him, for Him, and out of confidence in Him.[34]

28 15ª, Tr², 282ʳᵃ: Certe nec die nec nocte requiescit qui in peccato mortali est quia et ipsum facit. Sicut usura. Semper enim crescit, et nullus sapiens attingit usuram, ita est de peccato mortali.

29 19ᶜ, Le², 41ʳᵇ: ... sicut usurarius stercus et lutum; multum laborat ut acquirat, acquisita omni diligencia custodit ne perdat.

30 103ᶜ, Le², 140 ᵛᵃ⁻ᵛᵇ : Si sacerdos dicit usurario, renuntia usuris ; relinque multitudinem ; sequere fidelium paucitatem. Cui ille. Fodere non valeo; mendicare erubesco, preterea omnes vicini mei similiter faciunt. Quasi dicat. Paucitatem non curo, multitudinem non relinquam, immo sequitur eam ad penam eternam... . Usurarius videt nummum sed non videt Deum.

31 34ᵇ, Ar, 130ʳᵃ: Lupus iste est fenerator rapidus, qui pauperes Christi depascit... .

32 83ᵇ, Pa⁶, 62ʳᵇ: Ne simus sicut dolosi negociatores qui nolunt explicare pannos suos, sed involutos vendunt eos, et ita decipiunt emptores.

33 66ᵇ, Bs¹, 79ᵛᵃ: Siquis enim mercator aliquam rem ferret ad nundinas cuius rei magna esset copia in nundinis, eam male venderet. Unde boni mercatores res illas ferunt ad nundinas quarum illic non est copia, et ita propter raritatem illas bene vendunt... .

34 63, Bs¹, 131ʳᵇ: Constat ergo quod quilibet vivere vult cum eo, sed paucissimi sunt qui volunt pati et mori cum eo. Unde non est recta societas ista, nam sicut inter mercatores non est recta societas si alter semper velit esse particeps lucri et numquam dampni sive incommodi si forte acciderit, sic non est vera societas si velimus vivere cum Christo, et recusemus mori cum illo vel

Many are the usurers, robbers, and adulterers who call themselves Christians, observes Langton, but who vilify the name of Christ in the manner of the thief who, as he is dragged to the gallows, cries out that he is of noble blood.[35] Of the many vices condemned by Master Stephen, adultery, like usury, was denounced as a grave and enormous sin. Not only does it violate a divine precept, warned Langton, but it also disrupts the matrimonial bond. The adulterer's sin is therefore twofold: against God and his neighbor.[36]

That a man's neighbor is like a mirror is another of Langton's themes. If he is a good man, one ought to imitate his goodness; if, however, he is evil, one should avoid him, since happy is he who learns caution from the perils of others.[37] A man's life experience might well be compared to a ship: "In a ship the prow and stern are narrow; the keel broad. The beginning of life is narrow; the end likewise... the middle years are wider. Now man is at the peak of his strength; and even as the whole cargo is in the middle of the ship, so does [man] bear his whole burden in the middle of life."[38]

The images of the ship and the sea seem to have been popular with preachers at this time. Crusades and pilgrimages to the Holy Land apparently brought a greater awareness of the sea and ships, even to inhabitants of the most central provinces. Jacques de Vitry, for example, used the language of the sea in his sermons, calling forth the image of the four winds to describe pride, lust, mundane prosperity and adversity.[39] Comparisons between the sea and the world were long used in the tradition of the Church. Langton repeated the biblical aphorism: *Mare est mundus*, in his sermon on the twentieth Sunday after Pentecost.[40] On

pro illo. Sed sicut est recta societas ut mercatores in mercatura socii communiter participent dampna et lucra, sic vera societas est ut sicut volumus vivere cum Christo sic et pati et mori velimus cum eo, et pro eo, et in fide ipsius.

[35] 22[d], Le[2], 167[vb]: Multi licet usurarii, raptores, adulterii Christianos se nominant, in quo nomen Christi vilipendi faciunt, ad modum latronis qui dum ad patibulum trahitur, de alicuius nobilis sanguine se processisse testatur... .

[36] 33[b], Bs[1], 115[rb]: Sequitur de adulterio. O quam grave scelus et enorme peccatum adulterii iudicatur apud Dominum. Istud primo datum violat preceptum Domini, et istud dirumpit matrimoniale vinculum, istud directe se obicit in Deum et in proximum.

[37] 85, Le[2], 90[vb]: Tercium speculum est frater noster scil. proximus qui nobis est speculum, quia si bonus est debemus bonitatem illius imitari, si autem malus, ab eo cavere, quia felix quem faciunt aliena pericula cautum... .

[38] 117[d], Le[2], 184[va]: In navi prora et puppis angusta, carina lata, inicium vite angustum, finis similiter... medium vite latius est, nunc est homo in statu robusto, et sicut totum honus est in medio navis, ita totum honus in medio vite sustinet.

[39] Lecoy de la Marche, 419.

[40] 4, Ar, 115[ra]. *Cf.* Aug. *De Civ. Dei*, Lib. XVIII: c. 49 ("... et in hoc mundo, tamquam in mari... ." [Migne, *PL*, 41, 611], *cf. Matt.* 13: 47-48).

another occasion, the feast day of the Blessed Virgin, Master Stephen reiterated the lesson, but added this social message: "Notice that the sea is called the world, because of its varied tribulations. Just as in the sea, the greater fish devours the smaller one and digests it, so in this sea, the world, the greater fishes, i.e. princes and other nobles, devour lesser folk and digest their wealth."[41] Those who try to negotiate the perilous waters of this sea which is the world must follow the course of the star, who is the Virgin Mary. Does not her name *Maria* sound like the phrase *maris stella ?*[42]

Vox Dei

The image of the ship admirably suited Langton's descriptions of the Church and its clergy. "The Church," he said, "is signified by a ship whose helmsmen are the prelates... . Noah, helmsman of the ark, represents the prelates of the Church."[43] Although the number of sermons actually addressed to all-clerical audiences was small, Langton's comments on the Church and its clergy are frequent. This is understandable of the preaching of a reformer whose interests lay in the improvement of the religious life of the laity and who saw in the clergy an important instrument of that movement. Clerics had the task of education and setting an example for layfolk. In order to achieve a right order in society, preachers had to be teachers. Yet the Church, before it could effectively teach, had to set its house in order.

The welfare of the Church as a whole especially concerned Langton, and notably its wise administration by prelates.[44] In this passage Langton compared the Church to a vineyard, and its prelates to vinetenders and cultivators:

> By this vineyard is meant the Church whose vinetenders and cultivators are the prelates... . The Church is called a vine for three important reasons: it is dry in winter, but flourishes in summer. Thus, although the saints are despised in the winter of this life, in the summer of future resurrection, they will be glorious... . Second, a vineyard requires great labor, yet it perishes very easily. Thus, in order to bear fruit, the vine of our body must be tended diligently with the toil of vigils and fasts... . Third, a vine is good for nothing except for two things: to bear fruit or to feed a fire, something that is not

41 110^{b}, Le^{2}, 170va: ... quod mare appellatur mundus iste, propter tribulationes varias, et sicut in mari maior piscis devorat minorem et absorbet, sic in hoc mari mundo, scil. maiores pisces i.e. principes et alii nobiles suos minores devorant, et eorum substantias absorbent... .

42 *Ibid.*, f. 170vb. See p. 110, n. 7, *supra.*

43 62, Tr^{2}, 241ra: Navis ecclesiam significat. Rectores navis sunt prelati ecclesie... Noah... rector arche... . Owst, in his *Preaching in medieval England,* 37 and *Literature and pulpit in medieval England,* 68-69 cites the use of the same metaphor.

44 Powicke, *Christian life, etc.,* 140.

> true of any other wood. Whence Ezechiel [ch. 15]: Son of man, what shall become of the twig of the vine? Even as the twig of the vine which has been given to the fire to be consumed, so shall it be with the sinners of Jerusalem... and fire will consume them. Lust is fire, consuming even to perdition.[45]

In other sermons, Langton likened the priest to the doctor who bears the medicine of doctrine.[46] In his explanation of the meaning of *episcopus*, Langton underscored the prelate's supervisory powers: "*Episcopus* in Greek is *speculator* in Latin, and as the word indicates, it refers to one with supervisory powers."[47]

The preacher Stephen recognized that the responsibilities of the Church and its prelates were great because their privileges were greater. Ambition, natural to the prince, is a sin in the prelate.[48] Langton, like other medieval preachers, decried the ills of the Church. Simony, nepotism, the cupidity of the clergy and concubinage of priests were evils denounced in synod and pulpit alike.[49] Yet Langton's criticisms, in his commentaries at least, have been described as the "words of an observant man of affairs, rather than the objurgations of the ill-balanced preacher."[50]

This was also true of his remarks in his sermons. He addressed an audience of clerics assembled in synod as follows:

> The delight of the Lord ought to be the clerical order and especially the priesthood... . You are the ones who are entrusted with dispensing the ineffable sacrament of the body and blood of the Lord... . The root of all things is cupidity, as the apostle says (*I Tim.* 6: 10). But although it is reprehensible in anyone at all, it is detestable in a priest. There are, nevertheless, certain priests who turn the sacrament of the altar into a quest for worldly profit... .[51]

[45] 97[c], Le[2], 48[rb-va]: Per hanc vineam intelligitur ecclesia, cuius vinitores et cultores sunt prelati... . Ecclesia dicitur vinea maxime propter tria, arida est in hieme, sed floret in estate. Sic sancti in hieme huius vite licet sint despecti, in estate future resurrectionis erunt gloriosi... . Secundum in vinea est, quod magnum laborem requirit et facillime perit. Ita vinea corporis nostri ut fructum faciat, multo labore vigiliarum et ieiuniorum est excolenda... . Tercium in vinea est quod ad nichilum nisi ad duo valet, vel ut fructum faciat, vel ut ignem pascat, quod non est de aliis lignis. Unde Ezechiel. Fili hominis quid fiet de ligno vitis? Sicut lignum vitis quod traditum est igni ad devorandum, tradam peccatores Ierosolim... et ignis consumet eos. Luxuria est ignis usque ad perditionem devorans... .

[46] 38[b], PA[1], 110[ra]: Medicus est sacerdos... fert medicinam i.e. doctrinam. Qui sunt bene confessi penitus sunt curati. Eger morbo spirituali non potest corpus fatigare in servicio domini... .

[47] 9, Pa[16], 144[vb]: Episcopus grece latine speculator, et ut alludat vocabulo, dicitur quasi superintendens... . See Powicke, *Henry III and the Lord Edward*, I, 265 on the importance of the episcopal office in Langton's teaching.

[48] Powicke, *Christian life, etc.*, 144-45.

[49] See Lecoy de la Marche, 349-59.

[50] Powicke, *Christian life, etc.*, 140.

[51] 9, Pa[16], 142[vb]-143[vb]: Dilectus Domini esse deberet ordo clericalis et precipue sacerdotalis... . Vos estis quibus dispensatio ineffabilis sacramenti corporis et sanguinis Domini commissa... . Radix omnium est cupiditas, ut ait apostolus. Sed licet in quolibet sit reprehensibilis, in sacer-

Other priests abuse the sacrament by performing it ineptly.[52] Langton also denounced those prelates whose skill in giving advice about familial administration, about fund raising, and keeping in the good graces of the nobility exceeds their capacity to save souls.[53]

Like his contemporary, the bishop of Paris (and noted preacher), Maurice de Sully, Langton emphasized the duties of priests: to live a holy life, to instruct himself and others by preaching.[54] Were not prelates *genus electum, regale sacerdotium*[55] to be distinguished from the layfolk, the *laici simplices et idiote*?[56] Langton depicted the differences between clergy and laity in various ways. In his biblical commentaries, for example, the laity (or sometimes, the lesser clergy) were identified with the ten tribes of Israel; while the clergy (or more exactly, prelates) were signified by the remaining two tribes of Judah.[57]

In his sermons, Langton was very precise about the special relationship and responsibility of the clergy to the laity. It was by virtue of their singularity and exalted position that clerics were held to greater obligations than their lay brothers. In his lesson on *Joel* 1: 20 ("The beasts of the field cry also unto thee... ."), Langton remarked: "Who are the beasts of the field except the layfolk, those like simple beasts whom we ought to feed and nourish with spiritual food, and who like the thirsty plain seek from us the rain of spiritual teaching."[58] Clerics have the duty, therefore, to instruct the laity; even in their absence, the church itself shall be an open book: "Lest the layfolk try to excuse themselves by their ignorance because they do not understand Scripture, or because they are without preachers, whatever is contained in the holy church is displayed before them instead of a book.... The laity should have those letters by which they can know God, and above all, ought to love and praise [Him]."[59]

dote detestabilis. Sunt enim quidam sacerdotes qui sacramentum altaris convertunt ad questum lucri temporalis...

[52] 50^c^, Pa^16^, 37rb: ...quod hodie faciunt prelati cupidi qui per cupiditatem male dispensant Christi corpus.

[53] 93^a^, Tr^2^, 259rb: Plurimi (i.e. prelati) periti sunt in dandis consiliis de gubernatione familie, de colleccione opum, de conservando favore potentum, sed ad consulendum saluti anime hebetes sunt... . *Cf.* Kantorowicz, *op. cit.*, 124, n. 110, where the following remark is ascribed to Langton: "Sacerdotes etiam magis volunt vocari domini quam sacerdotes vel capellani."

[54] Lecoy de la Marche, 352-53.

[55] 9, Pa^16^, 143vb.

[56] *Ibid.*, f. 143rb.

[57] Smalley, *Study of the Bible in the Middle Ages*, 259.

[58] 59, Bs^1^, 122vb: (... bestie agri quasi area sitiens imbrem. *Ioel* 1: 20). Qui sunt bestie agri nisi laici? quos tamquam simplices bestias deberemus alimento spirituali nutrire et pascere, qui tanquam area sitiens a nobis imbrem spiritualis doctrine querunt.

[59] 85, Le^2^, 90va: Ne autem laici per ignorantiam se excusare valeant, quia scripturas non intelli-

Since the cleric was specifically trained for the instruction of laymen, his obligation was greater. It was also apparent that should he fail in carrying out the duties of his office, the defect was all the more pronounced. "Better by far are simple layfolk than indifferent clergy," said Langton.[60] The clerk may know better than the layman that which pertains to God's grace, but simple folk can feel the grace of God more than do subtle and proud clerks.[61]

The theme of the reinvigoration of Christian life by a rededicated clergy, devoted to the spread of popular piety, obtains ample emphasis in these sermons. Pope Innocent III recognized the importance of this popular preaching movement for the Church. In effect, the recognition given the mendicant orders institutionalized the apostolic movement that had begun years before in Paris. Stephen Langton, as a popular preacher interested in reform, was, insofar as we can judge by these sermons, in accord with the overall aims of his former Paris friend Innocent III. How then can we explain the absence of any references to the pope or any discussion relating to the papal office?

References to the pope in contemporary sermons generally appeared in the prayers of the people, especially those recited at the end of the sermon.[62] This feature may be helpful in explaining the absence of any mention of the pope in Langton's sermons. We have earlier described the transmission of these texts by *reportatio* and their subsequent collection in sermon manuals. In the process of this transmission, copyists may have eliminated references of a topical or contemporary nature which could be added orally by the preacher who used the model sermon. In a similar fashion, closing prayers were usually indicated in the manuscripts by standard formulae and these were either abbreviated or omitted entirely.[63] A special prayer for the pope might have been pronounced, but it would not necessarily appear in the manuscripts as we have them.

In short, given the condition of our texts, we cannot say with certainty that the pope was not mentioned in the prayers of the people. Since the procedure during this period generally called for such a prayer, this may well have been the case of Langton's sermons. What is clear, however, is the absence of any discussion relating to the papal office. We must notice,

gant, vel quia predicatoribus careant, quicquid in sancta ecclesia continetur, illis pro libro proponitur... . Habeant ergo laici istas litteras per quas Deum cognoscere possunt, et super omnia [eum] amare et laudare debent... .

60 38^{c}, Le^{2}, 68ra: Meliores multo sunt laici simplices, quam clerici torpentes... .

61 109^{d}, Le^{2}, 36vb: Sicut clerici melius sciunt quid sit stella [i.e. gratia Dei] quam laici, ita boni simplices melius agnoscunt Dei gratiam et senciunt, quam ipsi clerici suptiles et superbi.

62 Lecoy de la Marche, 343-45.

63 See Chap. III, *supra* on the transmission of the sermons.

first of all, that Langton's preaching in the evangelical movement of the late twelfth century had the support of the pope and hence it would be highly unlikely that the preacher addressing a popular audience would discuss the nature of the papal office. Nor would this kind of preaching be the place for discussing the kind of cases that attracted Langton's attention in the *Questiones*. These were of a very specific nature, e.g. the instance which related to the legitimacy of a particular papal decree on fasting.[64]

Furthermore, the emphasis given by Langton to the episcopate and the priesthood as instruments of reform has relevance here. Not only were bishops and priests to be the effectors of reform in local churches, but their special qualities coincided with those of a good pope. A story told by Peter the Chanter is most revealing. When someone told Alexander III that he was a good pope, saying: "What you do is papal," Alexander replied in the vernacular: "If I knew how to judge well, to preach well and to give repentance, I would be a good pope." In these three qualities, concluded the Chanter, is expressed the whole office of the prelate.[65] Peter the Chanter's lesson in the *Verbum Abbreviatum* fits in well with Langton's bias in favor of the importance of the duties of a prelate in the reform of the Church. The papal office itself would be seen in terms of the qualities associated with the good prelate, who worked for the good of the Church universal.

It is, in fact, the unity of *Christianitas* that Langton emphasizes. Both laity and clergy undoubtedly ought to believe, that all men have been liberated from sin, from eternal punishment, and from the death of the body by the Lord's passion.[66] The true religion that Langton describes in the following passage ignores the divisions among Christians, and underlines the importance of personal piety in this popular preaching: "We shall discover what is the true religion. In every religious person three things must be considered: namely piety in heart, sweetness in speech, and an absence of cupidity. Thus he who desires to have pure and true religion, let him be generous toward the poor, mild of speech, and let him not appropriate anything for himself."[67]

[64] See Chap. I, *supra*, p. 5, n. 26.

[65] *Verb. Abbrev.*, c. 75 (Migne, *PL*, 205, 199): Nec hoc est praetermittendum quod quidam, nescio quo animo, dixit Alexandro tertio: Domine, bonus papa es. Quidquid facis papale est. Et respondit Alexander in vulgari suo dicens: Si scirem, "Bien jujar, et bien predicar, et penitense donar, je seroie boene pape." Et ita his tribus expressit totum officium praelati. *Ibid.*, c. 76: Tripartitum officium praelati, scilicet judicare, poenitentiam dare, praedicare... .

[66] 63, Bs[1], 131[rb]: Tam laici quam clerici indubitanter debent credere, quod per passionem liberati sumus omnes a peccato, a pena eterna, et a morte corporis... .

[67] 85, Le[2], 91[ra]: In hoc igitur triplici speculo nos considerantes inveniemus quid sit vera religio. In omni autem religioso tria consideranda sunt, scil. pietas in corde, dulcedo in sermone, et quod

Langton's greatest praise was clearly reserved for those among the clergy who had renounced the things of this world to follow Christ, and who were examples of the ideals of the apostolic movement. Canons regular, hermits, and monks are mentioned by name.[68] These have entered the cloister and have given themselves up to religion. They speak of their property as *ours*, not *mine*; because nothing is one's own except sin, which alone can be called *mine*.[69] These religious have forsaken wives, sons, and great possessions; they have put aside their prebends and ecclesiastical dignities for the life of the cloister.[70] They are dissimilar from the secular clergy who are anxious about the administration of the household and devote their time to acquiring temporal goods.[71] The preacher Stephen also gives us this sketch of the hierarchy among regulars, where the right order is also desirable:

> Four orders are distinguished among religious: *prelati*, or abbots; *claustrales*, or the monks; *novitii*, or the novices; and *obedientiarii*... . Abbots ought to be like the Lebanon, i.e. the mountain... even as a mountain prominently dominates the plain, so should the life of the prelate excel in sanctity that of his subjects... . The good monks are [likened to] select myrrh—fervent are they in the management of their order; diligent are they in their holy work; not by fear of discipline but by spontaneous inclination — without coercion — are they proficient in good works... . The novices are the flowering vine; even as the blossom of the vine falls easily... so does the fervor of the novice swiftly fade should his superiors offer bad examples... . The *obedientiarii* are like the offering of the just... he has two responsibilities — to the world by the administration of temporal affairs... and to the order, by profession... .[72]

nichil cupiat. Sic qui mundam et veram religionem habere desiderat, sit pius erga pauperes mitis in sermone, nichil sibi approprict... .

[68] 38ª, Pa¹⁶, 67ᵛᵃ: ... canonici regulares, heremite, monachi... qui constituti sunt in arcta religione, qui relictis omnibus mundi secuti sunt Christum.

[69] 92ª, Bg², 37ʳᵇ: ... qui intrant claustrum quod se dederunt religioni. Item religiosi dicunt de rebus suis, nostrum, non meum, quia nichil proprium preter peccatum, illud solum potest dici meum.

[70] 6ᶜ, Le², 149ʳᵃ: Sunt enim quidam... qui huius mundi divicias et delicias abiecerunt, et se in claustris contulerunt, illi inquam considerant quod magna fecerunt pro Deo, quia uxores, filios, largas possessiones dimiserunt, illi qui prebendas suas, dignitates ecclesiasticas reliquerunt.

[71] 31ᵇ, Le², 184ʳᵃ: ... intellige seculares activos qui solliciti sunt de gubernatione familie, et acquirendis temporalibus vacant... .

[72] 17ᵇ, Ar, 12ᵛᵃ-13ʳᵃ: ... distinguantur ergo iiiiᵒʳ ordines [i.e. viris religiosorum]. Primus prelatorum, secundus claustralium, scil. eorum qui sunt in ordine provecti, tercius noviciorum, quartus obedientiariorum... . Prelati ergo debent esse quasi libanus i.e. mons... sicut mons terre planitiem altitudine superat, sic vita prelatorum debet excellere tam subditorum morem sanctitate... . Mirra electa sunt boni claustrales, in executione ordinis ferventes, in sancta operatione diligentes — qui non metu discipline sed spontanea voluntate sine coactione in bonis operibus proficiunt... . Vinea florens sunt novitii, sicut vinee flosculus de facili cadit... ita fervor novitii cito perit malo exemplo prelatorum... . Obedientiarii sunt quasi oblatio iusti... obedientiarius duobus tenetur

Among these regular clergy, the monk or *monachus* has a special singularity that is evident in the name itself. In a sermon for Passion Sunday, the preacher Langton emphasized the special obedience owed by monks to God, and contrasted these with seculars and layfolk, the saints and sinners who toil in the vineyard of the Church:

> You want an interpretation of your name, *cleric? Cleros* is the Greek word for the Latin *sors*, or this is also called *hereditas*. Hence you are called *clericus* because you have chosen your lot or inheritance (quia tuum sortem vel hereditatem elegisti)... . You interpret this name *clericus* when the priest blesses the tonsure for you, and you say: the Lord [is] a part of my inheritance... As for you, o monk who have vowed me special obedience... the *monachus* is custodian of one, or is interpreted as singular. Whatever he is, is because he should love me, not with other things, or before other things, but without other things. The layman can only love me together with other things, since he may not prefer his love of temporal goods to my love... . The cleric can love me before all else, because even if he should love mundane things, he is held much more to prefer my love to the love of worldly goods. But you [o monk] ought to love me without other things, since all things besides me... you should think of as dung. Hence you are called *monachus*, i.e. *singularis*.[73]

Vivat Rex Ipso Jure

Langton's *exempla* on kings and princes, on law and justice, appear frequently in the sermons because of their connections with the theme, God the King. References to earthly kings have a particular moral message and were fundamental to this popular preaching. When in the course of a sermon, Langton wanted to speak of the royal nature of Christ, he found his most effective examples drawn from the people's experience and image of earthly kingship. Divine law and justice were the more readily understood if translated into the language of the popular audience. After all, said Langton, if we are subject to the authority of an earthly king and must obey his edicts lest we suffer a capital penalty, how much more then must we obey the edicts of the *Summus Rex*, who is God Himself.[74]

scil. mundo per administrationem temporalium... et ordini per professionem. (An *obedientiarius* was an inferior officer or an advocate of a convent).

73 99ª, Pa¹¹, 229ra-va^: ... velles quod interpretarer nomen tuum. *Cleros* grece latine *sors*, vel hec *hereditas* dicitur. Inde *clericus* diceris, quia tuum sortem vel hereditatem elegisti... tu qui interpretaris hoc nomen *clericus* cum a sacerdote tibi corona benediceretur, dixisti namque dominus pars hereditatis mee... . Sed o tu monache qui mihi singularius obedientiam promisisti... *monachus* est custos unius vel singularis interpretatur; qualiter quia non cum aliis, vel pre aliis, sed sine aliis me diligere debet. Laicus enim cum aliis me diligere potest quia amorem temporalium potest non preferre amori meo... clericus me pre aliis diligere potest, quia et si diligat temporalia amorem meum amori temporalium multum preferre tenetur. Sed tu me debes diligere sine aliis, quia omnia preter me tamquam stercora reputare debes, et idcirco diceris *monachus* i.e. *singularis*... .

74 18^b, Le^2, 97va: Certe siquis preceptum regis terreni transgreditur, pena capitali punietur. Et

These were comparisons that were within the comprehension of his listeners and hence could be all the more useful in realizing the purpose of the sermon. The advent of Christ the King was brought even closer to the people by likening it to something they themselves had probably witnessed, the coronation procession of their prince.[75] The way in which Langton treated the themes of kingship and law, therefore, further reflects the popular element in his preaching.

These *exempla* on kings have, however, additional importance in that they are a part of this popular preaching movement which was devoted to the spread of reform. Langton's observations on these themes must be examined as reflections on the right order in the secular leadership of society. We must give notice therefore to the manner in which Langton defines the king and illustrates the tyrant; to the importance given the role of equity and justice in the land; and to the tasks that engage the earthly king in the conduct of his court, his army, and his kingdom.

These themes have, moreover, a special interest because of Langton's subsequent career as archbishop of Canterbury and his controversial role in the events that led to the drafting of Magna Carta. Langton's views on questions of a politico-ecclesiastical nature have been largely neglected. Powicke gave some attention to the problem in his writings on Stephen Langton, but his observations were largely restricted to, if not by, selected passages from the theological questions. Powicke has observed, for example, that in Langton's lectures there is no clearcut opinion on papal power over temporal princes. Present studies on the *Questiones* may add to and possibly revise our knowledge of Langton's thought in this area.[76]

si is taliter punietur, quis finis erit transgredientium preceptum et edictum omnipotentis Dei, qui potest corpus et animam mittere in gehennam? On the Royalty of Christ, see J. Leclercq, *L'idée de la royauté du Christ au moyen âge* (Paris, 1959). On its particular use as a sermon theme, see by the same author, "Le sermon sur la royauté du Christ au moyen âge," *Archives d'hist. doct. et litt. du m.a.*, XVIII-XX (1943-45), 143-80.

[75] 28[b], Be, 6ra: Item. Contra regis adventum nuper coronati, lutum tollendum est, platee spargende sunt floribus. Coronatus est rex noster in assumptione carnis. Corona signum est victorie, et dominus in carne assumpta vicit diabolum.

[76] See Professor John Baldwin's forthcoming study of Langton's Paris circle, which will shed additional light on the relevant passages in the *Questiones*. The *Questiones*, on problems moral and theological, touch on several issues that relate to preaching and also to the contents of some of these sermons. Notice, for example, these rubrics which appear in Miss Gregory's *Index* of the contents of the *Questiones* in St. John's Coll., Cambridge MS 57: (See Lacombe *et al.*, 231 ff.). Utrum opera legalia iustificarent... de clavibus... de officio ecclesie in adventu... utrum bona ecclesie a personis ecclesiasticis iure proprietatis an ex dispensatione possideantur... utrum prelatus plus quam alii ad opera misericordie teneatur... utrum temporalia absolute an sub conditione sint petenda... de preceptis decalogi et additionibus... . Quomodo sit intelligendum illud ius naturale... de contemplativa et activa... de decymis et primitiis... de usuriis... de usura... de matrimonio... de

Langton's comments on the nature of kingship and law, and the relationship between the powers spiritual and temporal, were reserved for the theological questions cited earlier and the lectures given to his students in Paris. In neither of these is there a cohesive body of political teaching. Nevertheless, discussions such as these were those of a potential reformer and must be examined in that light. Langton's students were the prelates of the future.[77] The lectures delivered by the master may well have provided the themes, if not the substance of many a sermon. The intimacy of biblical study and preaching, a persistent and recurrent motive in these studies, attaches special significance to Langton's remarks on kingship and law in a Christian society.[78]

The nature of his examples reflected his particular audience. The questions and the lectures had an educated, ecclesiastical audience. These were specialized discussions that dealt with more specific situations and problems. Notice, for example, that Langton had concluded in the *Questiones* that temporal lordship must be submitted to divine lordship.[79] In matters of political obedience, the king must be properly counselled. He is, however, subject to God, is bound by natural law, and must observe custom.[80] The Church had traditionally, in its view of kingship, stressed the idea of election and the suitability of the ruler. In his *Questiones*, Langton quoted the Lombard that the anointing of a king does not impart

helemosina... . Quando habeat esse ignorantia et utrum parvulus dicatur ignorare (*cf.* Utrum scientia naturali contraria sit ignorantia)... De ypocrisi... De libero arbitrio... De mendatio... De iuramento... De obedientia... De obedientia regum... . Quomodo dicatur unum genus operum magis bonum vel malum alio... . Miss Smalley, *Study of the Bible in the Middle Ages*, 200 has called attention to the more personal quality of the commentaries and the *Questiones*, as compared with the more theological tone and content of Langton's commentary on the *Sentences*. The following are some of the subjects treated in this work, edited by A. Landgraf, "Der Sentenzenkommentar des Kardinals Stephan Langton," *Beiträge zur Gesch. der Phil. und Theol. des Mittelalters*, Bd. XXXVII, Hft. 1 (1952), *passim*: liberum arbitrium... Plato and Aristotle... iustitia... equitas... Divina sapientia... homo iustus... sapientia... similitudo inter virum et uxorem; ratio... scientia et sapientia... distinctio inter intellectum et scientiam et sapientiam... periurium... homicidium.

[77] Smalley, *Study of the Bible in the Middle Ages*, 249. Langton apparently trained a group of teachers whose influence was felt in the development of academic thought between 1200-30. His pupils included Geoffrey of Poitiers (whose *Summa* has been shown to depend largely on Langton's *Questiones*); Richard Poore (later Bishop of Salisbury and Durham); Thomas of Marlborough (afterwards Abbot of Evesham); and possibly Henry of Sanford (future archdeacon of Canterbury). See Powicke, "Bibliographical note, etc.," 555-56; Cheney, "Earliest English Diocesan Statutes," 16; and R. Foreville in *Dict. Spirit.*, col. 1496.

[78] Powicke in *Christian life, etc.*, 142 (published in 1935) suggested that the sermons might yield "some idea of the principles which directed Langton's activities."

[79] See St. John's Coll., Cambridge MS 57, f. 195r and Powicke, *SL*, 94-95.

[80] *Ibid.*, 95.

a sacramental character to the office. It is not to the ministry, but to the service of the Church that the king is anointed.[81]

The sermons, however, as we have noted, were addressed to largely popular audiences, and the treatment given these subjects takes a form more suitable to the needs and interests of lay listeners. Like other preachers of the epoch, Langton tended to idealize the monarchy and feudal world of the high middle ages. Jolliffe's characterization of twelfth century monarchy: "Not power realized but power exercised..."[82] became, in the contemporary sermon, power idealized, for the purpose of emphasizing the right order in temporal leadership. To the preacher Jacques de Vitry, for example, the prince had to be noble in spirit. All Christians, says he, are kings, sons of the great Sovereign of the universe. Those who are personally consecrated to lead others have a special obligation to fulfill their duties. Theirs is the task of equity which consists of the elevation of the good, repression of evil, protection of churches and the poor, and the distribution of justice.[83]

Langton's actions bespeak a man who "believed that social relations must be rooted in unity and justice."[84] Later in his career, he insisted on the establishment of royal claims, if they were challenged: (e.g. when in 1223, prior to the reissue of the Charter, inquiries were made into the customs and liberties enjoyed by King John in 1215, before his conflict with the barons).[85] What of the early Langton, the master of theology and popular preacher in Paris ? How did he view questions of equity and justice ?

> Equity and iniquity, as you know, are opposites. Equity means that a man should return that which he owes. For any man is bound in three ways: He owes a debt to God, to his neighbor, and to himself. Should he not honor this debt, this is iniquity. Notice, that one does not use the singular, *iniquity*, but the plural, *iniquities*; since he owes many debts... not one iniquity but many iniquities does he make. Consequently, he is obligated to return those things which he owes, and to whom he owes them.[86]

[81] See St. John's Coll., Cambridge MS 57, f. 318^v and Powicke, *SL*, 108-09.

[82] Jolliffe, *op. cit.*, 85.

[83] Lecoy de la Marche, 376-78.

[84] Powicke, *Henry III and the Lord Edward*, I, 67.

[85] *Ibid.* On Langton's view of the theoretical rights of subjects of a deposed king, see his letter of 1207 (Gervase of Canterbury ii, p. lxxxii and Powicke, *SL*, 97). For other references, see Cheney, "The alleged deposition of King John," *op. cit.*, 102, n. 1. Also Painter, *Reign of King John*, 276.

[86] 91, Pa^{11}, 272ra: Equitas et iniquitas ut scitis contraria sunt. Equitas est ut homo reddat quod debet. Quilibet enim homo tribus modis ligatur. Debitum enim debet Deo, proximo et sibi ipsi, quod si non reddit, iniquitas est. Non dicit iniquitatem sed iniquitates, quia plura debita debet... non iniquitatem unam sed plures facit iniquitates. Tenetur ergo reddere ea que debet et quibus debet.

His comments on justice are scattered in various sermons. They are brief and traditional aphorisms, and eminently suited to his popular audiences. Justice, he said, is to render to each one that which is his.[87] There are two parts to justice, one is to turn away from evil, and the other is to do good.[88] Justice teaches obedience to one's superiors, counsel and aid to one's peers, and correction and protection of one's subjects.[89] The good judge will not permit robbers to flourish in the land.[90] Justice goes hand in hand with piety: "For the just man returns to each man that which is his... . Piety consists in having compassion for the pauper and distributing one's goods to the poor... ."[91]

In his observations on law as well, Langton's scriptural bias is obvious. In the *Questiones* he had written that all men are subject to the law of nature whose precepts are revealed in Scripture. Christ is the head of the Church, the pope, his mouthpiece and exponent of moral law. His decrees must therefore be observed. The prince is subject to the law of the community insofar as it is in accord with the law of nature. Secular government, as a part of divine order, has its own law, but is subject to moral law.[92]

The preacher Langton, in his definition of kings, took the position known as "political Augustinianism:" one is not a king unless he is a servant and minister of God.[93] Kings are those who rule themselves well and do justice in their land.[94] The lesson is repeated in more than one sermon: "On the contrary, all will be kings who serve Him, i.e. all rule themselves who serve the Lord. For no one is a king unless he rules himself, and this is in accord with divine precepts."[95] The good king acts justly: "If a king should order peace to be preserved in a land that is not his own and that he has conquered while, in his own state, thieves rob and despoil, he cannot be said to maintain justice."[96] The good king punishes counter-

[87] 33[a], Ar, 78[ra]: ... iustitia reddere unicuique quod suum est.

[88] 74[b], Pa[11], 210[rb]: Due sunt partes iusticie, alteram partem habuisti que est declinare a malo; aliam non habuisti, quia bona non fecisti que est consummatio perfectionis... .

[89] 80[b], Le[2], 181[vb]-182[ra]: Iustitia vero maioribus obedientiam, paribus consilium et auxilium inpendi precepit. In subditis vero correctionem et custodiam... .

[90] 19[c], Le[2], 41[vb]: Non diceretur bonus iudex qui terram aliorum pacificaret, et in propria latrones habitare permitteret... .

[91] 5[a], Bs[1], 137[ra]: ... enim iustus reddit unicuique quod suum est... . Est autem pietas pauperem misereri et distribuere pauperibus bona sua... .

[92] Powicke, *Christian life, etc.*, 143-44.

[93] 119, Tr[2], 289[ra]: Ipse enim rex non est nisi quidam servus et minister Dei.

[94] 33[a], Ar, 78[rb]: Reges sunt quicumque se bene regunt, et faciunt iustitiam in terra sua... .

[95] 5[a], Bs[1], 137[rb]: ... immo omnes erunt reges qui servient ei i.e. omnes regent se qui servient Domino. Nullus enim rex nisi regat se, et hoc secundum precepta Domini.

[96] 19[b], Bs[1], 142[vb]: Sequitur. Et iustitia. Si rex in terra sibi subdita et non propria pacem servari iubeat, in propria vero civitate eius fures spolient et furentur, non dicetur iustitiam observare... .

feitors.[97] One who disobeys his edicts may suffer a capital penalty.[98]

Langton also gave attention to the relationships between the king and his vassals. Again the emphasis is on the maintenance of law and order. The loyalty of one's subject should be investigated before entrusting him with a precious treasure,[99] or a king might take additional precautions: "If a king has some great princes in his kingdom, who are suspected of possible rebellion, he should demand hostages of them, lest they ever desert his cause, and they should hand over their sons."[100] It is incumbent upon the nobles who hold their fiefs of the king to render the services due him.[101] The terms of such service might be embodied in letters or in a charter and if fief — or terms are good, then all the more diligently should care be taken not to give bad service in return.[102] If someone betrayed the king, all his inheritance would devolve unto the king and could not be recovered except by someone of the same family who would win it back by diligence in the royal service.[103]

Feudal obligation consisted primarily of military service, and Langton liked to give examples which illustrated ideals of loyalty on the battlefield and sound military strategy: "A king who is about to do battle against a more powerful enemy ought first to assess his resources as against his opponent's strength. If he finds that he cannot resist, then, while still at a distance, he sends messengers to negotiate a peace..."[104] Any such treaty made by the king would be confirmed by letters that carried the royal seal.[105] If, however, the decision is to engage the enemy, fortifications must be made in strategic locations. Princes order their camps to be pitched on

[97] 74[a], Tr[2], 246[vb]: Sed attendite quod principes terre generaliter puniunt fabricatores false monete... .

[98] 18[b], Le[2], 97[va]: Certe siquis preceptum regis terreni transgreditur, pena capitali punietur... .

[99] 112, Tr[2], 287[vb]: Si rex terrenus aliquem preciosum thesaurum alicui suorum hominum vellet committere, prius multum investigaret an se diligeret... .

[100] 58[b], Le[2], 172[rb]: Sicut si rex habeat aliquos magnos principes in regno suo, qui suspecti sunt quod velint rebellare, petat ab eis obsides ne umquam recedant ab eo, et illi tradant ei filios suos... .

[101] 65[a], Tr[2], 254[ra]: Proceres feudum suum ab eo tenent, et prout incumbit eis debitis obsecuntur serviciis... .

[102] 58[b], Le[2], 173[va]: Siquis haberet feodum a rege, et litteras ut vulgariter loquar vel cartam ubi contineretur eiusmodi servicium quod deberet regi pro feodo, si bonum esset feodum multum diligenter caveret ne pro feodo male serviret... .

[103] 114[b], Le[2], 19[vb]: Lex iuris est quando aliquis prodicionem facit, omnis hereditas eius devolvitur ad regem; nec aliquis potest eam requirere nisi aliquis de genere eiusdem qui strenuitate sua et servicio regis requirat.

[104] 21[b], Le[2], 120[va]: Si rex preliaturus contra forciorem se, primo metitur vires suas, si sapiens est utrum ei resistere possit. Si resistere non potest, dum adhuc longe est mittit nuncios pro pace.

[105] 12, Pa[16], 38[rb]: Nonne si rex terrenus pacem alicui contulisset, et litteras sigillo suo confirmatas de pace servanda ei tradidisset... .

rocks and marshes where there is no easy access for the enemy, not in meadows or in flatlands that are open to invaders.[106] The obligation of defending the camp was paramount.[107] The king shows his great love for his soldiers by donning their uniform,[108] and to the experienced among them he entrusts the rearing and training of his sons.[109] The standard which is the sign of the royal office precedes those who march to battle.[110] So much importance was attached to this symbol that one who disrespectfully lowered the banner of his lord might deservedly be accused of treason.[111] Worse yet were those soldiers who, after the declaration of war, deserted to the ranks of the enemy, denying their lord and king. They are indeed faithless traitors.[112]

From the feudal host on the battlefield, Langton calls attention to other activities in which the king acts for the benefit of his subjects. The excitement of the coronation is evoked in the description of how the people fill the streets to see the king, and delight in the pomp and amusement of the occasion.[113] A royal visit to some poor place is preceded by legates who clear the way and proclaim the advent of the king.[114] On the question of petitions, Langton reminds his audience that one would do well to assure the favor of one of the king's familiars when submitting such a petition: "Should one want to be reconciled with the king, he should approach one of the king's familiars, and seek out his aid and counsel; and he should listen to him in all things so that he shall obtain the king's favor, and then fulfill his order [in deed]."[115] Suitable formality is required for those

[106] 57[b], Le[2], 160[va]: ... sicut principes firmant castra sua in rupibus et paludibus ad quas non est facilis accessus hostibus, non in pratis et locis planis que pervia sunt transeuntibus... . (*Cf.* use of the same *exemplum* in 72[b], Ar, 54[rb]).

[107] 8, Tr[2], 276[rb]: Preterea terrenus rex castrum custodiendum tibi tradidisset, multum deberes sollicitus esse custodiendo illud... .

[108] 44[a], Tr[2], 248[va]: Signum magne dileccionis esset, si rex vestem alicuius militis sui induet... .

[109] 119, Tr[2], 288[vb]: Reges terreni filios suos sapientibus militibus nutriendos et erudiendos tradunt... .

[110] 56, Bs[1], 133[va]: Scitis quod vexilla sunt signa regis que ad bella preferuntur...

[111] 102, Pa[16], 83[va]: Scitis quod signifer regis terreni si vexillum domini sui irreverenter depresserit, merito proditionis accusari poterit.

[112] 112, Tr[2], 288[ra]: Si enim aliquis miles post ictus belli, in medio hostium dominum suum et regem desereret et negaret, nonne infidelissimus et proditor diceretur?

[113] 28[b], Be, 5[vb]: Cum rex terrenus post susceptionem regii diadematis civitates ingreditur, platee inundantur; res preciose ad oblectamina vel oblectamenta videntium exponuntur... .

[114] 34[b], Ar, 129[rb]: ... quod si rex aliquis ad aliquem locum pauperem vellet descendere, multi precurrerent legati, ita adventum Filii Dei multi predixerunt prophete ut Ysayas et alii.

[115] 19[c], Le[2], 42[rb]: Nota. Siquis regi vellet reconciliari, ad aliquem familiarium regis petiturus consilium et auxilium accederet, et in omnibus ut regis gratiam consequeretur audiret, et iussa facto compleret.

having access to the prince. The magnate's messenger has greater precedence in the royal court and is readily received with honor.[116]

Like other contemporary preachers, Langton also attacked the vices of secular kingship: their pursuit of vain glory, the favors they granted to usurers and Jews, their attachment to games and to the hunt to the exclusion of the study of divine law, and the closer attention they gave to the advice of storytellers than to doctors and wise men. These were frequent complaints heard in the sermons of the age.[117] Langton had a few things to say about tyrants who persecuted the Church. When such a tyrant attacks the Church, the Lord shall not forsake her.[118] William Rufus was specifically cited as an example of an oppressor of the Church,[119] a theme that is elaborated in great length by Gerald of Wales in his book on princely instruction.[120] The book of *Maccabees*, Langton said, offers us an instance of a people's refusal to yield to tyranny: It is better for us to die than to disobey ancestral laws.[121] "So does the threat of a tyrant and secular persecution try to shake just men rooted in their faith; but they are invincible against the blows of adversity, and against persecutions, they are firm."[122] This was the tyrant, oppressor of Holy Church and antithesis of the good king who rules himself and his subjects with wisdom and justice.

116 60^{a}, Pa^{16}, 130ra: Sicut enim nuntius alicuius qui magnus et familiaris habetur in curia regis cum gaudio et expedite suscipitur et cum honore... .

117 Lecoy de la Marche, 381.

118 36^{a}, Tr^{2}, 250vb: Cum tyrannus infestat ecclesiam, Dominus eam non relinquit desolatam.

119 36^{b}, Bs^{1}, 144rb: Sicut quondam ut audivi pro certo dici de quodam rege Anglie Rufo pauperum et ecclesie oppressore manifeste ostendit... .

120 See Chap. I, *supra*, p. 8, n. 45.

121 30^{b}, Ar, 119rb: Melius est nobis mori quam patrias leges prevaricari... .

122 54^{b}, Ar, 60rb: Sic comminatio tirannica et persecutio secularis, iustos in fide radicatos concutere nititur, sed contra impulsus adversitatum sunt invincibiles, contra persecutiones rigidi... .

CONCLUSION

STEPHEN Langton emerges in these studies as a very important popular preacher in the evangelical movement in Paris in the second half of the twelfth century. This was an aspect of Langton's life and career that was previously little known and appreciated. We had the brief notices by various chroniclers of the archbishop's preaching to audiences on great occasions. Matthew Paris' life of Stephen Langton also included references to Langton's preaching, especially in North Italy and Flanders. In addition to these scanty remarks in the literature on Langton, we had to consider a long and complex sermon tradition. It was obvious that these sermons, nearly all in manuscript, had to be sorted out and identified before we could know more about the preacher Langton. Much of the preliminary work was done by Dr. Schneyer whose list of sermons and manuscripts was fundamental to the continuation of studies in the Langton sermons. The suggested connections between the sermons and Langton's Paris years demanded verification. We knew that some thirty years of Langton's career were spent in Paris. That these sermons were a part of that Paris experience (which has been proved by their connections with the schools, the liturgy, and references to France) assigns a special significance to their study, in that we now have an additional source from Langton's formative years, before becoming archbishop of Canterbury. Langton's later role in England (in his relationships with King John, the barons, the pope; and in his demands for the freedom of the English church), makes him a personage of considerable historical importance whose thought and activities have a special interest.

Much of this study has been concerned with the verification of texts and the confirmation of the nature of Langton's preaching to his audiences in Paris. Several steps preceded the establishment of a reliable body of source material. It was necessary to classify the manuscripts and the sermons according to the degree of their reliability, and to list the locations of all known texts (and their variants) to facilitate a future collation of the texts. Langton's sermons are scattered in many manuscript collections, often mingled with those of other Paris masters. Hence the importance of this verification procedure.

Our major source of material for these studies consisted of those sermons that appear in two or more authenticated manuscript copies. We have found that Stephen Langton, a notable popular preacher in Paris, was in the mainstream of the preaching of the age. His use of language and his stock of commonplaces and examples underline this as preaching *ad populum.* The range of subject themes, treated in a manner that would reflect the familiar experiences of his listeners, lends additional support to this thesis. Langton's sermon construction and his reliance on Scripture by way of example, direct quotation, and explication by the multiple senses, show him to be not only the traditional preacher, utilizing the various tools and conventions of the *ars praedicandi*, but also an important teacher of his students and his flock.

Langton's popular preaching was probably also intended to provide models and examples to other preachers. As master of theology, Langton had to be skilled in the art of preaching. He also commented on the Bible, and wrote theological questions and an exposition on the sentences of the Lombard. These works show similarities in subject matter with the sermons. Especially in the commentaries the connections with the sermons are prominent, in that sermon themes, if not large portions of the texts, grew out of the master's lectures. Major differences between the sermons and Langton's other writings are to be found in the treatment of subject matter, which reflected an audience of clerics or layfolk. Stephen Langton's students also preached to the people. Their master was himself an example of the effective preacher, who also furnished ideas and models of sermons. The process of the transmission of the sermon texts as manuals illustrates this purpose. The absence of contemporary and topical references may be explained by the nature of the manual which contained sermon exemplars that could be embellished by another preacher.

The content of these sermons eminently suited Langton's audiences of layfolk. They are reflective too of the effort of a reformer whose energies were directed toward the restoration of Christian teaching in all levels of society. These were moral teachings on matters of immediate interest and relevance to lay listeners. Langton's comments on usury and on the proper kind of personal and business relationships were applicable to the Paris bourgeois. His treatment of the themes of kingship and law is again indicative of popular preaching. Master Stephen's commonplaces about earthly kingship have as their intent the translation of moral teachings into the images familiar to medieval folk, and the inculcation of such precepts to serve the purpose of the right order in medieval society. Notably absent from these sermons are discussions on theological themes, such as the trinity, or the sacraments. These were distinctive themes in earlier twelfth-century preaching in the cloister and in the schools. Nor do we find any treatment of Church-State relations beyond Langton's traditional Augustinian view of kings as maintainers of justice and ministers and servants of God. Tyrants as oppressors of the Church must be punished;

but they are far removed: either in the book of *Maccabees* or at best in William Rufus.

Langton's reflections on the Church itself also have this popular quality, intent on reform. The clergy have the important function of instructing the laity and are held, therefore, to stricter requirements of discipline. In the clerical hierarchy, Langton singled out the monk as the closest to the ideal Christian life. When Master Stephen spoke of kings and princes, of law and justice, these were all colored and influenced by the teaching of the Church. In all this, the Church is supreme, for her preachers were teachers; their *exempla* were Bible stories, and the churches themselves, open picture books.

The similes used by Langton to describe the Church were well suited to his lay listeners. Images of ships and vineyards where prelates are helmsmen and saints are vinetenders were readily understandable to his audiences. In these comments on the Church and its clergy, there is, however, to my knowledge, no special discussion of the papal office and no reference to the pope himself. While prayers for the pope may have been added at the close of the sermon and hence may not be indicated in the manuscripts, the absence of any discussion on the papal office may be explained, first, by the nature of his audience. That is to say, that it was not politic for Master Stephen to air views about papal plenitude of power before popular audiences. Second, by the emphasis in the sermons on the priesthood and the episcopate whom Langton regarded as the instruments of reform in local churches. It is, in fact, the duty of the prelate that has Langton's major interest in this popular preaching. What is clear is that Langton's reflections on the Church show him to have the armory of any high prelate of his age who held to the doctrine of the supremacy of the spiritual power in a Christian society. It is also evident that Langton's role as a popular preacher in a movement that had the support of the papacy put him on the side of reform and undoubtedly made him a very attractive candidate for the archbishopric of Canterbury to Innocent III who was interested in a broad plan of reform in the Church.

Before turning to the implications of these conclusions for the later career of Stephen Langton, we might sum up the significance of our findings. With regard to Langton's formative years in Paris, we now have an additional source of information about his activities. The Paris years have been the most obscure in Langton's career since a full account depended upon the study of materials that are largely in manuscript. We have found that Langton, like many of his colleagues who were masters in the schools, was a popular preacher. He was of that circle of scholars who were interested and involved in the education of the laity and in the reform of the Church. These interests anticipate those of the mendicant orders, but it is notable that the beginnings of this popular evangelical movement are to be found among the intellectuals in the schools of Paris in the last part of the twelfth century.

We know more about Langton after his election as archbishop and consecration in 1207. In the period until 1213, when he took up the duties of the see of Canterbury, Langton was in exile. Like Thomas Becket many years before, Stephen Langton found a temporary refuge in the Cistercian monastery at Pontigny where he undoubtedly found time for contemplation and scholarly pursuits. Perhaps it was in these years of exile that these sermons of his were put together in useful handbooks or manuals under the title *Archbishop of Canterbury*. Langton, himself an illustrious preacher, would be aware of the importance of the art in the reinvigoration of Christian teaching among the laity.

Once the conventional popular preacher Stephen Langton returned to England, we see him the active prelate involved in the events that brought him to a position of leadership in the baronial party, to conflicts with John, and to an increasing divergence from the pope. It is of interest, therefore, to examine some of the events in Langton's later career in the light of what we now know of him as a preacher in the evangelical reform movement in Paris.

A notable quality of Langton's earlier preaching career is the conventional way in which he preached and in which he regarded the functions of his office. He was conventional in the tools of his preaching, and in the subject matter of his *exempla* to audiences of layfolk in Paris. While his interest in reform is an essential quality of these sermons, we must emphasize the different contemporary situations in France and in England. Preaching about the traditional themes of kingship and law in France where Philip Augustus was in firm control and where, in addition, there was a favorable climate of opinion among ecclesiastics about the good French kings, was one thing. Returning to England with such doctrines and to conditions that were in a state of flux, was quite another. John was faced with baronial discontent and rebellion and the possibility of foreign invasion. If Langton began to apply ideas of kingship and equity to the contemporary English situation, traditional and conventional ideas could have revolutionary effects. Ideas about the bad, tyrannous kings of England were not unheard of in this period. As we know, Gerald of Wales spoke at length about them in his book on the instruction of princes. Gerald was also a product of the Paris schools and that circle of masters that probably aroused John's suspicions about Langton when he was first elected archbishop. Langton's long residence in the city of the Capetian monarchs and his associations with that clique in Paris that was pro-Gallic would not especially endear Langton to King John.

Nor should we ignore the pro-Becket attitudes of these masters, which seem to have influenced Langton in the manner in which he regarded his office and significantly, in the independent direction of the English church. Langton's views on Becket appear in several instances. His master, Peter the Chanter, commented favorably on Becket's actions against simony in the archiepiscopal household. Caesar of Heisterbach reported that when the masters in Paris were discussing the death of Becket, the Chanter declared that he was a martyr, who was slain while defending the liberty of the Church. Langton himself spent part of his exile in Pontigny where the Cistercians had earlier welcomed the exiled Becket; and in his later career as archbishop of Canterbury, Langton preached on the occasion of the translation of the relics of Becket. By the time Langton returned to England to take up the duties of his archbishopric in 1213, he may well have been convinced that he was himself a successor to Becket. This also may help to explain John's opposition to the archbishop, despite Langton's persistence in carrying out his duties as advisor to the English monarch and as mediator between the barons and the king. If, however, the Becket thesis is a consistent theme in Langton's attitude, then his major effort woud be devoted to securing the freedom of the English church. That this was in fact the case is demonstrated by chapter one in Magna Carta. His alliance with the barons may be interpreted as an effort therefore to obtain this freedom from a wicked and tyrannical king. Recall the *exempla* in the sermons that stressed the importance of the mutual relationship between a king and his vassals.

Yet the issue did not remain so clear cut. When John took the Crusader's oath and became vassal to the pope, the previously harmonious relationship between Langton and Innocent became increasingly discordant. By and large, Langton was in agreement with the overall policy of reform that was being propounded by Innocent and which would form the subject of discussion at the Fourth Lateran Council, which Langton attended; and which would be effected in England by several provincial councils, which Langton supported. So long as these policies did not interefere with Langton's independent line in the English church, there was no essential quarrel with the pope. Once, however, it became apparent that this position was threatened, then the conflict with Rome was inevitable. We have mentioned the conventional way in which Langton regarded the duties of his office. This applies as well to the attitude taken by earlier archbishops of Canterbury toward Rome and papal legates. In the twelfth century, resistance to papal legates resulted in the granting of legatine powers to the archbishop himself. Langton's hostility toward legates from Rome was consistent with this earlier policy.

Stephen Langton challenged Rome on other issues as well. He refused to excommunicate the barons despite threats from Rome. This is all the more understandable in view of his alliance with the baronial opposition to the king. He insisted on the restitution of church property, even though the interdict was prolonged because of the delay in meeting this demand. His emphasis on canonical and valid elections, free of interference from papal legates and of intervention by the king, placed major emphasis on the suitability of the man for the office. The move obtains all the more significance if we apply it to the election of bishops and the importance that Langton attached to the episcopate in his scheme of reform. One must not forget the preacher Langton's preoccupation with the special functions and responsibilities of prelates. On the question of papal taxation, increasing objections by local clergy and magnates indicate a growing resistance in the English church toward these papal policies.

The divergence became all the more pronounced and emphatic once the pope became suzerain of England, a move which Langton himself criticized. Chenu has called attention to the significant shift in Innocent's policy after the French defeat of the Empire at Bouvines in 1214; namely, that this represented a break from the theocratic era of the papacy to an increasing temporal role which was not without its dangers for the Roman church.[123] So long as Innocent was the pope acting in the cause of reform and essentially having the qualities of the good prelate, Langton had no cause for argument. Once, however, papal policies threatened the freedom of the English church and its clergy, and furthermore became temporally allied with the very secular power from which the church wanted its freedom of action, then the conflict between Langton and the pope becomes more comprehensible. Stephen Langton set a pattern for the role of churchmen in the development of the English state during the thirteenth and fourteenth centuries. His initial role in the Magna Carta episode and his subsequent support for the reissue of the Charter, point the way to an ecclesiastical policy that would find natural allies among the baronial opposition to the king. Langton's effort to raise the standard of the English episcopate paved the way for reformers such as Grosseteste and Pecham, and for a wide participation by bishops in high offices in the fourteenth century.[124] While his immediate aims were to secure freedom of action for the English church, in the long run, any check on royal power has as its outcome the development of an effective parliamentary opposition, which was to be the story of a later age, when the laity were in a position to apply the lessons of their clergy. Stephen of the Thundering Tongue was one of the early teachers when he began practicing what he had preached!

123 Chenu, *La théologie au douzième siècle*, *op. cit.*, 398.

124 W. A. Pantin, *The English church in the fourteenth century* (Cambridge, 1955), 11 ff.

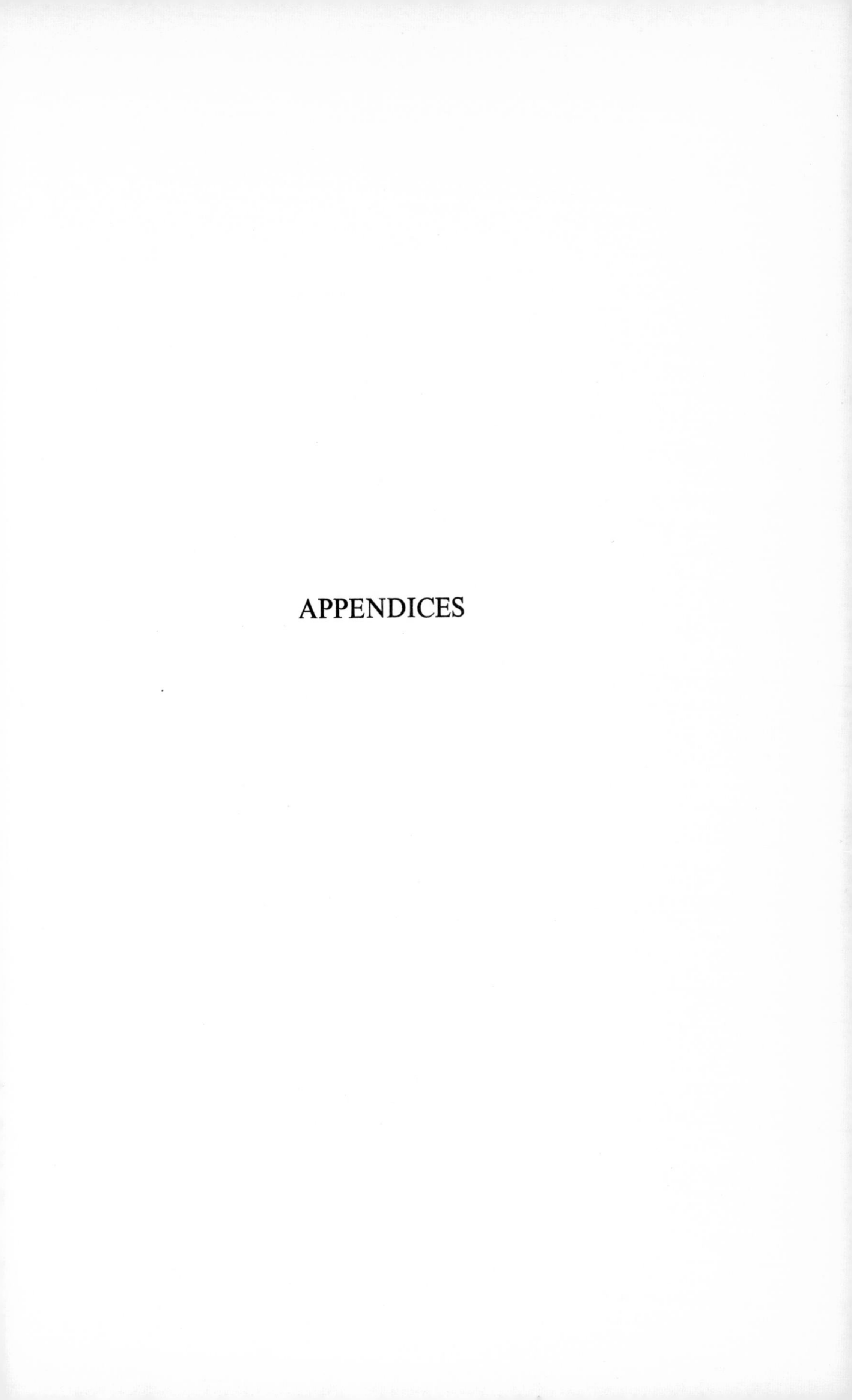

APPENDICES

CLASSIFICATION OF THE MSS

GROUP I. — MSS BEARING AN ATTRIBUTION TO LANGTON

Brugge: Stadsbibliotheek 28, XIII, Parch., 174 fols.
(= Bg[1]) (IRHT-film)

I. *Bibliog.*

De Poorter, *Cat. des mss... de Bruges, op. cit.*, 45-7.
Cf. Cave, II, 282.
Sander, 183.
Lacombe *et al.*, 6.
Glorieux, I, 255.

II. *Contents*

Mag. Steph. super iiii[or] Regum[1] et sermones eiusdem...
f. 2[ra]-21[vb]: Sermones magistri Stephani Cantuariensis archiepiscopi (contemp. hand, f. 2[r])

III. Sermons in the series attributed to SL: (*26*)

1) Doubtful; author unknown (2)
f. 10[va] Statue tibi speculam
19[ra] Ascendens christus

2) Copies and variants in other named MSS. (11)
Sermons No. 13[c], 17[c], 19[b], 50[d], 64[a], 70[a], 99[b], 101[b], 116[d], 118[b], 122[b].
Copies in other named MSS. (13)
2, 24, 35, 45, 52, 56, 59, 63, 73, 84, 108, 111, 113.

(N.B. All these sermons appear in Bs[1]. Copies may also be found in Le[2], Pa[11], Tr[2], Tr[4], PS).

Brugge: Stadsbibl. 278, XIV, Parch., 77 fols.
(= Bg[3])

I. *Bibliog.*

De Poorter, 314.
Lacombe *et al.*, 6.
Glorieux, I, 255.
Landgraf, *Einführung, etc.*, 127.

II. *Contents*

(Flyleaf:) Sermones Stephani Cantuariensis
f. 4ra: Sermones Steph. Cant. Arch. (contemp. hand)
76rb: Sermo Steph. Cant.
69ra: Oratio domina exposita a dom. Steph. Cant. archiep.

1 Langton's commentaries on Kings belong to the period 1187-93, while he was in Paris. Lacombe *et al.*, 166.

III. The series of sermons from f. 4ra has generally been attributed to Langton: (*40*)

1) f. 4ra-33vb Nicholas of Clairvaux[2] (19)
33vb Epistola, St. Bernard (1)
57ra-69ra Author unknown (6)
69ra Oratio (*supra*) (1)
71ra Author unknown (3)

2) *Copies and var. in other named MSS*:
77b, 118a. (2)
Copies in other named MSS:
9, 14, 75, 102, 121. (5)
Var. in other named MSS:
51b. (1)
Named only in this MS:
(Class II): Si abstuleris de medio (1)
Other attrib.:
(Cl. VI): Et quietum studium (1)

(Copies of the sermons are to be found in Bs¹, CUL, Le², PS, Tr², Tr⁴).

Brussels: Bibliothèque Royale II. 953, XIII, Parch., 184 fols. (= Bs¹)

I. *Bibliog.*

J. van den Gheyn, *Cat. des mss de la Bibl. Roy. de Belgique* (13 vols. Bruxelles 1901-48), III, 170, no. 1871.
Lacombe *et al.*, 6.
Glorieux, I, 255.
Schneyer, "Sermonesliste, etc.," 161 (from f. 65ra-151ra)
D'Alverny, 128, 134, 137.

II. *Contents*

f. 1v *Ex-libris*, Sir Thom. Phillips
2 Liber sancte Marie de Camberone
(Flyleaf:) In hoc volumine continentur isti libri Steph. Cant. archiep. super Genesim.[3]
Item eiusdem sermones numero LXXXIIII
Excepta (*sic*) quedam ex glosis Petri
Cantoris Parisiensis super Psalterium.
f. 65ra Sermo mag. Steph. in die sancto pent.

III. *Sermons in the series attributed to Langton* (*84*)

1) f. 49ra-64vb Author unknown (15)
87vb Ascendens christus[4] (1)
91vb In Syon erit salvatio (1)

[2] Schneyer, "Sermonesliste, etc.." 161, n. 12. Lacombe *et al.*, 6 call attention to a collection of 40 sermons in Arsenal MS 400, which allegedly appear in both MSS. See *infra*.

[3] Langton's commentary on the Heptateuch belongs to his Paris years, before 1206. Lacombe *et al.*, 163.

[4] *Inc*: Multiplex legitur descensus, multiplex ascensus... D'Alverny (128) assigns to Alain de Lille.

93vb	Egredimini filie Syon: Sicut nemo	(1)
96va	Statue tibi speculam	(1)
98vb	Dilectus meus descendit[5]	(1)
129ra	Ecce sacerdos magnus	(1)
138va	Iacet securis	(1)

2) *Copies and var. in other named MSS*: (15)
13^{c}, 17^{c}, 19^{b}, 50^{d}, 64^{a}, 70^{a}, 72^{a}, 77^{b}, 92^{b}, 99^{b}, 101^{b}, 114^{a}, 116^{d}, 118^{b}, 122^{b}.

Copies in other named MSS: (20)
2, 4, 10, 12, 14, 24, 35, 41, 45, 52, 56, 59, 63, 73, 75, 84, 102, 108, 111, 113.

Var. in other named MSS: (9)
5^{a}, 6^{b}, 30^{c}, 33^{b}, 36^{b}, 66^{b}, 78^{b}, 98^{d}, 106^{b}.

Named only in this MS: (16)

(Cl. II) Colligite que superaverunt
Convertetur ad Dominum
Deus Hebreorum vocavit nos
Ecce ego mittam piscatores
Frange esurienti panem tuum
Nescitis quia membra vestra
Prudentes virgines acceperunt oleum
Qui descendunt mare in navibus
Tempus est spargendi lapides
Vide arcum et benedic eum
Vincenti dabo

(Cl. III) Apertis thesauris
Puer natus est nobis
Sint lumbi vestri
Templum Dei estis
Trahe me post te

Other attrib.: (2)

(Cl. VI) Militia est vita hominis
Salvum me fac Deus

(Copies of the sermons are to be found in Bg^{1}, Bg^{3}, CUL, Le^{2}, OM, Pa^{11}, PS, Tr^{2}, Tr^{4}).

Cambridge: Corpus Christi Coll. 450 (Misc. R
(T. James 386, XIII-XIV, Vellum, 156 fols.
(= CCC 450) (IRHT-film)

I. *Bibliog.*

James, *Descrip. cat. of the MSS in the lib. of Corp. Chr. Coll., Camb.*, II, 364-72.

II. *Contents*

(291): Stephanus (de Langton) arch. ad suffraganeos suos de electione sua in archiepiscopum.

[5] Although a theme appearing in the Schneyer list, neither the incipit nor the contents of the sermon justify considering it as Langton's. Similarly elsewhere, where Langton themes appear in sub-section (1).

III. Single copy; listed by Schneyer among the MSS. Text does not have standard sermon form.

Cambridge: Corpus Christi Coll. 459 (N. 14
(T. James 178, XIII, Vellum, 162 fols.
(= CCC 459)

I. *Bibliog.*

James, *Descrip. cat. of the MSS in the lib. of Corp. Chr. Coll., Camb.*, II, 383-88.
Tanner, 468.
Lacombe *et al.*, 6.
Glorieux, I, 255.
Landgraf, *Einführung, etc.*, 44.

II. *Contents*

f. 147va: Sermo mag. Steph. Cantuar. Arch. (contemp. hand)
Ostende nobis (Cl. I, No. 68^{a})
148va: Item sermo eiusdem cuius est supra. Dominus prope est (No. 23^{b})
(Copies of the sermons in Pa^{11} and Tr^{4}. Var. in Le^{2} and Tr^{2}).

Cambridge: Univ. Lib. Ee.vi.10, XV-XVI,[6] Parch., 187 fols.
(= CUL)

I. *Bibliog.*

Cat. of the MSS in the lib. of the Univ. of Camb., II, 258-60, No. 1102.
Lacombe *et al.*, 6.
Glorieux, I, 255.

II. *Contents*

f. 108^{r}: Sermo mag. Steph. Arch. Cant. ad monachos.
Que est ista que progreditur
(Cl. I, No. 77^{b})
Copies of the sermon in Bs^{1}, Bg^{3}, Le^{2}, PS. A var. in Pa^{11}.
111^{r}: Sermo mag. Steph. Arch.
Qui sunt isti
113^{r}: Sermo mag. Steph. Arch. Cant.
In veteri
117^{r}: Sermo mag. Steph. Arch. Cant.
Despondi de enim vos
(In each of these, the rubric is in a contemp. hand. The above three sermons are listed in Cl. II. I have found no other copies or variants).

Leipzig: Universitäts-Bibliothek 364, XIII, Parch., 138 fols.
(= Le^{1})

I. *Bibliog.*

R. Helssig, *Katalog der HSS der Univ.-Bibl. zu Leipzig* (Leipzig, 1926-35), 540-42.

[6] This is the date assigned to the MS in the catalogue description. The above sermons, however, are written in a thirteenth century hand. T. J. H. Brown, Professor of Paleography at Kings Coll., London, supports my earlier date.

Cf. Feller, 97.
Tanner, 468.
Cave, II, 282.
Oudin, II, 1701.
Landgraf, *Einführung, etc.*, 127.

II. *Contents*

f. 123: (contemp. hand) Sermo magistri Steph. de nativ. sancte Marie. Numquid producis luciferum (Cl. I, No. 58^{b})
134: Item de eadem. Orietur stella (No. 67)

(Copies of both sermons in Le^{2})

Leipzig: Univ.-Bibl. 443, XIII, Parch., 196 fols.
(= Le^{2})

I. *Bibliog.*

Helssig, *cit. supra*, 716-18.
Cf. Feller, 150.
Cave, II, 282.
Oudin, II, 1701.
Landgraf, *Einführung, etc.*, 127 challenges attribution of these sermons to Langton, except f. 189^{v} (*infra*).
Schneyer, "Sermonesliste, etc.," 161, 163.

II. *Contents*

f. 1: (contemp. hand) Steph. Cant. arch. sive Steph. Langthon sive de Linguatona, Sermones de tempore et de sanctis.
189^{v}: Steph. Cant., Ad sacerdotes de decem plagis.[7]

III. *Sermons in the series attributed to Langton* (*139*)

1) *Doubtful; author unknown.* (4)

f. 21vb Rex noster coronatus
32vb Media nocte clamor
61va Miserere mei domine
186vb Homo quid nobilis

2) *Copies and var. in other named MSS:* (14)

13^{a}, 23^{c}, 28^{a}, 36^{a}, 38^{c}, 50^{a}, 54^{b}, 60^{a}, 74^{a}, 77^{b}, 81^{c}, 101^{b}, 116^{a}, 118^{a}.

Copies in other named MSS: (35)

3, 7^{a}, 9, 10, 11, 12, 16^{a}, 20, 27, 29, 34^{a}, 42, 43, 47, 48, 49, 53, 55, 58^{b}, 61, 63, 65^{a}, 67, 69, 73, 76, 85, 86, 87^{c}, 88, 89^{a}, 90, 91, 102, 112.

Var. in other named MSS: (35)

5^{b}, 6^{c}, 18^{b}, 19^{c}, 21^{b}, 22^{d}, 26^{b}, 31^{b}, 33^{a}, 40^{a}, 44^{b}, 46^{b}, 57^{b}, 64^{b}, 68^{c}, 70^{c}, 72^{c}, 78^{c}, 80^{b}, 82^{a}, 93^{b}, 97^{c}, 97^{d}, 98^{c}, 98^{e}, 103^{c}, 104^{b}, 105^{a}, 109^{c}, 109^{d}, 110^{b}, 114^{b}, 115^{b}, 117^{d}, 122^{a}.

(Copies of the sermons in Bg^{1}, Bg^{3}, Bs^{1}, CUL, Le^{1}, OM, Pa^{11}, PS, Tr^{2}, Tr^{4}, Pa^{14}).

Named only in this MS: (48)

(Cl. II) Amice, commoda mihi tres panes
Beati mortui qui in Domino moriuntur

[7] See *Hist. litt. de la France* (Paris, 1835), XVIII, 63.

Beatus es Simon bar Jona
Beatus ille servus
Convertimini ad me in toto corde
Cum inducerent puerum Jesum
Dilectus meus mihi
Ecce ascendimus Jerosolimam
Ecce positus est hic
Ecce qui mollibus vestiuntur
Ecce venit ad templum sanctum suum
Ecce vicit leo
Ego sum pastor bonus
Emitte spiritum bonum
Erat Jesus eiciens demonum
Estote imitatores mei
Et veniat super nos salutare tuum
Gaudete in Domino semper (2 copies)
Homo quidam erat dives
Homo quidam fecit cenam magnam
In diebus illis suscitabit
In salutari tuo anima mea
Iohannes cum audisset
Ipse vos baptizabit Spiritu Sancto
Nemo potest duobus dominis servire
Numquid elevabis in nebula
Numquid ingressus es
Obsecro vos tamquam advenas
Obtulerunt pro eo par turturum
Petite ut gaudium vestrum plenum sit
Qui crediderit in me
(Et) Qui preibant et qui sequebantur
Salvatorem expectamus
Simile est regnum celorum homini regi qui fecit nuptias
Surge tolle lectum tuum
Vexilla regis prodeunt
Vos sacerdotes Domini vocabimini

(Cl. III) Accingere cilicio
Apertis thesauris
Oculi mei semper ad Dominum — Isaias: Cor
——— In dominica precedenti
Petite et accipietis
Puer natus est nobis
Surgite, vigilemus
Trahe me post te — Karissimi, hodie Christus
——— Ne expectetis a me
Videte ne quis vestrum sit fornicator

Other attrib.: (3)

(Cl. VI) Et quietum studium
Memento quod cinis es
Misereor super turbam

London: British Museum, Arundel 292, XIII, Vellum, 116 fols.
(= LoA)

I. *Bibliog.*

Cat. of Arundel and Burney MSS (London, 1840), 86-87.
Tanner, 468.
Hist. litt., XVIII, 63.
C. E. Maurice, *Stephen Langton* (n.p. 1872), 103-04.
Norgate, *DNB*, XI, 569.
Lecoy de la Marche, 92-93; 195-98. (Doubts authenticity of the attribution. *Cf.* BN MS, lat. 16497, f. 74).
Glorieux, I, 259 (lists with spurious writings).

II. *Contents*

f. 38^r: Sermo mag. Steph. de Langedune arch. Cant. De sancta maria... Bele aliz... (See Cl. II, *inc.* Benedictione apostolica).
Ed. T. Wright, *Biog. Brit. Lit.* (2 vols., London, 1842-46), II, 446-47.
(Part. ed.): M. de la Rue, "Dissertation on the lives and works of several Anglo-Norman poets," *Archaeologia*, XIII (London, 1800), 231.

London: British Museum, Royal 8.A.X., *ca.* 1300, Vellum, 263 fols.
(= Lo^3)

I. *Bibliog.*

Warner & Gilson, *Cat. of Roy. MSS*, *op. cit.*, I, 212.
Glorieux, I, 255.
Cf. Hymn, V. Fortunatus: see U. Chevalier, *Repert. Hymn.* (6 vols., Louvain-Bruxelles, 1892-1920), I, No. 1889; and Migne, *PL*, 88, 265.

II. *Contents*

f. 36^r-53^v: (Colophon) Sermones Steph. mag. Cant. Arch. super ymnum Ave maris stella. (See Cl. II).
(See MSS Lo^2 and Lo^4 for anonymous copies).

Oxford: Magdalen Coll. 168, XIII-XIV, Parch., 162 fols.
(= OM)

I. *Bibliog.*

H. O. Coxe, *Catalogus codicum mss qui in coll. aulisque Oxon. hodie adservantur* (Oxon. 1852), ii, 77-78.
Powicke, *SL*, 170. (A table of 78 sermons including 18 ascribed to Langton on f. 50^v-51^v in the MS is reproduced on pp. 170-74; the incipits of the 11 extant sermons ascribed to Langton, on 175-76).

II. *Contents*

See table on f. 50^v-51^v.

III. *Extant sermons attributed to Langton* (*11*)

Copies and var. in other named MSS: (3)
81^c, 109^e, 120^b.
Copies in other named MSS: (3)
41, 49, 61.
(Copies of the sermons in Bs^1, Le^2, PS, Pa^{11}, Tr^4. For the themes of sermons no longer extant, but attributed to Langton, see Chapter II, *supra*).

Named only in this MS: (5)

(Cl. II) Benedicat nos Deus
Gaude et letare filia Edom
In omni ore quasi mel indulcabitur
Rorate celi desuper
(Cl. III) Sint lumbi vestri

Paris: Bibliothèque nationale, lat. 3227, I H XIII, Parch., 170 fols. (= Pa²)

I. *Bibliog.*

Ph. Lauer, *Bibl. nat.: Cat. gén. des mss lat.* (4 vols., Paris, 1939-58), IV,383-84.
(Regius 4126 in *Cat. mss Bibl. Reg.* (1744), III, 389).
Cave, II, 282.
Oudin, II, 1701.
Feret, I, 279.
Glorieux, I, 255.

II. *Contents*

f. 158ʳ: Sermo mag. Steph. Cant. arch. in assumpt. b. Dei genitricis virg. Marie. Vidi et super firmamentum...

(I have found no other copies of this sermon).

Paris: Bibl. nat., lat., 14859, XIII, Parch., 339 fols. (= Pa¹¹) (IRHT-file)

I. *Bibliog.*

Delisle, *Invent. des mss... St. Victor*, 53.
Cf. Oudin, II, 1701.
Cave, II, 282.
Feret, I, 279.
Lecoy de la Marche, 90.
Bourgain, 50 (on f. 205 sqq, sermons of Peter Cantor)
Lacombe, *Prévostin...*, 184.
Powicke, *SL*, 168.
Lacombe *et al.*, 6.
Glorieux, I, 255.
Landgraf, *Einführung, etc.*, 114.
Schneyer, "Sermonesliste, etc.," 161-62.
D'Alverny, 14, 121ff.

II. *Contents*

f. 178ʳ: Table of themes and rubrics of 75 sermons. (Nearly all the sermons are identified by author. See *supra*, Chapter III, p. 58, n. 127).

III. *Sermons from f. 209ᵛᵃ-282ʳᵇ attrib. to SL:* (*38*)

1) f. 225ʳᵃ Est puer unus hic (1)
(No attrib. in MS. Note IRHT attrib. to SL; see CL. V).
232ᵛᵇ Vulnerasti cor meum (1)
(Listed by Schneyer; no other copy; see Cl. IV).

2) *Copies and var. in other named MSS:* (7)
22^{a} (no attrib. in the MS) 23^{b}, 26^{a}, 54^{a}, 70^{a}, 83^{a}, 110^{a}.
Copies in other named MSS: (10)
16^{a}, 27, 47, 49, 69, 71, 86, 90, 91, 100^{a}.
Var. in other named MSS: (7)
17^{a}, 51^{a}, 74^{b}, 77^{a}, 94^{a}, 97^{a}, 99^{a}.
(Copies of the sermons in Bg^{1}, Bs^{1}, CCC 459, Le^{2}, OM, PS, Tr^{2}, Tr^{4}).
Named only in this MS: (11)
(Cl. II) Convertentur sedentes
Ecce Dominus vocat nos
Noli timere filia Sion
Ponite corda vestra
Reddet Deus mercedem
Si sciret paterfamilias
Solve iubente Domino
Surrexit Dominus vere
(Cl. III) Justus cor suum tradidit
Puer natus est nobis
Oculi mei semper ad Dominum
Other attrib. (1)
(Cl. VI) Homo natus de muliere

Paris: Bibl. nat., lat., 15025, XIII, Parch., 251 fols.
(= Pa^{14}) (IRHT-file-film)

I. *Bibliog.*
Delisle, *Invent. des mss... St. Victor*, 66.
MS not listed by Schneyer. For MS reference, see BN MS, lat. 2915, described in *Cat. gén.*, III, 274.

II. *Contents*
f. 222vb: (Contemp. hand): Lectio M. Stephani de Long. quam fecit in sua inceptione. Legimus filios Israel... (Cl. I, No. 48).
(Copy of the sermon in Le^{2}).

Paris: Bibl. Ste.-Gen. 1422 (D.I.27^{2}), XIII, Parch., 151 fols.
(= PS) (IRHT-file-film)

I. *Bibliog.*
Ch. Kohler, *Cat. des mss de la Bibl. Ste-Gen.* (2 vols., Paris, 1893-96), II, 16-17.
Feret, I, 279.
Lecoy de la Marche, 90.
Dargan, I, 233.
Powicke, *SL*, 168.
Lacombe *et al.*, 6.
Glorieux, I, 255.

II. *Contents*
f. 1: (Hand of XVIII) Mag. Steph. de Lingua Tonante
4: (Contemp. but other hand) Incipiunt sermones mag. Steph. de Linguatonante.

III. *Sermons from f. 4r-149r attrib. to SL:* (*60*)

1) *Sermons not listed by Schneyer; doubtful* (18)

f. 60v	Radix mea aperta est
68v	Ego sum panis vivus
84v	Comedi favum meum
95r	Reddite que sunt Dei Deo
97r	Justum deduxit Dominus
98r	Beati qui custodiunt iudicium
98v	In die vocabo Elyachim
100v	Ascendam in palmam[8]
106r	Tempus est ut iudicium
109r	Illos qui de mundo sunt
112r	Reddet Deus laborum
119r	Vir erat in terra Hus
120r	Assumpsit Ihesus Petrum
121v	Exaudi Domine vocem meam
125v	Vos estis genus electum
131r	Arcum meum ponam
137r	Adhuc esce
138v	Dispone domui

2) *Copies and var. in other named MSS:* (13)
6a, 13a, 22a, 26a, 38c, 50a, 50a (*sic*), 54b, 77b, 80a, 81a, 83a, 92b.
Copies in other named MSS: (22)
1a, 3, 3 (*sic*), 11, 12, 16a, 20, 32, 34a, 37a, 39a, 41, 42, 55, 55 (*sic*), 62, 75, 79, 88, 96, 119, 121.
Var. in other named MSS: (6)
17b, 38a, 46a, 57a, 60b, 70b.

(Copies of the sermons in Bg1, Bs1, Le2, OM, Bg3, CUL, Pa11, Tr2, Tr4).
Named only in this MS: (1)
(Cl. II) Sollempnitates vestras odivit

Rouen: Bibl. munic. 1468 (U. 136), XIII, Parch., 382 fols.
(= Ro) (IRHT-film)

I. *Bibliog.*

Cat. gén. des mss des bibl. publ. de France: Dép. I: Rouen (ed. H. Omont, Paris, 1886), 436-39.

Landgraf, *Einführung, etc.*, 126.

II. *Contents*

f. 377v: (Contemp. hand): Sermo mag. Steph. Cant. arch. Beatus vir qui in sapientia morabitur... Qui miserias hujus vite... (Cl. II)

No other copies.

Troyes: Bibl. munic. 862, XIII, Vellum, 146 fols.
(= Tr1)

I. *Bibliog.*

Cat. gén. des mss des bibl. publ. des départ. (Quarto ser. 7 vols., Paris, 1849-85), II; Troyes, 356-57.

[8] See Schneyer, *Wegweiser, op. cit.*, 41.

(Clairvaux O.83)
Cf. Oudin, II, 1701.
Cave, II, 282.
Lecoy de la Marche, 503.
Powicke, *SL*, 43, 169. (*Cf. Annal. Wav.*, II, 277)
Lacombe *et al.*, 6.
Glorieux, I, 255.
Landgraf, *Einführung, etc.*, 118.

II. *Contents*

f. 85rb: Sermo mag. Steph. Arch. Cant. ad populum. In Deo speravit... (Ed. G. Lacombe, *Cath. Hist. Rev.*, XV [1930], 408-20)
89rb: Eiusdem sermo in festo sancto martini. Justum deduxit Dominus...
121rb: Sermo mag. Steph. Cant. arch. in passione Domini. Cum venisset Saul...

No other copies. See Cl. II.

Troyes: Bibl. munic. 1100, XIII, Vellum, 309 fols.
(= Tr^{2}) (IRHT-file-film)

I. *Bibliog.*

Cat. gén., etc., cit. supra, II, 452-53.
(Clairvaux D.58)
Cf. Oudin, II, 1701.
Cave, II, 282.
Lecoy de la Marche, 503.
Powicke, *SL*, 169.
Lacombe *et al.*, 6.
Glorieux, I, 255.
Schneyer, "Sermonesliste, etc.," 161-62, 164.

II. *Contents*

f. 1: Liber sancte Marie Clarevallis. (Also f. 307^{v}). (See *Hist. litt.*, XVIII, 50-66).
238^{r}: (slightly later hand): Sermones magistri Steph. de Languetone numero LXX^{ta}

III. *Sermons from f. 238ra-307vb attrib. to SL:* (*74*)

1) f. 303va-305va Geoffrey of Babio[9] (IRHT) (4)
306va Proposuit David premium (1)
307vb Trahe me post te — Fiduciam habemus (1)

2) *Copies and var. in other named MSS:* (15)
6^{a}, 13^{a}, 22^{a}, 26^{a}, 28^{a}, 31^{a}, 36^{a}, 54^{a}, 72^{a}, 74^{a}, 81^{a}, 101^{a}, 114^{a}, 116^{a}, 118^{a}.
Copies in other named MSS: (24)
1^{a}, 3, 7^{a}, 8, 16^{a}, 24, 25^{a}, 29, 37^{a}, 39^{a}, 43, 53, 62, 65^{a}, 69, 76, 89^{a}, 95^{a}, 96, 100^{a}, 107^{a}, 112, 119, 121.
Var. in other named MSS: (15)
15^{a}, 18^{a}, 19^{a}, 21^{a}, 23^{a}, 30^{a}, 44^{a}, 66^{a}, 93^{a}, 98^{a}, 103^{a}, 104^{a}, 106^{a}, 109^{a}, 120^{a}.

(Copies of the sermons in Bg^{1}, Bg^{3}, Bs^{1}, Le^{2}, Pa^{11}, PS, Tr^{4}).

[9] See Chap. III, p. 41, n. 26.

Named only in this MS: (12)

(Cl. II) Christus assistens pontifex
Draco persecutus est mulierem
Omnis arbor que non facit fructum bonum
Quasi myrrha electa dedit suavitatem
Scimus quoniam diligentibus Deum
Super lapidem unum septem oculi sunt
Tres sunt qui testimonium dant
Ubicumque fuerit corpus

(Cl. III) Exemplum dedi vobis
Omne datum optimum
Petite et accipietis
Surgite vigilemus

Other attrib. (2)

(Cl. VI) Justum deduxit Dominus
Memento quod cinis es

Troyes: Bibl. munic. 1367, XIII, Vellum, 198 fols.
(= Tr^4)

I. *Bibliog.*

Cat. gén., etc., cit. supra, II, 568.
(Clairvaux M.54)
Cf. Oudin, II, 1701.
Cave, II, 282.
Lecoy de la Marche, 90, 503.
Powicke, *SL*, 169.
Lacombe *et al.*, 6.
Glorieux, I, 255.

II. *Contents*

f. 1^r-2^r: Table of 84 themes and rubrics.
15^r: (Contemp. hand): Incipiunt sermones mag. Steph. de Linguet. et quorumdam aliorum magistrorum Parisiensium ad populum.

III. *Sermons from f. 15^r-197^r, including those attrib. to SL:* (*80*)

1) The following are of unknown authorship; where themes used by SL appear, comparisons of incipits and of texts indicate that the sermon cannot be assigned to SL. (24)

f. 15^r Surgite vigilemus[10]
30^r In sole posuit taber
51^v Ascendit Deus in iubil.
53^r De antichristo primo
55^v Timor dicit morieris
63^r Ponite corda vestra
77^v Surrexit Dominus
84^r Egeni et pauperes
91^v Accingere cilicio

[10] *Wegweiser*, 472.

101^{v} Erat Jesus eiciens
105^{v} Dilectus meus descendit
115^{v} Ascendite in monte
116^{v} Emitte spiritum tuum
119^{r} Facite vobis sacculos
121^{r} Ductus est Jesus
122^{r} Fili memorare
135^{r} Petite et accipietis
147^{v} Veni in ortum meum
155^{v} Qui vestrum habebit amicum
157^{r} Confitemini alterutrum
165^{r} Qui Christi sunt
167^{r} Novate vobis novale
176^{v} Tempus est ut iudicium
194^{r} Est puer unus hic: Verba que propos

2) *Copies and var. in other named MSS:* (13)
13^{c}, 23^{c}, 26^{a}, 31^{a}, 54^{b}, 60^{a}, 68^{a}, 80^{a}, 99^{b}, 101^{a}, 109^{e}, 110^{a}, 120^{b}.

Copies in other named MSS: (26)
3, 4, 8, 9, 25^{a}, 29, 32, 34^{a}, 39^{a}, 41, 42, 49, 63, 69, 71, 75, 79, 85, 87^{c}, 89^{a}, 95^{a}, 96, 100^{a}, 107^{a}, 112, 119.

Var. in other named MSS: (11)
15^{b}, 28^{b}, 40^{b}, 70^{d}, 82^{b}, 83^{b}, 92^{a}, 94^{b}, 105^{b}, 115^{a}, 117^{a}.

(Copies of the sermons in Bg^{1}, Bg^{3}, CCC 459, Bs^{1}, Le^{2}, OM, Pa^{11}, PS, Tr^{2}. For the themes and rubrics of sermons no longer extant, but corresponding to Langton sermons in other named MSS, see Chapter II, *supra*).

Named only in this MS: (4)
(Cl. II) Tribularer si nescirem misericordiam tuam
Tu es qui venturus es
(Cl. III) Si quis cognoverit plagam
Videte ne quis vestrum sit fornicator

Other attrib. (2)
(Cl. VI) Justum deduxit Dominus
Memento quod cinis es

CLASSIFICATION OF THE MSS

GROUP II. — MSS CONTAINING ANONYMOUS TEXTS

Amiens: Bibl. munic., Fonds Lescalopier 30 (1073), XII, Parch., 145 fols. (unnumbered)
(= Am)

I. *Bibliog.*

Cat. gén. des mss des bibl. publ. de France: Dép. XIX: Amiens (ed. E. Coyecque, Paris, 1893), 475-76.

II. *Summary of contents*

1) Author unknown — Simile est regnum celorum homini patrifamilias

2) (Cl. IV) Sermo in Epiphania. Obtulerunt ei munera
Copy in Ar; var. in Pa³, Pa¹²

(Cl. I) Ecce vir prudens (No. 31ᵇ)
Copy in Le²
Var. in Tr², Tr⁴, Pa¹⁶ (anon.)

Egredietur fons de domo Domini (33ᵃ)
Copy in Le², Ar (anon.)
Var. in Bs¹

Plurima turba straverunt (70ᵃ)
Copies in Bg¹, Bs¹, Pa¹¹, Bs²
Var. in PS, Le², Tr⁴; Ar, Be, PA¹ (anon.)

(Cl. VI) Si conplantati fuerimus
Joh. de Abevilla; see Pa¹¹.

Homo natus de muliere
Copy in Pa¹¹, Pa¹⁵, Ni (anon.).

Arras: Bibl. munic. 222 (334), XIII, Vellum, 190 fols.
(= Ar)

I. *Bibliog.*

Cat. gén. des mss des bibl. publ. des départ., *op. cit.*, IV; Arras, 136.
Schneyer, "Sermonesliste, etc.," 161, 163.

II. *Summary of contents*

f. 3^{r-v}: Table of the contents of the MS: *Liber sermonum.*
The MS contains *106* extant sermons: (*106*)

1) Author unknown; doubtful

f. 21rb	Comedi favum
154rb	Proposuit David premium
172ra	Psallite Deo qui ascendit
173vb	Facta est quasi navis
179va	Ecce venit rex occurramus[11]

[11] *Wegweiser*, 191, 210.

2) (Cl. IV) A a a Domine Deus (23)
Auris mea audivit te
Consideravit semitas domus sue
Continuo relectis retibus
Deridetur iusti simplicitas
Dilectus meus descendit
Dissipat impios
(In Is. legitur): Dominus dedit mihi
Ecce quam bonum
Hec est dies, quam fecit Dominus
Hoc sentite
Introduxerunt archam Domini
Medicina omnium
Obtulerunt Magi Domino
Omnia vestra sunt
Ostende nobis Domine faciem tuam
Sicut ovis ad occisionem ducetur
Spiritus Domini replevit orbem terrarum
Stabat Jesus iuxta stagnum
Sub umbra illius
Veni in hortum meum
Vivit in Christo gemma sacerdotum
Zachee festinans descende
(Cl. V) Dominus prope est (2 copies) (8)
Ecce rex venit
Ecce sacerdos magnus
Homo quidam fecit cenam magnam
Semen quod cecidit in terram bonam
Tu es, qui venturus es
Viri Galilei quid statis
(Cl. II) Convertentur sedentes in umbra eius (14)
Convertimini ad me
Ecce ego mittam piscatores
Ecce positus est hic
Ecce vicit leo
Emitte spiritum tuum
Gaudete in Domino semper
In ingressu oraculi fecit Salomon
Nemo potest duobus dominis servire
Numquid elevabis in nebula
Prudentes virgines acceperunt
Quasi myrrha electa
Scimus quoniam diligentibus Deum
Sollempnitates vestras
(Cl. III) Apertis thesauris (5)
Justus cor suum tradidit
Omne datum optimum
Si quis cognoverit plagam
Videte ne quis vestrum sit fornicator

(Cl. I) (47)
Sermons No. 1[a], 3, 4, 7[a], 11, 13[a], 14, 16[b], 17[b], 18[a], 22[b], 25[b], 26[a], 26[b], 29, 30[b], 33[a], 34[b], 36[c], 39[a], 42, 46[a], 51[b], 54[b], 55, 58[a], 60[b], 62, 68[d], 69, 70[b], 72[b], 75, 77[b], 78[a], 79, 80[a], 87[c], 94[a], 97[b], 98[b], 101[a], 103[b], 109[c], 110[a], 115[a], 118[a] (Copies in Bs^1, Bg^3, Le^2, Pa^{11}, PS, Tr^2, Tr^4).

(Cl. VI) Memento quod cinis es (4)
Misereor super turbam
Que est ista que ascendit per desertum
Templum Dei sanctum est

Barcelona: Archivo de la Corona de Aragon, Ripoll 205 (187), XIII, Parch., 160 fols. (= Bar)

I. *Bibliog.*

"Códices Manuscritos de Ripoll," *Revista de Archivos Bibliotecas y Museos*, XXXV (1931), 162.

Z. Garcia, *Bibliotheca Patrum Latinorum Hispaniensis: II. Bd. nach den Aufzeichnungen Rudolf Beers* (Wien, 1915), 91.

II. *Summary of contents*

Otro libro de sermones; MS (num. mod. 16).

f. 10v: Sermo in capite ieiunii — Qui audit verba mea — Descendit pluvia...
(*Cf.* Cl. VI, Memento quod cinis es)

15r: Sermo in ram. palm. — Noli timere filia Sion — Fratres, si coram vobis...
(Cl. I, No. 51[a], copy in Pa^{11}; var., Bg^3)

Basel: Universitäts-Bibliothek, A.IX.2, mid XV, paper, 299 fols. (= Bas)

I. *Bibliog.*

G. Binz, *Die Deutschen HSS der Oeffentlichen Bibl. der Univ. Basel* (Basel, 1907), 110-26, I, HSS, Abt. A.

Schneyer, "Sermonesliste, etc.," 161 (f. 244 ?)

II. *Summary of contents*

f. 244r: Audite celi que loquor. Terret me consciencia mea scrutantem latebras...

Theme does not appear elsewhere, but notice the incipit (*Terret me*, etc.) in *Attendite vobis...* (Cl. I, No. 9 in Bg^3, Le^2, Tr^4).

Berlin: lat. fol. 764 (Görres 114), XIV, Parch., 139 fols. (= Be)

I. *Bibliog.*

Die HSS Verzeichnisse der Preussischen Staatsbibliothek zu Berlin: Verzeichnis der Latein. HSS (3 vols., Berlin, 1893-1919), III, 133-36.
(MS is now deposited in the Universitätsbibliothek Tübingen)

II. *Summary of contents*

f. 1ra-60vb Sermones de tempore et de sanctis (*46*)

1) Author unknown; doubtful (3)

f. 27rb Non enim vocavit nos Deus
43ra Si quis auditor est verbi
44vb Viri Galilei

2) (Cl. IV) Accepto responso in somnis (7)
Dilectus meus descendit
Diligite iustitiam
Erat Ninive civitas magna
Medicina omnium
Osculetur osculo oris sui
Pascha nostrum

(Cl. V) Erat Jesus eiciens demonium (1)

(Cl. II) Ecce positus est hic (8)
Ecce vicit leo
Emitte spiritum tuum
Ipse vos baptizabit
Si abstuleris de medio tui catenam
Surrexit Dominus vere
Tribularer si nescirem
Tu es qui venturus es

(Cl. III) Petite et accipietis (2)
Videte ne quis vestrum sit fornicator

(Cl. I) (21)
Sermons No. 7a, 12, 13b, 17b, 23b, 28b, 34a, 40b, 49, 51a, 60b, 68b, 69, 70b, 71, 72b, 89b, 94a, 101a, 109a, 118a (Copies in Bg3, Bs1, CCC 459, Le2, OM, PS, Tr2, Tr4, Pa11).

(Cl. VI) Erat Jesus eiciens demonium (4)
Justum deduxit
Memento quod cinis es
Si complantati fuerimus

Brugge: Stadsbibl. 93, XIII, Parch., 102 fols.
(= Bg2) (IRHT-film)

I. *Bibliog.*

De Poorter, *Cat. des mss.... de Bruges*, *op. cit.*, 110-14. (Catal. suggests Langton attribution).
(Prov. Abbey of Dunes, f. 102. *Cf.* Brugge MS 28)
Cf. Sander, 183.
Cave, II, 282.
Glorieux, I, 255.

II. *Summary of contents*

f. 34ra-52vb Series of sermons (*16*)
(Cl. IV) Rogate que ad pacem sunt (1)
(Cl. V) Ecce rex noster adveniet (1)

(Cl. II) Ipse vos baptizabit (3)
Numquid elevabis in nebula
Tu es qui venturus es
(Cl. III) Templum Dei estis (1)
(Cl. I) (10)
Sermons No. 7b, 16c, 22c, 37b, 40a, 49, 92a, 95b, 100b, 109a (Copies in Le², OM, Pa¹¹, Tr², Tr⁴).

Brussels: Bibl. Roy. II. 957, XIII, Parch., 255 fols. (= Bs²)

I. *Bibliog.*

Van den Gheyn, *op. cit.*, I, 106-08, No. 224.

II. *Summary of contents*

f. 1; 255- Liber sancte Marie de Camberone
255- *Ex-libris*, Sir T. P. Middle Hill, 352.
1v-7r: *Annotationes magistri Steph. Cathuariensis* (*sic*) *arch. in libro Iosue...*
245v: Sermo mag. Steph. in dominica septuag. - Circumdederunt me... (Cl. I, No. 13c)
13v-14v (2 sermons); 245v-251v (6 sermons) (*8*)

1) Not on Schneyer list; author unknown (3)
14v: Dabo vobis vallem Achor
248v: Memento homo... Dies presens dies
250r: Letare Ierusalem et conventum

2) (Cl. II) Ecce ego mittam piscatores (1)
(Cl. I) (3)
13c, 70a, 82b (Copies in Bg¹, Bs¹, Le², Pa¹¹, PS, Tr⁴).
(Cl. VI) Memento quod cinis es (1)

Brussels: Bibl. Roy. II. 962, XII-XIV, Parch., 235 fols. (= Bs³)

I. *Bibliog.*

Van den Gheyn, *op. cit.*, I, 102-06, No. 223.
Lacombe *et al.*, 6.
Glorieux, I, 255.

II. *Summary of contents*

f. 1: Liber sancte Marie de Camb.; *Ex-libris*, Sir T. P. Middle Hill, 357.
1v: *Tract. mag. Steph. Cant. arch. super librum numerorum...*
31r: *Tract. super Deut.*
(Cl. I) (*3*)
212ra: Que est ista — Dum singularem (Sermon No. 77b)
219ra: Infirma mundi — Si quis Christianus (No. 46a)
219vb: Spiritus oris — Primum canticum (No. 101a)

(Copies in Bg¹, Bg³, Bs¹, CUL, Le², PS).

Cambrai: Bibl. munic. 588 (546), XIII-XIV, Parch., 201 fols.
(= Ca)

I. *Bibliog.*

Cat. gén. des mss des bibl. publ. de France: *Dép. XVII: Cambrai* (ed. A. Molinier, Paris, 1891), 230.
Schneyer, "Sermonesliste, etc.," 161 (f. 31vb)

II. *Summary of contents*

(Cl. I) Viri Galilei — Magnum infirmitatis
(No. 121; copies in Bg^3, Tr^2, PS).

Douai: Bibl. munic. 495, XIV, Parch., 101 fols.
(= Do)

I. *Bibliog.*

Cat. gén. des mss des bibl. publ. des Dép. VI: *Douai* (Paris, 1878), 291.
Schneyer, "Sermonesliste, etc." 161 (f. 78ra)

II. *Summary of contents*

(Cl. V)
f. 79rb: Tu es qui venturus es
(Cl. I)
f. 78ra: Aspiciens a longe ecce video —
(No. 7^a, copies in Le^2, Tr^2).

Lincoln: Cathedral Chap. Lib. 239 (A.7.10), XIII, Vellum, 192 fols.
(= Li)

I. *Bibliog.*[12]

R. M. Woolley, *Catalogue of the MSS of Lincoln Cathedral Chapter Library* (Oxford Un. Pr., 1927), 171.

II. *Summary of contents*

f. 40^r: In sudore vultis tui — (Cl. I, No. 45)
(Copies in Bg^1, Bs^1).

London: British Museum, Royal 3.A.X., XIII, Vellum, 190 fols.
(= Lo^1)

I. *Bibliog.*

Warner & Gilson, *Cat. of Roy. MSS*, *op. cit.*, I, 69-70.
Schneyer, "Sermonesliste, etc." 161 (f. 95rb-115va)[13]

[12] The references to this Lincoln MS, Munich Clm. 12660 and the Vienna MS (*infra*) were sent to me by Dr. Schneyer in a private communication. They do not appear in his published list.

[13] F. 101va-115va contain no sermons that can be assigned to Langton. Although a few themes correspond, the incipits differ. F. 106ra-107ra, *Speculum confessionis*; f. 110ra-115va, misc. short pieces.

II. *Summary of contents*

f. 95rb-101rb Series of sermons (7)
(Cl. IV) Super manus meas depinxi (1)
(Cl. II) Nemo potest duobus dominis servire (1)
(Cl. I) (5)
Sermons No. 9, 10, 13a, 23c, 68a
(Copies in Bg³, Bs¹, CCC 459, Le², PS, Tr², Tr⁴).

London: British Museum, Royal 8.C.VII, XIII-XIV, Vellum, 172 fols. (= Lo²)

I. *Bibliog.*

Warner & Gilson, *Cat. of Roy. MSS.* I, 234-36.
Cf. Lo³ (*cit. supra*) Ave maris stella (Cl. II)

II. *Summary of contents*

(Cl. II)
f. 22v: Ave maris stella, etc.

London: British Museum, Royal 8.F.IV, XV, Vellum, 132 fols. (= Lo⁴)

I. *Bibliog.*

Warner & Gilson, *Cat. of Roy. MSS*, I, 262-63.
Cf. Lo³ (*cit. supra*) Ave maris stella (Cl. II)

II. *Summary of contents*

(Cl. II)
f. 125rb: Exposicio super Aue maris stella, etc. (Imperf. at end)

London: British Museum, Royal 10.A.VII, XIII, Vellum, 218 fols. (= Lo⁵)

I. *Bibliog.*

Warner & Gilson, *Cat. of Roy. MSS*, I, 304.

II. *Summary of contents*

MS contains *Distinctiones theol. a mag. Will. Lincoln. ecclesie cancellario collecte...* and various *Sermones de tempore...* (f. 117ra-140vb)
(Cl. I)
f. 122vb: Ponam desertum in delicias (No. 71; also in Pa¹¹, Tr⁴).
140rb: Produxit Deus (No. 75; also in Bs¹, Bg³, PS, Tr⁴).

Munich: Staatsbibl., Clm. 5998, XIII-XIV, 201 fols. (= Mu¹)

I. *Bibliog.*

Catalogus codicum Latinorum Bibliothecae Regiae Monacensis (ed. C. Halm *et al.*, 1873), III, 3.

J. B. Schneyer, "Beobachtungen zu lat. Sermoneshandschriften der Staatsbibl. München," *Bay. Akad. der Wissenschaft.-Phil. Hist. Kl. Sitz.* (München, 1958), Hft. 8, 48:

f. 11^{r}: Eine predigt auf das Fest der Assumptio Mariae v. Stephan Langton (Glorieux, I, 238-60).

II. *Summary of contents*

f. 11^{r}: Que est ista — Dum singularem
(Cl. I, No. 77^{b}).

(Copies in Bg^{3}, Bs^{1}, CUL, Le^{2}, PS).

Munich: Staatsbibl., Clm. 12660, XIV, 129 fols.
(= Mu^{2})

I. *Bibliog.*

(Communication from Dr. Schneyer; the MS does not appear in the published list).

Catalogus codicum Latinorum Bibliothecae Regiae Monacensis (1876), II, 2, 84.

II. *Summary of contents*

f. 34^{v}: Noli timere filia Sion: Ecce rex
(Cl. I, No. 51^{b}).

(Copy in Bg^{3}; var. in Pa^{11}).

Nîmes: Bibl. munic. 42 (13738), XIII, Parch., 96 fols.
(= Ni) (IRHT-film)

I. *Bibliog.*

Cat. gén. des mss des bibl. publ. des Dép: VII: Toulouse-Nîmes (Paris, 1885), 549-51.

D'Alverny, 128, 133.

II. *Summary of contents*

f. 81^{v}: Homo natus de muliere — Audi hoc
(Copy in Pa^{11}; See Cl. VI).

92^{v}: Viderunt eam hostes — Scitis fratres
(Cl. I, No. 118^{a}).

(Copies in Bg^{3}, Le^{2}, Tr^{2}).

Paris: Bibl. de l'Arsenal 400 (600 T.L.), XIII, Parch., 236 fols.
(= PA^{1})

I. *Bibliog.*

Cat. des mss de la bibl. de l'Arsenal (ed. H. Martin, Paris, 1885), I, 267-68. (Anon. sermons; attrib. fols. 49^{v}, 51^{v}, 73, 117 to Langton).

Feret, I, 279.

Powicke, *SL*, 169.

Lacombe *et al.*, 6.

Glorieux, I, 255.

Landgraf, *Einführung*, *etc.*, 85.

(In the Catalogue, *cit. supra*, there is a reference to a series of 40 sermons beg. f. 179ra (*Afferam paxillum aque*) and also appearing in Brugge MS 278. Lacombe and Powicke also cite the reference. I have examined the MSS and found that the *theme Afferam paxillum* appears in both; but the incipits differ. Furthermore, in this Arsenal MS, from f. 179ra-202vb, there are 11 sermons; from 202vb-216va, 20 brief passages developing the themes of sermons; and from f. 217, the *Penitentiale mag. Alani*).

II. *Summary of contents*

f. 45ra-$120bis^{rb}$ Series of sermons (*47*)

1) 96va-99va Geoffrey of Babion (2)

(See Schneyer, "Sermonesliste, etc.," 161)

2) (Cl. IV) (3)

Dentes tui sicut grex
Dilectus meus descendit
Videbam coram me vitem

(Cl. V) (3)

Ecce rex venit
Erat Jesus eiciens demonium
Novate vobis novale

(Cl. II) Ecce positus est hic (6)
Ipse vos baptizabit
Surrexit Dominus vere
Tres sunt qui testimonium dant
Tribularer si nescirem
Tu es qui venturus es

(Cl. III) Petite et accipietis (3)
Templum Dei estis
Videte ne quis vestrum sit fornicator

(Cl. I) (28)

Sermons No. 3, 6^a, 7^a, 8, 10, 10 (*sic*) 14, 15^b, 23^b, 25^a, 26^a, 28^b, 38^b, 39^a, 42, 49, 55, 65^a, 65^b, 68^a, 69, 70^b, 94^a, 100^c, 101^a, 109^a, 118^a, 121.

(Copies in Bg^3, Bs^1, CCC 459, Le^2, OM, Pa^{11}, PS, Tr^2, Tr^4).

(Cl. VI) Memento quod cinis es (2)
Si complantati fuerimus

Paris: Bibl. de l'Arsenal 854 (593 T.L.), 4 MSS in Vol., MS. A, XII-XIII, Parch., 146 fols.

(= PA^2) (IRHT-film)

I. *Bibliog.*

Cat. des mss de la bibl. de l'Arsenal, II, 134-37.
Schneyer, "Sermonesliste, etc.," 161 (f. 47^v)

II. *Summary of contents*

f. 47^v: In nativitate beate Marie sermo — Converti me ad viam porte — Ubicumque, fratres mei...

(No other copy in MSS cited).

Paris: Bibl. Mazarine 999 (958), XIII, Parch., 154 fols.

(= PM) (IRHT-file-film)

I. *Bibliog.*

A. Molinier, *Cat. des mss de la bibl. Maz.*, (4 vols., Paris, 1885-92), I, 500.
Lecoy de la Marche, 542.
Hauréau, "Bibliotheca Casinensis," *Journal des Savants* (1885), 298-308.
Schneyer, "Sermonesliste, etc.," 161 (f. 98-154)
(IRHT: although there is no attrib. to Langton in the MS, the 25 sermons from f. 110-154^v are regarded as his).

II. *Summary of contents*

f. 1: Table of sermons; all attrib. to Maurice de Sully (See *Hist. litt.*, XV, 156-58)

98-152vb Sermons (*35*)

(Cl. IV) Celebravit Salomon dedicationem (7)
Christus pro nobis passus est
Fluvius egressus est
In Ezek. legitur in visione templi
Isti sunt qui venerunt
Sapientiam sanctorum narrant populi
Vae genti peccatrici

(Cl. II) Nemo potest duobus dominis servire (3)
Scimus quoniam diligentibus Deum
Tribularer si nescirem

(Cl. I) (16)
Sermons No. 6^a, 9, 17^b, 34^a, 50^b, 54^c, 68^b, 69, 77^b, 80^b, 81^a, 94^b, 99^a, 116^c, 117^e, 118^a.
(Copies in Bg^3, Bs^1, CUL, Le^2, Pa^{11}, PS, Tr^2, Tr^4).

(Cl. VI) Amator pecunie servus est mammone (9)
Ave gratia plena
Duo ubera tua
Justus ut palma florebit
Memento quod cinis es
Qui sperant in Domino
Remittuntur ei peccata multa
Si sciret paterfamilias
Tulit David baculum

Paris: Bibl. nat., lat., 2915, XIII-XIV, Parch., 105 fols.
(= Pa^1) (IRHT-file)

I. *Bibliog.*

Bibl. nat.: Cat. gén. des mss lat., op. cit., III, 273-76.
Schneyer, "Sermonesliste, etc.," 161 (fols. 53^v, 60^v)
D'Alverny, 135.

II. *Summary of contents*

f. 42-105^v- heterog. group of 53 sermons. Some authors are identified: Alanus de Insulis; Iohannes Teutonicus; Innocentius III; Odo Cambrensis; Gebuinus; Stephanus Tornacensis; Serlo de Wilton. Others anon.

53^v-60^v Sermons (*4*)

(Cl. IV) Accepto responso in somnis (2)
Super manus meas depinxi

(Cl. I) Sermons No. 10, 48. (2)
(Copies in Bs^1, Le^2, Pa^{14}).

Paris: Bibl. nat., lat., 3495, XIII, Parch., 224 fols.
(= Pa^3) (IRHT-file)

I. *Bibliog.*

B. Hauréau, *Notices et extraits des mss de la Bibl. Nat. et autres bibl.* (ed. Acad.

des Inscrip. et Belles-Lettres, Paris, 1906), XXXVIII, ii, 397-447 on the contents of the MS.

—— *Notices et extraits de quelques mss lat. de la Bibl. Nat.*, *op. cit.*, II, 114 on the sermons (f. 176ra); 317 (f. 192^{v}-193^{v}); 173 (f. 201^{r}).

II. *Summary of contents*

f. 176ra-206^{v}		Series of sermons	(*18*)
	(Cl. IV)	Dedi flumina in deserto	(4)
		Ego sum panis vivus	
		Obtulerunt Magi Domino	
		Quemcumque osculatus fuero	
	(Cl. II)	Qui descendunt mare	(2)
		Sollempnitates vestras	
	(Cl. III)	Surgite vigilemus	(2)
		Videte ne quis vestrum sit fornicator	
	(Cl. I)		(10)
		Sermons No. 8, 29, 34^{a}, 51^{b}, 81^{c}, 87^{c}, 88, 89^{a}, 117^{c}, 118^{a}. (Copies in Bg^{3}, Bs^{1}, Le^{2}, OM, PS, Tr^{2}, Tr^{4}).	

Paris: Bibl. nat., lat., 3570, XIII-XIV, Parch., 218 fols.
(= Pa^{4}) (IRHT-file)

I. *Bibliog.*

Hauréau, *Notices et extraits... de la Bibl. Nat.*, II, 114.
Schneyer, "Sermonesliste, etc.," 161 (f. 185)

II. *Summary of contents*

f. 185^{r}: Que est ista — Dum singularem
(Cl. I, No. 77^{b}).
(Copies in Bg^{3}, Bs^{1}, CUL, Le^{2}, PS).

Paris: Bibl. nat., lat., 12420, XIII, Parch., 115 fols.
(= Pa^{6}) (IRHT-film)

I. *Bibliog.*

Delisle, *Invent. des mss... St. Germain-des-Prés*, 51.
Hauréau, *Notices et extraits... de la Bibl. Nat.*, II, 100-16, descr. contents of the MS.
Lecoy de la Marche, 534.
Powicke, *SL*, 168.
Lacombe *et al.*, 6.
Glorieux, I, 255.

II. *Summary of contents*

f. 36va-114ra		Sermons	(*24*)
	(Cl. IV)	Contra tres hostes est pugnandum	(2)
		Nisi Dominus edificaverit domum	
	(Cl. V)	Ecce rex venit	(3)
		Ecce sacerdos magnus	
		Trahe me post te	
	(Cl. II)	Qui crediderit in me	(3)
		Reddet Deus mercedem	
		Tribularer si nescirem	

(Cl. I) (15)
Sermons No. 9, 17^{b}, 34^{a}, 44^{a}, 50^{a}, 51^{b}, 67, 77^{b}, 83^{b}, 87^{b}, 100^{c}, 110^{a}, 116^{b}, 116^{c}, 117^{b}.
(Copies in Bg^{3}, Bs^{1}, CUL, Le^{1}, Le^{2}, Pa^{11}, PS, Tr^{2}, Tr^{4}).

(Cl. VI) (1)
Si complantati fuerimus

Paris: Bibl. nat., lat., 14470, XII-XIII, Parch., 342 fols.
(= Pa^{7}) (IRHT-film-file)

I. *Bibliog.*

Delisle, *Invent. des mss... St. Victor*, 17.
Hauréau, *Notices et extraits... de la Bibl. Nat.*, III, 68, compares series of sermons in this MS to sermons in lat. 14593, f. 45 sqq.
Lecoy de la Marche, 534.
Lacombe *et al.*, 7, n. 1; 6.
Glorieux, I, 255.
Landgraf, *Einführung, etc.*, 108.
D'Alverny, 132.

II. *Summary of contents*

f. 162^{v}-170^{v}; 195^{v}-321^{v} Sermons (*34*)

(Cl. IV) (Si) cognovit eum in benedictionibus (5)
Nuptie facte sunt
Pueri Hebreorum
Pulli aquile lambunt sanguinem
Retrahamus cum sole

(Cl. V) Ecce rex venit (5)
Ecce sacerdos magnus
Homo natus de muliere
Novate vobis novale
Orietur stella ex Jacob

(Cl. II) Convertentur sedentes in umbra eius (4)
Emitte spiritum tuum
Nemo potest duobus dominis servire
Numquid elevabis in nebula

(Cl. I) (17)
Sermons No. 1^{b}, 4, 9, 22^{a}, 26^{a}, 34^{a}, 39^{b}, 40^{a}, 46^{a}, 49, 50^{a}, 71, 77^{b}, 81^{a}, 107^{b}, 109^{b}, 110^{a}.
(Copies in Bg^{3}, Bs^{1}, CUL, Le^{2}, OM, PS, Pa^{11}, Tr^{2}, Tr^{4}).

(Cl. VI) Memento quod cinis es (3)
Scuto circumdabit te veritas eius
Templum Dei sanctum est

Paris: Bibl. nat., lat., 14525, XIII, Parch., 305 fols.
(= Pa^{8}) (IRHT-film-file)

I. *Bibliog.*

Delisle, *Invent. des mss... St. Victor*, 21.
Hauréau, *Notices et extraits... de la Bibl. Nat.*, II, 114, on f. 239^{v}.
Landgraf, *Einführung, etc.*, 77, 108.

II. *Summary of contents*

f. 233v-245v Sermons (*5*)
(Cl. I) Nos. 9, 10, 14, 77b, 121.
(Copies in Bg3, Bs1, CUL, Le2, PS, Tr2, Tr4).

Paris: Bibl. nat., lat., 14593, XIII, Parch., 352 fols.
(= Pa9)

I. *Bibliog.*

Delisle, *Invent. des mss... St. Victor*, 29.
Hauréau, *Notices et extraits... de la Bibl. Nat.*, III, 67-78, descr. contents of the MS; attributes some to Langton; compares series in this MS to sermons in lat. 14470, *supra.*
Feret, I, 279.
Lacombe *et al.*, 6.
Glorieux, I, 255.
Landgraf, *Einführung, etc.*, 107.
D'Alverny, 132.

II. *Summary of contents*

f. 46va-103va	Sermons	(*20*)
(Cl. IV)	Nuptie facte sunt	(4)
	Pueri Hebreorum	
	Pulli aquile lambunt sanguinem	
	Retrahamus cum sole	
(Cl. V)	Ecce rex venit	(5)
	Ecce sacerdos magnus	
	Homo natus de muliere	
	Novate vobis novale	
	Orietur stella ex Jacob	
(Cl. II)	Nemo potest duobus dominis servire	(1)
(Cl. I)		(9)
	Sermons No. 1b, 4, 26a, 39b, 40a, 46c, 81b, 107b, 109b.	
	(Copies in Bs1, Le2, Pa11, PS, Tr2, Tr4).	
(Cl. VI)	Templum Dei sanctum est	(1)

Paris: Bibl. nat., lat., 14804, XIII, Parch., 291 fols.
(= Pa10) (IRHT-file)

I. *Bibliog.*

Delisle, *Invent. des mss.... St. Victor*, 49.
Hauréau, *Notices et extraits.... de la Bibl. Nat.*, III, 141-74, descr. contents of the MS.
Lacombe, *Prévostin....*, 184.
Landgraf, *Einführung, etc.*, 114.
Schneyer, "Sermonesliste, etc.," 161 (f. 164ra)

II. *Summary of contents*

f. 159v: Qui descendunt mare — Domini mei
(Copy in Bs1; see Cl. II).
164ra: Veni Sancte Spiritus — Dum sollempnitatis
(Cl. I, No. 116c).

Paris: Bibl. nat., lat., 14925, XIII, Parch., 224 fols.
(= Pa¹²) (IRHT-file)

I. *Bibliog.*

Delisle, *Invent. des mss.... St. Victor*, 59.
Hauréau, *Notices et extraits... de la Bibl. Nat.*, III, 310-40, descr. contents of the MS.
Lacombe *et al.*, 6.
Glorieux, I, 255.
D'Alverny, 132.

II. *Summary of contents*

Sermons of Maurice de Sully; anon. sermons.

f. 106ᵛ-140ʳ	Sermons	(9)
(Cl. IV)	Obtulerunt Magi Domino	(2)
	Vivit in Christo gemma sacerdotum	
(Cl. II)	Qui crediderit in me	(2)
	Sollempnitates vestras	
(Cl. I)	Sermons No. 23ᶜ, 51ᵃ, 83ᶜ, 99ᵃ.	(4)
	(Copies in Le², Pa¹¹, PS, Tr⁴).	
(Cl. VI)	Si complantati fuerimus	(1)

Paris: Bibl. nat., lat., 14957, XIII, Parch., 251 fols.
(= Pa¹³) (IRHT-file)

I. *Bibliog.*

Delisle, *Invent. des mss.... St. Victor*, 62.
Hauréau, *Notices et extraits... de la Bibl. Nat.*, II, 110, on f. 69ᵛᵃ.
Schneyer, "Sermonesliste, etc.," 161 (f. 69ᵛᵃ)
D'Alverny, 129.

II. *Summary of contents*

(Cl. I)
f. 3ʳᵃ: Ductus est Jesus — Lectionis evangelice
(No. 24; copies in Bg¹, Bs¹, Tr²).
69ᵛᵃ: Noli timere filia Sion: Ecce rex tuus venit — Fratres, si coram vobis... et ex promissione
(No. 51ᵇ; copy in Bg³; var. in Pa¹¹).

Paris: Bibl. nat., lat., 15965, XIV-XV, Parch., 160 fols.
(= Pa¹⁵) (IRHT-file)

I. *Bibliog.*

Delisle, *Invent. des mss de la Sorbonne*, 31.
Lecoy de la Marche, 537, attrib. sermon on f. 12 to Langton, and prob. others in the series.
D'Alverny, 47, 123ff, 131ff, 252ff, 272ff.

II. *Summary of contents*

f. 12ʳᵃ: Homo natus de muliere — Audi hoc breve verbum
(Copy in Pa¹¹; see Cl. VI).

Paris: Bibl. nat., lat., 16463, XIII, Parch., 196 fols.
(= Pa[16])

I. *Bibliog.*

Delisle, *Invent. des mss de la Sorbonne*, 60.
Hauréau, *Notices et extraits... de la Bibl. Nat.*, V, 136-37, descr. contents of the MS.
Feret, I, 279.
Lacombe *et al.*, 6.
Glorieux, I, 255.
D'Alverny, 131, 135.

II. *Summary of contents*

f. 1v: Table listing rubrics of 90 numbered sermons.
Sermons of Maurice de Sully; others anon.

26ra-96ra; 130ra; 134ra-151ra Sermons (*50*)

(Cl. IV) Erat Ninive civitas magna (4)
Facta est quasi institoris
Super manus meas depinxi
Vivit in Christo gemma sacerdotum

(Cl. II) Ecce positus est hic (5)
Ego sum pastor bonus
Nemo potest duobus dominis servire
Scimus quoniam diligentibus Deum
Tribularer si nescirem

(Cl. III) Surgite vigilemus (3)
Trahe me post te
Videte ne quis vestrum sit fornicator

(Cl. I) (38)
Sermons No. 8, 9, 10, 12, 13[a], 14, 15[b], 20, 23[c], 31[a], 32, 34[a], 38[a], 46[b], 49, 50[c], 51[b], 54[b], 57[a], 60[a], 69, 71, 73, 75, 77[b], 79, 80[a], 81[a], 82[b], 83[a], 87[a], 89[a], 94[b], 102, 110[a], 115[a], 117[a], 118[a].
(Copies in Bg[1], Bg[3], Bs[1], CUL, Le[2], OM, Pa[11], PS, Tr[2], Tr[4]).

Paris: Bibl. nat., lat., 16502, XIII, Parch., 248 fols.
(= Pa[17])

I. *Bibliog.*

Delisle, *Invent. des mss de la Sorbonne*, 63.
Lecoy de la Marche, 538.
Schneyer, "Sermonesliste, etc.," 161 (f. 104ra)

II. *Summary of contents*

f. 104ra: Estote prudentes et vigilate
(No other copy in MSS cited).

Reims: Bibl. munic. 582 (F. 478), XIII, Parch., 186 fols.
(= Re) (IRHT-film)

I. *Bibliog.*

Cat. gén. des mss des bibl. publ. de France : Dép. XXXVIII: Reims (ed. H. Loriquet, Paris, 1904), I, 740-53.
Lacombe *et al.*, 6.
Glorieux, I, 255.

II. *Summary of contents*

f. 54v: Solve iubente Domino — Gloria mea semper
(Copy in Pa[11]; see Cl. II).

Troyes: Bibl. munic. 1227, XIII, Parch., 221 fols.
(= Tr[3])

I. *Bibliog.*

Cat. gén.... (Troyes), cit. supra, II, 504. (Clairvaux E. 47)
Lecoy de la Marche, 503, doubts authenticity of sermons generally ascribed to Langton in this MS.
Hauréau, *Notices et extraits... de la Bibl. Nat.*, II, 111.
Powicke, *SL*, 169-70.
Lacombe *et al.*, 6.
Glorieux, I, 255.

II. *Summary of contents*

(11 anon. sermons follow Langton on *Exodus*)
f. 87ra: Attendite vobis
(Copies in Bg[3], Le[2], Tr[4]; Cl. I, No. 9).
89ra: Sumite de optimis terre frugibus
(Copies in Bg[3], Bs[1], Le[2]; Cl. I, No. 102).

Vatican City: Biblioteca Apostolica Vaticana, Vat. lat. 634, XI-XIII, Parch., 93 fols.
(= Va)

I. *Bibliog.*

Codices Vaticani Latini (Rome, 1902), I, 478-83.
Schneyer, "Sermonesliste, etc.," 161.

II. *Summary of contents*

(There are 86 anon. sermons in the MS)

f. 46r-88r		Sermons	(*14*)
	(Cl. IV)	Pascha nostrum	(1)
	(Cl. II)	Nemo potest duobus dominis servire	(3)
		Nescitis quia membra vestra	
		Quasi myrrha electa	
	(Cl. I)	Sermons No. 7a, 20, 28a, 44a, 49, 65a, 67, 74a, 98a.	(9)
		(Copies in Bs[1], Le[1], Le[2], OM, Pa[11], PS, Tr[2], Tr[4]).	
	(Cl. VI)	Misereor super turbam	(1)

Vienna: Nationalbibliothek 1330 (Salisb. 193), XIV, 154 fols.
(= Vi)

I. *Bibliog.*

(Communication from Dr. Schneyer, MS does not appear in the published list).
Tabulae cod. MSStorum... in Bibl. Palat. Vindob. asservatorum (11 vols., 1864-1912), I, 220.

II. *Summary of contents*

f. 21r: Sermo in dominica in LXa: Semen est verbum Domini — Legitur in libro regum
(Copies in Le[2], Tr[2], Tr[4]; Cl. I, No. 89a).

CLASSIFICATION OF THE SERMONS

These lists contain the following:

1) references to all known copies of a given text.
2) evidence of individual attribution (where given).
3) rubric indicating audience and/or occasion (where available).
4) indication of variant by the symbol *; of a different sermon on the same theme, by the symbol ♯.
5) Roman numerals in the MS references indicate the number of the sermon in the series in that MS.
6) MSS of Group I are generally listed in the left column; MSS of Group II (anon.), on the right.
7) Only the sermons in Class I have been numbered; references to these sermons throughout the study are usually given as follows: number of the sermon; the MS reference; fol. no. — e.g., 121, Pa^{8}, 233^{v}. (In the Appendices, ordinarily only the number of the sermon is given).
8) References to Schneyer, *Wegweiser*, *op. cit.* = *Weg.*

Class I. — Sermons Appearing in More Than One Named Copy

(*Total:* 122 Sermons).

N.B. Some sermons appear with the same theme but in different versions: indicated by the sign *. Others, though having the same theme, are totally different sermons: indicated by the sign ♯. Named copies appear in the left column; anonymous in the right.

1a. Accingere cilicio (*Jer.* 6: 26) — Ad predicationis officium me minus idoneum esse profiteor et vos sensu pauperes ad intelligendum dominici sermonis mysterium... hoc est premium desiderabile.
PS, 45^{v}-8^{v}. — Ar, 35rb-7ra, In cap. ieiun., XXII.
Tr^{2}, 261vb-62vb.

1b. *——— Cavete vobis, karissimi, ne maledictionem Domini incurratis... hoc est premium desiderabile.
Pa^{7}, 248rb-50ra, In XL^{ma}, XLIII.
Pa^{9}, 75vb-8ra, XXXVIII.

2. Ad te Domine, clamabo, quia ignis comedit (*Joel* 1: 19) — Domini et patres reverendi, vobis ceciderunt funes in preclaris, etenim vobis preclara futura est hereditas in celis... in cellaria eterne beatitudinis introducat.
Bg^{1}, 18ra-9ra, In die pent.
Bs^{1}, 149va-51ra, *Ib.*, LXXXIIII.

3. Adam ubi es (*Gen.* 3: 9) — Cum Dominus Jeremiam ad officium predicationis assumeret, misit manum suam et tetigit os eius... ad eum per penitentiam redeamus.
Le^{2}, 45va-6rb, Dnca in LXX. — Ar, 32vb-4va, *Ib.*, XX.
PS, 39^{v}-42^{v}. — PA^{1}, 70rb-1vb.

PS, 115^{r}-17^{r}.
Tr^{2}, 262vb-63vb.
Tr^{4}, 97^{v}-9^{v}, *Ib.*, XXXI.

4. Amice, quomodo huc intrasti (*Matt.* 22: 12) — Intrante Israel in terram promissionis et pugnante contra Amalech victoria debetur illi orante Moyse... ut ei sociemur in gloria.
Bs^{1}, 84ra-^{vb}, Dnca xxi p. pent; XXX.
Tr^{4}, 146^{v}-47^{v}, Dnca xx^{a} p. pent; LV.
Ar, 114va-15va, *Ib.*, LXXIX.
Pa^{7}, 225rb-26va, *Ib.*, XXV.
Pa^{9}, 103va-04va, LX.

5a. Aperite portas nobis, quia nobiscum Dominus (*Jud.* 13: 13) — Nabuchodonosor volens omnem terram suo subiugare imperio... et erimus de familia Domini.
Bs^{1}, 136vb-37rb, In Adv; LXX. *Weg.*, 36.

5b. *——— In hodierno officio ait apostolus: Gaudete in Domino semper (*Phil.* 4: 4)... ad te, qui fons luminis es et totius claritatis valeamus pervenire.
Le^{2}, 23rb-5va, iiii Dnca adv.

6a. Aqua frigida bonus nuntius (*Prov.* 25: 25) — Isaias de filio Dei incarnando prophetans primo de beate virginis nomine designans... ad fruitionem dilectissimi filii introducat. Quod ipse meritis benignissimi matris concedere dignetur.
Tr^{2}, 260vb-61va.
PS, 53^{v}-5^{r}.
PA^{1}, 76rb-7va.
PM, 135va-37ra, De annunt. dnca.

6b. *——— Fratres, antequam Christus nasceretur, dixit Isaias, quod de Jesse nasceretur quedam virga... ut per te celum ingrediar.
Bs^{1}, 116vb-18rb, In adv; LIII.

6c. *——— Fratres karissimi, hodie est festus dies nuptiarum, in quo rex celorum dignatus est ad nostre cognationis mulierem nuptias celebrare... ad secreta regna celorum intromittat.
Le^{2}, 148vb-50ra, De annunt.

7a. Aspiciens a longe ecce video potentiam Dei — Salomon ait: Qui tantum verba sectatur, nichil habebit (*Prov.* 19: 7) ... Hiis verbis ostenditur, quod fructu verbi Dominici destituitur.... ut Salvator adveniens dignetur ea inhabitare per gratiam.
Le^{2}, 2va-4ra, De adv.
Tr^{2}, 298ra-^{vb}. *Weg.*, 44.
Ar, 147vb-49ra, *Ib.*, CVIII.
Be, 1ra-2rb, *Ib.*
Do, 78ra-9rb, LXIII.
PA^{1}, 85ra-6rb, Dnca i in adv.
Va, 46^{r}.

7b. *——— Salomon in Proverbiis docet nos, qualiter verbum Dei sit audiendum... ut per eam mundemini ab omni malicia et nequicia.
Bg^{2}, 44rb-5rb. *Weg.*, 44.

8. Assumpsit Jesus Petrum (*Matt.* 17: 1) — Sapiens quidam per Spiritum Sanctum loquens ait: Doctrinam oris audite filii (*Eccli.* 23: 7). Tante efficie non est quantecumque thesaurus pecunie... sicut illi viderunt in transfiguratione.
Tr^{2}, 275va-76vb.
Tr^{4}, 149^{r}-51^{r}, Dnca ii in XL^{a}; LVII.
PA^{1}, 104rb-06vb.
Pa^{3}, 181ra-83rb.
Pa^{16}, 76rb-^{vb}, In transfig. Domini; XLV.

9. Attendite vobis et universo gregi (*Act.* 20: 28) — Terret me latebras conscientie mee scrutantem illud (*Ps.* 49: 16): Peccatori dixit Deus: Quare tu enarras justitias meas... perveniatis ad premium eterne retributionis (beatitudinis), quam nobis prestare dignetur.
Bg^3, 38vb-41rb, In sinodo, XXII.
Le^2, 123rb-26ra, Ad sacerdotes.
Tr^4, 43^v-8^v, Ad episcopos et pastores; X.
Cf. Bas, 244^r.
Lo^1, 96va-7vb.
Pa^6, 55va-9va. *Weg.*, 47.
Pa^7, 206rb-09ra, In synodo ad prelatos, XII.
Pa^8, 245^v-48^v, *Ib.*
Pa^{16}, 142rb-45ra, *Ib.*, LXXVIII.
PM, 110ra-13ra, Sermo quomodo prelatus se habeat et de non appetenda prelatione.
Tr^3, 87ra-9ra, In synodo ad prelatos.
?Pa^9, 108va-09va, LXVI, *Weg.*, 46.

10. Beati pauperes spiritu (*Matt.* 5: 3) — Ut in *Ecclesiastico* (40: 1) legitur: Occupatio magna creata est... Beati pauperes spiritu.
Bs^1, 72vb-5ra, De omnibus sanctis; XXI.
Le^2, 177va-80ra, *Ib.*
?(Tr^4, LXXXIIII, (f. 2^r) Omnium sanctorum. *Theme only*)
Lo^1, 95rb-6va.
PA^1, 66va-9ra.
PA^1, 122^{ra-b}, *Ib.*
Pa^1, 53^v-5^v. (MS attrib. Iohannes Teutonicus)
Pa^8, 236^v-39^v, Omn. sanct. in capit. s. victoris.
Pa^{16}, 146vb-49vb, Omn. sanct; LXXX.

11. Bilibris tritici denario uno (*Apoc.* 6: 6) — Legimus, quod cum vir Domini Eliseus Samarie obsesse et fame laboranti tantam in crastino secuturam prediceret abundantiam.... malignorum spirituum vota satiamur.
Le^2, 137ra-39rb, De sancto Vincentio.
PS, 113^r-15^r.
Ar, 30va-2va, *Ib.*, XIX.

12. Bonum certamen certavi (*II Tim.* 4: 7) — Fratres, quanto magis preparat aliquis cor ad obsequendum Deo et tanto attentius attentatur a diabolo... sic fidem servavit restat ut detur ei corona. (reposita est mihi corona justitie).
Bs^1, 105va-06vb, De s. Paulo; XLV.
Le^2, 157va-59vb, *Ib.*
?(OM, LIX (f. 51^v), *Ib.* M. Steph. *Theme only*)
PS, 64^r-8^v.
Be, 58rb-60rb, *Ib.*
Pa^{16}, 37rb-9rb, *Ib.*, XXI.

13a. Circumdederunt me gemitus mortis (*Ps.* 17: 5) — Timere possumus, si consideremus verba apostoli dicentis: Terra super se venientem bibens imbrem (*Hebr.* 6: 7) ... nos ad novem ordines angelorum perducat omnipotens. Deus.
Le^2, 43va-5va, Dnca in LXX.
PS, 4^r-5^v.
Tr^2, 302va-03va.
Ar, 151ra-52ra, *Ib.*, CX.
Lo^1, 100va-01rb.
Pa^{16}, 30vb-3ra, *Ib.*, XVIII.

13b. *——— Timere debemus fratres, si consideremus verba Pauli dicentis... nos ponat in decimo ordine post diem iudicii.
Be, 17vb-9rb, *Ib.*

13c. *——— Paulus dicit: Terra... ut inter novem ordines predictos collocari mereamur.
Bg^1, 2vb-3rb, *Ib.*
Bs^1, 81va-2rb, *Ib.*, XXVIII.
Bs^2, 245^{v}-46^{r}, Sermo mag. Steph. in dnca septuag.
Tr^4, 104^{r}-05^{v}, In LXX^{a}; XXXIIII.

14. Consideravit agrum (*Prov.* 31: 16) — Legimus quod ad Jeremiam clausum (inclusum) in vestibulo carceris venit Ananeel patruclus eius... ad huius agri possessionem suspiremus et cum bonis operibus comparemus.
Bg^3, 54rb-7ra, De qualibet virgine, XXVIII.
Bs^1, 101va-03va, De s. Genovefa virg; XLII.
Ar, 90va-2vb, *Ib.*, LXIIII.
PA^1, 53ra-5vb.
Pa^8, 242^{r}-45^{v}, *Ib.*
Pa^{16}, 139rb-42rb, *Ib.*, LXXVII.

15a. Cum eiecisset Jesus demonium (*Luc.* 11: 14) — Hoc sumptum est de evangelio hodierno, in quo narratur, quod cum Dominus terram perambularet... et perfrui visione beatitudinis superne.
Tr^2, 282ra-83ra.

15b. *——— Verbum est evangelii. Cum Dominus in carne mortali predicaret, adductus est ad eum egrotus quidam... secundum arbitrium sacerdotis et vitam eternam mereri.
Tr^4, 130^{r}-32^{v}, In XL^{a}; XLVII.
PA^1, 106vb-08vb.
Pa^{16}, 64vb-6rb, Dnca iii XLe; XXXVII.

16a. Cum esset Stephanus plenus gratia (*Act.* 6: 8) — Si quis pauper haberet causam coram rege terreno, multum gauderet, si audiret, regem precipisse... obdormire in Domino cum beato prothomartyre Stephano. Quod precibus beati Stephani et sanctorum Nicomedis, Gamalielis atque Liborii.
Le^2, 166ra-67rb, De s. Stephano.
Pa^{11}, 249rb-50va, *Ib.*, S. M. Steph.
PS, 18^{r}-20^{v}, *Ib.*
Tr^2, 289vb-90va.

16b. *——— Scitis, fratres, quod cum pauper aliquid habet negotii in magna curia pertractandum... animas nostras in manum Salvatoris possumus offerre.
Ar, 68vb-9rb, *Ib.*, XLIII.

16c. *Cum esset Stephanus plenus Spiritu Sancto (*Act.* 7: 55) — Pauperes gaudent cum eis datur iudex liberalis in liberalitate confidentes. Nos sumus pauperes... et faciat exire a civitate peccati. de qua dicit Dominus: Ego civitatem non ingredior.
Bg^2, 41rb-2rb.

17a. Cum venerit Paraclitus, ille arguet mundum (*Joh.* 16: 8) — Bona gens, duplici intentione audit aliquis verbum alterius vel quia distincte loquitur vel quia amicus... et sanctos imitemur, ne iudicium timeamus.
Pa^{11}, 259vb-61rb, In ascens; XLVIII, S. M. Steph.

17b. *——— Scitis fratres, quod verbum alicuius libenter auditur vel ideo, quia magnus et potens est... directione gratie ad consummationem glorie, ad quam perducere dignetur Salvator noster.
PS, 140^{v}-43^{v}.
Ar, 11ra-3ra, In pasch; IIII.
Be, 54ra-5va, Dnca iii p. pascha.
Pa^{6}, 59va-61rb, Dnca i ascens.
PM, 118rb-20va, Dnca iiii p. pascha.

17c. *——— Notandum, quod sumus velut regio, per quam egreditur exercitus... cuius consolationem nobis prestante dignetur.
Bg^{1}, 20va-1ra, De pentecoste.
Bs^{1}, 113^{ra-vb}, *Ib.*, XLIX.

18a. Cum venerit Paraclitus, quem ego mittam (*Joh.* 15: 26) — Beatus Petrus in epistola hodierna docet, quid faciendum sit nobis, quando verbum Domini proferimus vel audimus dicens: Si quis loquitur quasi sermones Dei (*I Petr.* 4: 11)... ut eius directione perveniant ad statum glorie. Quod nobis largiatur, qui Spiritum Sanctum misit apostolis JCDN.
Tr^{2}, 264ra-65ra.
Ar, 44rb-6vb, In pasch; XXVIII.

18b. *——— Karissimi, Petrus, apostolus ait: Si quis loquitur... et per internam inspirationem gaudium futurum prelibare facit.
Le^{2}, 96vb-7va, Dnca p. ascens.

19a. Deficiente vino ait mater Jesu (*Joh.* 2: 3) — Qualiter audiendum sit verbum Domini, ostendit Salomon inquiens: Si quesieris sapientiam quasi pecuniam (*Prov.* 2: 4)... ut nobis in presenti conferat vinum gratie.
Tr^{2}, 254va-55va.

19b. *——— Evangelium duo facit, facta Christi recitat et docet, quid nobis sit faciendum... ut pro nostra salute fundat preces. amen.
Bg^{1}, 2ra, Dnca p. epiph.
Bs^{1}, 142^{va-vb}, *Ib.*, LXXVII.

19c. *——— Salomon (*Prov.* 2: 4): Qui thesauros effodit... Sic qui thesauros sapientie invenire desiderat, omne pondus terrenum a se reiciat... ad anteriora in eternum duratura extendamur.
Le^{2}, 41rb-2va, *Ib.*

20. Descendit dilectus meus in hortum suum (*Cant.* 6: 1) — Qui verbum Domini dicere vult vel audire, exemplum sumat de beata virgine. Cum angelus pastores admonuit de Christi nativitate... ad cuius gustum nos pure et caste ad salutem perducat...
Le^{2}, 146ra-47rb, In annunt.
PS, 144^{v}-47^{r}.
Pa^{16}, 89rb-90vb, *Ib.*, LIII.
Va, 55^{v}.

21a. Dicit Dominus: Scio, quid cogito (cogitem) super vos. Ego cogito cogitationes pacis (*Jer.* 29: 11) — Tobias instruendo filium ait illi: Audi, fili mi, verba oris mei et construe illa quasi fundamentum (*Tob.* 4: 2)... In fundamentis solent poni lapides impoliti et incompositi... et pacem eternitatis largietur.
Tr^{2}, 245rb-46rb.

21b. *——— Tobias ait filio suo: Audi fili... et de hac peregrinationis valle...
Le^{2}, 120rb-21va, Dnca xxiii p. pent.

22a. Dispersit dedit pauperibus (*Ps.* 111: 9) — Dominus populum Israel in deserto manna pavit, quia Dominus in deserto mundi huius dulcedine verbi sui reficit... habebitur ipsius veneratio in perpetuum. Ad cuius nos consortium.
Pa^{11}, 269vb-71ra, De s. Laurencio; LVII. Pa^{7}, 241vb-44ra, *Ib.*, XL.
PS, 20^{v}-3^{r}, *Ib.*
Tr^{2}, 290va-91va.

22b. *——— Cum populus Israeliticus per desertum in terram promissionis proficesceretur, Dominus eum manna collato cibavit... ad satietatem eterne felicitatis pervenire merebimur, quam nobis meritis.
Ar, 69rb-70va, *Ib.*, XLIIII.

22c. *——— Quando populus Israel ivit per desertum, Dominus pavit eum de manna, quod sapiebat unicuique quod volebat... huius lecti scil. contritio, confessio, satisfactio.
Bg^{2}, 42rb-3va.

22d. *——— Manna cuique saporem pro velle suo reddens... suffragiis beati Laurencii evadere mereamur.
Le^{2}, 167rb-68ra, *Ib.*

23a. Dominus prope est (*Phil.* 4: 5) — Sicut pugil protegit se clipeo ad repellendum ictus... Si dederimus pauperibus temporalia, dabo vobis eterna.
Tr^{2}, 283^{ra-b}, *Weg.*, 159.

23b. *——— Salomon ait (*Prov.* 30: 5): Sermo Domini ignitus clipeus est... Viri fratres, continua pugna est inter hominem et diabolum... ut digne illum hospitio nostro collocare valeamus. Quod ipse prestare dignetur, qui venturus est.
CCC 459, 148va-49^{v}. Be, 9^{ra-vb}, *Ib.*
Pa^{11}, 276^{ra-vb}, In adv. Mag. Steph. de Lang; LXIII. *Weg.*, 158. PA^{1}, 49va-50rb.

23c. *——— Ut dicit Salomon (*Prov.* 30: 5): Omnis sermo Domini clipeus est sperantibus in se. Pugil campum intraturus stultus est, si non orat, ut clipeo sibi tradito... hec fuit prima promissio, que nobis in ortu Salvatoris insonuit. Ad quam pacem.
Le^{2}, 28vb-30rb, *Ib.* Lo^{1}, 100^{ra-va}.
Tr^{4}, 141^{v}-43^{v}, *Ib.*, LIII. Pa^{12}, 139ra-40^{r}. *Weg.*, 157.
Pa^{16}, 44ra-5rb, *Ib.*, XXIII. *Weg.*, 159.

24. Ductus est Jesus in desertum (*Matt.* 4: 1) — Lectionis evangelice series non solum minoribus sed etiam majoribus timorem potest incurrere... fortiter confitendo peccata, ut simus participes victorie Christi.
Bg^{1}, 4va-5ra, In XL^{a}. *Cf.* Pa^{13}, 3ra-11ra, *Ib.*
Bs^{1}, 103va-04va, *Ib.*, XLIII.
Tr^{2}, 296^{ra-va}.

25a. Ecce Dominus veniet et omnes sancti eius (*Zach.* 14: 5) — Si quis existeret in belli discrimine nec haberet arma, quibus posset se defendere... in futuro lumine glorie sue illustrabit in celo.
Tr^{2}, 297rb-98ra. *Weg.*, 169. PA^{1}, 92rb-4rb.
Tr^{4}, 99^{v}-101^{v}, De omn. sanct; XXXII.

25b. *——— Si aliquis esset in bello inarmis et quidam amicus suus porrigeret ei scutum... et liberemur a gehenna.
Ar, 176vb-77vb, *Ib.*, CXXVIII. *Weg.*, 168.

26a. Ecce nunc tempus acceptabile (*II Cor.* 6: 2) — Salomon ait: Cor sapientis erudit os eius (*Prov.* 16: 23) — Non sunt sapientes, qui periti sunt terrena querere, sed qui cognoscere Deum student... sed merito vite bone perveniemus ad diem felicitatis eterne.
Pa^{11}, 266ra-67ra, In Quadrag; LIII, S. M. Steph.
PS, 48^{v}-50^{v}.
Tr^{2}, 259vb-60vb. *Weg.*, 183.
Tr^{4}, 158^{v}-61^{r}, *Ib.*, LXII.
Ar, 70va-2ra, *Ib.*, XLV.
PA^{1}, 73rb-4rb.
Pa^{7}, 247ra-48rb, *Ib.*, XLII.
Pa^{9}, 74rb-5vb, XXXVII.

26b. *——— Consideremus, fratres, terras, prata, vineas, arbores, ecce omnia virent... per commemorationem mortis eius divitemus luxuriam.
Le^{2}, 56va-7vb, *Ib.*
Ar, 177vb-78vb, *Ib.*, CXXVIIII. *Weg.*, 181.

27. ‡——— David: Invocavit me et ego exaudiam eum (*Ps.* 90: 15). Ecce pros missio Domini, qui invocantes se exaudit, in tribulationem descendentibu- assistit... ad pacem eterne iocunditatis valeamus pervenire.
Le^{2}, 57vb-8vb, *Ib.*
Pa^{11}, 218vb-19va, *Ib.*, XI, S. M. Steph.

28a. Ecce rex noster adveniet Christus (*Cf. Matt.* 21: 5; *Joh.* 12: 15) — In hodierno evangelio (*Luc.* 21: 33) dicitur: Celum et terra transibunt... In executione tremendi judicii terra combustione purgabitur... ut in adventu suo rex hic conferat gratiam, in futuro gloriam eternam.
Le^{2}, 16rb-7va, Dnca ii in adv.
Tr^{2}, 298vb-99va, *Weg.*, 184.
Va, 47^{r}.

28b. *——— In fine hodierni evangelii dicitur: Celum... ut in adventu suo.. gloriam eternam.
Tr^{4}, 192^{r}-94^{r}, *Ib.*, LXXVIII.
Be, 5va-6rb, *Ib.*
PA^{1}, 86rb-7va.

29. Ecce rex venit, occurramus Salvatori nostro (*Cf. Matt.* 21: 5; *Joh.* 12: 15) — Fratres karissimi, anime peccatrici utile est istud fieri, quod quandoque fit egrotanti... ut mereamur feliciter occurrere, cum ad iudicandum venerit.
Le^{2}, 1ra-2va, Dnca i adv.
Tr^{2}, 285rb-86ra. *Weg.*, 209.
Tr^{4}, 22^{v}-5^{r}, ii dnca. adv; III.
Ar, 185va-86ra, In adv; CXXXVI. *Weg.*, 190, 209.
Pa^{3}, 185vb-87va, In ram. palm.

30a. Ecce sacerdos magnus (*Cf. Num.* 35: 25) — Qui quasi flos rosarum in diebus vernis. (*Eccli.* 50 : 8)... sic fuit sanctus iste in domo Domini et quid orandum ab eo, qui audit istud Psalmista ostendit... et tandem ei consortes efficiamur in gloria.
Tr^{2}, 272ra-74ra.

30b. *——— Sic fuit sanctus iste in domo Domini. Quomodo audiendum sit verbum Domini, Psalmista ostendit et quid orandum ab eo... et tandem ei consortes efficiamur in gloria.
Ar, 118rb-20ra, De s. Germano Aut; LXXXIII.

30c. *——— Quando debemus audire verbum Domini debemus orare sicut David in Psalterio (87 : 3) ... ad celestia regna mereamur pervenire.
Bs^{1}, 86va-7vb, *Ib.*, XXXIII.

31a. Ecce vir prudens (*Cf. Prov.* 11: 12; 15: 21) — Scitis fratres, quod medicina sumi solet duabus de causis, a sanis, ut status sanitatis conservetur... eundem percipient denarium, quem nobis oratione beati Martini prestare dignetur DN.
Tr^{2}, 284ra-85rb.
Tr^{4}, 189^{r}-92^{r}, De b. Martino vel quolibet confessore; LXXVI.
Pa^{16}, 54vb-6va, De quolibet conf; XXXI.

31b. *——— Scitis quod medicina multis de causis sumitur. Sumi solet ut status sanitatis conservetur... in eterna retributione par habebunt Dominum.
Le^{2}, 182ra-84ra, De s. Martino.
Am, (unnumb. fol).

32. Ego sum via et veritas (*Joh.* 14: 6) — Orate, fratres, ut Deus det verbis suis virtutem, ut confortemur et emendemur... Christus est via, que ducit ad vitam.
PS, 38^{r}-9^{v}.
Tr^{4}, 133^{v}-35^{r}, Phil. et Iacob; XLIX.
Pa^{16}, 72ra-3ra (?p. pascha); XLII.

33a. Egredietur fons de domo Domini (*Joel* 3: 18) — Salomon dicit in *Proverbiis* (20 : 27): Lucerna Domini spiraculum hominis... nobis cum erit Deus.
Le^{2}, 4ra-5va, De adv.
Ar, 77rb-8rb, *Ib.*, L.
Am, (unnumb. fol.).

33b. *——— Fructum et commoditatem verbi Domini insinuat sub breviloquio vir sapiens, ubi ait: Lucerna Domini... penitus exterminetur.
Bs^{1}, 114ra-15vb, *Ib.*, LI.

34a. Egredietur virga de radice Iesse (*Is.* 11: 1) — Quidam Sapiens per Spiritum Sanctum loquens ait: Verbis cor accenditur, precibus serenatur... quod nobis precibus piissime tribuat gratia redemptoris Jesu Christi.
Le^{2}, 147rb-48vb, In annunt.
PS, 32^{r}-5^{r}, *Ib.*
Tr^{4}, 60^{r}-3^{r}, *Ib.*, XV.
Be, 53ra-4ra, *Ib.*
Pa^{3}, 176ra-78va, *Ib.*
Pa^{6}, 89va-92ra, De b. virg.
Pa^{7}, 276ra-78va, In annunt. sive in adv; LX.
Pa^{16}, 69rb-70vb, In annunt; XL.
Cf. PM, 149va-50rb, *Ib.*

34b. *——— Fratres karissimi, homo quidam a Spiritu Sancto edoctus loquitur dicens: Verbis cor accenditur... precibus illuminatur... Recolite ergo omnia predicta per ordinem.
Ar, 129rb-30rb, *Ib.*, LXXXX.

35. Egredimini et videte filie Sion (*Cant.* 3: 11) — Verba sunt matris nostre ecclesie loquentis ad dilectas suas, que sic ait: Egredimini... et hoc in die iocunditatis et letitie.
Bg^{1}, 16^{ra-va}, In pascha.
Bs^{1}, 126vb-27va, *Ib.*, LX.

36a. Emitte agnum Domine (*Is.* 16: 1) — Si quis ad flumen iret propter aquam et nihil reportaret... preparata ad gloriam. Ad quam nos precibus benignissime matris et meritis perducere dignetur SNJC.
Le^{2}, 150ra-51rb, De annunt.
Tr^{2}, 250rb-51vb. *Weg.*, 223.

36b. *——— Si quis ad hauriendum et deferendum ad magnum fluvium pergat et parum aut nihil afferat... et supplicia reproborum.
Bs^{1}, 142vb-44va, In adv; LXXVIII.
Weg., 223.

36c. *——— Scitis, karissimi, quod Secana vel fluvius alius, ubi iugis aquarum viget abundantia nemini rivos suos claudit... ab omnibus peccatis liberi efficiemur.

Ar, 133va-35va, In annunt., XCIIII.
Weg., 223.

37a. Erit iste pax, cum venerit Assyrius (*Mich.* 5: 5) — Quanto desiderio audiendum sit verbum Domini, ostendit Salomon dicens: Aqua frigida anime sitienti (*Prov.* 25: 25)... congrue igitur est vox martyrum. Erit iste pax...
PS, 16^{r}-8^{r}, De s. Vincentio.
Tr^{2}, 301va-02rb.

37b. *——— Salomon ostendit, quanto desiderio audiendum sit verbum Dei...
Bg^{2}, 52^{ra-vb}.

38a. Est puer unus hic (*Joh.* 6: 9) — Dominus noster reficiens turbam sublevavit oculos suos in celum per hoc nos instruens, ut intentionem nostre actionis ad Deum dirigamus... in die Pasche, quod nobis largiri dignetur, refector et redemptor noster Jesus Christus.
PS, 26^{v}-9^{v}.
Pa^{16}, 66rb-7vb, Dnca iiii^{a} XLe, XXXVIII.

38b. *——— Dominus noster turbam refecturus... in die Pasche, quod nobis largiri...
PA^{1}, 108vb-11ra.

38c. *——— Dominus, antequam apponeret populis panes, respexit in celum dans nobis exemplum... in futuro pane nos satiet eternaliter.
Le^{2}, 67vb-9rb, In XL^{a}.
PS, 147^{r}-49^{r}.

39a. Estote imitatores Dei (*Eph.* 5: 1) — Salomon in *Prov.* (22: 17) docet, quomodo audiendum sit verbum Domini dicens: Fili mi, inclina aurem tuam... in presenti per gratiam, in futuro per gloriam.
PS, 55^{v}-7^{v}.
Tr^{2}, 267ra-68rb.
Cf. Tr^{4}, 96^{r}-7^{v}, Dnca iii^{a} Quadrag. XXX.
Ar, 37ra-8vb, *Ib.*, XXIII.
PA^{1}, 77va-9rb.

39b. *——— Gaudium est matris et signum legitimi coniugii filius... satis facile est.
Pa^{7}, 267ra-68rb; LIIII.
Pa^{9}, 80vb-2rb; XLI.

40a. Exemplum dedi vobis (*Joh.* 13: 15) — Caveat quilibet, ne cadat retro... fragile est.
Le^{2}, 77ra-8rb, In cena Domini.
Bg^{2}, 35ra-6ra.
Pa^{7}, 251vb-53rb, *Ib.*, XLV.
Pa^{9}, 90va-2va; LI.

40b. *——— Attendere debent audituri verbum... ut in patria plene fruamur.
Tr^{4}, 143^{v}-46^{r}, *Ib.*, LIIII.
Be, 36vb-8ra, *Ib.*

41. Extendit rex virgam auream (*Esth.* 4: 11) — Rex iste est Deus Pater, virga aurea virgo Maria, manus regis Filius Dei, Hester anima a Deo per peccatum separata... interventu et imitatione beate virginis...
Bs^{1}, 86^{ra-va}, In nativ. s. Marie, XXXII.
OM, 57^{r-v}, De b. virg. Maria; III.
PS, 143^{v}-44^{v}.
Tr^{4}, 132^{v}-33^{v}, *Ib.*, XLVIII.

42. Hec est enim voluntas Dei (*I Thess.* 4:3) — Ne quis supergrediatur aut circumveniat in negotio fratrem suum... Si quis regi terreno familiaris litteras sub hac forma dirigeret... ad gaudium perveniemus eternum.
Le^{2}, 60rb-1va, Dnca ii^{a} (in XL^{a}). Ar, 72ra-4vb, *Ib.*, XLVI.
PS, 50^{v}-3^{v}. PA^{1}, 74va-6rb.
Tr^{4}, 173^{v}-76^{v}, *Ib.*, LXIX.

43. Homo quidam erat dives et induebatur (*Luc.* 16: 19) — Primo notandum, quod dicit: Homo quidam... Et non exprimitur nomen eius... nullo mortis metu affici.
Le^{2}, 101vb-03ra, Dnca i p. pent.
Tr^{2}, 171^{r}.

44a. Jerusalem surge (*Bar.* 5: 5) — Sapiens quidam dat nobis certam spem impetrandi quod pie petitur, cum dicitur: Respicite filii, nationes hominum (*Eccli.* 2: 11)... in secundo adventu letificemur gloria eterna.
Tr^{2}, 247va-48va. *Weg.*, 328. Pa^{6}, 11ra-^{vb}, In adv.
Cf. Va, 48^{r}.

44b. *——— Karissimi, quia nullus speravit in Domino et confusus est (*Eccli.* 2: 11)... in decore suo videre valeamus.
Le^{2}, 13rb-4vb, Dnca. ii^{a} in adv.
Weg., 328.

45. In sudore vultus tui (*Gen.* 3: 19) — Hec dicta sunt primo parenti nostro post peccatum. Scitote, quia multiplex est panis. Est panis materialis et visibilis... nec comedant, priusquam confiteantur si facultas assit.
Bg^{1}, 2ra-^{vb}, In Septuag. Li, 40^{r}-44^{v}.
Bs^{1}, 80ra-1va, *Ib.*, XXVII.

46a. Infirma mundi elegit Deus (*I Cor.* 1: 27) — Si quis christianus pugnaturus contra paganum fortissimum inveniret qui sibi gladium commodaret acutissimum... nos in numero prudentum virginum inveniat lampadibus plenis oleo.
PS, 8^{r}-10^{r}. Ar, 62ra-3rb, De s. Katherina, XXXIX.
Bs^{3}, 219^{ra-vb}.
Pa^{7}, 263vb-65va, *Ib.*, LII.

46b. *——— Si quis, fratres, alicui viro charactere insignito crucis et contra paganum pugnaturo gladium bene secantem traderet, ipse libenter eo se accingeret. ... ad amplexus sponsi transire merebimur, ad quos nos...
Le^{2}, 188ra-89rb, *Ib.* Pa^{16}, 52ra-3ra, *Ib.*, XXIX.

46c. *——— Ad conterendam superbiam diaboli... per flores enim virgines designantur sicut per fructus apostoli.
Pa^{9}, 46va-7vb, *Ib.*, XI.

47. Letatus sum in his que dicta sunt mihi (*Ps.* 121: 1) — Fratres, in hodierno legitur evangelio, quomodo turbe pauperum secute fuerant Dominum in desertum ... sic que expediti ibimus ad domum Dei, quam ipse prestare dignetur.
Le^{2}, 66vb-7vb, In XL^{a}.
Pa^{11}, 222^{ra-vb}, *Ib.*, XIIII, S. M. Steph. de Langt.

48. Legimus filios Israel profectos de Egypto — Farinulam conspersam in palliis ligatam in humeris suis portasse... in mei redemptoris obsequium linguam meam et mentem converto et eius gracie me et meum prepositum committo.
Le², 189-91, Epist. mag. Steph. de X plagis.
?(OM, LX (f. 51ᵛ), Lectio M. Steph. Cant. in Exod. *Theme only*)
Pa¹⁴, 222ᵛᵇ-26ᵛᵇ, Mag. Steph. de Lang; x plage Egipti.
Pa¹, 60ᵛ-4ᵛ.
BN lat. 2995, 135ᵛ-38ᵛ.

49. Maria Magdalena et Maria Jacobi (*Marc.* 16: 1) — Per os Sapientis Spiritus Sanctus locutus est dicens: Hominis est linguam preparare (*Cf. Prov.* 16: 1)... tunc dabitur septiformis gratia Sancti Spiritus, quam nobis prestare dignetur.
Le², 79ᵛᵃ-80ᵛᵇ, In resurrec.
OM, 57ᵛ-8ᵛ, Item eiusdem (i.e. Steph.) in pascha; IIII.
Pa¹¹, 278ʳᵃ⁻ᵛᵇ, *Ib.*, LXV, S. M. Steph.
Tr⁴, 139ᵛ-41ᵛ, *Ib.*, LII.
Be, 38ʳᵃ⁻ᵛᵇ, *Ib.*
Bg², 34ʳᵃ-5ʳᵃ.
PA¹, 117ʳᵇ-18ᵛᵇ.
Pa⁷, 197ᵛᵇ-200ʳᵃ; VIII.
Pa¹⁶, 76ᵛᵇ-8ʳᵇ, *Ib.*, XLVI.
Va, 72ʳ.

50a. Militia est vita hominis (*Job* 7: 1) — Dicit Dominus per Jeremiam prophetam (14: 5): Cerva peperit in agro... Anima sordibus peccati inquinata est... ut superne retributionis premium percipere mereamur.
Le², 82ʳᵃ-4ᵛᵇ, In oct. resurrec.
PS, 86ʳ-9ʳ.
PS, 103ʳ-06ʳ.
Pa⁶, 41ᵛᵇ-5ᵛᵃ.
Pa⁷, 272ᵛᵃ-76ʳᵃ, Sermo communis; LIX.

50b. *——— Jeremias (14: 5): Cerva peperit... Peccatores sicut porci...
PM, 113ʳᵃ-14ᵛᵃ, In Quadrag.

50c. *——— Valde memoranda est illa Jeremie sententia, que ait: Cerva peperit... Sic porcus volvens se in volutabro luti peccatorem significat in luto peccatorum se delectantem... prelati cupidi, qui per cupiditatem male dispensant Christi corpus.
Pa¹⁶, 35ᵛᵇ-7ʳᵇ, In pascha, XX.

50d. *——— Scitis dilectissimi, quod in hostilitatis tempore valde laboriosum est officium militare... ut superne retributionis premium percipere mereamur.
Bg¹, 16ᵛᵃ-7ᵛᵃ, *Ib.*
Bs¹, 111ʳᵃ-13ʳᵃ, *Ib.*, XLVIII.

51a. Noli timere filia Sion: Ecce rex tuus venit (*Joh.* 12: 15) — Fratres, si coram vobis positus esset mortuus et ex Dei promissione speraretis eius resurrectionem... in pacis visionem eternam scil. beatitudinem.
Pa¹¹, 255ʳᵇ-57ʳᵇ, In ram. palm; XLV, S. M. Steph.
?(Tr⁴, LXXXI (f. 2ʳ) *Theme only*)
Bar, 15ʳ-19ᵛ, *Ib.*
Leip. 345, 80.
Cf. Le³, 69 (*Kat. HSS Leip.*, 719, attrib. to Alain de Lille).
Pa¹², 136ᵛ-38ᵛ.
Be, 33ʳᵇ-5ʳᵃ, *Ib.*

51b. *——— Fratres, si coram vobis... et ex promissione Dei haberemus spem suscitationis eius... in pacis visionem eternam scil. beatitudinem.
Bg³, 65ra-7va, *Ib.*, XXXIIII. Ar, 124ra-27rb, *Ib.*, LXXXVII.
Mu², 34v-5r.
Pa³, 196v-201r.
Pa⁶, 50rb-4va.
Pa¹³, 69va-74rb, *Ib.*
Pa¹⁶, 33ra-5vb, *Ib.*, XIX.

52. ‡——— Sicut in evangelio quod paulo ante audivimus legitur: Dominus iturus Ierusalem cum venisset ad montem Oliveti... in pacis visionem scil. eternam beatitudinem.
Bg¹, 6va-8ra, In palmis.
Bs¹, 68rb-70va, *Ib.*, XIX.

53. Noli timere, quia redemi te (*Is.* 43: 1) — David ostendit, quare audiendum sit verbum Domini et quomodo... et beatitudinem in futuro.
Le², 168rb-vb, De s. Laurentio.
Tr², 241ra-vb.

54a. Non vos me elegistis (*Joh.* 15: 16) — Sciatis, fratres karissimi, quod cum quereretur a Domino a beato Juda, cur mundus gloriam eius visurus non esset... ut aridus ab humore gratie in futuro.
Pa¹¹, 222vb-24ra, De apostolis; XV, S. M. de Langt. *Weg.*, 383.
Tr², 279ra-80rb.

54b. *——— Fratres karissimi, cum Dominus loqueretur discipulis et promitteret se collaturum eis gloriam eternam... et eternam felicitatem promereris.
Le², 175rb-77rb, In die s. Symonis et Jude. Ar, 58rb-60va, *Ib.*, XXXVII. *Weg.*, 382.
PS, 10r-3r, *Ib.* Pa¹⁶, 137ra-39rb, *Ib.*, LXXVI.
Tr⁴, 68r-72r, *Ib.*, XVIII.

54c. *——— Loquente Domino ad discipulos...
PM, 138vb-40va, *Ib.*

55. Novate vobis novale (*Jer.* 4: 3) — Si aliquis rex litteras suas familiariter transmitteret... cor suum appellat.
Le², 51ra-2ra, In LXa. Ar, 34va-5rb, *Ib.*, XXI.
PS, 42v-5v. PA¹, 71vb-2ra.
PS, 117r-19r.

56. ‡——— Scitis, bone gentes, quod tempus dominice passionis modo inchoatum est... ad quam pacem perducat.
Bg¹, 6ra-va, In pass.
Bs¹, 133va-34rb, *Ib.*, LXVII.

57a. Numquid ingressus es thesauros nivis (*Job* 38: 22) — Micheas (2: 7) ait: Verba mea nonne bona sunt... cum eo, qui recte graditur... Sic conqueritur Dominus de nobis, qui sermones eius respuimus... et eius gratie me et meum propositum committo.
PS, 82v-4v, De Magd. Pa¹⁶, 39rb-43vb, *Ib.*, XXII.

57b. *——— Ita conqueritur Dominus de nobis, qui sermones eius respuimus... in presenti et in futuro vita eterna.
Le², 159vb-62ra, *Ib.*

58a. Numquid producis luciferum (*Job* 38: 32) — Plurimum me terrent verba quedam, que in ecclesia Dei proposita sunt heri scil. hec: Hortus conclusus Dei Genetrix... dedit Dominus audientibus verbum suum et custodientibus illud...

Ar, 82vb-5vb, In nativ. s. Marie; LVIII.

58b. *——— Terret me latebras mee conscientie... ut videant Deum Deorum in Sion.

Le^{1}, 123-34, S. mag. Steph. de nativ. s.m.
Le^{2}, 171rb-74ra, In nativ. s.m.

59. ‡——— Verba ista non sunt hominis, sed Dei loquentis ad amicum suum Job... sed iste sol iustitie lumen eterne glorie.

Bg^{1}, 14vb-5va, De pascha.
Bs^{1}, 122rb-23vb, *Ib.*, LVIII.

60a. Nunc scio vere (*Act.* 12: 11) — Qui verbum Dei audit, istud David et corde et ore habere debet: Appropinquet deprecatio mea in conspectu tuo, Domine (*Ps.* 118: 169)... eripuit me de manu Herodis et de omni expectatione Iudeorum, idest peccatorum.

Le^{2}, 155va-56va, In f. apost. Petri et Pauli.
Tr^{4}, 123^{r}-24^{v}, Ad vincula s. Petri; XLIIII.
Pa^{16}, 130ra-31vb, In f. Petri et Pauli, LXXIII.

60b. *——— Fratres, auscultaturi verbum Domini in corde et ore habeant quod dicit David: Appropinquet... de omnibus insidiis malignorum spirituum, quod nobis meritis beati Petri prestare dignetur.

PS, 69^{v}-72^{r}, (De) sancto Petro.
Ar, 56ra-7ra, *Ib.*, XXXV.
Be, 56vb-8rb, Petri et Pauli apost.

61. O radix Jesse, qui stas in signum (*Is.* 11: 10) — Si quis pauper regem in multis offendisset... frugem bonorum operum valeant atterere.

Le^{2}, 7va-8va, Dnca iiii (adv.)
OM, 88vb-90ra, Item eiusdem (i.e. Steph.) in annunt. XXXIIII.

62. Occidetur Christus (*Dan.* 9: 26) — Populus Christi est, qui fidem illius profitetur. Omnes de populo Domini esse debemus... a temporali vita ad gloriam eternam.

PS, 57^{v}-60^{v}.
Tr^{2}, 239va-41ra.
Ar, 38vb-41rb, In pass; XXIIII.

63. ‡——— Sicut dicit Paulus: Nemo sibi vivit (*Rom.* 14: 7) — Quia et vivere et mori debet homo in fide Jesu Christi... et vitam consequemur eternam.

Bg^{1}, 13ra-4ra, *Ib.*
Bs^{1}, 131rb-32vb, *Ib.*, LXV.
Le^{2}, 78rb-9va, In parasc.
Cf. Tr^{4}, 162^{v}-65^{r}, In pass., LXIIII.

64a. Omne datum optimum (*Jac.* 1: 17) — Fratres, in primo audiatis verbum Salomonis: Audi consilium et disce disciplinam (*Prov.* 19: 20)... ad tertium lumen perveniemus.

Bg^{1}, 15va-6ra, Dnca ante ascens.
Bs^{1}, 144va-45va, *Ib.*, LXXIX.

64b. *——— Salomon invitans ad audiendum verbum Dei ait: Audi consilium et suscipe disciplinam (*Prov.* 19: 20) Qui in presenti luxuria defluit... ex qua procedunt tria predicta lumina.
Le^2, 88ra-^{vb}, Dnca iiii p. pascha.

65a. Omnes de Saba venient (*Is.* 60: 5) — Salomon ait: Qui custodit Domini mandatum, custodit animam suam (*Prov.* 19: 16) Duo necessaria sunt ad hoc, ut custodiantur verba mandati dominici... ad visionem Salvatoris pertingere.
Le^2, 34vb-6rb, In epiph. — PA^1, 83va-4vb.
Tr^2, 253rb-54va. — Va, 51^{v}.

65b. *——— Hoc est verbum Isaie in epistola hodierna, in qua premittitur: Surge... Cum anima fidelis intelligit... et ad visionem Salvatoris pertingere.
PA^1, 79rb-81rb.

66a. Omnis vallis implebitur (*Luc.* 3: 5) — Heri cantabatur in ecclesia: Expectetur ut pluvia eloquium Domini et descendet super nos sicut ros Dominus. Scitis, fratres, quod colonus peritus agriculture... post terrorem iudicii nos perducat ad iocunditatem gaudii.
Tr^2, 251vb-53rb.

66^{b}. *——— Fratres, imprimis monet nos ecclesia per os Sapientis, ut audiamus verbum Dei diligenter... boni ad vitam eternam recipendam.
Bs^1, 78vb-80ra, In adv., XXVI.

67. Orietur stella ex Jacob (*Num.* 24: 17) — Hec sunt verba cuiusdam prophete perversi, qui missus erat ab Alac (Balac) rege infideli... clementissime matris sue prestare dignetur.
Le^1, 134-38, De nativ. s. Marie. — *Cf.* Pa^6, 81ra-2va.
Le^2, 174ra-75rb, *Ib.* — Va, 79^{v}.

68a. Ostende nobis, Domine, misericordiam tuam (*Ps.* 84: 8) — Bonus homo de bono thesauro (*Matt.* 12: 35) — Bonus thesaurus est verbum Dei... Ostende nobis, Domine — Ad hoc, karissimi, quod aliquid ostendatur, oportet, ut homo videat... ut eum digne recipere valeamus.
CCC 459, 147va-48va. — Lo^1, 99va-100ra.
Tr^4, 28^{r}-30^{r}, In adv., V. — PA^1, 48va-9va. *Weg.*, 396.

68b. *——— Fratres karissimi, ut Dominus ait in evangelio: Bonus homo de bono thesauro (*Matt.* 12: 35)... et se ipsum det nobis in premium.
Be, 3ra-4rb, *Ib.*
PM, 125va-28ra, *Ib.*

68c. *——— Sicut ait Dominus in evangelio: Bonus homo... Filius Dei datus est nobis.
Le^2, 9vb-11va, In adv.

68d. *——— Bonus homo... Qui verbum Dei audit et auditum in cordis armario recondit... in eterne glorificationis gaudium ab ipso suscipi mereamur.
Ar, 144ra-45vb, *Ib.*, CV. *Weg.*, 396.

69. Parate viam Domini (*Matt.* 3: 3) — Cavendum est nobis tripliciter, quod diabolus insidiatur nostris operibus tripliciter... ad contemplationem divine visionis ibimus. Ad quam ducat nos...
Le^{2}, 5va-7rb, In adv.
Pa^{11}, 276vb-78vb, In adv. sive in LX^{a}; LXIIII, S. M. Steph.
Tr^{2}, 286va-87va.
Tr^{4}, 25^{r}-8^{r}, In adv., IIII.
Ar, 182vb-84rb, *Ib.*, CXXXIIII.
Be, 4rb-5va, *Ib.*
PA^{1}, 47vb-8va.
Pa^{16}, 49ra-50rb, *Ib.*, XXVII.
PM, 140va-42rb, *Ib.*

70a. Plurima turba straverunt vestimenta sua (*Matt.* 21: 8) — Karissimi, auditor et narrator verborum Dei debeat more ministrorum ecclesie primum invocare divinum auxilium dicentes: Deus in adiutorium meum intende (*Ps.* 69: 2)... ut ad gloriam resurrectionis et hospitium celestis Jerusalem perveniamus, ad quam perducat Salvator noster Jesus.
Bg^{1}, 8ra-^{vb}, In ram. palm.
Bs^{1}, 100ra-01va, *Ib.*, XLI.
Pa^{11}, 231ra-32vb, *Ib.*, XX, S. M. Steph. de Langt.
Cf. Bs^{2}, 251^{v}-53^{r}, *Ib.*
Am (unnum. fol.)

70b. *——— Qui profert verbum et qui audit, exemplum sumat a sancta ecclesia et eius morem gerat... quatinus vel primo vel tertio vel quarto modo illum sequamur.
PS, 6^{r}-8^{r}.
Ar, 95rb-7va, *Ib.*, LXVII.
Be, 32ra-3rb, *Ib.*
PA^{1}, 59rb-61rb.

70c. *——— Qui verbum Dei dicit vel audit, sumat exemplum ab ecclesia... potest quia esse usurarius.
Le^{2}, 73vb-5vb, *Ib.*

70d. *——— Sacerdos initio matutinorum primo profert... ut ad futuram gloriam perveniamus.
Tr^{4}, 108^{r}-10^{v}, *Ib.*, XXXVI.

71. Ponam desertum in delicias (*Is.* 51: 3) — Scitis, quoniam qui peregre profectus redit domum memor miseriarum, quas in via sustinuit... hoc desertum posuit JCDN.
Pa^{11}, 279ra-80ra, In f.s. M. Magd; LXVI, S. M. Steph.
Tr^{4}, 72^{r}-4^{v}, *Ib.*, XIX.
Be, 60rb-^{vb}, *Ib.*
Lo^{5}, 122rb-24ra.
Pa^{7}, 244ra-45vb, *Ib.*, XLI.
Pa^{16}, 45rb-6vb, *Ib.*, XXIIII.

72a. Posuit me sicut sagittam electam (*Is.* 49: 2) — Qui habet sponsam, sponsus est (*Joh.* 3: 29) — Sponsus ecclesie est Christus... ut ipsum sequendo ad eternum perveniamus regnum.
Bs^{1}, 104va-05va, In vig. s. Iohannis Baptiste, XLIIII.
Tr^{2}, 277va-78rb, *Ib.*

72b. *——— Sanctissimus ille miles Christi, cuius festum instat, scil. Johannes Baptista dicit: Qui habet sponsam sponsus est (*Joh.* 3: 29)... in futura collatione felicitatis eterne.
Ar, 50vb-6ra, *Ib.*, XXXII.
Be, 55va-6vb, *Ib.*

72c. *——— Altissimus est ille dominus, cuius hodie festum celebramus, testante Domino qui ait: Inter natos mulierum... et sanati in eterna gloria iocundemur.
Le^{2}, 153va-55va, *Ib.*

73. Preceptor, tota nocte laborantes (*Luc.* 5: 5) — Ut Salomon ait: Cor fatui quasi vas confractum omnem sapientiam non tenebit (*Eccli.* 21: 17). Vas confractum lutum, quo polluitur... ut perveniat ad veras divitias, ad quas nos...
Bg^1, 21^{ra-vb}, Dnca vi^a p. pent.
Bs^1, 84vb-6ra, *Ib.*, XXXI.
Le^2, 105va-07ra, Dnca v^a p. pent.
Pa^{16}, 84va-6ra, *Ib.*, L.

74a. Preparare in occursum Dei tui (*Amos* 4: 12) — Salomon ait: Pauper et creditor obviaverunt sibi (*Prov.* 29: 13) — Nomine creditoris predicator intelligitur. Credit enim censum verbi divini auditoribus... in secundo adventu perducamur ad gloriam.
Le^2, 11va-3rb, De adv.
Tr^2, 246rb-47rb. *Weg.*, 414 .
Va, 47^v.

74b. *——— Fratres mei, priusquam hoc verbis aperiamus, verbum memoriale proponere vobis dignum duximus... et presentem conculei terrorem(?) non sentiamus.
Pa^{11}, 209va-11vb, *Ib.*, IIII, S. M.
Steph. de Langt. *Weg.*, 411.

75. Produxit Deus de terra omne lignum (*Gen.* 2: 9) — Omnium sanctorum merita sub una celebritate congesta hodie sacrosancta (ecclesia) recolit... gratias agamus Salvatori nostro.
Bg^3, 47ra-9vb, In fest. omn. sanct; XXV.
Bs^1, 70va-2vb, *Ib.*, XX.
PS, 76^v-80^v.
Tr^4, 38^v-43^v, *Ib.*, IX.
Ar, 121vb-24ra, *Ib.*, LXXXVI.
Lo^5, 140^{rb-vb}, *Ib.*
Pa^{16}, 151ra-53vb, LXXXII.

76. Protector noster aspice Deus (*Ps.* 83: 10) — Salomon ait: Egestas et ignominia... (*Prov.* 13: 18) — Omnia verba que in sacrosancta recitantur ecclesia, instituta sunt ad castigationem nostram... ad diem eternitatis, ad quam...
Le^2, 111ra-12va, Dnca xiiii (p. pent.).
Tr^2, 241vb-43ra.

77a. Que est ista, que progreditur (*Cant.* 6: 9) — Si igitur maris stelle claritatem considero et qua reverberata mercis mee actionis in meipsum reduco.... quando absterget Deus omnem lacrimam... ad quod nos perducat rex regum et Dominus dominantium.
Pa^{11}, 257rb-58vb, De b. virg., XLVI, S. M. Steph.
?(Tr^4, LXXXIII (f. 2^r) *Theme only*)

77b. *——— Dum singularem maris stelle claritatem considero... ad quod regnum perducat...
Bg^3, 52va-4rb, *Ib.*, XXVII.
Bs^1, 67ra-8rb, In assump. s. Marie; XVIII.
CUL, 108^r.
Le^2, 168vb-70rb, *Ib.*
PS, 92^r-4^r, *Ib.*
Ar, 127rb-28rb, De s. Maria, LXXXVIII.
Bs^3, 212ra-13ra.
Mu^1, 11^r-3^v, *Ib.*
Pa^4, 185^r.
Pa^6, 95ra-7va, *Ib.*
Pa^7, 238ra-39va, *Ib.*, XXXVIII
Pa^8, 239^v-42^r.
Pa^{16}, 145ra-46vb, *Ib.*, LXXIX.
PM, 121vb-24ra, *Ib.*

78a. Quare quasi colonus futurus es in terra (*Jer.* 14: 8) — Docet vir sapiens, qualiter cor vestrum debetis preparare ad audiendum verbum Dei.... utuntur ad malum.

Ar, 76va-7rb, Dnca i adv; XLIX. *Weg.*, 428.

78b. *——— Fratres dilectissimi, cum omne officium sancte matris ecclesie dulce sit ad audiendum... ut ita imitatores Domini Jesu Christi esse valeatis.

Bs^{1}, 115vb-16vb, In adv; LII. *Weg.*, 428.

78c. *——— Inter multa bonorum preconia etiam hec in laudem justi depromit ecclesia dicens: Justus cor suum tradet (*Eccli.* 39 : 6)... et contrariam ei conferat et per viam suam ad se ipsum perducat.

Le^{2}, 8va-9vb, Dnca iiii (in adv.)

79. Quasi arcus refulgens (effulgens) (*Eccli.* 50 : 8) — sic fuit sanctus iste in domo Domini. Salomon dicit: Cor hominis disponit viam suam (*Prov.* 16: 9)... sic temporali vita promeruit eternam.

PS, 80^{v}-2^{v}. Ar, 49va-50vb, *Ib.*, XXXI.
Tr^{4}, 124^{v}-27^{v}, De uno conf; XLV. Pa^{16}, 86ra-7vb, *Ib.*, LI.

80a. Quasi stella matutina (*Eccli.* 50: 6) — Scitis, fratres dilectissimi, quid dicitur predicatori a Salomone (*Prov.* 3: 5): Habe fiduciam in Domino Deo tuo... in futuro jubar stellis et sole clarius consequamur, ad quod nos perducat.

PS, 13^{r}-6^{r}. Ar, 60va-2ra, De sancto Germano Aut; XXXVIII.
Tr^{4}, 179^{r}-82^{r}, De quolibet conf; LXXI. Pa^{16}, 79vb-81vb, De quolibet Conf; XLVIII.

80b. *——— Scitis, fratres, quod predicatori a Salomon dicitur: Habe fiduciam... stellis et sole clarius consequemur.

Le^{2}, 180ra-82ra, De sancto Martino. PM, 128ra-30va, De quolibet sancto.

81a. Qui Christi sunt, carnem suam crucifixerunt (*Gal.* 5: 24) — Duo verba in sancta ecclesia hodie audivimus, que audituri sermonem Domini passionem ad memoriam debent revocare... ad eius corpus accedere secure poterimus.

PS, 29^{v}-32^{r}. Pa^{7}, 254ra-55rb, In Quadrag; XLVII.
Tr^{2}, 274ra-75va. Pa^{16}, 67vb-9rb, In pass; XXXIX.
PM, 150rb-52ra, *Ib.*

81b. *——— Qui ex familia Christi sunt... digne accipietis. Quod ipse vobis concedat.

Pa^{9}, 84va-5va, XLIIII.

81c. *——— Karissimi, vox Domini hodie in ecclesia insonuit: Hodie si vocem Domini audieritis... ad corpus ipsius digne accedere.

Le^{2}, 69rb-70vb, In pass. Pa^{3}, 213va-16ra.
OM, 86rb-8vb, Sermo mag. Steph. in pass; XXXIII.

82a. Qui preibant increpabant eum (*Luc.* 18: 39) — Ille, qui verbum predicationis aliis elucidat, est quasi nuntius missus ad predam tollendam... scil. sexte serie sabbati et dominice resurrectionis.

Le^{2}, 52vb-4ra, Dnca in L^{a}.

82b. *——— Qui dicit verbum Domini est quasi miles Domini, qui vult domini sui predam hosti suo auferre...; ut ad fructum dominice passionis, de quo sermo fuit in principio, prestante Domino possitis pervenire.
Tr^{4}, 184^{r}-86^{v}, *Ib.*, LXXIII.
Bs^{2}, 246^{r}-47^{v}, In dnca LXme.
Le^{3}, 78. (*Kat. HSS Leip.*, 720, attrib. to Alain de Lille).
Pa^{16}, 92vb-4va, In Quadrag; LV.

83a. Qui sperant in Domino (*Is.* 40: 31) — Ita dicit Isaias. Karissimi, cibo corporali apposito nobis premittimus benedictionem... dabit Dominus sabbatum pro sabbato, pacem super pacem, quam nobis prestare dignetur.
Pa^{11}, 280ra-81rb, Sermo communis, LXVII, S. M. Steph.
PS, 35^{r}-7^{v}.
Pa^{16}, 70vb-2ra, XLI.

83b. *——— Fratres mei, quando convenimus ad mensam comestionis... ascendere ad celestia, ad que nos perducat.
Tr^{4}, 197^{r}-98^{v}, In ieiun. et pass; LXXX.
Pa^{6}, 61rb-3va, In XL^{a}.

83c. *——— Sicut mensam corporalem debet precedere... crucis disponatur.
Pa^{12}, 138va-39ra.

84. Quod autem in terram bonam (*Luc.* 8: 15) — Auditurus de semine jacto in terram bonam cum David dicere debet: Expandi manus meas ad te (*Ps.* 87: 10) ... quoniam adventus Domini appropinquabit.
Bg^{1}, 3rb-4ra, In LX^{a}.
Bs^{1}, 132vb-33va, *Ib.*, LXVI.

85. Religio munda et immaculata (*Jac.* 1: 27) — Karissimi, quando aliquis semen suum seminat, ut multiplicetur, sollicite orat... ascensuri saltem in spe, postmodum autem in re.
Le^{2}, 90rb-1rb, Dnca v p. pascha.
Tr^{4}, 161^{r}-62^{v}, *Ib.*, LXIII.

86. Reminiscere miserationum tuarum (*Ps.* 24: 6) — Quia post omnia et ante omnia ad orationis presidium est confugiendum, ideo in principio sermonis... omnia cursum nostrum impedientia... propitiatus averte per DNJC^{m}.
Le^{2}, 58vb-60rb, In XL^{a}.
Pa^{11}, 219vb-21ra, *Ib.*, XII, S. M. Steph. de Langt.

87a. Respicite et levate capita vestra (*Luc.* 21: 28) — Scitis fratres, quod cibus paratur a matre puero lactanti... in die retributionis extreme gaudium celeste.
Pa^{16}, 58ra-9vb, De adv; XXXIII. *Weg.*, 356.
(IRHT: MS Peterhouse 255, f. 31^{v}).

87b. *——— Bene scitis, fratres dilectissimi... Vigilate itaque, quia nescitis diem neque horam. (*Matt.* 25: 13).
Pa^{6}, 46ra-7rb, In nat. Domini. *Weg.*, 351.

87c. *——— Si nutrix cibum puero parat, adhuc opus est, ut eum inde pascat... nec cogitari potest quanta felicitate plena erit.
Le^{2}, 14vb-6ra, In adv. *Weg.*, 356.
Tr^{4}, 19^{r}-22^{v}, *Ib.*, II.
Ar, 86va-7ra, *Ib.*, LXI.
Pa^{3}, 187vb-88vb (207va), *Ib.*

88. Sapientia edificavit sibi domum (*Prov.* 9: 1) — Venit Dei Filius vocare nos omnes, ducere nos secum vult in gloriam... non Deo qui curat dare.
Le^2, 108va-09rb, Dnca viii (p. pent.).
PS, 72^r-5^v.
Pa^3, 209vb-11ra.

89a. Semen est verbum Dei (*Luc.* 8: 11) — Legitur in libro Regum (*I Reg.* 16: 23), quod quando malignus spiritus vexabat Saulem, David percutiebat citharam... ad salutem anime et corporis.
Le^2, 49rb-50ra, In LX^a.
Tr^2, 278rb-79ra.
Tr^4, 48^v-51^v, *Ib.*, XI.
Pa^3, 178va-80ra.
Pa^{16}, 63ra-4va, *Ib.*, XXXVI.
Vi, 21^r-3^r, *Ib.*

89b. *——— Legitur in libro Regum, quod cum spiritus arripiebat Saulem... quod pro te pependit in cruce...
Be, 20vb-1vb, *Ib.*

90. Semen quod cecidit in terram bonam (*Luc.* 8: 8) — Karissimi, David dicit: Expandi manus meas ad te (*Ps.* 142: 6). Hec eadem Domino dicamus manus nostras in modum crucis expandentes... fructum vite eterne afferunt in patientia...
Le^2, 50^{rb-vb}, Dnca in LX^a.
Pa^{11}, 217va-18vb, *Ib.*, X, S. M. Steph.

91. Si iniquitates observaveris (*Ps.* 129: 3) — Scitote, karissimi, intelligentes, quod dicit Salomon: Omnis labor hominis in ore eius (*Eccle.* 6: 7)... ad portum salutis perpetue perducere dignetur.
Le^2, 117ra-18rb, Dnca xxii (p. pent.).
Pa^{11}, 272ra-73ra, Sermo communis, LIX, S. M. Steph.

92a. Si quis auditor est verbi (*Jac.* 1: 23) — Dominus dat nobis securitatem petendi, cum dicit in evangelio hodierno: Si quis petierit patrem in nomine meo, idest ad salutem, dabit vobis (*Joh.* 16: 23)... et sic aliis exemplo tuo ad superna viam monstres.
Tr^4, 182^r-84^r, Dnca p. pascha; LXXII.
Bg^2, 36ra-7rb.

92b. *——— O homo, tibi propositum est triplex speculum a Deo, speculum creature... ut ad eam bonis operibus tendas.
Bs^1, 120vb-21rb, Dnca ante ascens; LVI.
Cf. PS, 123^v-25^v.

93a. Si quis cognoverit plagam cordis sui (*III Reg.* 8: 38) — Consideremus in principio quoddam commendabile verbum Salomonis dicentis: Qui confidit in corde suo stultus est (*Prov.* 28: 26)... O quam felix erit, cuius operibus bonis... premium beatitudinis eterne.
Tr^2, 259^{ra-vb}.

93b. *——— Salomon: Qui confidit in corde suo... Hec verba, dilectissimi, attendens nihil de corde meo sicut stultus presumo... in futuro gloriam eternam.
Le^2, 128vb-29vb, In dedic.

94a. Si quis vult venire post me (*Matt.* 16: 24) — Salomon ait: Deprecatio pauperis... (*Eccli.* 21: 6). Pauper est quilibet peccator clamans ad Deum et penitens de peccatis... cum tribus regibus possidere possimus. Quod nobis prestare dignetur...
Pa^{11}, 281rb-82ra, In epiph; LXVIII, S. M. Steph.
Ar, 89ra-90va, *Ib.*, LXIII.
Be, 16va-7vb, *Ib.*
PA^{1}, 51vb-3ra.

94b. *——— Scriptum est: Deprecatio pauperis... Hec ideo dixi, quia plus confido, dum verba Dei pronuntio, in verbis auditoris quam in meis... qui prius agebatur torrente cupiditatis contra avaritiam.
Tr^{4}, 33^{v}-6^{r}, *Ib.*, VII.
Pa^{16}, 47vb-9ra, *Ib.*, XXVI.
PM, 120va-21vb, De penitentia.

95a. Sicut sol oriens (*Eccli.*26:21) — Principio sermonis mei bene competit verbum quoddam, quod dicit vir sapiens, qui preclarum verbum dixit, ait enim: Pauper cum obsecrationibus loquitur (*Prov.* 18: 23) ... construitur in celis vivis ex lapidibus.
Tr^{2}, 289^{ra-vb}.
Tr^{4}, 80^{r}-1^{v}, In assump. b. Marie; XXII.

95b. *——— Hic idem vir, qui hoc verbum dixit, ait: Pauper cum obsecrationibus loquitur... Ergo ego pauper scientia et vita, cum timore propono verbum Dei... que construitur in celis vivis ex lapidibus.
Bg^{2}, 43va-4rb.

96. Similabo eum viro sapienti (*Matt.* 7: 24) — David ait: Desiderium pauperum exaudivit Dominus (*Ps.* 10: 17). Pauperes a prophan vocantur qui defectum boni in se esse attendunt... ut in eo radicati et fundati perveniamus ad regnum celorum.
PS, 23^{r}-5^{r}, Unius confessoris.
Tr^{2}, 293vb-94va.
Tr^{4}, 85^{v}-7^{v}, S. Remigii vel alicuius confessoris sermo; XXV.

97a. Simile est regnum celorum (homini) patrifamilias (*Matt.* 20: 1) — Impius postquam transierit, non cognoscet eum amplius locus eius... Ne autem simile quid nobis contingat... claves, per quas regnum celorum aperitur, ad quod nos perducat Jesus Christus.
Pa^{11}, 215vb-16vb, In Septuag; VIII, S. M. Steph. Langt.

97b. *——— Dicitur in Job: Impius si (? cum) mortuus fuerit... sumamus cibum corporis et sanguinis Christi.
Ar, 128va-29rb, *Ib.*, LXXXIX.

97c. *——— Job ait: Impius postquam transierit... claves, per quas regnum celorum aperitur, ad quod...
Le^{2}, 48ra-9rb, *Ib.*

97d. *——— Salomon (*Prov.* 12: 15): Via stulti videtur sibi recta, sapiens autem audit consilia. Est via, que videtur homini recta... sed potius damnantur...
Le^{2}, 46va-8ra, *Ib.*

98a. Simile est regnum celorum regi, qui voluit rationem ponere (*Matt.* 18: 23) — Scitis, fratres, quod non potest in ratione reddenda domino suo satisfacere, qui nescit quid in dispensationis causam susceperit... nos in gaudium introducet eternum.
Tr^{2}, 243va-44va.
Va, 87^{r}.

98b. *——— Servus prudens predeliberando prevenit tempus reddende rationis... in loco pascue celestis nos collocet.
Ar, 18va-20ra, Ad clericos, X.

98c. *——— Tota vita nostra militia est. Cotidie in pugna sumus contra hostes invisibiles... Esurivi et non dedistis mihi... (*Matt.* 25: 42).
Le^{2}, 118rb-19ra, Dnca xxii (p. pent.).

98d. *——— Rex iste Deus, qui non solum corda regum et corpora habet in sua potestate, sed omnium, qui sunt... dicens: Esurivi...
Bs^{1}, 75^{ra-vb}, Dnca x p. pent; XXII.

98e. *——— Fratres, qui multa sub reddenda ratione accepisset, si a memoria sua evanuisset, quod accepit... ne in adventu suo cum impiis deputemur.
Le^{2}, 119ra-20rb, Dnca xxii (p. pent.).

99a. Simon dormis (*Marc.* 14: 37) — De vigiliis potius quam de sompno loqui debueram. Beatus enim ille est servus, quem Dominus... (*Luc.* 12: 37)... per vigilantiam fructuosi laboris pervenire valeamus ad sompnum eterne quietis. Quod nobis prestare dignetur JCDN...
Pa^{11}, 227vb-29vb, In pass., XVIII, S. M. Steph.
Pa^{12}, 106^{v}-09^{r}.
PM, 152vb-54vb, De arguendo torpore sompni.

99b. *——— Potius quam de sompno de vigiliis loqui debueram... ad sompnum eterne quietis. Quod nobis...
Bg^{1}, 14^{ra-vb}, In pass.
Bs^{1}, 140ra-41rb, *Ib.*, LXXV.
Tr^{4}, 56^{v}-60^{r}, De dormitione peccati; XIIII.

100a. Sint lumbi vestri (*Luc.* 12: 35) — Sicut est de sole, ita est de verbo Domini. Si fenestram soli aperias... convivio beatorum mediante trium superiorum executione.
Pa^{11}, 267^{ra-vb}, Ad populum; LIIII, S. M. Steph.
Tr^{2}, 300vb-01va.
Tr^{4}, 137^{r}-39^{v}, De confessoribus; LI.

100b. *——— Verbum Domini est ut radius solis, qui intrat domum aperta fenestra et clausa fenestra excluditur. A simili, si cor hominis clauditur, non intrabit verbum Dei... expectans dominum quando revertatur a nuptiis.
Bg^{2}, 37rb-8ra.

100c. *——— Sermo Domini comparabilis est quadam proprietate solari radio... et interesse convivio beatorum. Quod nobis prestare dignetur.
PA^{1}, 118vb-20$^{bis\,rb}$.
Pa^{6}, 108rb-11ra, De quolibet confessore.

101a. Spiritus oris nostri Dominus Christus (*Tren.* 4: 20) — Primus cantus, quem cecinit ecclesia in hac die in Matutinam laudem Dei fuit: Hodie si vocem eius audieritis... quo ad fruitionem gaudii in futuro.
Tr^{2}, 291va-92va.
Cf. Tr^{4}, 110^{v}-13^{r}, In pass; XXXVII.
Ar, 94ra-5rb, *Ib.*, LXVI.
Be, 30va-2ra, *Ib.*
PA^{1}, 57va-9rb.

101b. *——— Primum canticum noctis hodierne fuit: Hodie si vocem Domini audieritis... ut corporis et sanguinis eius participes esse mereamur.
Bg^{1}, 9va-10va, *Ib.*
Bs^{1}, 82rb-4ra, *Ib.*, XXIX.
Le^{2}, 70vb-2ra, *Ib.*
Bs^{3}, 219vb-20vb.

102. Sumite de optimis terre frugibus (*Gen.* 43: 11) — Legimus, quod fratres Joseph, quando fratrem suum minimum Benjamin ad Joseph ducendum a patre susceperunt.... eternam retributionem mereamur accipere. Quod nobis prestare dignetur pastor et episcopus animarum nostrarum.
Bg^{3}, 41rb-4rb, Sermo in sinodo ad omnes et maxime ad presbyteros; XXIII.
Bs^{1}, 106vb-09rb, In sinodo ad sacerdotes; XLVI.
Le^{2}, 126ra-28vb, *Ib.*
Pa^{16}, 81vb-4va, *Ib.*, XLIX.
Tr^{3}, 89ra-90vb.

103a. Surge, ingredere civitatem (*Act.* 9: 7) — Ante orationem prepara animam tuam (*Eccli.* 18: 23) — In his verbis sapientis insinuantur tria, que sunt audituris verbum Domini necessaria, scil. preparatio cordis, oratio devota, peccati vitatio... ad emendationem vite et ad adquisitionem glorie.
Tr^{2}, 255va-56va.

103b. *——— Verbum Sapientis egregium admodum auditoribus verbi Dei necessarium... nos ad hospitium bonum perducant.
Ar, 132rb-33va, De s. Paulo; XCII.

103c. *——— Salomon ait: Ante orationem... Tria dicit: Prepara, ora et Deum noli temptare... multas indomitas capit et decipit.
Le^{2}, 139rb-40vb, In conversione s. Pauli.

104a. Surgens Jesus imperavit ventis (*Matt.* 8: 26) — In principio notanda sunt verba Sapientis dicentis: Audi consilium et suscipe disciplinam... (*Prov.* 19: 20). Consilium istud infelix est, quod facit hominem male vivere... per huius tranquillitatis prelibationem perducat nos Salvator noster ad eternitatis quietem.
Tr^{2}, 249va-50rb.

104b. *———Audi consilium... Sine consilio prudentium et disciplina Domini vita humana non potest erigi... ad vitam eternam perducit.
Le^{2}, 42va-3va, Dnca ii p. epiph.

105a. Templum Dei estis (*I Cor.* 3: 16) — Gaudendum est in materialis templi consecratione propter bonorum operum excellentiam, orationum efficaciam, supernorum civium suffragia... diabolum dominum ac possessorem admittit.
Le^{2}, 129vb-31ra, In dedic.

105b. *——— In principio volo vobis ostendere quantum gaudium in ecclesie dedicatione... mereamur pervenire...
Tr^{4}, 151^{r}-54^{r}, *Ib.*, LVIII.

106a. Thesaurus desiderabilis et oleum (*Prov.* 21: 20) — Salomon ait: Cor sapientis erudiet (*Prov.* 16: 23) — Scitis fratres, quod sapientia consistit precipue in benefaciendo, non in docendo bona tantum... ut eo intercedente participes efficiamur celestis glorie.
Tr^{2}, 244va-45rb.

106b. *——— Inprimis attendite, quod dicit vir sapiens: Cor sapientis... et avaritie et superbie operibus vacat.
Bs^{1}, 75vb-6vb, In nat. s. Martini, XXIII.

107a. Tibi dixit cor meum, quesivi vultum tuum (*Ps.* 26: 8) — Licet seges bene crevit et in herba se bene ostenderit, eget tamen pluvia et rore... ut in futuro faciem judicis securi videamus et ut nos recipiat in eterna tabernacula.
Tr^{2}, 286^{ra-va}.
Tr^{4}, 154^{r}-55^{v}, In XL^{a}; LIX.

107b. *——— Cum pauper, cui offensus est dominus.... nos recipiat in eterna tabernacula...
Pa^{7}, 271rb-72va, Dnca intra octabas ascens; LVIII.
Pa^{9}, 79rb-80vb, XL.

108. Trahe me post te (*Cant.* 1: 3) — Hec verba sunt in libro Salomonis, qui dicitur Canticum amoris et non immerito... coronam regni celestis de manu Domini in extremo judicio recipias.
Bg^{1}, 17va-8ra, In ascens.
Bs^{1}, 148va-49va, *Ib.*, LXXXIII.

109a. Transeamus usque Bethlehem (*Luc.* 2: 15) — Sapiens quidam per Spiritum Sanctum loquens ait: Qui interrogationes manifestat, parabit verbum (*Eccli.* 33: 4)... hec sunt vie, quas debemus querere, ad quas perducat nos largitor omnium felicitatum.
Tr^{2}, 299va-300vb.
Be, 13ra-4rb, In natal. Domini.
Bg^{2}, 50rb-2ra.
PA^{1}, 94rb-6va.

109b. *——— Sapiens vir quidam docens, quales esse debeant qui verbum Dei aliis proponunt... et metam sermonis nostri appendite.
Pa^{7}, 230ra-32ra, *Ib.*, XXX.
Pa^{9}, 61rb-2vb, XXVII.

109c. *——— Fratres karissimi, omnis predicator debet habere tria, debet precogitare, quid dicat... tales passus perducunt ad visionem Dei.
Le^{2}, 38va-9rb, De epiph.
Ar, 135va-36rb, XCV.

109d. *——— Sapiens ait: Qui interrogationem manifestat... Hec verba Sapientis multum faciunt contra me... post decursum huius vite labilis recipere premium nostri laboris.
Le^{2}, 36rb-8rb, *Ib.*

109e. *——— Sicut vir quidam sapiens attestatur dicens: Qui interrogationem... et metam sermonis breviter apprehendite.
OM, 55^{v}-7^{r}, Item sermo eiusdem (i.e. Steph.) in apparit. Domini, II.
Tr[4], 89^{r}-91^{v}, *Ib.*, XXVII.

110a. Transite ad me omnes (*Eccli.* 24: 26) — Salomon ait: Melior est finis orationis (*Eccle.* 7: 9). Fatuus mercator est, qui non dat, quod minus valet pro eo, quod maioris valoris esse probatur... quod ipsa adiuvante mereamur obtinere a filio suo...
Pa[11], 271ra-72ra, De b. virg; LVIII, S. M. Steph.
Tr[4], 65^{r}-8^{r}, *Ib.*, XVII.
Ar, 57rb-8rb, *Ib.*, XXXVI.
Pa[6], 92ra-5ra, *Ib.*
Cf. Pa[7], 203vb-06rb, *Ib.*, XI.
Pa[16], 78rb-9vb, *Ib.*, XLVII.

110b. *——— Fratres, hodie beatissimi virgo Maria omnes ad sollempnem curiam nos invitat... nisi delictis filiorum provocetur.
Le[2], 170rb-71rb, *Ib.*

111. Tu cum ieiunas (*Matt.* 6: 17) — Vos, qui amici esse debetis Jesu Christi, qui christiani estis, scire debetis, quod modo venit tempus, in quo est vera probatio amoris... boni vero vitam eternam.
Bg[1], 4^{ra-va}, In cap. ieiun.
Bs[1], 134rb-35rb, *Ib.*, LXVIII.

112. Tu es pastor ovium (*Cf. Gen.* 46: 32) — Si rex terrenus dedisset alicui suorum familiarium potestatem talem super suos captivos incarceratos... Ipsi enim tradite sunt claves regni celorum, ad quod precibus beati Petri.
Le[2], 164va-66ra, De s. Petro.
Tr[2], 287va-88rb, *Ib.*
Tr[4], 36^{r}-8^{v}, *Ib.*, VIII.

113. Turba multa cum audisset (*Cf. Marc.* 12: 37) — Fratres, quantum ad me intelligo, indignus et insufficiens sum ad annuntiandum verbum Dei... subveniendo in eterna tabernacula.
Bg[1], 8vb-9rb, In palmis.
Bs[1], 121rb-22rb, *Ib.*, LVII.

114a. Unguento et variis odoribus delectatur cor (*Prov.* 27: 9) — Salomon ait: Aurem audientem et oculum videntem (*Prov.* 20: 12)... Aurem cordis erigit Dominus, erigit viro fideli, ut affectuose verbum sacrum audiat... justificati per gratiam perveniamus ad gloriam eternam.
Bs[1], 77va-8vb, In nativ. Domini, XXV.
Tr[2], 248va-49va.

114b. *——— Oculum videntem... — Non loquitur hic Salomon de oculo et aure exteriori... ad eternam vitam perveniemus.
Le[2], 18va-20ra, Dnca iii (adv.).

115a. Vado ad eum, qui misit me (*Joh.* 16: 5) — Viri fratres, si quis egregiorum militum, qui se zelo divine dilectionis signaculo crucis insignivit, in medio inimicorum statueretur... gaudium ineffabile, quod nemo tollet a nobis.
Tr[4], 113^{r}-15^{v}, Dnca v p. pascha., XXXVIII.
Ar, 8ra-11ra, In paschali tempore; III.
Pa[16], 134ra-37ra, Dnca iv p. pascha; LXXV.

115b. *——— Fratres, si militi inermi in medio hostium constituto daret quis gladium... introducat in eternam gloriam.
Le², 88vb-90rb, Dnca iiii (p. pascha).

116a. Veni Sancte Spiritus (*Cf.* Chevalier, *Rep. Hymn. II*, No. 21242) — Dum de sollempnitatis hodierne prerogativam merito loqui pertimesco... celestibus desideriis accensi fontem vite sitiamus DNJC^{m}.
Le², 97va-100ra, De Sancto Spiritu.
?(OM, LVIII (f. 51^{v}) M. Steph. in die Penth: Veni sancte Spiritus... *Theme only*)
Tr², 269va-71rb.

116b. *——— Si proprietates ignis pensantur... fontem vite sitiamus.
Pa⁶, 40vb-1vb.

116c. *——— Dum sollempnitatis hodierne prerogativam attendo... fontem vite sitiamus.
Pa⁶, 97va-101ra, In Pent.
Pa¹⁰, 164ra-66ra.
PM, 131ra-33vb, *Ib.*

116d. *——— Dum ineffabilem huius doni, quod petimus, attendo magnitudinem... fontem vite sitiamus.
Bg¹, 19va-20va, *Ib.*
Bs¹, 65ra-7ra, Sermo mag. Steph. in die sancto Pent., XVII.

117a. Venite post me (*Matt.* 4: 19) — Beatus Paulus magnam nobis prestat fiduciam orandi ad Dominum in epistola hodierna et securitatem impetrandi, si devote petierimus... ut possimus effici participes beatitudinis eterne eo intercedente, quod nobis...
Tr⁴, 186^{v}-89^{r}, De s. Andrea, LXXIV.
Pa¹⁶, 56vb-8ra, *Ib.*, XXXII.
PM, 137, *Weg.*, 505.

117b. *——— Fratres karissimi, magnam vobis fiduciam... in celis cum Deo mereamur fieri...
Pa⁶, 111vb-14ra, *Ib.*, *Weg.*, 506.

117c. *——— Rogat nos Dominus et pluribus modis... et reprobis auferetur...
Pa³, 183rb-85vb, *Weg.*, 512.

117d. *——— Beatus Paulus in epistola hodierna invitat ad orandum. Idem Dominus omnium, dives in omnes, qui invocant illum (*Rom.* 10: 12)... ut possimus effici participes beatitudinis eterne...
Le², 184^{ra-vb}, *Ib.*, *Weg.*, 505.

117e. *——— Qui periclitaretur in mari... regnemus in eternis.
PM, 99va-100ra, *Ib.*, *Weg.*, 511.

118a. Viderunt eam hostes et deriserunt sabbata eius (*Tren.* 1: 7) — Scitis fratres, quod licet vinum in se bonum sit et vinee electe, interdum tamen non bene sapit bibenti... tendentibus ad beatitudinem eternam, ad quam perducat nos JCDN.
Bg³, 44rb-7ra, In nativ; XXIIII.
Le², 30rb-2vb, *Ib.*
Ar, 97va-106rb, *Ib.*, LXVIII.
Be, 11rb-3ra, *Ib.*

Tr², 238ra-39va, *Ib.* Le³, 65 (*Kat. HSS Leip*, 719 attrib. to Alain de Lille).
Ni, 92v-3v, *Ib.*
PA¹, 61rb-3vb.
Pa³, 195r-96r.
Pa¹⁶, 26ra-8rb, *Ib.*, XVI.
PM, 133vb-35va.

118b. *——— Si quis statum suum diligenter velit attendere et sicut precipit propheta, cor suum super vias suas ponere... tendentibus ad beatitudinem eternam.
Bg¹, 11vb-3ra, De pass.
Bs¹, 109rb-11ra, *Ib.*, XLVII.

119. Videte, ne contemnatis (*Matt.* 18: 10) — Si dominus rex vellet a vobis redemptionem recipere... ubi non est luctus neque dolor (*Apoc.* 21: 4).
PS, 25r-6v.
Tr², 288va-89ra.
Tr⁴, 87v-9r, Michaelis archangeli, XXVI.

120a. Vidit Jesus hominem sedentem (*Matt.* 9: 9) — Salomon sententiam proponit magne promissionis explanativam omnibus dominici sermonis conservatoribus... ad rectam viam conversi interventu beati Matthei celestis glorie mereamur participes effici.
Tr², 292va-93vb.

120b. *——— Salomon dicit verbum quoddam, ex quo magnam spem possunt concipere, qui verbum Dei audiunt et faciunt... et delinquamus omnia ut peccatum, ut ad eum veniamus.
OM, 54r-5v, Sermo Mag. Steph. Cant. in f. Mathei; I.
Tr⁴, 81v-4r, *Ib.*, XXIII.

121. Viri Galilei, quid statis (*Act.* 1: 11) — Magnum infirmitatis mee solatium est, fratres karissimi, quod Dominus paucis panibus hordeaceis, quos puer ferebat, magnam pavit multitudinem... quo precessit delibatio sequitur et massa.
Bg³, 49vb-52va, In ascens.
Tr², 271rb-72ra.
PS, 89r-92r.
?(Tr⁴, LXXXII (f. 2r), *Theme only*).
PA¹, 63vb-6va.
Pa⁸, 233v-36v, In ascens. ... claustralibus et scolaribus.
Ca, 31vb-3vb.

122a. Vocavit Dominus Deus exercitum ad fletum et planctum (*Is.* 22: 12) — Apostolus ait ad Corinthios (*I Cor.* 13: 1): Si linguis hominum loquar... Si hoc dixit apostolus, quid ego miser dicam... ut in pascha Salvatorem nostrum digne recipere valeatis.
Le², 52ra-vb, In Quinquag.

122b. *——— Paulus vas electionis cum tot et tanta pro Domino esset passus... ut eius beneficio vitam eternam obtineamus.
Bg¹, 5ra-6ra, In diebus Quadrag.
Bs¹, 135rb-36vb, *Ib.*, LXIX.

Class II. — Sermons Appearing in Only One Named Copy

(*Total:* 82 Sermons).

Amice, commoda mihi tres panes (*Luc.* 11: 5) — Audiamus primo, karissimi, verbum illud Sapientis: Quid habet amplius stulto sapiens (*Eccle.* 6: 8)... vitam eternam adepturi sumus.
Le^{2}, 92rb-3va, In rogationibus.

Ave maris stella — In hoc versu continetur laus beate virginis quadripertita, quod ipse pre omnibus sanctis singulariter sit utilis...
Lo^{3}, 36^{r}-53^{v}, (Col:) Expliciunt sermones Steph. Cant. Arch. super ymnum Ave maris stella.
Lo^{2}, 23^{r}-36^{r}, In laudem BMV.
Lo^{4}, 125va-30vb, (Imperf.)

Beati mortui, qui in Domino moriuntur (*Apoc.* 14: 13) — Hec verba dicit Johannes in Apocalipsi, cui in captivitate posito Dominus multa revelavit... Ad quam requiem.
Le^{2}, 153^{ra-b}.

Beatus es Simon bar Jona (*Matt.* 16: 17) — Fratres, orate Dominum ut, sicut aperuit Petro os per confessionem veritatis, ita aperiat nobis corda et ora ad salutem nostram... et simplicitatem cum ipso possidere vitam eternam.
Le^{2}, 156va-57rb, De sancto Petro.

Beatus ille servus (*Matt.* 24: 46) — David (*Ps.* 18: 8) Lex Domini immaculata convertens animas etc. Nota, lex Domini est sermo ipsius, qui, licet pollutis labiis eum proferam, duo facit... in gaudium Domini sui ingredi mereatur.
Le^{2}, 145va-46ra, De sancto Gregorio.

Beatus vir, qui in sapientia morabitur (*Eccli.* 14: 22) — Qui miserias huius vite vigilanter attendit... sui memoriam cordibus imprimens.
Ro, 377^{v}-78^{r}, Sermo mag. Steph. Cant. arch.

Benedicat nos Deus, Deus noster (*Ps.* 66: 8) — Intuens Job incomprehensibilem diei maiestatis excellentiam... sic dictum est excludentur et dicetur eis amen...
OM, 90ra-3va, De trinitate, XXXV.

Benedictione apostolica. Benedicatur gens ecclesiastica, fugiat a nobis fraus diabolica et maneat semper fides catholica... Bele aliz matin leva... que portavit regem celorum et Dominum.
LoA, 38^{r}-9^{r}, Sermo mag. Steph. de Lang. arch. Cant. De sancta Maria.
(See MS Arundel 292, *supra*, for editions).

Christus assistens pontifex (*Hebr.* 9: 11) — Quia omnia alia verba sunt mortua respectu verbi Dei... persecutiones omnes sustineamus, ut ad eternam beatitudinem pertingamus.
Tr^{2}, 280rb-81vb, In dnca. pass. ?

Colligite que superaverunt (*Joh.* 6: 12) — Sermo Dei a quolibet devote et libenter debet audiri, in quo refectio anime recipit... ad quam felicem saturitatem perducat.
Bs^{1}, 137rb-^{vb}, Dnca ante adv; LXXI.
Weg., 70.

Convertentur sedentes in umbra eius (*Os.* 14: 8) — Ecce thema. Auctoritas est Joel. Notandum est, quod in Ecclesiastico (2: 11) legitur: Scitote, quia nullus speravit in Domino et confusus est... ad litus superne patrie perducat nos, quam meritis eius et precibus nobis assequi concedat, qui sine fine vivit et regnat.
Pa^{11}, 269ra-^{vb}, In f. beati Nicholai;
LVI, S. M. Steph.

*——— Per Sapientem quendam dicitur : Scitote... Perveniemus ad portum claritatis eterne.
Ar, 41rb-2vb, *Ib.*, XXV.

*——— Ait vir sapiens: Scitote... Perveniamus ad ipsum per ipsum qui cum patre, etc.
Pa^{7}, 268rb-69va, *Ib.*, LV.

Convertetur ad Dominum qui quievit in umbra eius — Fratres, qui hodie festum beati Nicolai celebratis, bene scitis, quod spes in homine posita sepe fallit... et a peste superbie nos liberet.
Bs^{1}, 120ra-^{vb}, De sancto Nicholao; LV.

Convertimini ad me in toto corde (*Joel* 2: 12) — Ait Dominus omnipotens. Septem sunt genera ieiuniorum. Est ieiunium avari... et tenebras ecclesias illuminando.
Le^{2}, 55ra-5va, In cap. ieiun.

*——— Fratres karissimi, dicit Dominus per prophetam (*Is.* 1: 2): Filios enutrivi... Summa est Dei misericordia... qui ignem venit mittere in terram non nisi ut arderet (*cf. Luc.* 12: 49) JCDN.
Ar, 139ra-40rb, In XL, XCVIIII. *Weg.*, 76.

Cum inducerent puerum Jesum (*Luc.* 2: 27) — Hodie sancta mater ecclesia representat illam processionem, que facta est in Jerusalem... celesti dulcedine perfruamur.
Le^{2}, 143vb-45rb, In purif. (BMV).

Cum venisset Saul ad civitatem Amalech (*I Reg.* 15: 5) — Notat causam cum dicit... nascentur virtutes in vobis.
Tr^{1}, 121rb-23va, Sermo mag. Steph.
Cant. arch. in pass. Domini.

Despondi enim vos (*II Cor.* 11: 2) — Doctor ecclesie est interlocutor sponsalium inter animam et Christum. Unde apostolus: Despondi enim vos... inter amplexos desiderabiles nos recipiat Salvator mundi.
CUL, 117^{r}-21^{r}, Sermo mag. Steph.
arch. de virginibus.

Deus Hebreorum vocavit nos ut eamus viam trium dierum (*Exod.* 3: 18) — Vos docete, qui nos omnes exemplo instruitis... qui hodie pro nobis oblatus est in templo JCDN.
Bs^{1}, 88rb-90ra, In purif. b. Marie,
XXXV.

Dilectus meus mihi (*Cant.* 2: 16) — Auctoritas speciei aromatice comparatur, quam qui integram glutit, nec odorem sentiet nec saporem... ut ad fructum eternum perveniant. Ad quem nos perducat filius virginis...
Le^{2}, 131ra-32ra, (In dedic).

Draco persecutus est mulierem (*Apoc.* 12: 13) — Verbum Dei, quod recolit ecclesia nostra, est lectio, ut patet per hodiernum evangelium, in quo legitur, quod draco antiquus... ut ad nostram patriam post transitum huius maris evolemus.
Tr^{2}, 296va-97rb.

Ecce ascendimus Jerosolimam (*Luc.* 18: 31) — DNJC descendit in carnem, ut nobis ostenderet humilitatem et iustitiam... Venite bendicti patris mei... (*Matt.* 25: 34).
Le^{2}, 73^{ra-va}, In pass.

Ecce Dominus vocat nos ad fletum (*Is.* 22: 12) — Inprimis, karissimi, attendamus illud verbum apostoli: Si linguis hominum loquar (*I Cor.* 13: 1)... et eo mediante vitam eternam adipiscamur, ipso prestante...
Pa^{11}, 216vb-17va, In Quadrag, IX, S. M. Steph. Langt.

Ecce ego mittam piscatores (*Jer.* 16: 16) — Si a quolibet nostrum fratres queratur, utrum velit esse beatus... de aquis mundane voluptatis nos piscari dignetur.
Bs^{1}, 130rb-31rb, In nat. ss. Petri et Paul; LXIIII.
Bs^{2}, 13^{v}-4^{v}, In nat. s. Petri.

*——— Si quereretur ab aliquo, an vellet beatificari, responderet se velle... ad octavum eterne beatitudinis et vos et subditi vestri pervenietis.
Ar, 120ra-21vb, *Ib.*, LXXXIIII.

Ecce positus est hic (*Luc.* 2: 34) — Fratres, scire debetis, quod non verbum Domini eo modo audire debetis, quo cantilenas mimorum... in domum Dei non intrabunt.
Le^{2}, 34^{ra-vb}, Dnca infra oct.
Pa^{16}, 46vb-7vb, In purif. b. virg., XXV.

*——— Cum Dominus locutus fuit ad turbas, eius sermo quibusdam placuit... ut signa Christi imitari possimus et in die iudicii cum militibus coronari.
Ar, 87rb-9ra, In natal. Domini, LXII.
Be, 14rb-5va, *Ib.*
PA^{1}, 50rb-1vb.

Ecce qui mollibus vestiuntur (*Matt.* 11: 8) — Beatus Johannes Baptista, cum esset in vinculis Herodis, audivit miracula Christi... causa omnium malorum, a quibus nos defendat.
Le^{2}, 21^{va-b}, Dnca iii in adv.

Ecce venit ad templum sanctum suum (*Cf. Mal.* 3: 1) — Domini et fratres mei, miser ego et virtutum omnimodis vacuus et ieiunus... ut ipsum non punitorem, sed eternorum largitorem invenire possimus in patria.
Le^{2}, 141ra-43ra, In purif. s. Marie.

Ecce vicit leo (*Apoc.* 5: 5) — Dum fleret Johannes, quia nemo dignus inventus est aperire librum... ut ad dexteram Dei transferamur.
Le^{2}, 80vb-2ra, De resurrect...
Ar, 22va-3ra, *Ib.*, XV.
Be, 40vb-2ra, *Ib.*

Ego sum pastor bonus (*Joh.* 10: 11) — Necessarium fuerat, fratres et patres karissimi, ut diei presentis exhortationem lingue torrenti et fecundo pectori commisissem ... ad quam gloriam nos inducere, deducere, et perducere dignetur...
Le², 85ʳᵃ-6ᵛᵇ, Dnca ii p. pascha.
Weg., 216.

*——— Karissimi fratres, intuendum nobis est... amittat regnum.
Pa¹⁶, 149ᵛᵇ-51ʳᵃ, LXXXI. *Weg.*, 215.
Ste. Gen. 2787, 159ᵛ-160ᵛ. (See D'Alverny, 131).

Emittes spiritum tuum (*Ps.* 103: 30) — Nituntur seculares, ut habitu splendeant, ut vestes decentes habeant... supra multa constituat in regno glorie.
Le², 100ʳᵃ-01ᵛᵇ, De Sancto Spiritu. Pa⁷, 287ʳᵇ-89ʳᵇ, In Pent; LXVII.

*——— Fratres, scitis et videtis, quod homines in magnis sollempnitatibus desiderant et nituntur habere vestes pretiosas... in futuro vita glorie.
Ar, 46ᵛᵇ-9ᵛᵃ, De Spiritu Sancto; XXX.
Be, 46ᵛᵇ-8ᵛᵇ, In Pent.

Erat Jesus eiciens demonium (*Luc.* 11: 14) — Adversarius genus humanum tripliciter impugnat, ablatione temporalium, lesione corporis... absterget Deus omnem lacrimam ab oculis sanctorum (*Apoc.* 7: 17; 21: 4).
Le², 65ʳᵇ-6ᵛᵇ, Dnca iii (Quadrag.)

Estote imitatores mei (*I Cor.* 4: 16; 11: 1) — Sicut filii karissimi et ambulate in dilectione sicut et Christus dilexit nos... Salomon: Fili, inclina aurem tuam (*Prov.* 22: 17)... Deum Deorum in Sion videamus cum gaudio.
Le², 64ʳᵇ-5ʳᵇ, Dnca iiiᵃ (adv.)
?OM, XLIII (f. 51ʳ), M. Steph. Cant. (*theme only*)

Et veniat super nos salutare tuum — Hodie sancti et beati senis Simeonis adimpletur desiderium, et quod promisit misericordia solvit veritas... fructum celestis vite reperimus.
Le², 151ʳᵇ-53ʳᵃ, In purif.

Frange esurienti panem tuum (*Is.* 58: 7) — Dominus docet nos per prophetam, quod ieiunium sit ei acceptabile... Cor autem sapientis... lutum amittit.
Bs¹, 47ᵛᵃ-8ᵛᵇ, De elemosina, I.

Gaude et letare filia Edom (*Tren.* 4: 21) — Cum sol vitream quandam tenuem et lucidam penetrat et illuminat... et glorie quam precibus beate Magdalene, etc.
OM, 65ʳ-7ᵛ, Steph. Cant. In festo b. Marie Magd; X.

Gaudete in Domino semper (*Phil.* 4: 4) — Fratres karissimi, iste quattuor virtutes sunt sorores, gaudium, modestia, petitio, pax... quia sic adquiritur Dei gratia.
Le², 22ᵛᵃ-3ʳᵇ, iiiiᵃ Dnca (adv.) Ar, 178ᵛᵃ-79ʳᵇ, In adv; CXXX.
Ib., 134ᵛᵇ-35ʳᵇ, *Ib.*

Homo quidam erat dives, qui habebat villicum (*Luc.* 16: 1) — Homo iste dives Deus est, eius, villicus est quicumque homo quasi ville custos sicut dicit *Eccli.* (15: 14) Deus ab initio constituit hominem... recipere mereamur id, quod nostrum est.
Le², 109ᵛᵃ-10ᵛᵇ, Dnca ixᵃ (post pent.)

Homo quidam fecit cenam magnam (*Luc.* 14: 16) — Fratres karissimi, non spe temporalis mercedis, sed potius eterne remunerationis semen Dei inter vos seminare proposui... ubi rex veritas, lex est caritas, possessio eternitas.
Le², 103ra-05rb, Dnca ii (p. pent.)

In Deo speravit cor meum (*Ps.* 27: 7) — Audivimus, fratres karissimi, et bene scimus, quod optimis plena est civitas ista doctoribus... tandem perveniatis ad gaudia paradisi. Quod nobis et vobis prestare dignetur.
Tr¹, 85rb-9rb, Sermo Mag. Steph. Arch. Cant. ad populum; Londini 25.VIII.1213.
(See MS Troyes 862, *supra*, for edition).

In diebus illis suscitabit Deus regnum celi (*Dan.* 2: 44) — Sciatis, karissimi, quod Deus qui creavit celum et terram, et omnia, que in eis sunt pro nostra salute... Oremus ergo Dominum, ut nos a fune triplici liberet.
Le², 133rb-34vb, In adv.

?In ingressu oraculi fecit Salomon duo ostia (*III Reg.* 6: 31) — Domini et patres reverendi, venio ad vos non in sublimitate sermonis... percipiatis incomparabile eterni regni premium.
OM, LXIII (f. 51^{v}) M. Steph. in sollempnitate apostolorum Petri et Pauli; (*Theme only*)
Ar, 140rb-41rb, In nativ. apost; C.

In omni ore quasi mel indulcabitur (*Eccli.* 49: 2) — Vere felix est sanctorum memoria, que nulli dulcedini comparatur... quatinus pro labore nostro similem ipsi fructum repertemus.
OM, 68^{r-v}, M. Steph. Cant. unius conf; XII.

In salutari tuo anima mea — Tria sunt que hominem gravant, infirmitas peccati, tribulatio et temptatio... coronam triumphalem recipere de manu Domini.
Le², 116ra-17ra, Dnca xxi^{a} (post pent.)

In Veteri Lege offerebat sacerdos diversa sacrificia secundum peccatorum genera, unde nunc hyrcus, nunc agnus, nunc aries, nunc vitulus et multa talia genera... crux Christi commendat.
CUL, 113^{r}-14^{r}, Sermo Mag. Steph. Arch. Cant.

Johannes cum audisset (*Matt.* 11: 2) — Hec erat causa, quare Johannes misit discipulos ad Jesum, quia ipsi audierant de eo, quod maiora opera faceret... perducere ad gaudia vite perpetue.
Le², 25va-7ra, Dnca iii (adv.)

Ipse vos baptizabit Spiritu Sancto (*Matt.* 3: 11) — Si beatus Johannes Baptista, cui Dominus testimonium perhibuit... collocemur in gloria eterna.
Le², 27rb-8vb, Dnca iii (adv.)

*——— Si quis verba beati Johannis Baptiste diligenter attendat timere sibi potest, si verbum Domini predicare presumat indigne... ad statum felicitatis eterne, quam nobis conferre velit Redemptor noster.
Be, 7vb-9ra, In quarta dnca adv.
PA¹, 90rb-2rb.

*——— Dominus ait de Johanne: Inter natos mulierum non fuit maior Johanne Baptista (*Matt.* 11: 11). Et ipse Johannes ait de Domino: Non sum dignus solvere corrigiam (*Joh.* 1: 27)... A simili nos obliti sumus beneficium nativitatis Domini nostri idest Christi.

Bg², 46va-8ra.

Justum deduxit Dominus per vias rectas (*Sap.* 10: 10) — Vellem, karissimi, ad vos venire... impinguant et fructificare faciunt.

Tr¹, 89rb-90va, Eiusdem (i.e. Steph.) sermo in festo s. Martini.

Nemo potest duobus dominis servire (*Matt.* 6: 24) — Isaias docet, quomodo verba Domini sint audienda. Dominus: Audite verbum Domini, qui timetis verbum eius... et Christi domino adherere perseverant ipso adiuvante.

Le², 112va-14rb, Dnca xv (post pent.)

Ar, 164ra-66ra, *Ib.*, CXVII.
Lo¹, 98va-9va.
Pa⁷, 311ra-12va, *Ib.*, LXXXIII.
Pa⁹, 99vb-102rb, LVIII.
Pa¹⁶, 91ra-2vb, *Ib.*, LIIII.
PM, 114va-16vb, In xv^a^ dnca post trin.
Cf. Va, 85^v^.

Nescitis, quia membra vestra templum sunt Spiritus Sancti (*I Cor.* 6: 19) — Fratres, verba ista apostoli vero corde a quolibet nostrum audiri debent... et veram pervenias inchoationem.

Bs¹, 128rb-29ra, In dedic. eccl., LXII.

Cf. Va, 84^r^.

Noli timere filia Sion: Ecce enim evangelizo vobis gaudium magnum (*Luc.* 2: 10) — Sicut in hac nocte legimus in Isaia, dicit Dominus predicatoribus et illis, qui debent alios movere ad benefaciendum: Loquimini ad cor Israel (*cf. Is.* 40: 2)... ad lumen, quod numquam deficit, ad quod...

Pa¹¹, 261rb-62va, In nativ. Domini; XLIX, S. M. Steph.

Numquid elevabis in nebula vocem tuam (*Job* 38: 34) — Scitis fratres, quod mos est pauperum gaudere in celebratione festorum... satiabimur in meridie in eterne claritatis beatitudine.

Ar, 65vb-8vb, De Magdalena, XLI.

*——— Pauperes in diebus festis magis letantur... ad patriam in presenti celestem nos perducat.

Le², 162ra-63vb, *Ib.*

Pa⁷, 239vb-41vb, *Ib.*, XXXIX.

*——— Pauperes gaudent in festo propter dationem elemosine, que tunc solet fieri maxime. Qui plus habet peccati, plus pauper est. Hodie festum est Magdalene... comprehendit sub primo vel secundo.

Bg², 40rb-1rb.

Numquid ingressus es in profundum maris (*Job* 38: 16) — Quis est, qui in profundum huius maris potest ingredi? Nemo nisi Deus. Mare istud appellatur cor hominis... delicta imitari valeamus in aliquo.

Le², 163vb-64va, De s. Maria Mag.

Obsecro vos tamquam advenas (*I Petr.* 2: 11) — Considerandum in principio, fratres et amici, quod torrens mollit terram, per quam transit... gaudium quod nemo tollet a vobis (*cf. Joh.* 16: 22).
Le², 86vb-7vb, Dnca iii (p. pascha).

Obtulerunt pro eo par turturum (*cf. Luc.* 2: 24) — DJC tribus vicibus oblatus est, primo in templo, secundo in ligno, tertio in celo... ut cum Christo offeramur in celo.
Le², 143^{ra-vb}, In purif. (BMV).

Omnis arbor, que non facit fructum bonum (*Matt.* 7: 19) — Fratres karissimi, festum dedicationis huius ecclesie in crastino annua revolutione celebratur... angelis associari in eterna felicitate.
Tr², 294va-95rb, Sermo in festo ded. eccl. (Marg.)

Petite, ut gaudium vestrum plenum sit (*Joh.* 16: 24) — In hodierna epistola monet beatus Jacobus apostolus quoslibet fideles, ut sint factores verbi.... nec in cor hominis ascendit. (*I Cor.* 2: 9).
Le², 91rb-2rb, Dnca v (p. pascha).

Ponite corda vestra (*Ps.* 47: 14) — Salomon narrat quedam (quoddam ?) cavendum in necessitate cure circa finem... in qua ipse glorificetur....
Pa¹¹, 274vb-75vb, In exalt. sancte crucis, LXII, S. M. Steph.

Prudentes virgines acceperunt oleum (*Matt.* 25: 4) — Que sunt sapientes virgines, que ita dicunt et faciunt sicut antique sapientes femine dixerunt... ut ad generales nuptias introire valeatis.
Bs¹, 76vb-7va, Sermo de virginibus; XXIIII.

*——— Cum beatus Paulus ab accusatoribus suis Romam duceretur, ut coram imperatore sisteretur... coruscabunt corpora iustorum in gloria, quam Salvator noster...
Ar, 115va-17rb, Ad sanctimoniales; LXXXI.

Quasi myrrha electa dedit suavitatem odoris (*Eccli.* 24: 20) — Legitur in *Apoc.* (22: 2) quod duodecim sunt fructus ligni vite, id est verbi Christi... qui reddetur vel retribuetur pro carnis mortificatione.
Tr², 256va-57vb. Ar, 130va-32rb, XCI. *Cf.* Va, 57^{r}.

Qui crediderit in me, flumina de ventre eius (*Joh.* 7: 38) — Si quis ad elemosinam vocaret pauperes, statim convenirent propter panis desiderium... Ecce quantum Deo placet oratio justi.
Le², 132ra-33rb, In pass.

*——— Fratres karissimi, sicut pauperes... vocem illam sanctissimam et dulcissimam ex ore Salvatoris.
Pa⁶, 38rb-40vb, De sancto spiritu.

* (?)——— Dum clamatur "manjue pain" pauperes undique leti concurrunt...
Pa¹², 135^{v}-36^{r}.

Qui descendunt mare in navibus (*Ps.* 106: 23) — Domini mei et patres, verbum Sapientis, immo verbum Sapientie est (*Prov.* 27: 7): Anima saturata calcabit favum... suscipere opus ultime retributionis.
Bs[1], 123vb-26vb, Sermo ad episcopos; LIX. Pa[3], 201^{r}-06^{v}. Pa[10], 159^{v}.

(Et) Qui preibant et qui sequebantur (*Marc.* 11: 9) — Cum mundus tempore nostro ad tantam peccatorum ignominiam devenerit... recipiant vos in eterna tabernacula.
Le[2], 75vb-7ra, In palmis.

Qui sunt isti, qui ut nubes volant (*Is.* 60: 8) — Verba ista et presenti congruunt sollempnitati et vestre possunt assignari conversationi. Qualiter autem conveniunt huic sollempnitati videmus. Isaias previdens in spiritu futuram conversionem gentium... ubi cum Moyse faciem Dei videaris.
CUL, 111^{r}-13^{r}, Sermo mag. Steph. arch.

Reddet Deus mercedem (*Cf. Sap.* 10: 17) — Salomon ait (*Prov.* 19: 16): Qui custodit animam suam... Quis est ille, qui custodit viam suam, quis est ille, qui negligit viam suam... precibus et meritis beati Stephani protomartyris obtinere valeamus, ipso prestante.
Pa[11], 268ra-69ra, De quolibet martyre; LV, S. M. Steph.

*——— Salomon (*Prov.* 19:16): Qui custodit precepta Domini... Quidam sunt, qui nolunt querere verba Dei... et sicut sanctus Stephanus pro eo mortem subiit.
Pa[6], 103va-05rb, De beato Stephano.

Rorate celi desuper (*Is.* 45: 8) — Sancta mater ecclesia his diebus prophetarum recitat suspiria... In beatitudine nos salvet...
OM, 67^{v}-8^{r}, In adv; XI. *Weg.*, 450.

Salvatorem expectamus (*Phil.* 3: 20) — Volo vos, fratres, non ignorare tempus visitationis vestre... ad quam... vitam, que exsuperat omnem sensum (*Phil.* 4: 7) nos perducat.
Le[2], 17va-8va, Dnca iii adv.

Scimus, quoniam diligentibus Deum (*Rom.* 8: 28) — Legitur in *Ez.* (47: 12): Erunt fructus in cibum... Fructus sunt bona opera, folia sermo Domini... quod ipsum videre mereamur.
Tr[2], 283rb-84ra. *Weg.*, 455.

*——— Bene ait Ez. loquens de Christo: Erunt fructus eius... ut per erogationem elemosinarum et abstinentiam desideriorum...
Ar, 162ra-63vb, CXVI.

*——— Ezechiel loquens sub figura...
PM, 142rb-44va, De apostolis (in) commune.

*——— Ut ait Ez. loquens de Christo: Erunt fructus eius in cibum... Arbor vite est Christus, cuius fructus cibus est... transferat nos Christus ad celeste convivium.
Pa[16], 50va-2ra, De pluribus sanctis, XXVIII. *Weg.*, 456.

Si abstuleris de medio tui catenam (*Is.* 58: 9) — Legimus Dominum ad opera misericordie nos invitantem dixisse... participes nos faciat misericors et miserator Dominus.
Bg^3, 37rb-8vb, Sermo ad claustrales in Quadrag... XXI. Be, 28rb-30va, *Ib.*

Simile est regnum celorum homini regi, qui fecit nuptias (*Matt.* 22: 2) — Legitur quod cum Dominus misisset Josue contra Amalech, Moyses ascendit, ut oraret... pedibus illuc currere non possumus.
Le^2, 115rb-16ra, Dnca xx p. pent.

Si sciret paterfamilias (*Luc.* 12: 39) — Sepe contingit, quod quando alique cum magno labore acquiruntur, magis amantur et carius observantur... doceat familiam nostram regere, etc.
Pa^{11}, 245^{ra-va}, Sermo communis, XXXVI, S. M. Steph. de Langt.

Sollempnitates vestras odivit anima mea (*Is.* 1: 14) — Cibus delicatus hominem habentem sanum palatum reficit competenter... negotium nostrum fideliter pertractabit.
PS, 75^{v}-6^{v}.
Ar, 113^{ra-vb}, De quolibet sancto; LXXVII.
Le^3, 76 (*Kat. HSS Leip*, 719; the sermon is attrib. to Alain de Lille).
Pa^3, 192^{v}-93^{v}.
Pa^{12}, 132^{v}-33^{v}.

Solve iubente Domino terrarum Petre cathenas — Gloria mea semper innovabitur... (*Job* 29: 20) Omnis autem gloria in presenti esse deberet, ut seipsum primo corrigeret... ut pateant celestia regna beatis. Ad que nos meritis et precibus beati Petri et aliorum Sanctorum pervenire concedat DNCJ.
Pa^{11}, 282rb-83vb, In festiv. b. Petri; LXVIIII, S. M. Steph. Re, 54^{v}-5rb.

*——— Vir quidam sapiens ait:... pervenire concedat DNJC.
Pa^6, 101ra-03va, *Ib.*

Super lapidem unum septem oculi sunt (*Zach.* 3: 9) — Karissimi, Dominus et Salvator noster hunc diem triplici beneficio consecravit, scil. passionis sue initio... ut Jesum Christum Salvatorem nostrum digne percipere possimus.
Tr^2, 257vb-58va.

Surge, tolle lectum tuum (*Matt.* 9: 6) — Ad hanc domum convenit hec captatio. Convenerunt ad David, qui erant constituti in angustia... qui operatus est predictum miraculum.
Le^2, 114rb-15rb, Dnca xix p. pent.

Surrexit Dominus vere (*Luc.* 24: 34) — Apostolus oravit Colossenses (3: 16): Hoc verbum habitet in vobis abundanter. In illis non habitat verbum... et sic de aliis apparitionibus.
Pa^{11}, 258vb-59vb, In resurrect; XLVII, S. M. Steph.

*——— Proficuum est audituris verbum Domini, ut sic postulent effici... cognitionem Salvatoris habebimus hic per spem, quod nobis largiatur idem Deus...
Be, 39va-40vb, In pascha.
PA^1, 114va-16vb.

Tempus est spargendi lapides (*Eccle.* 3: 5) — Fratres karissimi, de me misero et insufficiente et dolente possum hoc vere dicere illud verbum, quod dicit beatus Job... ut in fine mundi colligantur cum fructu centuplo.
Bs[1], 127va-28rb, De omnibus sanctis,
LXI.

Tres sunt, qui testimonium dant in terra (*I Joh.* 5: 8) — Qualiter audiendum sit, verbum Domini, docet Sapiens, cum ait: Audi tacens... (*Eccli.* 32: 9) Tres sunt, qui... Hec sunt verba Johannis evangeliste. Prima medietas verborum pertinet ad festa, que precesserunt... in gaudium eternum intrare mereamur.
Tr[2], 268rb-69rb. PA[1], 81rb-2vb.

Tribularer si nescirem misericordiam tuam, Domine. — Sicut legitur in evangelio hodierno, per tria temptatus fuit Dominus, per superbiam... facienda est.
Tr[4], 171^{v}-73^{v} Dnca i Quadrag; Be, 21vb-2va, *Ib.*
LXVIII.

*——— Tu dixisti: Nolo mortem peccatoris (*Ez.* 33: 11). Qui Chananeum et publicanum vocasti ad penitentiam et Petrum lacrimantem suscepisti, misericors Dominus, quam utile sit audire verbum Domini... ad quietem eterne felicitatis mereamur pervenire.
PA[1], 102rb-04rb.
Pa[6], 84rb-7ra, *Ib.*
Pa[16], 74vb-6rb, *Ib.*, XLIIII.

*——— Quam utile sit audire...
PM, 147vb-49va, De misericordia et iudicio.

Tu es, qui venturus es (*Matt.* 11: 3) — Cum precursor Christi vinculatus ab Herode opera illius audiret... in futuro transferet ad gloriam, quam nobis largiri dignetur Redemptor propitius.
Cf. Tr[4], 74^{v}-7^{v}, In adv., XX. Be, 6rb-7vb, *Ib.*
Bg[2], 48ra-50rb.
PA[1], 87va-90rb.

Ubicumque fuerit corpus (*Matt.* 24: 28) — Corpus Domini nostri Jesu Christi iam consecrabitur in altari divina virtute et ministerio novi sacerdotis... ut interminabilis gaudii participes efficiamini. Quod vobis largiri dignetur.
Tr[2], 243^{ra-va}.

Vexilla regis prodeunt — Fratres mei, quando rex in exercitu suo precepit, vexillum suum a terra tolli... idioma suum mutabit hiis, qui modo non mutant.
Le[2], 72rb-3ra, In passione Domini.

Vide arcum et benedic eum (*Eccli.* 43: 12) — Cum vir spiritum Dei habens sacerdotem magnum describens arcui celesti illum comparat... vel si peccatores sumus nos visitare dignetur.
Bs[1], 118rb-19vb, De sancto Maglioro;
LIIII.

Vincenti dabo (*Apoc.* 2: 7, 17) — Solet vulgariter dici: Qui bene diligit, tarde obliviscitur. Est autem triplex amor, quia quidam diligit carnem... cum electis Dei in eternum victuri.
Bs[1], 145va-46va, De sancto Vincentio;
LXXX.

Vos sacerdotes Domini vocabimini (*Is.* 61: 6) — Materiam planam et evidentem vobis proponimus, quia occulta et profunda ad presens investigare non intendimus... vere eritis sacerdotes Domini et ministri Dei altissimi...
Le[2], 121va-23rb, Ad sacerdotes.

Class III. — Addenda: Sermons Appearing in Only One Named Copy (*Total:* 25 Sermons).

N.B. It will be noted that the *themes* in the following sermons appear elsewhere in other named copies. In many cases, it has been found that differences in *incipits* indicate a sermon that is in content a version of the named sermon. (See, *supra*, sermons appearing in more than one named copy). In the following, however, this is not the case, and investigation has shown that these are *different* sermons having neither copies nor variants in other named MSS.

Accingere cilicio (*Jer.* 6: 26) — Dilectissimi, indignus ego scientia et vita ad verbum Domini annuntiandum... stolam anime et corporis.
Le[2], 55va-6va, In cap. ieiun.

Apertis thesauris (*Matt.* 2: 11) — Bone gens, hodierna festivitas cum maxima sollempnitate debet venerari... felicitatis eterne recipiet claritatem.
Bs[1], 147va-48va, In epiph., LXXXII.

‡——— Scio, dilectissimi, quod ignitum est verbum Domini (*Cf. Ps.* 118: 140). Unde Jeremias in persona Domini ait: Nonne verba mea sunt quasi ignis (*Jer.* 23: 29)... ad regnum triumphans, cuius participes.
Le[2], 39va-41rb, De epiph.

*——— Hec verba mystice intellecta fidem nostram roborant et mores instruunt... ut alii videntes glorificent patrem nostrum, qui in celis est.
Ar, 78rb-9ra, *Ib.*, LII.

Exemplum dedi vobis (*Joh.* 13: 15) — Rex aliquis in sua coronatione post omnia discrete petita tribuit et exaudit... Jesu Christo compatiamur, ut cum eo regnemus.
Tr[2], 258va-59ra.

Justus cor suum tradidit ad vigilandum (*Eccli.* 39: 6) — Splendidum cor bonum in epulis (*Eccli.* 30: 27) — Epule enim illius diligentes fuerunt... artam sanguinis sui manu teneat. Quod ipse prestare dignetur, qui in Trinitate perfecta vivit.
Pa[11], 224ra-vb, De quolibet martyre vel confessore; XVI, S. M. Steph.
?(OM, XLI [f. 51r], M. Steph. Cant. in unius confessoris — *Theme only*)

*——— *Eccli.* (30: 27) dicit: Splendidum cor... ad mensam Patris digne in die Pasche accedere valeamus.
Ar, 79vb-81va, De uno conf; LIIII.

Oculi mei semper ad Dominum (*Ps.* 24: 15) — Fratres, cum Dominus adhuc esset in carne mortali, curavit surdum et mutum... continet ille locus, ad quem nos perducat Jesus Christus.
Pa[11], 221ra-22ra, In Quadrag; XIII, S. M. Steph. de Langt.

♯——— Isaias (32: 4): Cor stultorum intelliget sapientiam (scientiam)... Lingua balbutientis nimis brevis est... tandem ad vitam eternam perducat.
Le², 62va-3ra, Dnca iii in Quadrag.

♯——— In dominica precedenti clamavit ecclesia ad Dominum dicens: Reminiscere miserationum tuarum Domine (*Ps.* 24: 6)... totius beatitudinis plenitudo, ad quam perducere...
Le², 63ra-4rb, Dnca iii in Quadrag.

Omne datum optimum (*Jac.* 1: 17) — Firma nititur columpna, qui in rebus gerendis consilio munitur sapientis... et perveniemus ad lucem glorie. Quam nobis conferre dignetur pater luminum.
Tr², 266ra-67ra. Ar, 42vb-4rb, In paschali tempore; XXVI.

Petite et accipietis (*Joh.* 16: 24) — Sapiens ait (*Prov.* 5: 7): Audi me fili, quod non recedas a verbis oris mei... et coronam immarcessibilem recipiatis.
Le², 93vb-4vb, In rogationibus.

*——— Sapiens quidam per Spiritum Sanctum loquens sententiam profert commendabilem, qua evidenter ostenditur, quod necessarium est audire verbum Dei... ad gaudium superne felicitatis mediantibus illis.
Be, 42ra-3ra, In Letania maiore.
PA¹, 112va-14va.

♯——— Beatus Jacobus in hodierna epistola nos instruit, ut sermonem Domini in opus producamus, alioquin nosmetipsos seducimus... ut gaudium quod hic prelibamus in gratia, nobis impleatur in gloria.
Tr², 265ra-66ra.

Puer natus est nobis (*Is.* 9: 6) — Libenter audiret incarceratus rumores sue liberationis, pauper rumores regni suscipiendi... illum magnum nuntium: Venite benedicti... (*Matt.* 25: 34).
Pa¹¹, 241rb-vb, In nativ; XXX; S. M. Steph. de L.

♯——— Dominus dominantium rex regum, cui nomen omnipotens, humane infirmitatis consortium non aspernatus nec dedignatus... unde ei sit honor et gloria.
Bs¹, 90ra-1vb, *Ib.*, XXXVI.

♯——— Dominus noster sex gaudia nuntiavit nobis, primum per Isaiam et alios prophetas: Ecce virgo concipiet... Hoc est in cordibus principum et potentium.
Le², 33va-4ra, *Ib.*

Si quis cognoverit plagam cordis sui (*III Reg.* 8: 38) — Ut idem Salomon ait: Qui docet fatuum quasi qui compaginat... (*Eccli.* 22: 7). Vere testa est fatuus... ad eterne glorie perducat coronam.
Tr⁴, 127v-29v, In dedicat., XLVI. Ar, 158ra-59va, *Ib.*, CXIIII.

Sint lumbi vestri (*Luc.* 12: 35) — Filiis Israel exeuntibus de Egipto precepit Dominus facere farinam... Vigilemus igitur et expectemus vitam eternam...
OM, 59v-61r, M. Steph. Cant. unius confessoris, VI.

♯——— Verbum Domini attento et diligenti animo a quolibet vestrum debet audiri, quia in eo est veritas et vita... (*Matt.* 25: 34): Venite benedicti...
Bs¹, 146va-47va, In purif. s. Marie; LXXXI.

Surgite, vigilemus, venite adoremus — Hec est prima cantilena, quam hodie summe mane cantavit... adoremus contra superbiam et ita habemus regnum Dei.
Tr[2], 295va-96ra. *Weg.*, 472.

♯——— Audivimus in evangelio hodierno, quod Johannes Baptista vocavit duos de discipulis suis... ut possimus in die Domini a dexteris eius collocari.
Le[2], 20ra-1rb, Dnca iii (adv.)   Pa[3], 207vb-09vb. *Weg.*, 472.
Pa[16], 59vb-61ra, Dnca iiii in adv., XXXIIII. *Weg.*, 472.

Templum Dei estis (*I Cor.* 3: 16) — Hoc est verbum beati Pauli, fratres, dulce bonis et timendum malis et horribile... ut ad eternam beatitudinem mereamur pervenire.
Bs[1], 141rb-42va, In dedicat; LXXVI.

*——— Fratres karissimi, congratulari debent fideles in festo dedicationis ecclesie... stabiliter tribus iam dictis modis... templum.
PA[1], 120$^{bis rb}$-21ra.

*——— Magna species habenda est in dedicatione ecclesie... hic in corpore et ibi in anima.
Bg[2], 39rb-40rb.

Trahe me post te (*Cant.* 1: 3) — Karissimi, hodie Christus discipulis suis convescens exprobravit illis duritiam cordis eorum... ipso preduce gregis humilitas subsequatur.
Le[2], 94vb-5vb, In ascens.

♯——— Ne expectetis a me sermonem politum, quia non sapientia verbi loquor vobis, ne evacuetur crux Christi... pax persecutionem patientibus, ad quam nos perducat, qui sine fine...
Le[2], 95vb-6vb, *Ib.*   Pa[16], 87vb-9ra, LII.

♯——— Estimet unusquisque quanto affectu et desiderio apostoli viderunt Dominum ascendentem... absterget Deus omnem lacrimam ab oculis sanctorum.
Bs[1], 113vb-14ra, *Ib.*, L.

Videte, ne quis vestrum sit fornicator (*Hebr.* 12: 16) — Structura stabilis edificii fieri nequit vel post constructionem custodiri, nisi celestis edificator manum gratie dignetur apponere... cum Esau vitio gule privemini hereditate celesti.
Le[2], 135rb-36vb, In cap. ieiun.   PA[1], 99va-102rb.
Pa[3], 211rb-13va.
Pa[16], 73ra-4vb, In Quadrag., XLIII.

♯——— In *Ps.* (126: 1) legitur: Nisi Dominus edificaverit domum... per varias iniurias et peccata remeavit.
Tr[4], 178^{r}-79^{r}, In Quinquag.   Ar, 180ra-82vb, In XL^{a}, CXXXII.
Be, 22va-3va, *Ib.*

Class IV. — Sermons Appearing Only in Anonymous Copies [1]
(*Total:* 51 Sermons).

A a a Domine Deus, nescio loqui (*Jer.* 1: 6) — Si Iheremias ab utero sanctificatus, a Domino propheta electus, a criminali macula alienus, divina inspiratione edoctus, timens predicationis officium assumere... ne coram ipso homine sua fateri crimina vereatur.
Ar, 141rb-42rb; CI, *Weg.*, 1.

Accepto responso in somnis (*Matt.* 2: 12) — Coartor nimis e duobus mentem meam distrahentibus... Deus et Salvator, testis, advocatus, et iudex, una cum spiritu sancto per infinita seculorum secula. amen.
Be, 15va-6va; In epiph.
Pa^1, 57^r-8^v; *Ib.*

Auris mea audivit te — Sicut ex prophetico colligitur eloquio quasi ignis est dominicus sermo... penitentiam condignam faciatis.
Ar, 81va-2vb; In cap. ieiun; LVI.

Celebravit Salomon dedicationem (*II Macc.* 2: 12) — Considerantes, quanta fuerit sollempnitas... quam edificabitis mihi.
PM, 109ra-^{va}; In ded. eccl.

Christus pro nobis passus est (*I Pet.* 2: 21) — Christo igitur carne passo... contra omnem impugnationem hostis.
PM, 106vb-07va; In parascheve.

(Si) Cognovit eum in benedictionibus suis (*Eccli.* 44: 26) — Duplex est benedictio glorie et gratie... recumbens et pacificans.
Pa^7, 246ra-^{vb}; De sancto Martino.

Consideravit semitas domus sue (*Prov.* 31: 27) — In hiis verbis Salomonis sex ad presens notanda occurrunt, que beatissime Rictrudi conveniunt... perveniamus ad regna polorum et beatitudine perfruamur.
Ar, 74vb-6va; De beata Rictrude; XLVIII.

Continuo relectis retibus (*Matt.* 4: 20) — Bona gens, quando redeo ad meipsum, valde deterreor de verbo, quod hodie audimus... in mundo non habet, unde delectetur.
Ar, 106rb-07va; De sancto Andrea; LXXII. *Weg.*, 441.

Contra tres hostes est pugnandum, quia, ut ait Job (7: 1), militia est vita hominis super terram... ad cuius pugne victoriam perducat nos Deus.
Pa^6, 54va-5va; Cap. ieiun.

Dedi flumina in deserto (*Is.* 43: 20) — Proverbialiter et vere dicitur: Qui non ardet, non incendit... servare curetis. Quod nobis... prestare dignetur, etc.
Pa^3, 190^v-92^v.

[1] On the significance of these anonymous texts in Cl. IV and V, see Ch. II on the classification of the MSS, *supra*.

Dentes tui sicut grex (*Cant.* 6: 5) — Sub hac figura commendatur ecclesie quadripartita convenientia. Commendatur enim a communione fidelium... ut cum venerit ad iudicium recipiat te in celi habitaculo.
PA^1, 69ra-70ra.

Deridetur iusti simplicitas (*Job* 12: 4) — In prima dominica adventus evangelium facit nobis mentionem de primo Domini adventu, qui fuit humilitatis et misericordie... Ad quas sollempnitates.
Ar, 142ra-43vb; In adv; CII. *Weg.*, 122.

Dilectus meus descendit in hortum suum (*Cant.* 6: 1) — Viri fratres, qui auscultavit verbum Dei... Fratres, sermo iste, quem a principio dixi: Dilectus meus... canticum est ecclesie... ad salutem corporis et anime.
Ar, 92vb-4ra; In annunt. Domini; LXV.
Be, 50ra-1va; *Ib.*
PA^1, 55vb-7va.

Diligite iustitiam, qui iudicatis terram (*Sap.* 1: 1) — Eloquia Domini sunt eloquia casta... qui venturus est iudicare vivos et mortuos...
Be, 51va-3ra; Exhortatorius sermo.

Dissipat impios (*Prov.* 20: 26) — Victoris hodierni gloriosum certamen trepidanter predico, quia proprie indignitatis mee defectus cognosco (agnosco)... et nobis largiri dignetur gloriam eternam.
Ar, 117rb-18rb; De sancto Victore; LXXXII.

(In Is. legitur:) Dominus dedit mihi linguam eruditam (*Is.* 50: 4) — Fratres, quando proponitur ab aliquo sancto huius verbum non est iactantia elati... sicut in precedentibus distinctum est.
Ar, 138^{ra-vb}; XLVIII.

Ecce quam bonum (*Ps.* 132: 1) — Licet hec verba generalem unitatis ecclesiastice commendationem contineant... transibitis ad plenitudinem gaudii...
Ar, 23ra-4rb; Ad claustrales; XVI.

Ego sum panis vivus (*Joh.* 6: 41) — Hic est panis in clibano coctus... et sanam doceant et discant doctrinam.
Pa^3, 196^{r-v}.

Erat Ninive civitas magna (*Ion.* 3: 3) — Narrat beatus Gregorius, quod quidam eger pessimus monachus in quadam basilica erat et — infirmaretur usque ad mortem... ad gloriam future resurrectionis DNJC leti perveniamus.
Be, 24vb-6ra; In XL^a.
Pa^{16}, 61ra-3ra; *Ib*; XXXV.

Facta est quasi institoris (*Prov.* 31: 14) — Veniens in hoc undo Dei Filius querere et salvum facere quod perierat, mirabili usus est genere communi... ut omnes... transferamur in portum salutis eterne. Prestante Domino nostro.
Pa^{16}, 28rb-30vb; De sancta Genovefa; XVII.

Fluvius egressus est de loco voluptatis (*Gen.* 2: 10) — Mater quecumque, cum habet filium languidum... gratias agamus Salvatori nostro.
PM, 124ra-25va; De iiii fluminibus paradisi.

Hec est dies, quam fecit Dominus (*Ps.* 117: 24) — Multa sunt mala, que in colatu huius mundi abundant... ad quam nos puer hodie natus perducat...
Ar, 17rb-8va; De resurrect; VIII.

Hoc sentite (*Phil.* 2: 5) — Exordium sermonis sumemus a quadam notabili sententia beati Pauli dicentis: Verbum crucis pereuntibus stultitia est (*I Cor.* 1: 18)... pervenire mereamur ad gloriam exoptate resurrectionis.
Ar, 15rb-7rb; In ram. palm; VII.

In Ezechiele legitur in visione templi: Exibant aque (47: 1)... amaritudo pene eterne.
PM, $152^{ra\text{-}va}$; De baptismo.

Introduxerunt archam Domini (*II Reg.* 6: 17) — Sicut dicit Dominus in evangelio, adventum regis magni multa precedent signa... hostie impiorum, que ex scelere offeruntur.
Ar, 136va-37va; In adv; XCVI. *Weg.*, 344.

Isti sunt, qui venerunt ex magna tribulatione (*Apoc.* 7: 14) — Ab initio nascentis ecclesie... glorie consortes.
PM, 144va-46va; De martyribus in commune.

Medicina omnium (*Eccle.* 43: 24) — Unde proveniunt infirmitates... et consolationem spiritus sancti et die pentecostes.
Ar, 20rb-1rb; In adv. Domini; XI. *Weg.*, 363.

*——— Unde proveniant infirmitates et in quibus sint, quas ista nebula et eius medicina expellit... et in eterno regno ex ea sine fine reficiamur.
Be, 2rb-3ra, *Ib.*, *Weg.*, 363.

Nisi Dominus edificaverit domum (*Ps.* 126: 1) — Fratres, videtur, si quis vestrum sit fornicator... velut scriptura utriusque testamenti.
Pa^{6}, 87ra-9va; (In cap. ieiun. ?)

Nuptie facte sunt (*Joh.* 2: 1) — Veritas dicit in evangelio (*Joh.* 8: 47): Qui est ex Deo verba Dei audit. Qui enim libenter verba Dei audit... usque ad mortem desudare appetunt.
Pa^{7}, 212vb-14ra; Dominica post oct. epiph; XVI.
Pa^{9}, 63vb-4va; XXIX.

Obtulerunt Magi Domino (*cf. Matt.* 2: 11) — Dicit *Eccli.* (31: 28): Splendidum in panibus benedicent labia multorum... myrrham quia peccavimus corpore.
Ar, $79^{ra\text{-}vb}$; De epiph; LIII.
Am (unnumb. fol.), *Ib.*

*——— Si quis (gravatus) egritudine medicinam corporalem... ut eum qui vera pax est invenire et habere mereamur.
Pa^{3}, 193^{v}-95^{r}.
Pa^{12}, 133^{v}-34^{r}.

Omnia vestra sunt (*I Cor.* 3: 22) — Terra super se sepe venientem imbrem bibens (*Hebr.* 6: 7)... Christus pro nobis factus pontifex in eternum.
Ar, 186ra-87vb; CXXXVII.

Osculetur osculo oris sui (*Cant.* 1: 1) — Natura humana vulnerata in naturalibus et spoliata... quia in his est meritum et prelibatio eterne iocunditatis...
Be, 9vb-11rb; In adv.

Ostende nobis, Domine, faciem tuam (*Ps.* 79: 4) — Apostolus dicit in epistola ad Romanos verbum bonum: Quecumque scripta sunt (15: 4). Magna cura notatur apud scriptores... neque pedi liceat deviare in latitudine claudorum.
Ar, 175rb-76vb; In adv; CXXVI. *Weg.*, 395.

Pascha nostrum immolatus (*I Cor.* 5: 7) — Hodie sancta ecclesia facit sollempnitatem paschalem... et conscius meus in excelsis. ad quam resurrectionem...
Be, 38vb-9va, In pascha.
Cf. Va, 73.

Pueri Hebreorum tollentes ramos — Isti pueri figura fuerunt sanctorum, qui in iudicii resurgent... tollentes ramos olivarum et non ramos palmarum.
Pa^{7}, 215va-16rb; In ram. palm; XVIII.
Pa^{9}, 89ra-^{vb}; XLVIII.

Pulli aquile lambunt sanguinem (*Job* 39: 30) — Aquila non dedignatur volare ad cadaver... de fonte, qui eminavit de latere eius.
Pa^{7}, 209ra-10vb; De fide passionis; XIII.
Pa^{9}, 85va-7ra; XLV.

Quemcumque osculatus fuero (*Matt.* 26: 48) — Pie Jesu, ego puer sum et loqui nescio... quem nobis conferre dignetur...
Pa^{3}, 189^{r}-90^{v}.

Retrahamus cum sole claritatem gaudii pristini, ut doleamus cum Salvatore — Ecce patet, quomodo asina respondit peccatori... in pacis visionem eternam scil. beatitudinem.
Pa^{7}, 259vb-61vb; In ram. palm; L.
Pa^{9}, 89vb-90rb; XLIX.

Rogate que ad pacem sunt (*Ps.* 121: 6) — Si quis dominum divitem, munificum et sapientem ab eo remunerationem peteret, si indigeret et si gratiam ipsius haberet... omnem sensum in futuro teneamus.
Bg^{2}, 38ra-9rb.

Sapientiam sanctorum narrant populi (*Eccli.* 44: 15) — Que sit ista sapientia...
PM, 107va-09ra, In f. omn. sanct.

Sicut ovis ad occisionem ducetur (*Is.* 53: 7) — Legitur in evangelio Johannis, scil. in passione Domini, que vi. feria legitur, quod nuntii Judeorum missi sunt, ut tenerent Jesum... ad dexteram Dei Patris eidem coeternus et consubstantialis JCDN...
Ar, 159va-62ra; In palmis; CXV.

Spiritus Domini replevit orbem terrarum (*Sap.* 1: 7) — Exultemus hodie, fratres karissimi, unanimiter in honorem Sancti Spiritus, per quem omnis catholica ecclesia sanctificatur... amor Patris et Filii.
Ar, 184rb-85va, De Spiritu Sancto; CXXXV.

Stabat Jesus iuxta stagnum (*Cf. Luc.* 5: 1) — Qui stat iuxta stagnum, non est in stagno, sed extra. Stagnum significat fluxum mortalis vite... idest vix remittetur.

Ar, 107va-12ra; Ad claustrales; LXXIII.

Sub umbra illius (*Cant.* 2: 3) — Horum verborum seriem tripliciter exponemus, ut et congruat martyri, cuius sollemnitas hodie agitur... transeatis ad gaudia celestis vite.

Ar, 13ra-5rb; De sancto Thoma martyre; VI.

Super manus meas depinxi muros tuos — Sicut Salomon, perambulemus loca florida scripturarum, nihil vita sacerdotali beatius, nihil timorosius... percipiatis immarcessibilem coronam glorie.

Lo^{1}, 97vb-8va.
Pa^{1}, 55^{v}-7^{r}; Ad prelatos.
Pa^{16}, 94va-6ra; Ad sacerdotes; LVI.

Vae genti peccatrici (*Is.* 1: 4) — Hodie sollempnitatem adventus... per gratiam ibi habitare dignetur.

PM, 146va-47vb; In adv... dominica i.

Veni in hortum meum (*Cant.* 5: 1) — Karissimi, quod prius concepi, nunc pariam, quod aliquando texui, nunc evolvam... et torrente voluptatis potabit eterne, ad quam nos perducat Salvator noster.

Ar, 6vb-8ra; In cap. ieiun; II.

Videbam coram me vitem (*Gen.* 40: 9) — O quam necessarium erat sic obdormisse, qui canit consolationis verbum... simul in martyrio et actione.

PA^{1}, 82vb-3va.

Vivit in Christo gemma sacerdotum — Fratres, si quis haberet electuarium dulce et circa quemlibet morbum efficax, istud recondet in munda pixide... hospitium glorie habeamus in dextera parte cum sanctis collocati.

Pa^{16}, 53ra-4vb; De sancto Martino; XXX.

*——— Unusquisque nostrum si haberet electuarium pretiosum et efficax ad expellendum omnia genera morborum... et ad eternam habitationem perducat.

Ar, 152ra-54rb; *Ib.*; CXI.
Cf. Pa^{12}, 140^{r}-43^{r}.

Vulnerasti cor meum (*Cant.* 4: 9) — Loquitur ad sponsam Christus et se illius pulchritudine vulneratum ingeminans amoris ostendit... et apertos dare videt, et recte discernit.

Pa^{11}, 232vb; Sermo communis.
(This sermon appears with a series of texts individually assigned by author. It appears with other Langton sermons, but has no attrib. See, Pa^{11}, *supra*).

Zachee festinans descende (*Luc.* 19: 5) — Fecit Deus duo luminaria (*Gen.* 1: 16) — Per luminare maius possunt mystice intelligi prelati sive doctores... ut nos tecum maneamus per participationem glorie. Ad quam gloriam...

Ar, 167va-69vb; In ded. eccl; CXXI.

Class V. — Addenda: Sermons Appearing Only in Anonymous Copies (*Total:* 17 Sermons).

N.B. It will be noted that the *themes* in the following sermons appear elsewhere in named copies. In many cases, it has been found that differences in *incipits* indicate a sermon that is in content a version of the named sermon. In the following, however, this is not the case, and investigation has shown that these are *different sermons* and have neither copies nor variants in the named MSS.

Dominus prope est (*Phil.* 4: 5) — Affectuose solet audire relatio nuntii desiderati, quo recreantur desolati... per excellentiam sanctitatis. Quod nobis concedere dignetur, qui pro nobis nasci voluit.

Ar, 5ra-6vb, In vigil. natal. Domini, I., *Weg.*, 153.
Ar, 145vb-47va, *Ib.*, CVI. *Weg.*, 157.

Ecce rex noster adveniet Christus — Dominus dicit in evangelio: Celum... verba autem mea non transient ante principes celi, scil. Petrum, Paulum, et alios sanctos.

Bg^{2}, 45rb-6va, In natal. Domini? *Weg.*, 184.

Ecce rex venit, occurramus Salvatori nostro — Nota sex homini necessaria esse currere volenti... ad liliata campestria perducet.

Ar, 113vb-14va, In adv., LXXVIII.
Pa^{6}, 107va-08rb.
Pa^{7}, 167va-68rb, *Ib.*
Pa^{9}, 53rb-4ra, XVIII.

——— Pater omnipotens filium in mundum mittente volens monet nos per prophetas ut obviemus... tanto maior corpus ei paratur.

PA^{1}, 116vb-17rb.

Ecce sacerdos magnus — Jesus Filius Sirach sacerdotem magnum multipliciter describens et multas similitudines ad eius commendationem inducens... huius ergo misericordie participes nos faciat misericors et miserator Dominus.

Ar, 24rb-30va; De sancto Martino; XVII.
Pa^{7}, 201rb-03vb; De uno confessore; X.
Pa^{9}, 48vb-51rb; XIII.

Ecce sacerdos magnus — Item dicitur a Sapiente (*Eccli.* 22: 24). Pungit cor et prodiet sensus... et terrena subpeditare et habere vilia. Quod ipse prestare dignetur.

Pa^{6}, 105rb-06vb, De sancto Germano.

Erat Jesus eiciens demonium (*Luc.* 11: 14) — In fine hodierni evangelii quedam verba proponit Salvator, quorum consideratione confert fidelibus affectum audiendi verbum Dei... quatinus possimus esse participes illius beatitudinis.

Be, 23va-4vb, Dnca iii in XL^{a}.
PA^{1}, 45ra-6va, *Ib.*

Est puer unus hic (*Joh.* 6: 9) — Non invitamus vos, fratres dilectissimi, ad mensam illius divitis... consummato in fine apprehendat cui se probavit DNJC^{m}...
Pa^{11}, 225ra-27vb, In XL^{a} ad claustrales et religiosos quoslibet; XVII. (?Steph. Lang., IRHT)

Homo natus de muliere (*Job* 14: 1) — In huius itaque exilii miseriam dignatus est Filius Dei descendere... Multi enim sunt vocati... (*Matt.* 20: 16).
Pa^{7}, 214ra-15va, XVII.
Pa^{9}, 57^{ra-vb}, XXII.

Homo quidam fecit cenam magnam (*Luc.* 14: 16) — Multos invitavit ad hanc cenam ille homo secundum historiam evangelii et noluerunt venire... eorum mors vivet in suppliciis.
Ar, 112ra-13ra, Dnca ii p. pent., LXXVI.

Novate vobis novale (*Jer.* 4: 3) — Verbum Jeremie prophete consonat in parte parabole evangelice, in qua mentio fit de semine, quod inter spinas... metetis gaudium ineffabile.
PA^{1}, 72ra-3rb.

‡——— Hic est familiaris modus instructionis, ut per visibilia fiat doctrina de invisibilibus... pace scil. incommutabili requiescam in futuro.
Pa^{7}, 216rb-18vb, De cultura anima, XIX.
Pa^{9}, 66vb-8va, XXI.

Orietur stella ex Jacob (*Num.* 24: 17) — Quod dicitur: Orietur stella, pertinet ad primum adventum... querunt vestes, conspergunt adipem.
Pa^{7}, 269va-70va, De adv., LVI.
Pa^{9}, 56va-7ra, XXI.

Semen quod cecidit in terram bonam (*Luc.* 8: 8) — Rex dives et prepotens nuper cum suis habuit colloquium. In preterita scil. dominica ibi sermo magnificus habitus est... qui in hoc gaudio perseveraverit, ad gaudium perveniet eternum.
Ar, 166ra-67va, Dnca LX^{a}, CXVIII.

Trahe me post te (*Cant.* 1: 3) — Fratres, immo domini mei, si apostolus, qui sapientissimus et eloquens erat... sed audiamus illam vocem sanctissimam.
Pa^{6}, 36va-8rb, In ascens.

Tu es, qui venturus es (*Matt.* 11: 3) — Sicut legitur hodie in evangelio, inter beneficia, que contulit Christus humano generi hoc reputatur precipuum, ut pauperes evangelizantur... illo participare gaudio, quo angeli fruuntur in celo.
Ar, 149ra-51ra, In adv., CVIIII.
Do, 79rb, LXIIII.

Viri Galilei, quid statis (*Act.* 1: 11) — Notate fratres, quod Dominus noster quadruplicem fecit ascensum. Ascendit enim in carnem vel super carnem... gloria, quam nec oculus vidit.
Ar, 137va-38ra, De ascens., XCVII.

Class VI. — Sermons That Have Been Otherwise Attributed (*Total:* 20 Sermons).

N.B. A number of sermons that appear in the Schneyer List have, in these subsequent investigations, been found to be assigned to other preachers. In several cases, the source is a file compiled by a researcher at the IRHT in Paris, or references to the MS in the literature. In others, the writer has noticed a copy and/or variant of a text in a MS where the author is mentioned.

Amator pecunie servus est mammone — Dederet Dominus homini... ad vitam eternam perducat.
PM, 102rb-03rb, De s. Iohanne Evangelista.
(? Steph. of Tournai, IRHT)

Ave gratia plena (*Luc.* 1: 28) — Si quis esset iuxta fluvium... ad portum vite eterne.
PM, 103rb-04ra, In annunt.
(? Steph. of Tournai, IRHT)

Duo ubera tua quasi duo hinnuli (*Cant.* 4: 5) — Merito pauperes venerantur illos... in conspectu Domini in celis.
PM, 104vb-05va, Apostolorum Petri et Pauli.
(? Steph. of Tournai, IRHT)

Erat Jesus eiciens demonium (*Luc.* 11: 14) — In hodierno evangelio tria docentur gravitates infirmitatis... donec videatur Deus Deorum in Sion.
Be, 26ra-7rb, In iii^{a} dnca XLe.
Pa^{11}, 253ra-54rb, S. M. Iohannis de Abevilla in Quadrag.
(IRHT: Iohannes Halgrinus de Abbatisvilla: *Summa Sermonum*, f. 1^{v}-203; BN, lat. MSS 2909, 85^{v}; 2910, 69; 2911A, 40; 2911, 105; MS Troyes 876, 40rb).

Et quietum studium et attentum silentium et tanta tanti viri festivitas monent, immo compellunt alique dicere... sponsus ecclesie filius Marie, qui est benedictus.
Bg^{3}, 23vb-5va, De s. Andrea.
Le^{2}, 184vb-86vb, *Ib.*
(IRHT: Peter Damian, *PL*, CXLIV, 828 or Nicholas of Clairvaux, *PL*, CLXXXIV, 1049).

Homo natus de muliere (*Job* 14: 1) — Audi hoc breve verbum tue brevis vite compendiose dispendiosam complectens miseriam... Deus erit omnia in omnibus. (*Cf. I Cor.* 15: 28).
Am (unnum. fol.)
Ni, 81^{v}-2^{v}, Sermo communis.
Pa^{11}, 248rb-49rb, Sermo de miseria hominis; XXXIX, S. M. Steph.
Pa^{15}, 12ra-^{vb}.
(D'Alverny, 132-33, indicates that the MS tradition authenticates this sermon as that of Alain de Lille. See MSS Dijon 219, f. 80-81: Item sermo eiusdem <Alani> de contemptu mundi; Toulouse 195, f. 115-16^{v}; Périgueux, Arch. Départ. fonds Cadouin 23, f. 66-66^{v}; BN, lat. 3818, f. 62-62^{v}).

Justum deduxit Dominus per vias rectas (*Sap.* 10: 10) — Salvator noster discipulis suis loquens... et remunerabit in eterna felicitate.
Be, 48vb-50ra, De primo confessore.
Pa[11], 250va-51vb, De quolibet s. confessore, S. M. Iohannis de Abbeville.
Tr[2], 300ra.
Tr[4], 169^{v}-71^{v}, *Ib.*

Justus ut palma florebit (*Ps.* 91: 13) — Arbores, que cito fructificare solent... in ecclesia triumphari.
PM, $104^{ra\text{-}vb}$, S. Iohannis Baptiste.
(? Steph. of Tournai, IRHT)

Memento, quod cinis es (*Cf. Gen.* 3: 19) — Legimus in evangelio Dominum dicentem: Qui audit verba mea et facit ea... (*Matt.* 7: 24). Oportet fratres, ut domus nostra fundata sit super firmam petram... hoc modo interficiuntur hostes David scil. diabolus et complices eius in quadragesima. Quam victoriam.
Ar, 85vb-6va, In cap. ieiun.
(?) *Cf.* Bar 10^{v}-13^{v}, *Ib.*
PA[1], 46va-7vb, *Ib.*
Le[3], 74 (Note the attrib. to Alain de Lille in *Kat. HSS Leip.*, 719, but notice *infra* that a version of the text appears in Pa[11] under the name, Iohannes de Abbevilla).
Tr[2], 276vb-77va. *Weg.*, 364.

*——— Ait Dominus: Qui audit verba mea... quia si compatimur et conregnabimus.
Be, 19rb-20vb, *Ib.*
Bs[2], 247^{v}-48^{v}, *Ib.*
Le[2], 54ra-5ra, *Ib.*
Pa[7], 255rb-58ra, *Ib.*
Pa[11], 254rb-55rb, *Ib.*, S. M. Iohannis (de Abbevilla).
PM, 116vb-18rb, *Ib.*
Tr[4], 94^{r}-6^{r}. *Ib.*, (see also LXXVII, f. 2^{r}, *theme only* not extant).

Militia est vita hominis (*Job* 7: 1) — O homo in his brevibus verbis vitam tuam lege, tuum statum intellige... de hoc fluctu ad portum.
Bs[1], 139rb-40ra, De libro Iob.
Pa[11], 235ra-36ra, Ad scolares, Sermo eiusdem (i.e. Alani de Insulis).
(IRHT: MS Dijon 219, f. 76; MS Toulouse 195, f. 112^{v}).
(D'Alverny, 134; See also BN, lat. 3818, f. 60^{v}-62, Ad religiosos; 15965, f. 3^{v}-4; Vat. lat. 10807, f. 12-12^{v}, inc.)

Misereor super turbam (*Marc.* 8: 2) — Scitis, quod cum puer esuriens petit panem a patre et impetrat, si postea proiciat acceptum... in futuro gloriam eternam.
Ar, 63rb-5vb, Dnca vii p. pent.

*——— Si quis puer a patre suo crebro panem peteret et acceptum conculcaret, patrem offenderet... ad fruendum cum eis pane vite, qui est Christus.
Le[2], 107ra-08va, *Ib.*
Pa[11], 263vb-64vb, *Ib.*, vel In XL^{a}; S. M. Iohannis de Abevilla.
Va, 88^{r}.

Que est ista, que ascendit per desertum (*Cant.* 3: 6) — Imperfectum meum viderunt oculi mei, dum de beatissima matre Salvatoris cogitarem aliquid ad edificationem loqui... ad desertum summe beatitudinis.
Ar, 170ra-71vb, In assumpt. s. Marie.
(IRHT: Adam Perseniae, *Coll. sermonum et epistolarum*, MS Douai, f. 194rb) (*sic*).

Qui sperant in Domino (*Is.* 40: 31) — Solet quilibet ostendere... sanitatem restituet.
PM, 98vb-9va, De s. Katerina.
(? Steph. of Tournai, IRHT)

Remittuntur ei peccata multa (*Luc.* 7: 47) — Si quis aliqua gravi infirmitate... societatis ipsius participes simus in celis.
PM, 105va-06va, De s. Marie Magd.
(? Steph. of Tournai, IRHT)

Salvum me fac, Deus, quoniam intraverunt aque (*Ps.* 68: 2) — Hec brevis oratio, fratres karissimi, totam nostram miserie summam comprehendit... spe ut suspiremus ad gloriam.
Bs^{1}, 138^{ra-va}, De pass.
Pa^{11}, 237vb-38vb, In XL^{a} (anon.)
(IRHT: Alain de Lille, MS Dijon 219, f. 81^{v}) (See D'Alverny, 137).

Scuto circumdabit te veritas eius (*Ps.* 90: 5) — Dicit Abacuch (3: 3): Quia Deus ab austro veniet... a timore iudicii et a merore producet ad gloriam.
Pa^{7}, 258ra-59va, Dnca i XLe.
Pa^{11}, 244ra-45ra, In LXX^{a}, S. M. Iohannis de Abevilla.

Si complantati fuerimus (*Rom.* 6: 5) — Fratres, in evangelio dicit Dominus: Qui ex Deo est, verba Dei audit. (*Joh.* 8: 47) Non loquitur de auditu corporis... Si ergo complantati facti sumus... similes et participes erimus.
PA^{1}, 111ra-12va.
Pa^{11}, 264vb-66ra, In pass., S. M. Iohannis de Abevilla.
Pa^{12}, 136^{r-v}.
Am (unnumb. fol.)

*——— Veritas dicit in evangelio: Qui ex Deo est... illud dulce verbum percipere valeamus...
Be, 35ra-6vb, *Ib.*
Pa^{6}, 47rb-50rb.

Si sciret paterfamilias (*Luc.* 12: 39) — Divites, qui habent magnum thesaurum... vivamus in eternis.
PM, 100va-01rb, De s. Nicholao.
(? Steph. of Tournai, IRHT)

Templum Dei sanctum est (*I Cor.* 3: 17) — Legimus, quod Salomon dedicato templo... ut spiritus sanctus in nobis habitare dignetur.
Ar, 171vb-72ra, In dedic.
Cf. Pa^{7}, 278va-80ra, *Ib.*
Pa^{9}, 97vb-9vb.
Pa^{11}, 251vb, Prévostin.

Tulit David baculum (*I Reg.* 17: 40) — Miles, qui multos habet hostes... exaltari et gloriari.
PM, 101rb-02rb, De s. Stephano.
(? Steph. of Tournai, IRHT)

Appendix A

SERMONS CLASSIFIED BY AUDIENCE

Sermons identifiable by rubric and/or some clear form of address in the text:

(1) *Ad populum* — Sermon No. 50, 64, 83, 91, 100 (5)
(2) *Ad clericos* — 2, 9, 48, 77, 98, 99, 102, 121 (8)
(N.B. 83, 100, 9, and 99 are in Tr^4).

Sermons judged according to content, and addressed:

(3) *Ad populum* — 1, 3, 4, 5, 6, 7, 8, 10, 11, 12, 13, 14, 15, 16, 17, 18, 19, 20, 21, 22, 23, 24, 25, 26, 27, 28, 29, 30, 31, 32, 33, 34, 35, 36, 37, 39, 40, 41, 42, 43, 44, 45, 46, 47, 49, 51, 52, 53, 54, 55, 56, 57, 58, 60, 61, 63, 65, 66, 67, 68, 69, 70, 71, 72, 73, 74, 75, 76, 78, 79, 80, 81, 82, 84, 85, 86, 87, 88, 89, 90, 92, 94, 95, 96, 97, 101, 103, 104, 105, 106, 107, 108, 109, 110, 111, 112, 113, 114, 115, 116, 117, 118, 119, 120, 122 (105)
(4) *Ad clericos* — 38, 59, 62 ?, 93 ? (4)

Total (122)

Sermons listed above in section (3), *Ad populum*, copies and/or variants of which appear in Tr^4 which has the general rubric: *Sermones... ad populum*:

3, 4, 8, 13, 15, 23, 25, 26, 28, 29, 31, 32, 34, 39, 40, 41, 42, 49, 54, 60, 63, 68, 69, 70, 71, 75, 79, 80, 82, 85, 87, 89, 92, 94, 95, 96, 101, 105, 107, 109, 110, 112, 115, 117, 119, 120 (46)
(N.B. Of the 105 sermons judged according to content to have been addressed to largely popular audiences, 46 of these are to be found in Tr^4).

Appendix B

ARRANGEMENT OF SERMONS ACCORDING TO THE ECCLESIASTICAL CALENDAR IN LEIPZIG MS 443

Reproduced below are the rubrics of the sermons in Le^2 in the order in which they appear in the MS, corresponding to the ecclesiastical calendar:

Sermon No.	Fol. No. Le^2	Rubric
29	1ra	Dnca i in adv.
7^a	2va	Adv.
33^a	4ra	”
69	5va	”
61	7va	Dnca iiii (Adv.)
78^c	8va	” ” ”
68^c	9vb	Adv.
74^a	11va	”

Sermon No.	Fol. No. Le^{2}	Rubric
44^{b}	13rb	Dnca ii (Adv.)
87^{c}	14vb	Adv.
28^{a}	16rb	Dnca ii in adv.
114^{b}	18va	" iii (Adv.)
5^{b}	23rb	iii Dnca adv.
23^{c}	28vb	Adv.
118^{a}	30rb	In nativ.
65^{a}	34vb	Epiph.
109^{d}	36rb	"
109^{c}	38va	"
19^{c}	41rb	Dnca p. epiph.
104^{b}	42va	Dnca ii p. epiph.
13^{a}	43va	Septuag.
3	45va	"
97^{d}	46va	"
97^{c}	48ra	"
89^{a}	49rb	Sexag.
90	50rb	Dnca in LX
55	51ra	Sexag.
122	52ra	Quinquag.
82^{a}	52vb	Dnca in L
26^{b}	56va	Quadrag.
27	57vb	"
86	58vb	"
42	60rb	Dnca ii in XL
47	66vb	Quadrag.
81^{c}	69rb	Pass.
101^{b}	70vb	"
70^{c}	73vb	Ram. palm.
40^{a}	77ra	Cena Dni.
63	78rb	In paras.
49	79va	In resurrec.
50^{a}	82ra	In oct. resurrec.
64^{b}	88ra	Dnca iiii p. pascha
115^{b}	88vb	" " "
85	90rb	" v " "
18^{b}	96vb	Dnca p. ascens.
116^{a}	97va	De sancto spiritu
43	101vb	Dnca i p. pent.
73	105va	" " v "
88	108va	" viii "
76	111ra	" xiiii "
91	117ra	" xxii "
98^{c}	118rb	" " "
98^{e}	119ra	" " "
21^{b}	120rb	" xxiii "

(De Sanctis, etc.)

Sermon No.	Fol. No. Le²	Rubric
9	123rb	Ad sacerdotes
102	126ra	In sinodo
93b	128vb	In dedicatione
105a	129vb	" "
11	137ra	St. Vincent
103c	139rb	Conv. S. Paul
20	146ra	Annunt.
34	147rb	"
6c	148vb	"
36a	150ra	"
72c	153va	Vig. S. Joh. Bap.
60a	155va	Peter and Paul
12	157va	St. Paul
57b	159vb	De Magd.
112	164va	St. Peter
16a	166ra	St. Stephen
22d	167rb	St. Laurence
53	168rb	" "
77b	168vb	Assump. S. Marie
110b	170rb	B. virg.
58b	171rb	In nativ. s. m.
67	174ra	" " "
54b	175rb	In die S. Simonis et Jude
10	177va	All Saints
80b	180ra	St. Martin
31b	182ra	" "
117d	184ra	St. Andrea
46b	188ra	St. Katherine
48	189	Epistola de x plagis.

Brugge MS 28

Reproduced below are the rubrics of the sermons in Bg¹ in the order in which they appear in the MS, according to the ecclesiastical calendar:

Sermon No.	Fol. in Bg¹	Rubric
19b	2ra	Dnca p. epiph.
45	2ra	Septuag.
13c	2vb	"
84	3rb	Sexag.
111	4ra	Cap. ieiunii
24	4va	Quadrag.
122b	5ra	Diebus Quadrag.
56	6ra	Dnca in pass.
52	6va	In palmis
70a	8ra	Ramis palm.
113	8vb	Dnca in palm.
101b	9va	Pass. Dni
118b	11vb	" "

Sermon No.	Fol. in Bg[1]	Rubric
63	13ra	Pass. Dni
99b	14ra	" "
59	14vb	Pascha
64a	15va	Dnca ante ascens.
35	16ra	In pascha
50d	16va	" "
108	17va	Ascensione Dni
2	18ra	Pentecost
116a	19va	"
17c	20va	"
73	21ra	Dnca vi p. pent.

Appendix C

SOURCES OF THE LANGTON THEMES (SCRIPTURE)

Where a (?) appears, this indicates that the theme is not directly quoted from the source, but is related to the scriptural passage.

Old Testament

Historical books

Gen. Sermon No. 3, 45, 75, 102, 112 (?)
Exod. 48
Num. 30(?), 67
III Reg. 93
Esther 41
Iudith 5

Didactic books

Job 50, 57, 58, 59
Psalms 13, 22, 47, 68, 76, 86, 91, 107
Proverbs 6, 14, 31(?), 88, 106, 114
Cant. Cant. 20, 35, 77, 108
Ecclesiasticus 79, 80, 95, 110

Prophetic books

Isa. 34, 36, 53, 61, 65, 71, 72, 83, 122
Jer. 1, 21, 55, 56, 78
Tren. (Lamentations) 101, 118
Baruch 44
Daniel 62, 63
Joel 2, 33
Amos 74
Michaea 37
Zach. 25

New Testament

Historical books: Gospels and Acts

Matt. 4, 8, 10, 24, 69, 70, 94, 96, 97, 98, 104, 111, 117, 119, 120
Marc. 49, 99, 113(?)
Luc. 15, 43, 66, 73, 82, 84, 87, 89, 90, 100, 109
Ioh. 17, 18, 19, 32, 38, 40, 51, 52, 54, 115
Act. 9, 16, 60, 103, 121

Didactic books: Epistles

I Cor. 46, 105
II Cor. 26, 27
Gal. 81
Eph. 39
I Thess. 42
II Tim. 12
Phil. 23
Iac. 64, 85, 92

Prophetic: Apoc. 11
Hymn, Veni Sancte Spiritus 116
Unclassified: 7, 28, 29 (*Cf. Matt.* 21: 5; *Ioh.* 12: 15)

Appendix D

A NOTE ON WILLIAM DE MONTIBUS AND HIS WRITINGS

In addition to the *Similitudinarius*, William de Montibus compiled other useful handbooks for preachers. These have an interest, especially since they include materials contemporaneous to Langton and thus represent a body of material common to medieval preachers of this period. A *Versarius* contains a metrical exposition of scriptural terms and subjects, arranged alphabetically. The book is ascribed to William de Montibus and may be found in BM MS, add. 16, 164. (The following extracts may be found on fols. 17^{r}, 18^{r-v}, 20^{v}): Amor bonus vel malus; Avaritia; Adulatio; Baptismus; Brevitas vite... (for the order of terms). (For the content of terms, e.g.): Arundo-debilis et vacua, levis, et radice lutosa... Castellum... fossa (timore vel humilitas)... collis (contemplacio vel desiderium supernorum sursum corde), ac muris (constancia, celsaque turris), (Christus vel caritas). In his *Speculum penitentis* (BM MS, Cotton, Vesp. D. XIII, fols. 63va-67ra): ... De vii viciis principalibus; De indignacione; De confessione; De statu monachorum et regularium; De vita et honestate clericorum.... A collection of *Tropi*, also arranged alphabetically, contain some of the following rubrics (in BM MS, Cotton, Vesp. E. X, fols. 49^{v}-52^{r}): ... Corpus Christi; Caritas; Conscientia; Causa; Deus, etc. In this same MS, on fols. 129^{v}-134^{r}, these examples from the *Numerale*:... Duo gladii... sunt gladii, materialis et spiritualis... potestates ecclesiastica scil. et secularis... . Tres persone in trinitate. ... De tribus muneribus Magorum aurum, thus, et mirra.... Hec offerre debemus Deo. Igitur aurum preciosissimum metallorum, caritas est superlativa virtutum.... Porro thus oratio est.... Mirra penitentia est.... A book of *Distinctiones* has also been attributed to William de Montibus. The following rubrics from this alphabetical collection are drawn from the text in BM MS, Roy. 10.A.VII, fols. 16^{r}-17^{v}: ... Beneficia; Cena; Caput; Capilli; Civitas; Cogitationes; Cor; Curvacio; Cupiditas; Confusio; Consilia reproba, etc.

APPENDIX E

KINDS AND OCCASIONS OF THE LANGTON SERMONS

Jan.

(3) St. Genovefa - Sermon No. 14
(6) Epiphany - 65, 94
Sun. after Epiph. - 19
Second Sun. after Epiph. - 104
(22) St. Vincent - 11, 37
(25) Conv. St. Paul - 103

Feb.

(22) St. Peter - 112

Mar.

(25) Annuntiation Sun. - 6, 20, 34, 36

Apr.

May

(1) Phil. & Jacob - 32

June

(29) Peter & Paul - 60
(30) St. Paul - 12

July

(22) M. Magdalene - 57, 71
(31) St. Germanus - 30, 80

Aug.

(10) St. Laurence - 22, 53
(15) Assump. B. Virg. - 77, 95, 110

Septuagesima - 3, 13, 45, 97
Sexagesima - 55, 84, 89, 90
Quinquagesima - 82, 122

Ash Wednesday - 1, 111
Lent - 8, 15, 24, 26, 27, 38, 39, 42, 47, 83, 86, 107
Passion Sun. - 56, 62, 63, 81, 99, 101
Palm Sun. - 51, 52, 70, 113
Holy Thursday - 40
Easter - 17, 35, 49, 50, 59
Sun. after Easter - 92
Rogation Sunday - 64, 85, 115
Ascension Day - 108, 121
Sun. after Ascen. Day - 18
Pentecost - 2, 116

i Sun. after Pent. - 43
vi ” ” ” - 73
viii ” ” ” - 88
xiiii ” ” ” - 76
xx ” ” ” - 4

xxii ” ” ” - 91, 98
xxiii ” ” ” - 21

Sept.

(8) Nativ. S. Mariae - 41, 58, 67
(21) Matthew ap. - 120
(29) Michael Archangel - 119

Oct.

(1) St. Remigius - 96
(28) Simon & Iud. - 54

Nov.

(1) All Saints - 10, 25, 75
(11) St. Martin - 31, 106
(25) St. Catherine - 46
(30) St. Andrew - 117
Advent - 5, 7, 23, 28, 29, 33, 44, 61, 66, 68, 69, 74, 78, 87

Dec.

(25) Christmas - 109, 114, 118
(26) St. Stephen - 16
(27) John Baptist - 72

Misc. sermons

Synod - 9, 102
On Confessors - 79, 100
Dedication - 93, 105
Inaugural lecture as master of theology - 48

Appendix F

BIBLICAL SOURCES IN THE LANGTON SERMONS

(No attempt has been made to collect *every* scriptural reference in these sermons. The following citations are by way of illustration; where there is more than one reference to a given book in one sermon, this is only listed once. The numbers refer to the list of sermons in Class I).

Historical Books of the OT

E.g. *Gen.* 2, 13, 29, 65, 71, 75, 77, 103, 110. *Exod.*, 9, 10, 16, 35, 49, 77. *Levit.*, 91. *Num.* 112. *Deut.* 14, 62, 78, 98, *Iud.*, 30. *Lib. reg.* 13, 15, 21, 33, 39, 50, 57, 59, 86, 89, 102. *Tobias* 14, 21, 23, 79, 118. *Iudith* 5, 44, 66. *Esther* 33. *Macc.* 30, 59, 69, 97, 116. (For New Testament books, see *infra*).

Prophetic Books

Ezek. 1, 2, 9, 10, 12, 21, 40, 57, 74, 80, 83, 94, 97, 98, 102, 110, 112, 114.

Jer. 1, 3, 8, 9, 10, 12, 13, 14, 15, 18, 19, 21, 23, 26, 29, 30, 34, 37, 39, 42, 44, 46, 49, 50, 51, 54, 57, 60, 62, 63, 65, 66, 70, 74, 75, 77, 78, 87, 89, 93, 96, 97, 98, 101, 102, 103, 104, 107, 114, 116, 117, 118, 119.

Isa. 1, 3, 5, 6, 7, 8, 9, 10, 13, 14, 15, 17, 20, 23, 25, 28, 29, 31, 32, 33, 35, 36, 37, 39, 40, 44, 46, 50, 51, 53, 57, 59, 61, 62, 63, 64, 65, 66, 67, 68, 69, 70, 71, 72, 73, 75, 77, 79, 81, 82, 83, 84, 85, 87, 90, 91, 93, 96, 98, 100, 101, 102, 103, 104, 106, 109, 110, 111, 112, 114, 116, 117, 118, 119, 122. *Cf. Dan.* 17, 59, 62. *Amos* 42, 80, 98, 118, 120.

Joel 1, 2, 15, 30, 50, 59, 62, 63, 68, 91.

Osee 2, 9, 10, 15, 19, 29, 33, 51, 59, 63, 66, 68, 84, 86, 90, 104, 118.

Zach. 11, 25, 33, 51, 61, 62, 63, 66, 70, 77, 92, 102.

Malach. 9, 10, 29, 39, 59, 74, 77, 91, 116, 118. *Cf. Michea* 11, 16, 25, 37, 42, 57, 65, 110. *Habac.* 2, 37, 39, 50, 69, 95, 118.

Didactic Books

Cant. Cant. See e.g. 6, 15, 30, 34, 46, 51, 54, 57, 72, 75, 93, 94, 95, 101, 102, 108, 116.

Job 2, 5, 6, 9, 10, 11, 13, 14, 15, 20, 21, 23, 25, 26, 29, 30, 31, 33, 36, 37, 38, 39, 44, 46, 49, 50, 51, 54, 56, 57, 58, 59, 62, 64, 65, 66, 70, 72, 73, 74, 75, 77, 80, 83, 88, 89, 96, 97, 98, 99, 101, 102, 103, 105, 106, 109, 110, 111, 112, 113, 115, 117, 118, 119, 120.

Psalms 10, 11, 13, 14, 15, 23, 26, 27, 29, 30, 36, 39, 44, 50, 57, 58, 59, 62, 65, 68, 73, 74, 75, 77, 80, 81, 84, 89, 90, 96, 100, 102, 106, 108, 109, 116, 117, 118.

Prov. 2, 7, 23, 26, 33, 36, 37, 39, 58, 64, 65, 74, 76, 79, 80, 93, 95, 97, 98, 104, 106, 114.

Ecclesiasticus 8, 10, 13, 17, 29, 30, 31, 33, 44, 46, 51, 54, 59, 74, 76, 78, 80, 92, 93, 94, 95, 97, 100, 103, 109, 110, 113, 115, 116, 120, 121. *Cf. Ecclesiastes* 25, 65, 90, 91, 97, 110, 115. *Lib. sap.* 2, 3, 6, 7, 9, 10, 13, 19, 20, 22, 54, 58, 59, 75, 77, 80, 82, 97, 105, 106, 115, 116, 121.

(References e.g... *sicut ait Salomon* or *Salomon dicit.*) See e.g. 3, 5, 6, 7, 8, 13, 14, 19, 21, 23, 25, 26, 28, 29, 33, 35, 36, 44, 46, 51. 53, 54, 57, 64, 66, 68, 72, 73, 74, 79, 80, 81, 83, 84, 87, 91, 93, 95, 96, 97, 104, 109, 117, 118.

New Testament

Matt. 51, 68, 82, 92. *Marc.* 82. *Luc.* 16, 28, 89, 99. *Ioh.* 9, 13, 72, 80, 92, 95, 97, 115, 116. *Act.* 10, 100. *Epistles* 11, 13, 15, 18, 26, 31, 34, 39, 46, 54, 62, 63, 65, 66, 72, 75, 80, 98, 100, 103, 104, 109, 115, 122. *Iac.* 13, 23, 50, 57, 64, 80, 116. *Petr.* 18, 68. *Apoc. Ioh.* 11, 24, 37, 51, 58, 74, 75, 87.

Appendix G

TEXT OF LANGTON'S INAUGURAL LECTURE AS MASTER OF THEOLOGY (1180)

The text of Langton's lecture that follows is based upon Leipzig MS 443, ff. 189va-191vb (= A). It has been fully collated with all other known texts: Paris BN, lat. MSS 2915, ff. 60^{v}-64^{v} (= B); 2995, ff. 135^{v}-138^{v} (= C); and 15025, ff. 222vb-226vb (= D).

A has been selected as the basis of this text because of its long and established tradition as an authentic MS copy of this sermon-lecture. Now Leipzig MS 443, the MS was noticed by Feller in the catalogue of the MSS in the Pauline library in the Leipzig Academy in 1686.[1] Subsequent notices and descriptions of the MS appear in Oudin, Cave and in the modern catalogue edited by Helssig.[2]

Texts in B, C, or D have been selected when they offer a better reading, or to supplement omissions in A. (The sermon appears as no. 48 in Class I; for additional references and bibliography, see the separate MSS as listed in the section on MSS.)[3]

Langton's sermon-lecture has been selected as an exemplar of his sermon technique and methodology. In order to establish a final text, it would be necessary to examine all the MSS and the numerous variants of Langton's sermons to assess the MS tradition and to obtain a thorough familiarity with the author's language and style. For the purposes of this particular exemplar, however, we submit the following collation which represents a tentative text, and is sufficient to illustrate Langton's preaching.

The sermon was Langton's inaugural lecture as master of theology and was addressed to an audience of clerics. As an *inceptio*, or introductory sermon of a course, it might obviously have been entitled *de laudibus sacre scripture*. It is in its structure a sermon, and does not follow the customary pattern of an *accessus*.[4] Consisting largely of a commentary on various passages in the book of *Exodus*, the sermon has as its subject the study of Scripture and the qualities necessary for learning and teaching Sacred Scripture. Thus the account of the ten plagues (*Exod.* 7-12) teaches the lessons of the calamities of mortal life. The story of the Exodus (*Ibid.*, 12: 37-51) emphasizes the importance of scriptural study, and likens Scripture to the manna in the wilderness (*Ibid.*, ch. 16). The sermon draws widely on other books in the Old and New Testament and has references to the writings of Gregory the Great.

Passages from Scripture and from the works of Gregory (whether quoted directly or paraphrased) have been identified and italicized in the text. Scriptural sources are generally given in parentheses in the text itself. Significant variants from biblical quotations are indicated in the apparatus. References to the works of Gregory also appear in the footnotes. In addition to italicizing the quotation when it first appears, subsequent repetitions of various words and phrases of the text under examination are also italicized. This procedure is most useful as an indication of Langton's method of commenting on the text, and his reliance on authority.

Obvious errors have been eliminated and variants are shown in the apparatus. Punctuation and capitalization of the manuscripts have not been retained, and spelling has been normalized.

[1] Feller, *op. cit.*, Repositorii Theolog. III Ser. II in fol., p. 150, no. 36: (Sermones item [i.e. Steph. Cant.] ad sacerdotes de decem plagis...)

[2] For full citations, see the section in chap. II, "The Langton Sermons: A Bibliographical Survey," (*supra*) and Leipzig MS 443 in Group I MSS.

[3] (A and D in Group I; B in Group II). For a full description of the contents of C = BN, lat. MS 2995 (XIII, Parch., 176 fols.), see *Bibl. nat.*: *Cat. gén. des mss lat.*, *op. cit.*, III, 380-83.

[4] On the *accessus*, see E. A. Quain, "The medieval Accessus ad Auctores," *Traditio*, III (1945), 215-64.

Epistola Magistri Stephani de Decem Plagis[1]

Legimus filios Israel de Egypto profectos[2] *farinam*[3] *conspersam in palliis ligatam in humeris suis portasse, de qua panes subcinericios sibi*[4] *fecerunt.* (*Exod.* 12: 34, 39) *Deinde in deserto manna celeste acceperunt,*[5] (*Ibid.*, 16) *tandem in terra*[6] *promissionis constituti, fructus* [7]*regionis illius*[7] *comederunt.* Sic et nos [8]tamquam veri filii Israel,[8] antequam ad terram superne[9] promissionis veniamus, et fructus [10]terre illius[10] comedamus, duplici cibo spirituali in presenti pasci debemus — farinam de Egypto portantes et manna celeste degustantes.

Ut vilescant nobis temporalia, *portetur de Egypto farina* i.e. discutiatur mundi fallacia. Perit enim[11] [12]sophisma cum deprehenditur,[12] transit[13] mundus et concupiscentia eius, [14]et preterit[14] figura huius mundi. Ut dulcescant nobis eterna, *degustetur* [15]*manna celeste*[15] i.e. cognoscatur Sacra Scriptura. Verbum enim[16] Domini manet in eternum. [17]De Egypto exire monuit[17] qui dixit: *Nolite diligere mundum, neque*[18] *ea que in mundo*[19] *sunt.* (*I Ioh.* 2: 15) Farinam monstravit cum subiunxit: (*I Ioh.* 2: 16) *Quoniam omne quod est in mundo* [20]*aut concupiscentia est*[20] *oculorum, aut concupiscentia carnis, aut superbia vite.* Ut autem sciamus ex quibus granis hanc farinam[21] colligere debeamus,[22] plagas Egypti ad memoriam revocemus ut ex qualitate percussionis elucescat calamitas vite mortalis.

Prima Egypti percussio est[23] *aque in sanguinem*[24] *conversio, pro aqua sanguis in Egypto inundat.*[25] (*Cf. Exod.* 7: 17) Quia in hoc mundo pro refrigerio boni operis, habundat corruptio vite carnalis.[26] Dicente propheta: (*Osee* 4: 1-2) [27]*Non est veritas, non est misericordia,*[27] *non est scientia Dei in terra.* [28]*Maledictum, mendacium, furtum,*[28] *adulterium, homicidia*[29] *inundaverunt, et sanguis sanguinem tetigit.*

Secunda plaga Egyptiorum est multitudo ranarum. (*Cf. Exod.* 8: 1) *Rane Egypti* sunt vaniloquia huius seculi de quibus scriptum est: (*I Cor.* 15: 33) [30]*Corrumpunt mores bonos colloquia prava.*[30] *Has ranas* [31]*Egypti fluvius*[31] *ebullit,* (*Cf. Exod.* 8: 3) quia sermones vanitatis habundantia temporalis producit et nutrit. *Ingrediuntur he rane cubiculum lectuli*[32] *Pharaonis, stratum eius et*[33] *reliquias ciborum eius,* (*Ibid.*) quia apud eos[34] habundant vaniloquia; [35]teste propheta:[35] (*Cf. Amos* 6: 4-6) *Qui*[36] *dormiunt in lectis*[37] *eburneis, lasciviunt in stratis suis. Qui comedunt agnum de grege et vitulum de medio armenti, qui canunt ad vocem psalterii et nichil patiuntur super contricione*[38] *Ioseph i.e. pauperis.* Ranas Egypti arcere

[1] Title in A. B has no rubric and beginning initial "L" is lacking. C has rubric, *De plagis Egipti* in a contemp. hand; beginning initial "L" is lacking. D has rubric in later hand, *Magistri Stephani de Langueton* and in a contemp. hand, *Lectio M. Stephani quam fecit in sua inceptione.*
[2] *om.* A. [3] farinulam A. [4] ibi BCD. [5] *om.* B. [6] terram C. [7] illius regionis B.
[8] tamquam veri Hebrei vel filii Israel B, tamquam filii veri Israel C. [9] *om.* CD.
[10] illius regionis B, regionis (*om.* illius) CD. [11] enim mundus (mundus *del.* in A), *om.* enim C.
[12] sophismatum et deprehenditur B. [13] transmisit C. [14] preterit enim A. [15] celeste manna BCD. [16] *om.* A. [17] De Egipti monuit exire C. [18] nec AD. [19] eo A.
[20] aut est concupiscentia BCD. [21] farinulam A. [22] debemus D. [23] fuit B, *om.* C.
[24] sanguine B. [25] redundat A. [26] mortalis B. [27] Non est misericordia, non est veritas A.
[28] Maledictum furtum, mendacium AB. [29] homicida D. [30] Corrumpunt mores bonos confabulationes pessime AB. Corrumpunt bonos mores prava colloquia C. Corrumpunt bonos mores colloquia prava D. (*I Cor.* 15: 33 reads... *colloquia mala.*) [31] fluvius Egipti BC. [32] lecti B. [33] i.e. A. [34] eum D. [35] qui teste propheta BC, quia teste propheta D. [36] *om.* BCD. [37] lectulis C. [38] contricionem BC.

voluit [39]Apostolus cum ait:[39] (*Ephes.* 5: 3-4) [40]*Fornicatio et omnis immundicia, aut avaricia, nec nominetur in vobis, aut turpitudo,*[40] *aut stultiloquium, aut scurilitas,* [41]*que ad rem non pertinet sed magis gratiarum actio.*[41]

Tercia plaga Egyptus percutitur cum[42] *pulvis terre in* [43]*ciniphes convertitur.*[43] (*Cf. Exod.* 8: 16) Stimulus ciniphis est aculeus nocivi[44] sermonis. Bene autem natura culicis exprimit qualitatem lingue mordacis. Hoc enim[45] animal modicum est (189[vb]) sed[46] inquietum. [47]Magna impetit[47] et acriter pungit. Et teste beato *Iacobo* (3: 5): *Lingua modicum membrum est et magna exaltat.* (*Ibid.* 3: 8): *Inquietum*[48] *malum est et*[49] *plena veneno mortifero.* Hanc plagam [50]significat Eliphas[50] et[51] loquens ad beatum *Iob* (5: 19) cum enim dixisset: *In sex tribulationibus liberabit te Dominus, et in septima non tanget te*[52] *malum.* Quibusdam premissis[53] subiungit: (*Iob* 5: 21) *Et a flagello lingue absconderis. Flagellum lingue* [54]ut ait Gregorius[54] *est exprobratio*[55] *illate contumelie. Sancta igitur*[56] *anima a flagello lingue absconditur, quia dum in hoc mundo honorem laudis non querit* [57]*nec contumeliam detractionis sentit.*[57] [58]Hinc David ait: (*Ps.* 91: 3) *Ipse liberavit me de laqueo, etc.*[58] *Asperitatem verbi evadere est irrisiones detrahentium*[59] *dissimulando calcare.* [60]Ciniphes fugare voluit *Paulus* cum ait:[60] (*Ephes.* 4: 31) [61]*Omnis amaritudo et ira et indignatio,*[61] *et clamor tollatur a vobis cum omni malicia.*

Quarta igitur[62] *plaga est musca gravissima.* (*Cf. Exod.* 8: 21) [63]*Gravissima musca* est[63] mundane[64] sollicitudinis cura, vel remordens conscientia. [65]Unde Gregorius: *Nichil enim est laboriosius*[65] *quam terrenis desideriis estuare; nichil quietius quam in hoc mundo nichil appetere. Hinc est quod Israel custodiam sabbati accepit*[66] *in munere.* (*Ibid.* 16: 29) *Egyptus percutitur muscarum multitudine.* (*Ibid.* 8:21) *He*[67] *sunt musce morientes, que perdunt suavitatem unguenti,* (*Eccle.* 10: 1) *quia dum cure multiplices in corde nascuntur* [68]*et deficiunt et suavitatem*[68] *devotionis corrumpunt et distrahunt.*[69] *Hec musca* secundum prophetum (*Cf. Isa.* 7: 18) *habitat in* [70]*extremo fluminum*[70] *Egypti. Flumen Egypti* est [71]voluptas huius seculi[71] que[72] cito effluit[73] et[74] in mare i.e. in amaritudinem defluit.[75] *Labia enim*[76] *meretricis mel distillant et novissima illius*[77] *amara quasi*[78] *absynthium.* (*Prov.* 5: 3-4) *Utramque*[79] *extremitatem huius fluvii Egypti musca occupat.* (*Cf. Isa.* 7: 18) [80]Quia plenus anxietatis est voluptatis appetitus, satietas vero anxietas penitentie.[80] Utrumque[81] ergo amaritudo. [82]Unde

[39] cum dixit A. [40] Fornicatio et omnis immundicia non nominetur in vobis, aut avaricia, aut turpitudo A, Fornicatio aut immundicia aut avaricia non nominetur in vobis aut turpitudo C. [41] *om.* C. [42] dum BCD. (*Exod.* 8: 16 reads... *sciniphes.*) [43] cynifex vertitur A. [44] nocui B, noscivi D. [45] autem D. [46] et A. [47] Magno impetu B. [48] Et inquietum B. [49] *om.* BCD. [50] significavit eliphath B, significavit eliphas CD. [51] *om.* BCD. [52] *om.* A. [53] pretermissis A. [54] *om.* A. [55] exprobatio A. See *Moral. in Iob*, Lib. VI, c. 28 (Migne, *PL*, 75, 754). [56] ergo A. [57] contumeliam detractionis non sentit A. [58] Hinc Ysayas ait: Ipse liberabit me (te in B) de laqueo, etc. BD. Hinc Psalmista ait: Ipse liberavit me de laqueo, etc. C. [59] detrahantium A. [60] Cinifes Paulus fugare (*superscr. et mg.*) voluit A, Ciniphes voluit fugare apostolus cum ait BC. [61] Omnis amaritudo et ira et omnis indignatio A, Omnis amaritudo, ira et et indignatio D. [62] *om.* A. [63] *om.* C. [64] *add.* videlicet C. [65] ... est laboriosius *Corr.* A. Nichil enim est ut ait Gregorius BD. Nichil est enim ut ait Gregorius C. See *Moral. in Iob*, Lib. XVIII, c. 43 (Migne, *PL*, 76, 78). [66] accipit BCD. [67] hec C. [68] et deficiunt suavitatem ABC. [69] distraunt B, destruunt C. [70] eterno flumine C. [71] *corr.* in A. [72] qui C. [73] fluunt B. [74] que A, *om.* B. [75] defluunt B, diffluit C. [76] *om.* A. [77] eius BCD. [78] velud ABD. [79] Utram A. [80] Quia... appetitus, satietas vero pecunie A. Quia voluptatum appetitus plenus est anxietatis, sacietas vero anxietas penitentie B. Quia voluptatis plenus est anxietatis appetitus, sacietas vero penitentie CD. [81] Utrique BCD. [82] Hinc propheta ait BCD.

propheta:[82] (*Ioel* 2: 20) *Eum*[83] *qui ab aquilone est longe faciam a vobis,* [84]*faciem eius ad mare orientale*[84] *et extremum eius ad mare novissimum. Mare orientale* est amaritudo perveniens;[85] *mare novissimum* est[86] amaritudo subsequens.[85]

Quinta plaga est [87]*mors pecorum.*[87] (*Cf. Exod.* 9: 6) *Pecora* sunt de quibus ait[88] beatus *Iudas* apostolus (-10): *Quecumque*[89] *tamquam muta*[90] *animalia norunt*[91] *in his*[92] *corrumpuntur.* Que autem sit mors horum[93] pecorum consequenter ostendit, cum enim premisisset:[94] (*Ibid.*, 12-13) *Hi*[95] *sunt in epulis suis macule,*[96] *convivantes sine timore, pascentes semetipsos, nubes sine aqua, arbores autumnales infructuose bis mortue; fluctus feri maris, despumantes confusiones suas, sidera*[97] *errantia* — in fine subiunxit — *quibus procella tenebrarum conservata*[98] *est in eternum.* Horum etiam pecorum describens beatus *Iob* miserabilem exitum, [99]ut de adultero ait:[99] (*Cf. Iob* 24: 19-20) *ad*[1] *calorem nimium* [2]*transeat ab aquis nivium,*[2] *et peccatum illius sit usque ad inferos. Obliviscatur eius misericordia,*[3] *dulcedo illius vermes*[4] *non sit in recordatione et conteratur quasi lignum infructuosum.*

[5]*Sexta plaga est vesicarum turgentium multitudo.*[5] (*Cf. Exod.* 9: 9) *Turgens vesica* est inflatio superbie virulenta.[6] Hec est plaga tumens que secundum prophetam (*Cf. Isa.* 1: 6) *non*[7] *est circumligata fasciis preceptorum* (190ra) *nec curata medicamine penitentie neque*[8] *fota oleo divine misericordie. Bene autem cinis camini de manu Moysi proicitur* [9]*et ita hec plaga producitur.* (*Cf. Exod.* 9: 10) *Cinis camini* est homo estuans desideriis seculi. *Cinis iste de manu Moysi proicitur,*[9] dum homo qui cinis est legem abicit et a lege abiectus ostenditur. *Cinis iste in celum spargitur,* dum homo per superbiam elatus extra se funditur nec per humilitatem intra[10] se colligitur.

Septimum genus percussionis fuit impetus grandinis. (*Cf. Exod.* 9: 22) *Grando contundens*[11] est potestas secularis pauperes opprimens. Habundat[12] enim in hac Ninive secundum prophetam: (*Nah.* 3: 2) *Vox flagelli et vox impetus rote. Vox flagelli* in paupere conquerente, *vox impetus rote* in divite opprimente.[13] Unde advertendum est *qualis*[14] *grando primitivis nocuit, sed serotina non lesit.* (*Cf. Exod.* 9: 32) Primitivi sunt qui festinant accipere temporalia, serotini sunt[15] qui reservant se ad eterna. De primitivis[16] ait *Salomon*: (*Prov.* 20: 21) *Hereditas ad quam festinatur in principio in novissimo benedictione carebit.* De serotinis [17]ait iterum *Salomon*:[17] (*Ibid.*, 28: 28) *Cum surrexerint impii, abscondentur*[18] *homines, et cum illi perierint*[19] *multiplicabuntur iusti.* De serotinis simul et primitivis ait: (*Ibid.*, 13: 11) *Substantia festinata minuetur, que autem paulatim manu*[20] *colligitur multiplicabitur.* Grando igitur primitiva ledit, [21]sed non serotina.[21] Quia ut ait *Salomon*: (*Ibid.*, 12: 21) *Non contristabit iustum quicquid ei acciderit,*[22] *impii autem replebuntur malo.*

[83] cum D. [84] *om.* A. [85] *mg.* C. [86] *om.* A. [87] mors peccorum B, mors peccatorum pecorum D. [88] dicit BCD. [89] Quicumque AC. [90] bruta AB. [91] noverit CD. [92] hiis BCD. [93] *om.* B. [94] premisset B. [95] Hii BD, Hec C. [96] male *add. mg.* C. [97] fideri C, secunda D. [98] conversa C. [99] ait de adultero A, ait de adulterio B, ut de adulterio ait C, ut de adulterio D. [1] Transibunt ad B. [2] *om.* B. [3] et *add.* B. [4] vermis ABCD (*Iob* 24: 20 reads... *vermes*). [5] Sexta plaga Egiptorum est numerus vesicarum sive multitudo turgentium BD, Sexta plaga Egyptorum est multitudo vesicarum turgencium C. [6] *om.* A. [7] nec CD. [8] nec AD. [9] *om.* A. [10] *infra* C. [11] contondens B, contendens D. [12] habundant ABC. [13] conculcante BCD. [14] quod BCD. [15] *om.* AC. [16] serotinis D. [17] idem ait C, Salomon *om.* D. [18] absconduntur A. [19] perierunt D. [20] *om.* A. [21] serotina non A. [22] acciderat D.

Plaga octava percutiens est locusta consumens. (*Cf. Exod.* 10: 12) *Locusta depascens* est adulatio demulcens. Bene autem lingua adulatoris locuste comparatur.[23] Sicut[24] enim locusta tempore frigoris torpescit, [25]in calore autem[25] alacriter exilit; sic adulator tempore adversitatis se sub silentio claudit, sed tempore[26] prosperitatis impudenter se exerit.[27] Bene itaque[28] scriptum est (*Ibid.*) *quia*[29] *quod grando reliquit*[30] *locusta consumpsit.*[31] Sepe enim bonum quod non minuit adversitas frangens, perimit adulatio demulcens.[32]

Nona est plaga caliginis. (*Ibid.* 10: 21) Bene autem post plagam locustarum sequitur plaga tenebrarum. Qui enim peccatum[33] alterius palpat, ipsum peccatorem excecat. Unde *Salomon* ait:[34] (*Prov.* 29: 5) *Homo qui blandis*[35] *fictisque sermonibus loquitur cum amico suo rete expandit gressibus*[36] *eius.* Et propheta ait:[37] (*Isa.* 3: 12-13) *Popule meus, qui* [38]*te beatum*[38] *dicunt, ipsi*[39] *te decipiunt et viam gressuum tuorum dissipant.* [40]*Stat ad iudicandum Dominus et stat ad iudicandos populos, etc.*[40] Quanta autem [41]sit huius plage[41] temptatio ostendit *Salomon* cum ait: (*Prov.* 27: 21) *Sicut in conflatorio probatur*[42] [43]*argentum et in fornace aurum,*[43] *sic probatur*[44] *homo ore laudantis.* Hoc exponens beatus[45] Gregorius ait: *Argentum et*[46] *aurum quale sit ignis ostendit. Si*[47] *reprobum est igne consumitur, si probum est*[48] *igne declaratur. Si enim* [49]*laudibus suis*[50] *auditis*[49] *in altum se extollit,*[51] *quid aliud quam* [52]*aurum reprobum*[52] *fuit*[53] *quod*[54] *fornax lingue*[55] *consumpsit. Si autem ad divini iudicii* [56]*considerationem redit*[56] *et ne laudibus suis gravetur metuit, ex*[57] *igne purgationis excrescit in augmentum*[58] *caritatis.*[59]

Decima plaga[60] *est mors primogenitorum.* (*Cf. Exod.* 12: 29) Hoc nomen primogenitus non semper refertur ad etatem, immo interdum ad dignitatem. [61]*Primogeniti* igitur *Egypti* sunt potentes[62] huius seculi.[61] Ad hanc plagam [63]filii Israel non tantum[63] exire[64] monentur, verum etiam compelluntur.[65] (190rb) Sicut scriptum est: (*Exod.* 12: 33) *Urgebant* [66]*etiam Egyptii populum velociter exire*[66] *dicentes omnes morimur.* Dum enim [67]aliquis potens huius seculi[67] inprovisa morte [68]de medio tollitur,[68] adeo [69]ut ei competat[69] quod scriptum est: (*Iob* 16: 13) *Ego ille quondam opulentus, repente contritus sum.* Ad fugiendum Egypti sordes videtur[70] non tantum nos invitare verum etiam[71] compellere, [72]sicut in *Ecclesiastico* dicitur:[72] (38: 23) [73]*Memento iudicii mei sic enim erit et tuum;*[73] [74]*meum heri, tuum hodie.*[74] Mundus iste [75]advocatus est[75] contra se ipsum. [76]Ut enim ait beatus Gregorius: *Contempnendus esset hic mundus etiam*[76] *si rebus*

[23] *Cf.* Greg. *Moral. in Iob*, Lib. XXXI, c. 25 (Migne, *PL*, 76, 598-99). [24] Sic A. [25] in calescente die BCD. [26] in tempore A. [27] excutit A. [28] autem A. [29] *om.* ABD. [30] dereliquit B. [31] consumpserit D. [32] blandiens BC, blandientis D. [33] peccant D. [34] *om.* A. [35] blanditur BCD. [36] *del.* A, pedibus BCD (*Prov.* 29: 5 reads... *gressibus*) [37] *om.* A. [38] beatum te BD, te *om.* C. [39] illi BD. [40] *om.* BCD. [41] huius plage sit CD. [42] (?) examinatur A, probatum B. [43] aurum et argentum in fornace C. [44] *om.* A. [45] *om.* ABD. *Cf. Moral. in Iob*, Lib. XVI, c. 32 (Migne, *PL*, 75, 1141). [46] vel BD. [47] sed A. [48] *om.* A. [49] auditis laudibus suis CD. [50] *om.* A. [51] excellit A. [52] reprobum aurum BCD. [53] fuerit B. [54] quam CD. [55] *om.* A. [56] redit considerationem A, reddit C. [57] et ex A, *om.* D. [58] aue mentum A. [59] est *add.* D. [60] *om.* B. [61] Primogenita Egypti sunt potentes A. [62] *om.* D. [63] ad tantum filii Israel B. [64] orare D. [65] exire compellunt B. [66] Egyptii populum Israel exire A, etiam *om.* BD. [67] potens A. [68] tollitur de medio A. [69] quod ei competat A, ut competat ei B. [70] *om.* A, videntur B. [71] immo BCD. [72] de ore si quidem eius videtur sonare quod in Ecclesiastico legitur BCD. [73] enim *om.* A,... sic erit meum et tuum C, sic enim *om.* D. [74] *mg.* A. [75] est advocatus A. [76] Unde Gregorius. Odio habendus esset mundus A. *Cf.* Greg. *Super lib. Eccli.*, c. 24 (Migne, *PL*, 79, 939-40).

16

prosperis animum demulceret. At ubi tot adversitates[77] *ingeminat, tot calamitatibus animum pulsat, quid aliud quam*[78] *ne diligatur clamat?*[79]

Dum hec et alia [80]incommoda huius mundi[81] tamquam Egypti plagas[80] attendimus, grana in usum farine colligimus. Dum autem singula diligenter discutimus grana comminuimus et tamquam[82] in farinam redigimus. Hanc farinam quidam habent, sed in humeris non portant; quia mundum contemptibilem sciunt nec tamen contempnunt. Sunt qui in humeris portant sed in palliis non ligant, quia quodam[83] tedio affecti[84] et[85] adversitate pulsi,[86] mundum[87] deserunt sed contemptum illum ad caritatem non referunt. [88]Hoc autem pallium breve est[88] quod[89] utrumque operire non potest. Hoc est pallium laudis quod datur pro spiritu meroris. *Debemus igitur farinam habere*, (*Cf. Exod.* 12: 34) i.e. [90]vanitates mundi[90] attendere, *habitam*[91] *in humeris portare*, i.e. quod contemptibile scimus contempnere, et quod[92] inscientia scimus[93] opere exhibere. Et ut bene feramus *debemus farinam in palliis nostris ligare*, i.e. contemptum mundi ornamento caritatis informare. *Farina ista*[94] *conspergitur* dum scientia lacrimarum effusione solidatur. Qui enim apponit scientiam apponit et dolorem, *conspersio est farina aqua glutinata.*[95] *De farina conspersa* [96]*panes subcinericios*[96] *facere*, (*Cf. Exod.* 12: 39) est conditionem nostre mortalitatis ad memoriam reducere,[97] et quod homo [98]cinis et pulvis est[98] [99]prudenter advertere.[99]

Vidimus qualiter[1] portetur de Egypto farina, nunc videamus qualiter[2] in deserto colligendum sit manna. Manna est Sacra Scriptura, quod facile perpendere poterimus,[3] si ea que leguntur de manna ad memoriam reducamus. Primo igitur[4] consideremus quod legitur. (*Ibid.* 16: 13) *Cum descenderet ros* [5]*super castra*[5] *descendebat pariter et manna. In suavitate roris* [6]intelligitur benignitas[6] divine miserationis. Bene igitur *cum rore manna descendit* quia Dominus [7]genus humanum[7] oculo benignitatis[8] respexit cum tenebras nostre mortalitatis illustravit lumine[9] Scripture celestis. Sicut scriptum est: (*Ps.* 118: 105) *Lucerna pedibus meis verbum tuum* [10]*et lumen semitis meis.*[10] (*Ps.* 18: 9): [11]*Preceptum Domini lucidum illuminans oculos.*[11] *Non solum autem cum rore descendisse sed in modum roris in circuitu castrorum*[12] *legitur*[13] *iacuisse*, quia per virtutem verbi divini castra milicie nostre circumquaque[14] [15]protegit et[15] defendit misericordia Domini. Sicut scriptum est: (*Prov.* 30: 5) *Omnis sermo Domini ignitus clipeus est sperantibus*[16] *in se.*[17]

Secundo [18]occurrit considerandum[18] (190va) quod legitur: (*Exod.* 16: 14) *Apparuit manna in solitudine minutum et quasi pilo tunsum.* Granum pilo tunditur [19]ut folliculus[19] exuatur. Sic et littera[20] pilo expositionis comminuitur[21] dum eius intellectus aperitur. Bene igitur *quasi pilo tunsum apparet manna*, quia facilis reputatur[22] Sacra Scriptura. *Sed licet manna sit quasi pilo tunsum est tamen minutum.* In minutiis exprimitur virtus subtilitatis. Bene igitur *manna*[23] *est et minutum et quasi pilo tunsum* quia[24] Sacra Scrip-

[77] amaritudines A. [78] nisi A. [79] *mg.* C. [80] Egypti incommoda cernimus A. [81] *om.* C. [82] quasi A. [83] quidam A. [84] effecti B. [85] vel BCD. [86] pusilli A, pressi B. [87] nondum C. [88] Hoc est pallium breve BCD. [89] et C. [90] mundi vanitates BCD. [91] *om.* A. [92] qualis A. [93] novimus BCD. [94] itaque A. [95] conglutinata A. [96] subcinericios panes A. [97] revocare A. [98] pulvis et cinis est C. [99] diligenter attendere A. [1] quomodo A. [2] quomodo A. [3] potimus D. [4] *om.* A. [5] *om.* A. [6] benignitas intelligitur BCD. [7] humanum genus BCD. [8] pietatis BCD. [9] claritate A. [10] *om.* A. [11] Preceptum tuum lu. A. [12] roris D. [13] dicitur BCD. [14] circumque B. [15] *om.* A. [16] spiritualibus A. [17] in se *om.* C. [18] considerandum occurrit BCD. [19] ut in se folliculis C. [20] scriptura C, lucerna D. [21] minuitur C. [22] apparet C. [23] *om.* B. [24] *add.* -que A.

tura simplicibus [25]facilis videtur[25] intelligentie et ab acutis reperitur subtilitatis inexhauste.[26] Unde bene filii Israel [27]manna videntes leguntur dixisse: (*Ibid.*, 16: 15) *Manhu,*[27] *quod interpretatur: quid est hoc?*[28] Quia[29] inter filios Israel sunt devoti et humiles; sunt[30] superbi et arrogantes. [31]Humiles sunt *manna minutum*[31] considerantes pre admiratione cordis obstupescunt et dicunt, (*Ibid.*) *quid est hoc*? Qui[32] vero superbi sunt *manna* [33]*quasi pilo tunsum*[33] considerantes[34] contempnunt et illusorie dicunt, *quid est hoc*?

Tercio considerandum[35] est *quod manna in modum pruine* [36]*super terram videtur iacuisse.*[36] (*Ibid.*, 16: 14) Verbum Domini[37] et ignis est[38] et[39] pruina. Ignis est [40]sicut scriptum est:[40] (*Cf. Ier.* 23: 29) *Nonne verba mea quasi ignis et quasi malleus conterens*[41] *peccatum?*[42] *Ignis est*[43] quia ad bonum opus inflammat. *Pruina est* quia contra vitiorum incentiva refrigerat. Bene [44]igitur *manna in modum*[44] *pruine* [45]*super terram iacet*[45] quia verbum Domini[46] carnalia desideria reprimit et cohibet.

Quarto attendendum est[47] quod[48] Scriptura tempus et modum colligendi manna determinat. De tempore scriptum est: (*Exod.* 16: 21) *Mane colligebant manna.* [49]Vere mane[50] colligendum est manna,[49] quia peccati mortalis nocte fugata, dum recens est ingenii perspicacitas[51] addiscenda est Sacra Scriptura. Scriptum est (*Ibid.* 25: 2 ff.) *quod filii Israel* [52]*iussi sunt rerum suarum primitias offerre*[52] *in constructionem*[53] *tabernaculi.* Eorum igitur exemplo ingenii nostri primitie, non feces Domino essent consecrande. Et tamen siquis [54]reliquias ingenii[54] per multa distracti[55] [56]et multitudine scientiarum tamquam exhausti[56] ei[57] offerre vellet, benigne reciperet.[58] Sed[59] eum a quo omnia[60] habemus, vix etiam reliquiis[61] dignum iudicamus. Si artem recte [62]vel ornate loquendi velles[63] addiscere,[62] senectutem studeres prevenire. Artem bene vivendi scire proponis, et usque in senium expectabis?

Scriptum preterea est[64] de manna (*Ibid.* 16: 18) [65]*quod qui plus collegerat, non habebat plus; nec qui minus habuit minus.*[65] Tantum de manna colligis, quantum de Sacra Scriptura intellectu[66] percipis. Tantum vero habes, quantum operatione exhibes. Sepe enim[67] *qui minus colligit* non[68] minus habet quia quod minus est in scientia supplet [69]operatio bona.[69] [70]*Plus autem colligens,* non ideo plus possidet;[70] plurimumque[71] enim[72] torpescit in opere cui plus dinoscitur habere scientie. Non est autem[73]

[25] videtur facilis BC. [26] exhauste CD. [27] leguntur dixisse manna videntes, manu A. [28] (The next passage beginning *Quia inter filios...* and ending *illusorie dicunt, quid est hoc* is omitted in C.) [29] *om.* BD. [30] *om.* A. [31] Humiles sunt manna minutum esse BD. [32] (The passage beginning *Qui vero superbi...* and ending *quid est hoc* is omitted in D.) [33] *om.* A. [34] perpendentes B. [35] attendendum BCD. [36] legitur iacuisse A, super terram perhibetur iacuisse B, super terram dicitur iacuisse C. [37] et enim B. [38] *om.* C. [39] *om.* D. [40] unde Iere. A. [41] contundens A, contra C. [42] peccata B. (*Ier.* 23: 29 reads... *conterens petram*). [43] *om.* A. [44] *om.* A. [45] *om.* A. [46] *om.* A. [47] *om.* D. [48] quia BCD. [49] *om.* D. [50] *mg.* A. [51] perspicacia BC. [52] rerum suarum primicias iussi sunt offerre BCD. [53] constructione ABC. [54] ingenii reliquias CD. [55] discussi A, districti B, destructi D. [56] et tamquam per multitudinem scientiarum exhausti A. [57] *om.* B. [58] susciperet A. [59] Si B. [60] totum BCD. [61] reliquii B. [62] loquendi vel ordinem velles addiscere A. [63] vellet D. [64] *om.* C. [65] nec qui plus colligerat (collegit in D) habuit plus, nec qui minus colligerat (collegit in D) habuit minus BD; nec qui plus collegit plus habuit, nec qui minus minus C. [66] interdum A. [67] igitur CD. [68] nec C. [69] bona operatio B. [70] *om.* D. [71] plerumque CD. [72] *om.* C. [73] *om.* B.

silentio pretereundum (*Ibid.* 16: 16) *quod tantum unusquisque collegit quantum ad vescendum sufficere potuit.* [74]Quis studii vestri[75] finis esse debeat[74] ex hoc facto manifeste perpenditur. Tunc enim [76]recte manna colligitur[76] cum ea intentione. [77]Cibus (190vb) Sacre Scripture acquiritur[77] ut hoc alimento homo interior reficiatur. Unde non vacat (*Ibid.* 16: 20) *quod manna in* [78]*diem alterum*[78] *reservatum*[79] *scatere cepit vermibus atque computruit. Cum autem*[80] *in sabbatum fiebat reservatio, eam nulla sequebatur putrefactio.* (*Ibid.* 16: 24) Cum sapientie thesaurus colligitur ut eterna requies obtineatur, *manna in diem*[81] *sabbati reservatur.* Cum autem[82] ex avaricia congregatur et in usum bene vivendi non assumitur, [83]*manna non in sabbatum sed in diem alterum colligitur,*[83] *sic collectum*[84] *vermes generat.* Sic enim[85] colligentes expectat vermis — *qui non moritur et ignis qui*[86] *non extinguitur* (*Cf. Marc.* 9: 43). *Manna ad vescendum*[87] colligitur,[88] monuit *Salomon* [89]cum ait:[89] (*Prov.* 5: 15) *Bibe aquam de cisterna tua* [90]*et fluenta putei tui. Aquam de cisterna sua*[90] *bibit et fluenta putei sui haurit,* qui scientiam suam et verba in opus convertit. *Manna in diem alterum reservari*[91] noluit *Salomon* cum ait: (*Ibid.*, 16) *Aquas tuas in plateis*[92] *divide.* Deinde subiungit: (*Ibid.*, 17) *Habeto eas solus.* Mirabili modo *aquas dividit et solus eas*[93] *retinet,* qui scientiam cum humilitate dispensat nec tamen aure popularis inania captat.

Nunc attendamus *quod manna induruit ad ignem, et liquefiebat ad solem.* (*Cf. Exod.* 16: 21) Possumus ad presens [94]*per solem*[94] solem iusticie, [95]*per ignem*[95] spiritus sancti gratiam intelligere. [96]Et providentia huius gratie *manna aliquando liquefit aliquando indurescit,*[96] quia superna dispensante [97]gratia Sacre Scripture[97] intelligentia interdum est liquida et aperta et[98] interdum obscura. *Liquefit*[99] *manna* ut [1]donum celestis gratie[1] agnoscamus; *indurescit* ne nostre infirmitatis inmemores de ingenii perspicacia superbiamus. Sicut spiritus[2] prophetie corda prophetarum interdum tangebat, interdum se[3] subtrahebat. *Tangebat*[4] *teste beato Gregorio ut scirent* [5]*quid a Deo haberent.*[5] *Subtrahebat se*[6] *ut scirent quid essent* [7]*de semetipsis.*[7]

Nunc consideremus quod[8] tripliciter determinat[9] Sacra Scriptura quem saporem habuit manna. [10]Legitur enim[10] (*Num.* 11: 8) *quod populus colligens manna frangebat illud mola sive* [11]*terebat in mortario coquens in olla*[11] *et faciebat ex eo tortulas, saporis quasi panis oleati.* Alibi legitur (*Exod.* 16: 21) *quod gustus eius*[12] *erat quasi*[13] *simile cum melle.* Legitur iterum, (*Sap.* 16: 20) *paratum panem de celo prestitisti*[14] *eis sine labore*; *omne delectamentum* [15]*in se habentem*[15] *et omnis saporis suavitatem.* Vere Sacra Scriptura *simile*[16] *sapit cum melle* quia refectionem [17]pariter continet[17] et dulcedinem. (*Cf. Cant.* 4: 11): *Mel enim*[18] *et*[19] *lac sub lingua sponse et favus distillans labia eius.* Volumen quod comedit

[74] Quis finis studii nostri esse debeat A. [75] nostri B. [76] recte *mg.* A, colligitur manna B, manna recte colligitur C. [77] Sacre Scripture cibus adquiritur B, Scripture Sacre cibus acquiritur CD. [78] die altera B. [79] reservant C. [80] *om.* B. [81] die BC. [82] vero ACD. [83] manna in diem alterum non in sabbatum A. [84] facta collectio BCD. [85] eam C. [86] *mg.* A. [87] advescenditur A. [88] colligi ABD. [89] dicens A. [90] *om.* B. [91] servari A. [92] puteis A. [93] *om.* BCD. [94] in sole BCD. [95] in igne BCD. [96] Nunc liquefit *add.* A. Huius gratie providentia manna nunc indurescit nunc liquescit (liquefit in B) BCD. [97] clementia Scripture Sacre BCD. [98] *om.* ACD. [99] liquefecit B. [1] gratie celestis donum BCD.
[2] Sic BCD. [3] *om.* A. [4] Tangebat ut C. [5] quod habebant a Deo A, quid haberent a Deo BC. *Cf.* Greg. *Super Exod.*, c. 24 (Migne, *PL*, 79, 733). [6] *om.* A. [7] ex semetipsis A. [8] quid BCD. [9] decretat D. [10] Legimus A. [11] coquebat in olla vel terebat in mortario A.
[12] *om.* BD. [13] *om.* A. [14] dedisti A. [15] habentem in se A. [16] *mg.* A. [17] continet pariter B. [18] *om.* A. [19] *om.* D.

Ezechiel (3: 1-3) *factum est in ore eius dulce*[20] *sicut mel.* Liber devoratus a *Iohanne* (*Apoc.* 10: 9) *sicut mel fuit in ore eius,*[21] *licet ventrem faceret*[22] *amaricare.* (*Ps.* 118: 103): *Quam dulcia faucibus meis eloquia tua super mel ori meo.* Sed quid est quod omnem saporem habuisse dicitur, et tamen spirituali[23] similitudine sapor eius exprimitur cum dicitur *saporem habuisse simile cum melle et panis oleati*? Si attendere voluimus[24] dum [25]ita spiritualiter sapor eius exprimitur,[25] per consequens omnem saporem habere[26] perhibetur. (191ra) Quoniam *omne tulit punctum qui miscuit utile dulci.*[27] Dulcedo notatur in simile cum melle, utilitas in oleato pane. Oleum enim[28] reficit esurientes, recreat lassos, luci pabulum prestat, vulneratos sanat. Similiter quatuor usus celestis discipline assignat apostolus scribens *Timotheo*: (*II Tim.* 3: 16) *Omnis scriptura divinitus inspirata utilis est ad docendum, ad arguendum, ad*[29] *corripiendum,*[30] *ad erudiendum.* Merito igitur *manna*[31] [32]*saporem habet*[32] *panis oleati, mola comminutum vel in mortario tritum et in olla coctum.* Dum enim verbum Domini mola lectionis comminuitur vel pilo disputationis teritur et postmodum in olla mentis sedula[33] meditatione decoquitur, *docet et*[34] *arguit, corripit*[35] *et erudit,* et ita more olei pascit et[36] recreat, sanat et illuminat.

Vidimus qualis sit [37]Sacra Scriptura;[37] nunc videamus qualiter sit addiscenda, qualiter docenda. Discenti quinque sunt admodum necessaria — vite mundicia, cordis simplicitas, attentio mentis, humilitas et mansuetudo.

Vite mundicia [38]necessaria est[38] quia in malivolam animam non introibit sapientia nec [39]habitabit[40] in corpore subdito peccatis.[39] Electuarium preciosum si haberes in pixide munda reponeres et electuarii [41]omnia sanantis[41] receptaculum non mundabis? Scriptum est: (*Sap.* 16: 12) *Non herba non malagma sanavit eos, sed sermo tuus Domine qui sanat omnia.* Et propheta ait:[42] (*Ezech.* 47: 12) *Erunt fructus eius in cibum et folia eius*[43] *in medicinam.* Et *Iohannes* ait: (*Cf. Apoc.* 22: 2) *Folia lignis vite erunt in sanitatem gentibus.*

Legimus Dominum precepisse per Moysen ut populus legem accepturus[44] *sanctificaretur, vestimenta sua lavaret et ab uxoribus abstineret.* (*Cf. Exod.* 19: 10) Multo fortius tu legem evangelicam[45] auditurus debes[46] sanctificare corpus tuum[47] quod [48]anime vestimentum est;[48] diligenter abluere et te ab omni immundicia impollutum conservare.[49] Ut secundum *Salomonem*: (*Eccle.* 9: 8) *Omni tempore* [50]*sint vestimenta tua*[50] *candida. Legimus iterum* [51]*Dominum precepisse per Moysen*[51] *ut cinerem*[52] *vitule rufe* [53]*vir mundus*[53] *colligeret, et aquam expiationis cui cinis erat admixtus homo mundus aspergeret.* (*Cf. Num.* 19: 9) *Vitule rufe cinis* [54]memoriam Dominice passionis significat.[54] *Hunc cinerem aspergit* qui evangelium legit. *Colligit* qui audit. *Mundus itaque*[55] *debet esse et*[56] *aspergens et colligens,* quia impollutus debet esse evangelium et[57] docens et audiens.

Simplicitas [58]cordis iterum[58] necessaria est; sicut scriptum est: (*Sap.* 1: 1) *Sentite de*[59] *Domino in bonitate et in*[60] *simplicitate cordis querite illum.* [61]Et iterum:[61] (*Ibid.*, 1: 5)

[20] *om.* C. [21] *om.* BCD. [22] faciat A. [23] *om.* A, speciali B. [24] voluerimus BC. [25] sapor eius ita spiritualiter exprimitur A, ita sapor eius specialiter exprimitur B. [26] habuisse C. [27] Horace, *Ars Poetica* 343. [28] *om.* A. [29] et C [30] corrigendum A. [31] Sacra Scriptura A. [32] habet saporem C. [33] assidua A. [34] *om.* AD. [35] corrigit A. [36] *om.* A. [37] Scriptura Sacra CD. [38] est necessaria A. [39] in corpore subdito peccatis habitabit B. [40] inhabitabit A. [41] sanantis omnia B. [42] *om.* A. [43] *om.* BCD. [44] precepturus BD, recepturus C. [45] dominicam C. [46] deberes C. [47] *om.* D. [48] est anime vestimentum A. [49] servare A, custodire C. [50] vestimenta tua (sua in D) sint BCD. [51] per Moysen Dominum precepisse A. (The passage beginning... *iterum Dominum* and ending *per Moysen* is omitted in B.) [52] cineres A. [53] mundus vir A. [54] significat memoriam Dominice passionis A, memoriam significat Dominice passionis CD. [55] ita B. [56] *om.* B. [57] *om.* B. [58] iterum cordis BD, etiam cordis C. [59] in A. [60] *om.* B. [61] item A, et B.

Spiritus sanctus discipline effugiet fictum. [62]Beatus Gregorius ait:[62] *Nullus sapientiam que Deus est plene recipit nisi qui* [63]*se ab omnium carnalium cogitationum fluctuatione*[64] *retrahit.*[63] *Unde scriptum est*: (*Eccli.* 38: 25) *Sapientiam scribe*[65] *in*[66] *tempore vacuitatis et qui minoratur actu percipiet eam. Et in Psalmo*: (45: 11) *Vacate et videte quoniam ego sum Deus, etc. Hinc est quod Israel re-* (191rb) *quiem sabbati accepit.* (*Exod.* 16: 29) *Egyptum* [67]*muscarum multitudo*[67] *vexavit.* (*Ibid.*, 8: 21) [68]*Qui enim Deum sequitur et querit*[68] *a carnalium desideriorum strepitu requiescit.*[69] *Egyptus vero*[70] *i.e. mundus muscis percutitur quia curis insolentibus*[71] *vexatur et affligitur. De hiis muscis scriptum est*: (*Eccle.* 10: 1) *Musce morientes perdunt suavitatem unguenti. Dum enim cogitationes superflue in corde nascuntur* [72]*et deficiunt*[72] *suavitatem unguenti,*[73] *i.e. dulcedinem celestis pabuli, et devotionem mentis corrumpunt et destruunt.* Hinc *Psalmista*[74] cum premisisset: (118: 2) *Beati qui scrutantur*[75] *testimonia eius.* Eleganter subiunxit: (*Ibid.*) *In toto corde exquirunt eum.* Qui enim scrutantur [76]testimonia Scripture[76] non dimidio sed toto corde Deum debent exquirere.

Necessaria [77]est iterum[77] cordis attencio. *Non enim fastidientes sed* [78]*sitientes invitantur*[78] *ad aquas.* (*Cf. Isa.* 55: 1) Cibus enim[79] Sacre Scripture cum quadam [80]spirituali aviditate sumendus est.[80] Hinc [81]est quod[81] [82]*Iohanni* dictum est:[82] (*Apoc.* 10: 9) *Accipe librum et devora illum.*[83] Quid est librum[84] devorare nisi verbum Domini[85] avide percipere? Ad[86] attentionem invitat et attentos confortat, quod de sapientia scriptum est: (*Sap.* 6: 13-15) [87]*Clara est et que nunquam*[88] *marcescet sapientia. Et facile videtur ab hiis qui diligunt eam et invenietur ab hiis qui querunt illam.*[89] *Preoccupat eos qui se concupiscunt et illis se prior*[90] *ostendit.*[87] *Qui de* [91]*luce vigilaverit*[91] *ad illam non laborabit, assidentem enim* [92]*illam foribus suis inveniet.*[92]

Necessaria [93]est iterum[93] humilitas. Unde *Psalmista*:[94] (118: 71) *Bonum mihi quia humiliasti me* [95]*ut discam iustificationes tuas.*[95] Et propheta ait: (*Isa.* 28: 9) *Quem docebit*[96] *scientia et intelligere faciet auditum nisi ablactatos a lacte apulsos ab uberibus*? Quod [97]tamquam Salvator exponens in evangelio ait:[97] (*Matt.* 11: 25) *Confiteor tibi patri* [98]*celi et terre,*[98] *quia*[99] *abscondisti hec a sapientibus et prudentibus et revelasti ea parvulis.* Et *Sapientia* ait: (*Prov.* 9: 4) *Siquis parvulus est veniat ad me.* Quam necessaria autem[1] sit humilitas eleganter ostenditur[2] in *libro Regum. Cum enim congregati essent*[3] *tres reges contra regem Moab et*[4] *aqua carentes ad*[5] *auxilium Helisei confugerent,*[6] *dixit Heliseus*: (*IV Reg.* 3: 16-17) *Facite alveum*[7] *torrentis huius fossas et fossas. Hec enim*[8] *dicit Dominus:*

[62] *mg.* Gregorius A. dicit in C. Greg. *Super lib. Eccli.*, c. 24 (Migne, *PL*, 79, 939) and *Moral in Iob*, Lib. XVIII, c. 4 (*Ibid.*, 76, 78). [63] ab omnium carnalium cogitationum se fluctuatione retrahit B; ab omnium carnalium se cogitationum fluctuationibus retrahit CD. [64] cura A. [65] scribes C. (*Eccli.* 38: 25 begins *Sapientia scribe*...) [66] *om.* C. [67] multitudo muscarum B. [68] Qui enim Deum credit A. [69] quiescit A. [70] *om.* A. [71] *om.* C, sollicitis D. [72] minuunt C. [73] perdunt A. [74] David A. [75] custodiunt A. [76] verba Sacre Scripture AB, *om.* D. [77] enim A, item B. [78] sitientes venite B, scientes vocantur CD. [79] *om.* A. [80] ...sumendus est aviditate AD, sumendum est spirituali aviditate C. [81] *om.* C, est *om.* D. [82] dictum est Iohanni A. [83] *om.* A. [84] verbum D. [85] Dei A. [86] *mg.* A. [87] Clara est inquam marcescet quod facile videtur ab hiis qui diligunt eam et invenietur ab hiis qui querunt illam. Preoccupat qui se concupiscunt et illis se prior ostendit B. [88] nusquam A. [89] eam A. [90] priora A. [91] *mg.* C. [92] foribus suis illa invenit A. [93] est (iterum *om.*) A, item B, est *om.* CD. [94] *om.* A. [95] *om.* A, etc., B. [96] docet B. [97] tamquam exponens ait Dominus in evangelio A, Salvator tamquam... C, tamquam Salvator in evangelio ait D. [98] *om.* ACD. [99] qui BCD. [1] *om.* A. [2] signatum est BC, significatum est D. [3] fuissent CD. [4] *om.* BCD. [5] et ad C. [6] confugientes C. [7] in alveum C. [8] *om.* A.

Non videbitis ventum nec pluviam et [9]*alveus iste replebitur*[9] *aquis et bibetis vos et familie vestre et iumenta vestra.* Tamquam *alveus torrentis* est receptaculum humani cordis. Sicut enim per alveum torrens[10] defluit, sic per [11]cor humanum[11] multipliciter[12] cura decurrit. Faciende sunt in hoc alveo fosse — [13]nec unica tantum fossa,[13] nec tantum fosse, sed fosse et fosse. [14]Fossas facere est humiliare se Deo interius et exterius.[14] Facere iterum[15] fossas est[15] humiliare se proximo[16] dupliciter. *Fossas igitur et fossas* [17]*in alveo facere* est[17] tam Deo quam [18]proximo se interius et exterius devote humiliare.[18] Si ita precesserit[19] diversitas fossarum sine vento et pluvia [20]sequitur habundantia aquarum.[20] Ventus est disputatio contentiosa; tamquam gutte pluviales sunt verba ornata et similiter cadentia. *Sine vento igitur*[21] *et pluvia fosse replentur*[22] *aqua* quia sine ornatu apparate[23] orationis, sine[24] strepitu litigiose disputationis mentes humilium celesti[25] habundant scientia.[26]

[27]Necessaria item est mansuetudo[27] (191va) sicut scriptum est: (*Eccli.* 5: 13) *Esto mansuetus ad audiendum verbum Domini.*[28] Et beatus[29] *Iacobus* ait: (1: 21) *In mansuetudine suscipite* [30]*insitum verbum.*[30] [31]Et *Psalmista* ait:[31] (24: 9) *Docebit mites vias suas.* Humilitatis [32]pariter et mansuetudinis fructum[32] insinuans *Ysaias* ait: (30: 23) *Pascetur in possessione*[33] *tua agnus spaciose.* Illi enim[34] in Sacra Scriptura habundantia inveniunt pascua qui prediti sunt humilitatis et mansuetudinis gratia.

Vidimus qualiter addiscenda sit Sacra Scriptura. Docenti quatuor [35]admodum sunt[35] necessaria: scientia et[36] vita, humilitas et[37] mansuetudo. Scientiam esse necessariam eleganter signatum[38] est in *Ezechiele*: (3:4) *Cum enim volumen comedisset dictum est ei: Fili*[39] *hominis, vade ad domum Israel* [*et*] *loqueris*[40] *ad eos verba mea.* Tunc enim recte[41] sequitur verborum[42] predicatio cum precessit[43] voluminis incorporatio.[44] Hoc est volumen volans quod ostensum est *Zacharie.* (*Cf.* 5: 1-2) *Cum igitur volans sit non poterit ad illud* [45]*pertingere qui non habuerit*[45] *alas vite et scientie.*

Vitam etiam maxime [46]necessariam esse[46] significatum[47] est in *Ezechiele.* (*Cf.* 2: 23-24) *Cum enim visa gloria Domini in faciem suam*[48] *cecidisset; postmodum* [49]*in eum spiritus*[49] *ingressus statuit eum super*[50] *pedes suos et dixit ei: Fili hominis, mittam*[51] *te ad filios Israel. Qui enim gloriam Domini*[52] *vidit,* i.e. archana Sacre Scripture consideravit, et[53] *visa gloria in faciem suam cadit,* i.e. consideratis Dei mirabilibus, humilitatis [54]iugo se subicit.[54] *Super pedes suos statuitur,*[55] i.e. ad bene operandum erigitur, ut sic[56] tandem *ad filios Israel mittatur,* i.e. ad[57] verbum Domini[58] predicandum[59] ydoneus[60] habeatur.[61]

[9] replebitur alveus iste A. [10] torrentes A. [11] humanum cor B. [12] multiplex B, multiplici CD. [13] *om.* BCD. [14] Facere fossas est humiliare coram Deo exterius et interius A. Facere fossas est humilare se Deo interius et exterius CD. [15] item B. [16] pro Christo A. [17] facere est in alveo A. [18] pro Christo interius et exterius devote se humiliare A. [19] precessit A. [20] habundantia sequetur aquarum BCD. [21] *om.* B. [22] repluntur A. [23] aptate A, *om.* D. [24] vel sine C. [25] *om.* A. [26] milicia CD. [27] Mansuetudo etiam est necessaria A, Necessaria est igitur mansuetudo CD. [28] Dei BC. [29] *om.* BCD. [30] verbum insitum A. [31] *om.* A. [32] et mansuetudinis paratum fructum A, et mansuetudinis pariter fructum B. [33] passione B. [34] *om.* B. [35] sunt admodum CD. [36] *om.* A. [37] *om.* A. [38] significatum D. [39] Filii D. [40] loquens CD (*Ezech.* 3: 4 reads... *et loqueris*). [41] *om.* C. [42] *om.* A. [43] precesserit A. [44] incorporatum A. [45] attingere qui non habet (habuit in CD) BCD. [46] esse *om.* B, esse necessariam CD. [47] signatum C. [48] *om.* B. [49] spiritus in eum BCD. [50] supra ABD. [51] mitto BCD. [52] Dei B. [53] i.e. BD, *om.* C. [54] se iugo subdit A. [55] statuit A. [56] *om.* A. [57] *om.* C [58] Dei C. [59] poterit predicare C. [60] extraneus D. [61] *om.* C.

Hinc etiam sponsus loquens ad sponsam ait: (*Cant.* 2: 14) *Ostende mihi faciem tuam; sonet vox tua in auribus meis. Vox enim*[62] *tua dulcis et facies tua*[63] *decora.* Faciem mentis depingit qualitas conversationis. Bene igitur [64]primo iubetur facies[64] ostendi ut deinde vox melius[65] audiri; quia si[66] facies decora, vox dulcis. Quia accepta est predicatio, quam honesta commendat conversatio. Quia teste beato[67] Gregorio: *Sermo dulcedinem non habet quem vita remordet.* Hinc etiam[68] de labiis sponse dicitur: (*Cant.* 4: 3) *Sicut vitta*[69] *coccinea labia tua et eloquium tuum dulce.* Cum doctores [70]maceratione carnis[70] attenuati et ardore caritatis [71]sunt coccinei, capiti[71] capillos astringunt, [72]hoc est[72] fideles Christo coniungunt nec [73]dissolutos fluctuare permittunt.[73] *Eloquium est*[74] *dulce quia* [75]*sicut vitta*[75] *coccinea sunt labia.* Hinc etiam sponsa ait in *Canticis*: (5: 5) *Surrexi ut aperirem dilecto meo; manus mee distillaverunt myrram et*[76] *digiti mei pleni sunt myrra probatissima.* In illis sponsa[77] [78]*dilecto suo aperit,*[78] per quos[79] verbum predicationis[80] ad alios transmititt.[81] Bene igitur[82] postquam *surrexit aperire dum* [83]*manus suas dicit myrram distillare,*[83] quia decens est ut[84] per mortificationem carnis exemplum [85]amaritudinis habeant in opere,[85] qui verbum sacre[86] predicationis habent in ore.

Quod[87] autem meritum vite necessarium sit[88] docentibus pene [89]singule sacre[89] pagine[90] testantur simile. Sufficiat tamen ad presens testimonium *Ieremie. Legitur* (32: 6-15) [91]*enim quod*[91] *cum emisset Ieremias agrum in Anathoth ab Ananeel patrueli suo accepit in testimonium* [92]*possessionis librum*[92] *signatum et librum apertum qui repositi sunt in vase fictili. Econtrario autem appendit argentum:*[93] *septem stateres et decem argenteos. Agrum emere* est eterne hereditatis possessionem comparare. Bene autem[94] eterna[95] possessio *per agrum Anathoth* intelligitur. *Anathoth enim*[96] interpretatur obedientia. Fructus autem obedi- (191vb) entie est acquisitio [97]hereditatis eterne.[97] *Hec possessio duobus libris confirmatur*[98] *aperto et clauso,* i.e. veteri testamento[99] et novo. *Uterque autem liber in vase fictili reponitur* quia utriusque testamenti intellectus [1]ruditate littere[1] et simplicitate reconditur. *Hos libros accipit*[2] qui Sacre Scripture intelligentiam percipit.[3] *Sed libros hos*[4] *accipiens argentum debet appendere,*[5] quia qui[6] intellectum a Domino percipit[7] bona opera [8]debet econverso rependere.[8] Qualiter autem appendi[9] debeat argentum docet vir sapiens cum ait: (*Eccli.* 28: 29) *Argentum et aurum tuum*[10] *confla et facito verbis tuis stateram. Argentum et aurum tuum*[11] *conflare* est doctrine operationem coniungere. *Ille autem verbis suis stateram facit* qui sue predicationi [12]bene vivendo pondus adiecit.[12] [13]Unde idem *Salomon*:[13] (*Eccli.* 21: 28) *Labia inprudentium* [14]*stulta narrabunt; verba autem prudentium*[14] *statera*[15] *ponderabuntur.*

[62] *om.* A. [63] *om.* C. [64] facies primo iubetur BCD. [65] *om.* BCD. [66] *om.* A. [67] *om.* B. Greg. *Super Cant. Cant.*, c. 2: 14 (Migne, *PL*, 79, 500). [68] est quod B. [69] vita ABC. [70] eius maceratione sunt A. [71] coccinei capitis BC, sunt *om.* D. [72] Hii B. [73] fluctuare permittunt dissolutos B, ...permittant D. [74] enim B. [75] *om.* A. [76] *om.* ACD. [77] *om.* A. [78] aperit dilecto suo B, meo in A. [79] quorum CD. [80] predicatio C. [81] committit A, transit C. [82] autem A. [83] manus su- (*eras.*) distillare myrram A. [84] post B. [85] habeant amaritudinis (amaritudinis habeant *corr.*) in corpore A. [86] *om.* A. [87] licet BCD. [88] esse BD, sic C. [89] sacre singule B. [90] scripture A. [91] *om.* A, enim *om.* B. [92] possessionis *om.* AC, *mg.* B. [93] *om.* A. [94] ergo D. [95] *om.* BCD. [96] *om.* AB, autem C. [97] eterne hereditatis B, hereditatis superne CD. [98] comparatur A. [99] *om.* A. [1] in littere ruditate B. [2] accepit A. [3] precipit A. [4] *om.* BCD. [5] apprehendere A. [6] *om.* ABD. [7] precipiens AB, percipientur D. [8] debet equo impendere (rependere in D) AD, econverso debet rependere B. [9] apprehendi A. [10] *om.* D. [11] *om.* ACD. [12] pondus bene vivendi adiecit A. [13] Ut idem Sapiens ait B, Sapiens ait CD. [14] *om.* D. [15] *om.* C.

[16]Necessaria iterum est[16] humilitas proponendi[17] verbum Domini. Quod[18] bene significatum est in *Ieremia*, (1: 6, 9) *cum enim dixisset a a a Domine Deus ecce*[19] *nescio loqui, quia puer ego sum. Consequenter missa est ad eum*[20] *manus Domini et tetigit os eius et dictum est ei*: *Ecce dedi verba mea in ore tuo.* Idem [21]etiam eleganter[21] significavit *Ysaias* cum enim[22] premisisset: (30: 22) *Contaminabis laminas sculptilium argenti tui et vestimentum*[23] *conflatilis auri tui et disperges ea sicut*[24] *immundiciam menstruate.* Postmodum subiungitur: (30: 23) *Dabitur pluvia semini tuo ubicumque seminaveris in terra et panis frugum terre* [25]*erit uberrimus.*[25] *Per laminas* [26]*sculptilium argenti*[26] [27]intelligitur ornata et polita eloquentia.[27] *Per vestimentum auri conflatilis* humane sapientie fulgor designatur.[28] Si igitur[29] hoc contaminaveris et quasi[30] immunda abieceris et [31]nec de eloquentia nec de sapientia tua presumpseris,[31] *Ubicumque seminaveris semini tuo dabitur pluvia* quia predicationem tuam et doctrinam celestis diriget gratia,[32] *et panis tuus erit* [33]*uberrimus* quia sermo tuus ad docendum erit efficacissimus.

Mansuetudo iterum[34] necessaria est.[35] Unde beatus *Iacobus* ait: (3: 13) *Quis sapiens et*[36] *disciplinatus inter vos? Ostendat ex bona conversatione operam suam in mansuetudine sapientie.*[37] In cuius verbi expositione dicitur: *quis ex vobis* [38]est a Deo[38] *sapiens* cognitione[39] *et disciplinatus* exercitio vite, ut audeat magisterium sibi assumere. [40]Prius discat bene operari[40] [41]quam alios docere[41] ut *bene conversando* [42]inter vos[42] exemplum aliorum[43] possit esse. Et hoc *in mansuetudine* ne propter suam sapientiam et [44]operationem bonam[44] alios despiciat. Hinc etiam beatus *Petrus* ait: (*I Petr.* 3: 15-16) *Parati estote semper*[45] *ad satisfactionem omni poscenti vos rationem* [46]*de hac que in*[47] *vobis est*[46] *fide et spe, sed tamen cum modestia et timore* [48]*conscientiam habentes bonam.*[48] In hiis verbis [49]forma doctoribus[49] prescribitur. [50]Quatuor enim notantur hic doctoribus necessaria[50]: sollicitudo doctrine, puritas conscientie, timor humilitatis, modestia mansuetudinis. Quid ad hoc dicturus sum[51] qui nec vite nec scientie[52] eminentiam habeo et tamen cathedram[53] magistralem ascendo. Sed superne pietatis[54] inexhaustam bonitatem[55] pocius quam humanum presumptionem attendens in mei redemptoris obsequium linguam meam et mentem converto et eius gratie me et [56]propositum meum[56] committo. Amen.[57]

[16] Necessaria item est B, Necessaria est iterum C. [17] proponenti BC. [18] quia C. [19] *om.* A, ecce ego B. [20] ipsum C. [21] autem eleganter C, *om.* A. [22] *om.* A. [23] vestimenta D. [24] tamquam A. [25] *om.* B. [26] argenti sculptilis BD, argenti C. [27] ornata et polita intelligitur eloquentia ABD. [28] intelligitur C. [29] ergo A. [30] ut A. [31] et nec de sapientia nec de eloquentia presumpseris B, et de eloquentia et sapientia tua non presumpseris C. [32] gloria D. [33] *om.* B. [34] item B. [35] *om.* B. [36] *om.* A. [37] tue *add.* C. [38] a Deo est B. [39] cognomine A. [40] bene operari prius discat C. [41] et postea doceat C. [42] *om.* A. [43] *om.* A. [44] bonam operationem BCD. [45] *om.* A. [46] reddere de ea que in vobis est C. [47] *om.* A. [48] habentes bonam conscientiam B. [49] doctoribus forma BCD. [50] *om.* A. - Quatuor enim doctoribus sunt necessaria A. [51] sim A. [52] conscientie C. [53] *mg.* A. [54] bonitatis A. [55] pietatem A. [56] meum propositum A. [57] *om.* ACD.

Appendix H

INDEX OF PROMINENT THEMES IN THE LANGTON SERMONS

E

F

G

H

I

L

M

Q

R

S

T

U, V

Y

BIBLIOGRAPHY

CONTENTS

I. PRIMARY SOURCES

A. Manuscripts

Austria
  Vienna
    Nationalbibl. 1330

Belgium
  Brugge (Bruges) 28
    93
    278
  Brussels
    Bibl. royale II.953
    II.957
    II.962

England
  Cambridge
    Corpus Christi Coll. 55
    450
    459
    Peterhouse Coll. 112
    119
    255

St. John's Coll. 57
C 12
University Library Ee.vi.10
Ii.vi.5

Lincoln
Cathedral Lib. 239
Record Office
Ancaster 16/1

London
British Museum
Add. 16, 164
Arundel 292
346
Cotton Vesp. D. XIII
Vesp. E. X
Harleian 325
Royal 2.D.XXXVII
3.A.X
8.A.X
8.C.VII
8.D.IV
8.F.IV
10.A.VII
Lambeth Palace Lib. 71

Oxford
Bodleian Lib.
Hatton 37
Magdalen Coll. 168

FRANCE
Amiens
Fonds Lescalopier 30
Arras 222
Cambrai 588
Douai 495
Nîmes 42
Paris
Arsenal 400
854
Mazarine 999
Bibl. nat., lat. 1112
2915
2995
3227
3495
3570
3995
12420
14470
14525

Bibl. nat., lat. 14593
14804
14859
14925
14957
15025
15965
16463
16502
16875
Ste. Geneviève 93
1422
Reims 582
Rouen 1468
Troyes 862
1100
1227
1367
[Vitry-le-François] 73
75

GERMANY
[*Berlin*] *Tübingen*
lat. fol. 764 (Görres 114)
Leipzig
Univ. Bibl. 364
443
444
Munich
Staatsbibl. Clm. 5998
12660

SPAIN
Barcelona
Ripoll 205

SWITZERLAND
Basel
Univ. Bibl. A.IX.2

VATICAN CITY
Biblioteca Apostolica Vaticana, Vat. lat. 634

B. PRINTED SOURCES

Alain de Lille. See *PL.* and D'Alverny, M.-Th.
Andrieu, M. *Les Ordines Romani du haut moyen âge.* 4 vols. Louvain, 1931-56. See also *PL.*
Annales Monastici. Ed. H. R. Luard. 5 vols. *Rolls Series.* London, 1864-69.
Augustine. *De Doctrina Christiana. Corpus Christianorum, Ser. Lat.*, 32 (1962). See also *PL.*

Caesar of Heisterbach. *Dialogus Miraculorum*. Ed. J. Strange. 2 vols. Cologne, 1851.

—. *Die Fragmente der Libri VIII Miraculorum des Caesarius von Heisterbach*. Ed. A. Meister. Rome, 1901.

Cheney, C. R., and Semple, W. H., edd. *Selected letters of Pope Innocent III concerning England, 1198-1216. Nelson's Medieval Texts*. Edinburgh, 1953.

Chronique des Ducs de Normandie par Benoît, Trouvère Anglo-Normand du XIIe siècle. Ed. Fr. Michel. 3 vols. Paris, 1836-44.

Conciliorum Oecumenicorum Decreta. Edd. J. Alberigo, *et al.* Freiburg-Rome-Vienna, 1962.

D'Achery, L., ed. *Veterum Scriptorum Spicilegium*. 3 vols. Paris, 1723.

D'Alverny, M.-Th. *Alain de Lille: Textes inédits, avec une introduction sur sa vie et ses œuvres, Études de Philosophie Médiévale*, LII. Paris, 1965.

Denifle, H., et Chatelain, A., edd. *Chartularium universitatis Parisiensis*. 4 vols. Paris, 1889-97.

Dickson, Marcel et Christiane. "Le cardinal Robert de Courson: sa vie," *Archives d'histoire doctrinale et littéraire du moyen âge*, IX (1934), 53-142.

Eadmer. See *PL* and Southern, R. W., ed.

Foreville, R. *Le Jubilé de Saint Thomas Becket du XIII*[e] *au XV*[e] *Siècle, 1220-1470: Étude et documents*. Paris, 1958.

Gerald of Wales. *Opera*. Ed. J. S. Brewer. 8 vols. *Rolls Series*. London, 1861-91.

—. "De Principis Instructione Liber," in *Opera*, VIII, 3-329.

Gervase of Canterbury. *Historical Works*. Ed. W. Stubbs. 2 vols. *Rolls Series*. London, 1879-80.

Saint Gregory the Great: *Dialogues*. Tr. O. J. Zimmerman. *Fathers of the Church*. New York, 1959.

Gregory the Great. See *PL*.

Guibert de Nogent. See *PL*.

Henry of Ghent. *Liber de Scriptoribus Ecclesiasticis*. Ed. A. Miraeus. *Bibliotheca Ecclesiastica*. Antwerp, 1639.

Henry of Knighton. *Chronicon*. Ed. J. R. Lumby. 2 vols. *Rolls Series*. London, 1889-95.

L'histoire de Guillaume le Maréchal, Régent d'Angleterre de 1216 à 1219. Ed. P. Meyer. 3 vols. *Soc. de l'hist. de France*. Paris, 1891-1901.

Hunt, R. W. "The Disputation of Peter of Cornwall against Symon the Jew," *Studies in Medieval History presented to F. M. Powicke*. Oxford, 1948. 143-56.

Jacques de Vitry. *Libri duo, quorum prior Orientalis, sive Hierosolymitanae; alter, Occidentalis...* Duaci, 1597.

—. *The History of Jerusalem, A.D. 1180*. Tr. A. Stewart. Abbrev. London, 1896.

—. *Lettres de Jacques de Vitry, 1160/-70-1240, évêque de Saint-Jean-d'Acre*. Ed. R. B. C. Huygens. Leiden, 1960.

Liebermann, F., ed. See Matthew Paris.

Major, K., ed. *Acta Stephani Langton Cantuariensis Archiepiscopi. Canterbury and York Series*, No. 50. Oxford, 1950.

Materials for the history of Thomas Becket, Archbishop of Canterbury. Ed. J. C. Robertson. 6 vols. *Rolls Series*. London, 1875-85.

Matthew Paris. *Chronica Majora*. Ed. H. R. Luard. 7 vols. *Rolls Series*. London, 1872-83.

—. *Vita sancti Stephani archiepiscopi Cantuariensis*. Ed. F. Liebermann. In *Ungedruckte Anglo-Normannische Geschichtsquellen*. Strassburg, 1879. 318-29.

—. *Ex vita Stephani archiepiscopi Cantuariensis*. *MGH: SS*, XXVIII. Hannover, 1888. 441-43.

Memorials of St. Edmund's Abbey. Ed. T. Arnold. 3 vols. *Rolls Series.* London, 1890-96.
—. *The Chronicle of Bury St. Edmund's, 1212-1301.* Ed. A. Gransden. *Nelson's Medieval Texts.* London-Edinburgh, 1963.
Monumenta Germaniae Historica: *Leges, Poetae, Scriptores.* Edd. G. H. Pertz, G. Waitz, *et al.* [Cited as *MGH*].
—. *Capitularia. Legum,* I. Hannover, 1835.
—. *Chronica Alberici Monachi Trium Fontium. SS,* XXIII. 1874.
—. *Willelmi Chronica Andrensis. SS,* XXIV. 1879.
—. *Roberti Autissiodorensis Chronicon. SS,* XXVI. 1882.
Patrologiae Cursus Completus: *Series Latina.* Ed. J. P. Migne. 221 vols. Paris, 1844-64. [Cited as *PL*].
—. Augustine. *De Doctrina Christiana.* 34, 15-122.
—. Gregory the Great. *Moralium libri sive expositio in librum B. Iob.* 75, 509-1162; 76, 9-782.
—. —. *Homiliae in Ezechielem prophetam.* 76, 785-1072.
—. —. *XL Homiliae in Evangelia.* 76, 1075-1312.
—. —. *Liber regulae pastoralis.* 77, 13-128.
—. *Ordines Romani.* 78, 937-1368.
—. Guibert de Nogent. *Liber quo ordine sermo fieri debeat.* 156, 21-32.
—. Eadmer. *Liber de S. Anselmi Similitudinibus.* 159, 605-708.
—. Stephen Langton. *Tractatus de translatione Beati Thomae.* 190, 407-24.
—. Peter Comestor. *Historia Scholastica.* 198, 1054-1722.
—. Peter the Chanter. *Verbum Abbreviatum.* 205, 23-370.
—. Alain de Lille. *Summa de arte praedicatoria.* 210, 109-98.
—. Various sermons in vols. 39, 156, 158, 162, 171, 172, 175, 178, 184, 189, 191, 192, 196, 198, 202, 207, 210, 211, 212, 217.
Powicke, F. M., and Cheney, C. R., edd. *Councils and synods, with other documents relating to the English Church*: *II, A.D. 1205-1313.* 2 vols. Oxford-New York, 1964.
Ralf de Diceto. *Opera Historica.* Ed. W. Stubbs. 2 vols. *Rolls Series.* London, 1876.
Ralph of Coggeshall. *Chronicon Anglicanum.* Ed. J. Stevenson. *Rolls Series.* London, 1875.
Ranulf of Higden. *Polychronicon.* Ed. J. R. Lumby. 9 vols. *Rolls Series.* London, 1865-86.
Regesta Pontificum Romanorum inde ab a. post Christum natum 1198 ad a. 1304. Ed. A. Potthast. 2 vols., repr. Gratz, 1957.
The Register of St. Osmund. Ed. W. H. R. Jones. 2 vols. *Rolls Series.* London, 1883-84.
Rerum Britannicarum medii aevi scriptores. 244 vols. London, 1858-96. [Cited as *Rolls Series*].
Roger of Wendover. *Flores Historiarum.* Ed. H. G. Hewlett. 3 vols. *Rolls Series.* London, 1886-89.
Royal and other historical letters illustrative of the Reign of Henry III. Ed. W. W. Shirley. 2 vols. *Rolls Series.* London, 1862-66.
Rymer, T., ed. *Foedera.* 20 vols. London, 1704-35.
Southern, R. W., ed. *Eadmeri monachi Cantuariensis Vita Sancti Anselmi archiepiscopi Cantuariensis* (The Life of St. Anselm, Archbishop of Canterbury by Eadmer). *Nelson's Medieval Texts.* London-Edinburgh, 1963.
Stubbs, William. *Historical Introductions to the Rolls Series.* Ed. A. Hassall. London, 1902.
—. *Select Charters and other Illustrations of English Constitutional History.* Ed. H. W. C. Davis. 9th ed., rev. Oxford, 1960.
Walter of Coventry. *Memoriale.* Ed. W. Stubbs. 2 vols. *Rolls Series.* London, 1872-73.
Wharton, H., ed. *Anglia Sacra.* 2 vols. London, 1691.
Wilkins, D., ed. *Concilia Magnae Britanniae et Hiberniae.* London, 1737.

II. SECONDARY SOURCES

A. Catalogues of Manuscript Collections

Austria

Vienna. Tabulae codicum manuscriptorum praeter graecos et orientales in Bibliotheca Palatina Vindobonensi asservatorum. 11 vols. Vienna, 1864-1912.

Belgium

Sanderus, A. *Bibliotheca Belgica Manuscripta.* Insulis, 1641.

Brugge (Bruges). *Catalogue des manuscrits de la bibliothèque publique de la ville de Bruges.* Ed. A. De Poorter. Gembloux-Paris, 1934.

Brussels. Catalogue des manuscrits de la Bibliothèque Royale de Belgique. Edd. J. Van den Gheyn, *et al.* 13 vols. Bruxelles, 1901-48.

England

Botfield, B. *Notes on the Cathedral Libraries of England.* London, 1849.

De Ricci, S. *English Collectors of Books and Manuscripts* (*1530-1930*) *and their marks of ownership.* Cambridge, 1930.

Ker, N. R. *Medieval libraries of Great Britain: list of surviving books.* 2d ed. rev. London, 1964.

Cambridge. A catalogue of the Manuscripts preserved in the library of the University of Cambridge. 6 vols. Cambridge, 1856-67.

—. Corpus Christi Coll. *A descriptive catalogue of the Manuscripts in the library of Corpus Christi College, Cambridge.* Ed. M. R. James. 2 vols. Cambridge, 1912.

—. Peterhouse Coll. *A descriptive catalogue of the Manuscripts in the library of Peterhouse, Cambridge.* Ed. M. R. James. Cambridge, 1899.

—. St. John's Coll. *A descriptive catalogue of the Manuscripts in the library of St. John's College, Cambridge.* Ed. M. R. James. Cambridge, 1913.

Canterbury. James, M. R. *The ancient libraries of Canterbury and Dover.* Cambridge, 1903.

—. *A catalogue of the manuscript books in the library of Christ Church, Canterbury.* Ed. C. E. Woodruff. Canterbury, 1911.

—. Woodruff, C. E. and Danks, W. *Memorials of the Cathedral and Priory of Christ in Canterbury.* London, 1912.

Lincoln. Catalogue of the Manuscripts of Lincoln Cathedral Chapter Library. Ed. R. M. Wooley. Oxford Un. Pr., 1927.

—. *Historical Manuscripts Commission, Report: MSS of the Earl of Ancaster.* Dublin, 1907.

London. British Museum: Department of MSS. *Index*: *Early sermons and theological treatises, Latin.* 3 vols. n.d. I.

—. British Museum. *Catalogue of Additions to the Manuscripts in the British Museum, 1846-47.* London, 1864.

—. British Museum. *Catalogue of Arundel and Burney Manuscripts.* Ed. J. Forshall. 3 pts in 1. London, 1834-40.

—. British Museum. *A Catalogue of the Manuscripts in the Cottonian Library.* Ed. J. Planta. London, 1802.

—. British Museum. *A Catalogue of the Harleian Manuscripts in the British Museum.* Edd. R. Nares, *et al.* 4 vols. London, 1808-12.

—. British Museum. *Catalogue of western Manuscripts in the Old Royal and King's Collections.* Edd. G. F. Warner and J. P. Gilson. 2 vols. London, 1921.

—. Lambeth Palace. *A Catalogue of the Archiepiscopal Manuscripts in the Library at Lambeth Palace.* Ed. H. J. Todd. London, 1812.

—. Lambeth Palace. *A descriptive catalogue of the Manuscripts in the library of Lambeth Palace: the medieval MSS.* Ed. M. R. James. Cambridge, 1932.

Oxford. A summary catalogue of western manuscripts in the Bodleian Library at Oxford. Edd. F. Madan, *et al.* 7 vols. Oxford, 1895-1953.

—. *Catalogus codicum mss qui in collegiis aulisque Oxoniensibus hodie adservantur.* Ed. H. O. Coxe. Oxonii, 1852.

—. Powicke, F. M. *The medieval books of Merton College.* Oxford, 1931.

FRANCE

Catalogue général des manuscrits des bibliothèques publiques des départements. Quarto Ser. 7 vols. Paris, 1849-85.

II (1855): Troyes, n.n.

IV (1872): Arras. Ed. J. Quicherat.

VI (1878): Douai. Ed. C. Dehaisnes.

VII (1885): Toulouse-Nîmes. Ed. A. Molinier.

Catalogue général des manuscrits des bibliothèques publiques de France, Départements. Octavo Ser. 51 vols. Paris, 1886-1956.

I (1886): Rouen. Ed. H. Omont.

XIII (1891): Vitry-le-François. Ed. G. Hérelle.

XVII (1891): Cambrai. Ed. A. Molinier.

XIX (1893): Amiens. Ed. E. Coyecque.

XXXVIII (1904): Reims. Ed. H. Loriquet.

Leroquais, V. *Les manuscrits liturgiques latins du haut moyen âge à la Renaissance.* Paris, 1931.

—. *Les pontificaux manuscrits des bibliothèques publiques de France.* 3 vols. Paris, 1937.

—. *Les sacramentaires et les missels manuscrits des bibliothèques publiques de France.* 4 vols. Paris, 1924.

Paris. Bibliothèque de l'Arsenal. *Catalogue des manuscrits de la bibliothèque de l'Arsenal.* Ed. H. Martin. 7 vols. Paris, 1885-96.

—. Bibliothèque Mazarine. *Catalogue des manuscrits de la bibliothèque Mazarine.* Ed. A. Molinier. 4 vols. Paris, 1885-98.

—. *Catalogus Codicum Manuscriptorum Bibliothecae Regiae.* 4 vols. Paris, 1739-44.

—. Bibliothèque Nationale. *Catalogue général des manuscrits latins.* 4 vols. Paris, 1939-58. [lat. MSS 1-3277].

—. Delisle, L. "Inventaire des manuscrits latins de Saint-Germain-des-Prés, conservés à la Bibliothèque Impériale, sous les numéros 11504-14231 du fonds Latin," *Bibliothèque de l'École des Chartes,* XXIX (1868), 220-60.

—. Delisle, L. "Inventaire des manuscrits latins de l'Abbaye de Saint-Victor, conservés à la Bibliothèque Impériale, sous les numéros 14232-15175 du fonds Latin," *Ibid.,* XXX (1869), 1-79.

—. Delisle, L. "Inventaire des manuscrits latins de la Sorbonne, conservés à la Bibliothèque Impériale, sous les numéros 15176-16718 du fonds Latin," *Ibid.,* XXXI (1870), 1-50; 135-61.

—. Delisle, L. "Inventaire des manuscrits latins de Notre-Dame et d'autres Fonds, conservés à la Bibliothèque Nationale, sous les numéros 16719-18613 du fonds Latin," *Ibid.,* XXXI (1870), 463-565.

—. Hauréau, B. *Notices et extraits de quelques manuscrits latins de la Bibliothèque Nationale.* 6 vols. Paris, 1890-93.

Paris. Hauréau, B. *Notices et extraits des manuscrits de la Bibliothèque Nationale et autres bibliothèques*. Académie des Inscriptions et Belles-Lettres, Paris, 1906. XXXVIII, ii, 397-447.

—. Bibliothèque Sainte-Geneviève. *Catalogue des manuscrits de la bibliothèque Sainte-Geneviève*. Ed. Ch. Kohler. 2 vols. Paris, 1893-96.

GERMANY

[*Berlin*]. *Die Handschriften-Verzeichnisse der Preussischen Staatsbibliothek zu Berlin* (*Vierzehnter Bd.*): *Verzeichnis der Lateinischen Handschriften*. 3 vols. Berlin, 1893-1919. III, *Die Görreshandschriften*.

Leipzig. Feller, Io. *Catalogus Codicum Manuscriptorum Bibliothecae Paulinae in Academia Lipsiensi*. Lipsiae, 1686.

—. *Katalog der Handschriften der Universitäts-Bibliothek zu Leipzig*. Ed. R. Helssig. Leipzig, 1926-35.

Munich. *Catalogus codicum latinorum Bibliothecae Regiae Monacensis*. Edd. C. Halm, *et al*. 2 vols. in 7 pts. Munich, 1868-81.

—. Schneyer, J. B. "Beobachtungen zu lateinischen Sermones-handschriften der Staatsbibliothek München," *Bayerische Akademie der Wissenschaften, Phil.-Hist. Kl. Sitzungsberichte*, München, 1958. Hft. 8.

SPAIN

Barcelona. "Códices Manuscritos de Ripoll," *Revista de Archivos Bibliotecas y Museos*, XXXV (1931), 162.

—. Garcia, Z. "Bibliotheca Patrum Latinorum Hispaniensis; II Band nach den Aufzeichnungen Rudolf Beers," *Sitzungsberichte der Kaiserlichen Akademie der Wissenschaften* [Vienna] *Philos.-Hist. Klasse*, CLXIX (1915), no. 2.

SWITZERLAND

Basel. *Die deutschen Handschriften der Oeffentlichen Bibliothek der Universität Basel. Bd. I: Die Handschriften der Abteilung A*. Ed. G. Binz. Basel, 1907.

VATICAN CITY

—. *Codices Vaticani Latini*. I. Ed. M. Vattasso and P. Franchi de' Cavalieri. Rome, 1902.

B. BIOGRAPHICAL AND BIBLIOGRAPHICAL WORKS

Bale, J. *Index Britanniae Scriptorum*: *John Bale's Index of British and other writers*. Ed. R. L. Poole with M. Bateson. Oxford, 1902.

Baxter, J. H., *et al*. *An Index of British and Irish Latin Writers A.D. 400-1520. Extrait du Bull. du Cange*, VII. Paris, 1932.

Brucker, Joh. *Historia critica philosophiae*. 6 vols. Leipzig, 1766-67.

Cave, W. *Scriptorum ecclesiasticorum historia literaria... ad saeculum XIV*. 2 vols. Oxford, 1740-43.

Ceillier, R. *Histoire générale des auteurs sacrés et ecclésiastiques*. Nouv. éd. 18 vols. Paris, 1868-69.

Chevalier, U. *Répertoire des sources historiques du moyen âge. Bio-bibliographie*, I. Paris, 1905; *Topo-bibliographie*, II. Paris, 1894-99.

—. *Repertorium Hymnologicum*. 6 vols. Louvain-Bruxelles, 1892-1920.

De Visch, Ch. *Bibliotheca Scriptorum Sacri Ordinis Cisterciensis.* Duaci, 1649.

Emden, A. B. *A biographical register of the University of Oxford to A.D. 1500.* 3 vols. Oxford, 1957-59.

Fabricius, Io. *Bibliotheca latina mediae et infimae aetatis.* 6 vols. Leipzig, 1754.

Glorieux, P. *Répertoire des maîtres en Théologie de Paris au XIIIe siècle.* 2 vols. Paris, 1933.

Hardy, T. D. *Descriptive catalogue of materials relating to the history of Great Britain and Ireland.* 3 vols. *Rolls Series.* London, 1862-71.

Jöcher, C. G. *Gelehrten-Lexikon.* 3 vols., repr. Hildesheim, 1960-61.

Leyser, P. *Historia poetarum et poematum medii aevi.* Halae, 1721.

Morin, F. (Migne). *Dictionnaire de philosophie et de théologie scolastiques.* 2 vols. Paris, 1856.

Oudin, C. *Commentarius de scriptoribus ecclesiae antiquis.* 3 vols. Leipzig, 1722.

—. *Supplementum de scriptoribus vel scriptis ecclesiasticis a Bellarmino omissis, ad annum 1460.* Paris, 1686.

Pelzer, A. *Répertoires d'incipit pour la littérature latine, philosophique et théologique du moyen âge.* Rome, 1951.

Pits, Io. *De illustribus Angliae Scriptoribus. Relationum Historicarum de Rebus Anglicis.* Paris, 1619.

Potthast, A. *Bibliotheca historica medii aevi.* 2 vols. Berlin, 1896.

Rouse, R. H. "Bostonus Buriensis and the Author of the *Catalogus Scriptorum Ecclesiae,*" *Speculum,* XLI (1966), 471-99.

Russell, J. C. *Dictionary of writers of thirteenth century England. Bull. Inst. Hist. Research, Suppl.* no. 3. London, 1936.

Stegmüller, F. *Repertorium biblicum medii aevi.* 7 vols. Madrid, 1950-61.

Tanner, Th. *Bibliotheca Britannico-Hibernica: sive de scriptoribus qui in Anglia, Scotia, et Hibernia ad saeculi XVII initium floruerunt.* London, 1748.

Thomson, S. H. *The writings of Robert Grosseteste, bishop of Lincoln 1235-53.* Cambridge, 1940.

Tritheim, Ioh. *Liber de ecclesiasticis scriptoribus.* Ed. J. A. Fabricius. *Bibliotheca Ecclesiastica,* 1718, in fol.

Twysden, R. *Historiae Anglicanae Scriptores.* London, 1652.

Wright, T. *Biographia Britannica Literaria.* 2 vols. London, 1842-46.

C. Stephen Langton: Bibliography on His Writings

1. *Biblical Commentaries*

Kürzinger, J. "Neuere Forschungen zur Exegese des Kardinals Stephan Langton," *Biblica,* XIII (1932), 385-98.

Lacombe, G; Smalley, B; Gregory, A. L. "Studies on the commentaries of Stephen Langton," *Archives d'histoire doctrinale et littéraire du moyen âge,* V (1930), 5-266. [Cited as Lacombe, *et al.*].

M.-B. de Vaux Saint. "Les deux commentaires d'Étienne Langton sur Isaïe," *Revue des sciences philosophiques et théologiques,* XXXIX (1955), 228-36.

Smalley, B. "Biblical commentaries of the 12th and 13th centuries, viewed as historical material, with special reference to the commentaries of Stephen Langton." Unpublished Ph. D. thesis, University of Manchester, 1929.

—. "Exempla in the commentaries of Stephen Langton," *Bull. John Rylands Lib.,* XVII (1933), 121-29. [Cited as *BJRL*].

Smalley. "Stephen Langton and the four senses of Scripture," *Speculum*, VI (1931), 60-76.

2. *Theological Writings*

a. *Questiones*

Antl, L. "An introduction to the Quaestiones theologicae of Stephen Langton," *Franciscan Studies*, XII (1952), 151-75.

Gregory, A. L. "The Cambridge Manuscript of the Questiones of Stephen Langton," *The New Scholasticism*, IV (1930), 165-226.

Lacombe, G. "The Questiones of Cardinal Stephen Langton," *The New Scholasticism*, III (1929), 1-18.

Lacombe, G., and Landgraf, A. "The Questiones of Cardinal Stephen Langton," *The New Scholasticism*, III (1929), 113-58; IV (1930), 115-64.

Landgraf, A. "Quelques collections de Questiones de la seconde moitié du XIIe siècle," *Recherches de théologie ancienne et médiévale*, VI (1934), 368-93; VII (1935), 113-28. [Cited as *RTAM*].

b. *Summa*

De Ghellinck, J. "La somme théologique d'Étienne Langton," *Recherches de science religieuse*, IV (1913), 255-62.

Lacombe, G. "The authenticity of the Summa of Cardinal Stephen Langton," *The New Scholasticism*, IV (1930), 97-114.

Landgraf, A. M. *Einführung in die Geschichte der theologischen Literatur der Frühscholastik*. Regensburg, 1948.

—. "Echtheitsfragen bei Stephan von Langton," *Philosophisches Jahrbuch*, XL (1927), 306-18.

—. "Some unknown writings of the early scholastic period," *The New Scholasticism*, IV (1930), 1-22.

—. "Zur Chronologie der Werke Stephan Langtons," *RTAM*, III (1931), 70 ff.

Lottin, O. "L'authenticité de la 'Summa' d'Étienne Langton," *RTAM*, I (1929), 497-504.

—. "Un nouveau manuscrit fragmentaire de la Somme d'Étienne Langton," *RTAM*, I (1929), 373-76.

Van den Eynde, D. "Hugues de Saint-Victor, source du pseudo-Étienne Langton," *RTAM*, XVII (1950), 61-78.

c. *Comm. in Sententias*

Beumer, Joh. "Zur Ekklesiologie der Frühscholastik," *Scholastik*, XXVI (1951), 364-89.

Landgraf, A. M. "Der Sentenzenkommentar des Kardinals Stephan Langton," *Beiträge zur Geschichte der Philosophie und Theologie des Mittelalters*, Bd. XXXVII, Hft. 1 (1952).

—. "The first Sentence Commentary of Early Scholasticism," *The New Scholasticism*, XIII (1939), 101-32.

—. "Kannte Langton das original der collectanea des Lombarden?" *RTAM*, III (1931), 72-75.

—. "Sentenzenglossen des beginnenden 13. Jahrhunderts," *RTAM*, X (1938), 40-42.

d. Spiritual doctrine, etc.

Antl, L. "Stephen Langton's principle of determining the essence of a sacrament," *Franciscan Studies*, XIV (1954), 336-73.

De la Rue, M. "Dissertation on the lives and works of several Anglo-Norman poets of the thirteenth century: Stephen of Langton," *Archaeologia*, XIII (1800), 231-34.

Dulong, M. "Étienne Langton versificateur," *Mélanges Mandonnet*. Paris, 1930. II, 183-90.

Lottin, O. "Les premiers linéaments du traité de la syndérèse au moyen-âge," *Revue néo-scolastique de philosophie*, XXVIII (1926), 422-54.

Thurston, H. "Notes on familiar prayers: The Veni Sancte Spiritus of Cardinal Stephen Langton," *The Month*, CXXI (1913), 602-16.

Van den Eynde, D. "Stephen Langton and Hugh of St. Cher on the causality of the sacraments," *Franciscan Studies*, XI (1951), 141-55.

Veal, J. F. *The sacramental theology of Stephen Langton and the influence upon him of Peter the Chanter*. Rome, 1955.

D. Stephen Langton: Political and Ecclesiastical History

Cantor, N. F. *Church, kingship, and lay investiture in England: 1089-1135*. Princeton, 1958.

Cazel, F. A., Jr. "Hubert de Burgh." Unpublished Ph. D. thesis, Johns Hopkins University, 1948.

—. "The last years of Stephen Langton," *English Historical Review*, LXXIX (1964), 673-97. [Cited as *EHR*].

Cheney, C. R. *Episcopal visitation of monasteries in the thirteenth century*. Manchester, 1931.

—. *English Synodalia of the Thirteenth Century*. Oxford, 1941.

—. *English Bishops' Chanceries 1100-1250*. Manchester, 1950.

—. *From Becket to Langton: English Church Government 1170-1213*. Manchester, 1956.

—. "A neglected record of the Canterbury election of 1205-06," *Bull. Inst. Hist. Research*, XXI (1948), 233-38.

—. "King John and the Papal Interdict," *BJRL*, XXXI, no. 2 (1948), 295-317.

—. "The Letters of Pope Innocent III," *BJRL*, XXXV, no. 1 (1952), 23-43.

—. "The eve of Magna Carta," *BJRL*, XXXVIII, no. 2 (1956), 311-41.

—. "The papal legate and English monasteries in 1206," *EHR*, XLVI (1931), 443-52.

—. "Legislation of the English medieval church," *EHR*, L (1935), 193-224; 385-417.

—. "The earliest English Diocesan Statutes," *EHR*, LXXV (1960), 1-29.

—. "The alleged deposition of King John," *Studies presented to Powicke* (q.v.), 100-16.

—. "King John's reaction to the Interdict on England," *Trans. Roy. Hist. Soc.*, 4th ser., XXXI (1949), 129-50.

Chew, H. M. *The English ecclesiastical tenants-in-chief and knight service especially in the XIIIth and XIVth centuries*. London, 1932.

Collins, A. J. "The documents of the Great Charter of 1215," *Proc. Brit. Acad.*, XXXIV (1948), 233-79.

Daunou, M. "Étienne Langton," *Hist. litt. de la France*, XVIII (Paris, 1835), 50-66.

Ellis, C. *Hubert de Burgh: a study in constancy*. London, 1952.

Fliche, A. et Martin, V. *Histoire de l'Église depuis les origines jusqu'à nos jours.* 21 vols. Paris, 1938-52.

Foreville, R. "Étienne Langton," *Dictionnaire de Spiritualité Ascétique et Mystique doctrine et histoire.* 4 vols. Paris, 1937-61. IV, ii, cols. 1495-1502.

Gibbs, M., and Lang, J. *Bishops and Reform, 1215-1272, with special reference to the Lateran Council of 1215.* Oxford, 1934.

Haskins, G. L. "Charter witness lists in the reign of King John," *Speculum,* XIII (1938), 319-25.

Hefele, C. J., et Leclercq, H. *Histoire des conciles.* 11 vols. Paris, 1907-52.

Holdsworth, C. J. "John of Ford and the Interdict," *EHR,* LXXVIII (1963), 705-14.

Holt, J. C. *The Northerners: a study in the reign of King John.* Oxford, 1961.

—. *Magna Carta.* Cambridge, 1965.

—. "The barons of the Great Charter," *EHR,* LXX (1955), 1-24.

—. "The making of Magna Carta," *EHR,* LXXII (1957), 401-22.

Hurter, F. *Geschichte Papst Innocenz III.* 4 vols. Hamburg, 1834-42.

Janssen, W. *Die päpstlichen Legaten in Frankreich: (1130-98).* Köln, 1961.

Jolliffe, J. E. A. *Angevin Kingship.* London, 1955.

Kantorowicz, E. H. *The King's Two Bodies: a study in medieval political theology.* Princeton, 1957.

Knowles, M. D. "The Canterbury Election of 1205-06," *EHR,* LIII (1938), 211-20:

Kuttner, S. and Rathbone, E. "Anglo-Norman Canonists of the Twelfth Century: An Introductory Study," *Traditio,* VII (1949-51), 279-358.

Lawrence, C. H. *St. Edmund of Abingdon: a study in hagiography and history.* Oxford, 1960.

Luchaire, A. *Innocent III.* 6 vols. Paris, 1904-08.

Malden, H. E., ed. *Magna Carta Commemoration Essays.* London, 1917.

McKechnie, W. S. *Magna Carta: a commentary on the Great Charter of King John.* Glasgow, 1905.

Major, K. "Familia of Archbishop Stephen Langton," *EHR,* XLVIII (1933), 529-53.

Moore, J. C. "Pope Innocent III and his relations with the French princes." Unpublished Ph. D. thesis, Johns Hopkins University, 1959.

Norgate, K. *England under the Angevin Kings.* 2 vols. London, 1887.

—. *John Lackland.* London, 1902.

—. "Stephen Langton," *Dictionary of National Biography.* Ed. S. Lee. London, 1909. XI, 563-69. [Cited as *DNB*].

—. *The minority of Henry the Third.* London, 1912.

Packard, S. R. "King John and the Norman Church," *Harvard Theological Review,* XV (1922), 15-40.

Painter, S. *William Marshal, knight errant, baron, and regent of England.* Baltimore, 1933.

—. *The reign of King John.* Baltimore, 1949.

—. "Magna Carta," *American Historical Review,* LIII (1947), 42-49. [Cited as *AHR*].

Pantin, W. A. *The English church in the fourteenth century.* Cambridge, 1955.

Parker, T. M. "The terms of the interdict of Innocent III," *Speculum,* XI (1936), 258-60.

Petit-Dutaillis, Ch. *Étude sur la vie et le règne de Louis XIII, 1187-1226.* Paris, 1894.

—. *Studies and notes supplementary to Stubbs' Constitutional History down to the Great Charter.* Tr. W. E. Rhodes. 2d ed. Manchester, 1911.

Poole, A. L. *From Domesday Book to Magna Carta 1087-1216.* 2d ed. Oxford, 1955.

Power, E. *Medieval English Nunneries: c. 1275 to 1535.* Cambridge Univ. Pr., 1922; repr. 1964.

Powicke, F. M. *Stephen Langton: being the Ford Lectures delivered in the University of Oxford in Hilary Term 1927.* Oxford, 1928. [Cited as *SL*].

—. *The Christian life in the Middle Ages and other essays.* Oxford, 1935.

—. *King Henry III and the Lord Edward: the community of the realm in the thirteenth century.* 2 vols. Oxford, 1947.

—. *Ways of medieval life and thought: essays and addresses.* London, 1950.

—. *The Loss of Normandy 1189-1204.* 2d ed. rev. Manchester, 1961.

—. *The Thirteenth Century 1216-1307.* 2d ed. Oxford, 1962.

—. "The bull 'Miramur plurimum' and a letter to Archbishop Stephen Langton, 5 Sept. 1215," *EHR*, XLIV (1929), 87-93.

—. "Bibliographical note on recent work upon Stephen Langton," *EHR*, XLVIII (1933), 554-57.

—. "Stephen Langton: an oration delivered at Canterbury," *Theology*, XVII (1928), 83-96.

Richardson, H. G. "The morrow of the Great Charter," *BJRL*, XXVIII, no. 2 (1944), 422-43.

—. "Addendum," *BJRL*, XXIX, no. 1 (1945), 184-200.

Richardson, H. G. and Sayles, G.O. *The Governance of Mediaeval England from the Conquest to Magna Carta.* Edinburgh, 1963.

Stubbs, Wm. *The Constitutional History of England: in its Origin and Development.* Oxford, 1880. I.

Thompson, F. *Magna Carta: its role in the making of the English Constitution, 1300-1629.* Minneapolis, 1948.

Tillmann, H. *Die päpstlichen Legaten in England bis zur Beendigung der Legation Gualas 1218.* Bonn, Diss., 1926.

Vaughan, R. *Matthew Paris.* Cambridge, 1958.

Warren, W. L. *King John.* London, 1961.

Wilkinson, B. *The Constitutional history of England: 1216-1399 with select documents.* London, 1948. I, *Politics and the Constitution.*

—. "The 'political revolution' of the thirteenth and fourteenth centuries in England," *Speculum*, XXIV (1949), 502-09.

Wood, S. *English monasteries and their patrons in the thirteenth century.* Oxford, 1955.

E. Sermons, Preaching, and Aids for Preachers

Baldwin, Ch. S. *Medieval rhetoric and poetic.* New York, 1928.

Belfour, A. O., ed. *Twelfth-century homilies in MS Bodley 343. Early English Text Soc.*, orig. ser. 137. London, 1909.

Blench, J. W. *Preaching in England in the late Fifteenth and Sixteenth Centuries: a study of English Sermons 1450-c.1600.* Oxford, 1964.

Bourgain, L. *La chaire française au XIIe siècle d'après les manuscrits.* Paris, 1879.

Caplan, H. *Medieval Artes praedicandi: a handlist. Cornell Studies in Classical Philology*, nos. 24-25. Ithaca, 1934-36.

—. "Classical rhetoric and medieval theory of preaching," *Classical Philology*, XXVIII (1933), 73-96.

—. "The four senses of scriptural interpretation and the medieval theory of preaching," *Speculum*, IV (1929), 282-90.

Charland, Th. M. *Artes praedicandi*. Paris-Ottawa, 1936.

Châtillon, J. "Sermons et prédicateurs victorins de la seconde moitié du XIIe siècle," *Arch. d'hist. doct. et litt. du m.a.*, XXXII (1965), 7-60.

Crane, T. F. *The exempla or illustrative stories from the Sermones Vulgares of Jacques de Vitry. London Folklore Soc.*, no. 26. London, 1890.

—. *Medieval sermon-books and stories and their study since 1883. Proc. Amer. Philos. Soc.*, LVI, no. 5, repr. 1917.

Cruel, R. *Geschichte der deutschen Predigt im Mittelalter*. Detmold, 1879.

Dargan, E. C. *A history of preaching, from the apostolic fathers to the great reformers A.D. 70-1572*. 2 vols. New York, 1905.

Davy, M. M. *Les sermons universitaires parisiens de 1230-31: Contribution à l'histoire de la prédication médiévale*. Paris, 1931.

Delhaye, P. "La vertu et les vertus dans les œuvres d'Alain de Lille," *Cahiers de civilisation médiévale*, VI (1963), 13-25.

De Poorter, A. "Un manuel de prédication médiévale, le ms 97 de Bruges," *Revue néo-scolastique de philosophie*, XXV (1923), 192-209.

Devlin, M. A., ed. *The sermons of Thomas Brinton, bishop of Rochester 1373-89. Camden Third Ser.*, LXXXV-LXXXVI. London, 1954.

Douie, D. "Archbishop Pecham's Sermons and Collations," *Studies presented to Powicke* (q.v.). 269-82.

Frenken, G. *Die Exempla des Jacob von Vitry: Ein Beitrag zur Geschichte der Erzählungsliteratur des Mittelalters*. Munich, 1914.

Friend, A. M. "Master Odo of Cheriton," *Speculum*, XXIII (1948), 641-58.

Funk, P. *Jakob von Vitry: Leben und Werke. Beiträge zur Kulturgeschichte des Mittelalters und der Renaissance*, Hft. 3. Leipzig-Berlin, 1909.

Gilson, E. "Michel Ménot et la technique du sermon médiéval," *Revue d'histoire franciscaine*, II (1925), 301-60.

Glorieux, P. "Sermons universitaires parisiens de 1267-68," *RTAM*, XVI (1949), 40-71.

Grundmann, H. *Religiöse Bewegungen im Mittelalter. Historische Studien*. Hft. 267. Lübeck, 1965.

Haring, N. M. "A Christmas sermon by Gilbert of Poitiers," *Medieval Studies*, XXIII (1961), 126-35.

Harjunpaa, T. "Preaching in England during the later Middle Ages," *Acta Academiae Aboensis, Ser. A.*, XXIX (1965), [Abo, Finland].

Haskins, C. H. "The University of Paris in the sermons of the XIIIth century," *AHR*, X (1904), 1-27.

Hauréau, B. "Sermonnaires," *Hist. litt. de la France*, XXVI (Paris, 1873), 387-468.

Herbert, J. A. *Catalogue of romances in the Department of MSS in the British Museum*. London, 1910. III.

Hervieux, L. "Eudes de Cheriton et ses dérivés," *Les fabulistes Latins*. 5 vols. Paris, 1893-99. IV.

Howie, M. D. *Studies in the use of exempla: with special reference to middle high German literature*. London, 1923.

Hunt, R. W. "Alexander Neckham." Unpublished thesis, Oxford D. Phil., 1936.

Kaeppeli, Th. "Un recueil de sermons prêchés à Paris et en Angleterre, conservé dans le MS de Canterbury, Cathedr. Libr. D7," *Archivum fratrum praedicatorum*, XXVI (1956), 161-91.

Klapper, J. *Exempla aus Handschriften des Mittelalters*. Heidelberg, 1911.

Krappe, A. H. "The Indian provenance of a medieval exemplum," *Traditio*, II (1944), 499-502.

Lacombe, G. *Prepositini Cancellarii Parisiensis (1206-10) Opera Omnia, I: La vie et les œuvres de Prévostin. Revue des sciences philos. et théolog.*, 1927.

—. "An unpublished document on the Great Interdict 1207-13," *Catholic Historical Review*, XV (1930), 408-20.

Lampen, W. "De sermonibus Gaufredi Babionis scholastici Andegavensis," *Antonianum*, XIX (1944), 145-68.

Langlois, Ch.-V. "L'Éloquence sacrée au moyen âge," *Revue des Deux Mondes*, CXV (1893), 170-201.

—. "Sermons parisiens de la première moitié du XIIIe siècle contenus dans le ms 691 de la Bibliothèque d'Arras," *Journal des Savants* (nouv. sér., 1916), 488-94; 548-59.

Lebreton, M.-M. "Recherches sur les principaux thèmes théologiques traités dans les sermons du XIIe siècle," *RTAM*, XXIII (1956), 5-18.

Leclercq, J. *L'idée de la royauté du Christ au moyen âge*. Paris, 1959.

—. "Le sermon sur la royauté du Christ au moyen âge," *Arch. d'hist. doct. et litt. du m.â.*, XVIII-XX (1943-45), 143-80.

—. "Le Magistère du Prédicateur au XIIIe siècle," *Arch. d'hist. doct. et litt. du m.â.*, XXI (1946), 105-47.

—. "Recherches sur d'anciens sermons monastiques," *Revue Mabillon*, XXXVI (1946), 1-14.

Leclercq, J., et Figuet, J. "La Bible dans les homélies de S. Bernard sur *Missus est*," *Studi medievali* (3^a s., V, fasc. II, 1964), 613-48.

Lecoy de la Marche, A. *La chaire française au moyen âge, spécialement au XIIIe siècle: d'après les manuscrits contemporains*. 2d ed. Paris, 1886.

Lee, A. E. "Preaching in Elizabethan and Jacobean Drama." Unpublished Ph. D. thesis, Columbia University, 1953.

Little, A. G. *Liber exemplorum ad usum praedicantium saeculo XIII compositus a quodam fratre minore anglico de provincia Hiberniae. British Soc. of Franciscan Studies*, I. Aberdeen, 1908.

Little, A. G., and Douie, D. "Three sermons of Friar Jordan of Saxony, the successor of St. Dominic, preached in England, 1229," *EHR*, LIV (1939), 1-19.

Lynch, K. F. "Three sermons on the Doctor Evangelicus by John de la Rochelle," *Franciscan Studies*, XXIII (1963), 213-37.

Mandonnet, P. *Saint Dominique*. 2 vols. Paris, 1938.

McDonnell, E. W. *The Beguines and Beghards in Medieval Culture: with special emphasis on the Belgian scene*. Rutgers Univ. Pr., 1954.

MacKinnon, H. "The life and works of William de Montibus." Unpublished thesis, Oxford D. Phil., 1959.

Morris, R., ed. *Old English Homilies of the Twelfth Century. Early Eng. Text Soc.*, 2nd ser. London, 1873.

—. *Old English Homilies and Homiletic Treatises of the XII and XIII Centuries. Early Eng. Text Soc.*, orig. ser. 29. London, 1867. repr. 1907.

Mosher, J. A. *The exemplum in the early religious and didactic literature of England*. New York, 1911.

Murphy, J. J. "The Medieval Arts of Discourse: an introductory bibliography," *Speech Monographs*, XXIX (1962), 71-78.

Owst, G. R. *Preaching in medieval England: an introduction to sermon manuscripts of the period, c. 1350-1450*. Cambridge, 1926.

—. *Literature and pulpit in medieval England: a neglected chapter in the history of English letters and of the English people*. 2d ed. rev. Oxford, 1961.

Pfander, H. G. *The popular sermon of the medieval friar in England.* New York, 1937.
—. "The medieval friars and some alphabetical reference books for sermons," *Medium Aevum,* III (1934), 19-29.
Robertson, D. W. "Frequency of preaching in thirteenth century England," *Speculum,* XXIV (1949), 376-88.
Robson, C. A. *Maurice of Sully and the medieval vernacular homily.* Oxford, 1952.
Rochais, H. M., *et al.*, edd. *S. Bernardi Opera, I: Sermones super Cantica Canticorum 1-35.* Rome, 1957.
Ross, W. O. "A brief Forma predicandi," *Modern Philology,* XXXIV (1937), 337-44.
Schneyer, J. B. "Eine Sermonesreihe des Mgr. Alexander von Hales in der Hs. Pavias Univ. Aldini 470 f. 128ra-180vb," *Archivum Franciscanum Historicum,* LVIII (1965), 537-51.
—. "Predigten Alberts des Grossen in der Hs. Leipzig, Univ. Bibl. 683," *Archivum fratrum praedicatorum,* XXXIV (1964), 45-106.
—. "Die Sittenkritik in den Predigten Philipps des Kanzlers," *Beiträge zur Geschichte der Philosophie und Theologie des Mittelalters,* XXXIX, 4 (Münster, 1963).
—. "Eine Sermonesliste des Jacobus von Lausanne," *RTAM,* XXVII (1960), 67-132.
—. "Eine Sermonesliste des Kardinals Stephan Langton Erzbischofs von Canterbury," *RTAM,* XXIX (1962), 159-205.
—. "Beobachtungen bei der Sammlung von Predigtinitien des 13. Jahrhunderts," *Scholastik,* XXXII (1957), 72-81.
—. "Die Erforschung der scholastischen Sermones und ihre Bedeutung für die Homiletik," *Scholastik,* XXXIX (1964), 1-26.
—. *Wegweiser zu lateinischen Predigtreihen des Mittelalters. Bayerische Akademie der Wissenschaften.* München, 1965.
Smalley, B. *English friars and antiquity in the early fourteenth century.* Oxford, 1960.
—. "Robert Holcot O.P.," *Archivum fratrum praedicatorum,* XXVI (1956).
Stinglhamber, L. "Prédicateurs au moyen âge," *Nouvelle revue théologique,* LXIX (1947), 651-64.
Studies in Biblical and Jewish Folklore. Edd. R. Patai, *et al.* Indiana Univ. Pr., 1960.
Sweet, J. "Some thirteenth-century sermons and their authors," *Journal of Ecclesiastical History,* IV (1953), 27-36.
Teetaert, A. "Nicolas Biard," *Dictionnaire de théologie catholique.* Paris, 1931. XI, 591.
Tubach, F. C. "Exempla in the decline," *Traditio,* XVIII (1962), 407-17.
Van den Eynde, D. "Le recueil des sermons de Pierre Abélard," *Antonianum,* XXXVII (1962), 17-54.
Welter, J. T., ed. *Le Speculum Laicorum: Édition d'une collection d'exempla, composée en Angleterre à la fin du XIIIe siècle. Thesaurus exemplorum,* fasc. V, Paris, 1914.
—. *La tabula exemplorum secundum ordinem alphabeti: Recueil d'exempla compilé en France à la fin du XIIIe siècle. Thesaurus exemplorum,* fasc. III. Paris, 1926.
—. *L'Exemplum dans la littérature religieuse et didactique du moyen âge.* Paris, 1927.
Williams, W. *St. Bernard of Clairvaux, Of Conversion. A sermon to the clergy.* (*De conversione ad clericos*). London, 1938.

F. Arts and Theology: The Schools: The Liturgy

Andrieu, M. *Le pontifical Romain au moyen-âge.* 4 vols. Vatican, 1938-41.

Berger, S. *Histoire de la Vulgate pendant les premiers siècles du moyen âge.* Paris, 1893.

Bishop, E. *Liturgica historica: papers on the liturgy and religious life of the western church.* Oxford, 1918.

Bolgar, R. R. *The Classical Heritage and its Beneficiaries: from the Carolingian Age to the end of the Renaissance.* Harper Torchbook, 1964.

Budinszky, A. *Die Universität Paris und die Fremden an derselben im Mittelalter. Ein Beitrag zur Geschichte dieser hohen Schule.* Berlin, 1876.

Bulaeus. (Égasse du Boulay, C.). *Historia universitatis Parisiensis.* 6 vols. Paris, 1665-73. II-III.

Chenu, M.-D. *Introduction à l'Étude de Saint Thomas d'Aquin. Publications de l'Institut d'Études Médiévales,* XI. Montreal, 1950.

—. *La théologie au douzième siècle. Études de philosophie médiévale,* XLV. Paris, 1957.

—. *La théologie comme science au XIIIe siècle.* 3rd ed. Paris, 1957.

De Ghellinck, J. *L'essor de la littérature latine au XIIe siècle.* 2 vols. Paris, 1946.

—. *Le mouvement théologique du XIIe siècle.* 2d ed. Bruges-Paris, 1948.

DeLubac, H. *Exégèse médiévale. Les quatre sens de l'Écriture.* 4 vols. Paris, 1959-64.

De Wulf, M. *History of medieval philosophy.* Tr. E. C. Messenger. 2 vols. 3rd ed. London, 1935-38. I.

Ebner, A. *Quellen und Forschungen zur Geschichte und Kunstgeschichte des Missale Romanum im Mittelalter. Iter Italicum.* Freiburg-i-Br., 1896.

Faral, E. *Les arts poétiques du XIIe et du XIIIe siècle. Recherches et documents sur la technique littéraire du moyen âge.* Paris, 1924.

Feret, P. *La faculté de théologie de Paris et ses docteurs les plus célèbres: Moyen-Age.* 4 vols. Paris, 1894-97. I.

Frere, W. H. *The use of Sarum.* 2 vols. Cambridge, 1898-1901.

Friedmann, A. *Paris, ses rues, ses paroisses du moyen âge à la révolution: Origine et évolution des circonscriptions paroissiales.* Paris, 1959.

Grabmann, M. *Die Geschichte der scholastischen Methode.* 2 vols. Freiburg-i-Br., 1909-11. II.

—. *Die Geschichte der katholischen Theologie seit dem Ausgang der Väterzeit.* Freiburg-i-Br., 1933.

Hailperin, H. *Rashi and the Christian Scholars.* Univ. of Pittsburgh Pr., 1963.

Hunt, R. W. "English learning in the late twelfth century," *Trans. Roy. Hist. Soc.,* 4th ser., XIX (1936), 19-42.

Jones, C. W. *The Saint Nicholas Liturgy and its literary relationships (ninth to twelfth centuries).* Univ. of Calif. Pr., 1963.

Jungmann, J. A. *The mass of the Roman rite: its origins and development (Missarum Sollemnia).* Tr. F. A. Brunner. 2 vols. New York, 1951-55.

Kennedy, V. L. "The calendar of the early thirteenth-century curial missal," *Mediaeval Studies,* XX (1958), 113-26.

King, A. A. *Liturgy of the Roman Church.* London, 1957.

Langlois, Ch. V. *La vie en France au moyen âge d'après des moralistes du temps.* 4 vols. Nouv. éd. Paris, 1925-28.

Lecoy de la Marche, A. *Le treizième siècle littéraire et scientifique.* Bruges, 1894.

Lottin, O. *Psychologie et morale aux XIIe et XIIIe siècles.* 6 vols. in 8. Louvain-Gembloux, 1942-60.

Mangenot, E. "Chapitres de la Bible," *Dictionnaire de la Bible*. Ed. F. Vigouroux. 5 vols. in 10. Paris, 1926-28. II, 559-65.

Manitius, M. *Geschichte der lateinischen Literatur des Mittelalters*. 3 vols. München, 1911-31.

Martin, J. P. P. *Introduction à la critique générale de l'Ancien Testament*. 3 vols. Paris, 1887-89. II.

—. "Le texte parisien de la Vulgate latine," *Le Muséon*, VIII (1889), 444-65.

Michaud, M. *Les livres liturgiques: des Sacramentaires au Missel. L'église dans sa liturgie et ses rites*, Xme partie. Paris, 1961.

Michaud-Quantin, P. *Sommes de casuistique et manuels de confession au moyen-âge* (*XIIe-XVIe siècles*). *Analecta mediaevalia Namurcensia*, 13. Louvain, 1962.

Rand, E. K. "The classics in the XIIIth century," *Speculum*, IV (1929), 249-69.

Rashdall, H. *The Universities of Europe in the Middle Ages*. Edd. A. B. Emden and F. M. Powicke. 3 vols. Oxford, 1936.

Robert, G. *Les écoles et l'enseignement de la théologie pendant la première moitié du XIIe siècle*. Paris, 1909.

Rost, H. *Die Bibel im Mittelalter: Beiträge zur Geschichte und Bibliographie der Bibel*. Augsburg, 1939.

Schneyer, J. B. "Die Scholastischen Sermones als Quellen der Liturgiewissenschaft," *Theologie und Philosophie* (1966), 228-42.

Schnürer, G. *Kirche und Kultur im Mittelalter*. 3 vols. Paderborn, 1924-30. II.

Siegmund, A. *Die Überlieferung der griechischen christlichen Literatur in der lateinischen Kirche bis zum zwölften Jahrhundert*. München, 1949.

Smalley, B. *The Study of the Bible in the Middle Ages*. 2d ed. rev. Oxford, 1952.

—. "Some XIIIth century commentaries on the Sapiential books," *Dominican Studies*, II (1949), 318-55; III (1950), 41-77; 236-74.

Southern, R. W. *Saint Anselm and his biographer: a study of monastic life and thought 1059-c.1130*. Cambridge, 1963.

Spicq, P. C. *Esquisse d'une histoire de l'exégèse latine au moyen âge. Bibliothèque Thomiste*, XXVI, 1944.

Ueberweg, F. *Grundriss der Geschichte der Philosophie*. Berlin, 1928.

Wilmart, A. *Auteurs spirituels et textes dévots du moyen âge latin: études d'histoire littéraire*. Paris, 1932.

Wright, F. A., and Sinclair, T. E. *A history of later Latin literature from the middle of the IVth to the end of the XVIIth century*. London, 1935.

INDEX OF MANUSCRIPTS

(*Note* — On classification of MSS, 25ff, 131, 139-67. Page citations in italics indicate references where MS is quoted. Numbers followed by asterisk refer to pages where MS is described. References to MSS in Groups I & II, *passim*. CR = Catalogue reference in bibliography).

GENERAL INDEX

(*Note* — The names of medieval writers and chroniclers are usually indexed under their first names).